Gender and Trauma since 1900

Gender and Trauma since 1900

Edited by
Paula A. Michaels and
Christina Twomey

BLOOMSBURY ACADEMIC
LONDON • NEW YORK • OXFORD • NEW DELHI • SYDNEY

BLOOMSBURY ACADEMIC
Bloomsbury Publishing Plc
50 Bedford Square, London, WC1B 3DP, UK
1385 Broadway, New York, NY 10018, USA
29 Earlsfort Terrace, Dublin 2, Ireland

BLOOMSBURY, BLOOMSBURY ACADEMIC and the Diana logo are trademarks of
Bloomsbury Publishing Plc

First published in Great Britain 2021

Copyright © Paula A. Michaels, Christina Twomey and Contributors 2021

Paula A. Michaels and Christina Twomey have asserted their right under the Copyright, Designs and Patents Act, 1988, to be identified as Authors of this work.

For legal purposes the Acknowledgements on p. xiii constitute an extension of this copyright page.

Cover design: Terry Woodley
Cover image: *Untitled II – African Aids Epidemic*, 1991 (oil on board) © Bayo Iribhogbe / Bridgeman Images

All rights reserved. No part of this publication may be reproduced or transmitted in any form or by any means, electronic or mechanical, including photocopying, recording, or any information storage or retrieval system, without prior permission in writing from the publishers.

Bloomsbury Publishing Plc does not have any control over, or responsibility for, any third-party websites referred to or in this book. All internet addresses given in this book were correct at the time of going to press. The author and publisher regret any inconvenience caused if addresses have changed or sites have ceased to exist, but can accept no responsibility for any such changes.

A catalogue record for this book is available from the British Library.

Library of Congress Cataloging-in-Publication Data
Names: Michaels, Paula A., 1966- editor. | Twomey, Christina, editor.
Title: Gender and trauma since 1900 / edited by Paula A. Michaels and Christina Twomey.
Description: London; New York, NY: Bloomsbury Academic, 2021. | Includes bibliographical references and index. |
Identifiers: LCCN 2020049935 (print) | LCCN 2020049936 (ebook) | ISBN 9781350145351 (paperback) | ISBN 9781350145375 (ebook) | ISBN 9781350145382 (epub)
Subjects: LCSH: Psychic trauma–Case studies. | Women–Violence against–Case studies. | War–Psychological aspects–Case studies. | Victims of violent crimes–Case studies.
Classification: LCC BF175.5.P75 G45 2021 (print) | LCC BF175.5.P75 (ebook) | DDC 616.85/21–dc23
LC record available at https://lccn.loc.gov/2020049935
LC ebook record available at https://lccn.loc.gov/2020049936

ISBN: HB: 978-1-3501-4536-8
PB: 978-1-3501-4535-1
ePDF: 978-1-3501-4538-2
ePub: 978-1-3501-4537-5

Typeset by Deanta Global Publishing Services, Chennai, India

To find out more about our authors and books visit www.bloomsbury.com and sign up for our newsletters.

For my mentors John Starkes Bushnell and Donald J. Raleigh
PAULA A. MICHAELS

For Patricia Grimshaw, who taught me about gender and history
CHRISTINA TWOMEY

CONTENTS

List of Illustrations   ix
Notes on Contributors   x
Acknowledgements   xiii

1. Gender and Trauma since 1900 *Paula A. Michaels and Christina Twomey*   1

2. Trauma in post-First World War Italy: Experiences, erasures and denials *Martina Salvante*   19

3. Trauma, child refugees and humanitarians in the Spanish Civil War and the Second World War: A case study of Esme Odgers *Joy Damousi*   41

4. Servitude, displacement and trauma: Jewish refugee domestics in Great Britain 1938–45 *Jennifer Craig-Norton*   59

5. 'Combat exhaustion' versus 'psychoneurosis': American psychiatrists and the terminology of war trauma during the Second World War *Rebecca Jo Plant*   79

6. POWS into citizens: Repatriation, gender and the Civil Resettlement Units in Great Britain *Elizabeth Roberts-Pedersen*   101

7. Soviet maternity care and competing narratives of trauma *Paula A. Michaels*   123

8. Trauma and sexual violence: Narratives and cases in late twentieth-century Australia *Lisa Featherstone*   143

9	Embodied, psychological and gendered trauma in militarized Kampala (Uganda) *Benjamin Twagira*	163
10	'The missing ones': Vietnamese diasporic memory and women's narratives of loss *Nathalie Huynh Chau Nguyen*	185
11	Refiguring trauma: Women's narratives of suffering in post-conflict Timor-Leste *Hannah Loney*	201
12	Changing the story: Women and trauma in Australian narratives of mental illness *Katie Holmes*	221

Consolidated bibliography — 241
Index — 266

ILLUSTRATIONS

Figures

1.1 André Brouillet, Une leçon clinique à la Salpêtrière, [A Clinical Lesson at the Salpêtrière], 1887 2

2.1 Mural (1969) memorializing Italian casualties from the Battle of Caporetto 30

Table

2.1 Number of Executions per Offence Perpetrated 28

CONTRIBUTORS

Jennifer Craig-Norton is a visiting fellow at the Parkes Institute for the Study of Jewish/Non-Jewish Relations at the University of Southampton. Her publications include *Migrant Histories and Historiographies: Essays in Honour of Colin Holmes* (2018), co-edited with Christhard Hoffman and Tony Kushner and *The Kindertransport: Contesting Memory* (2019). She is currently writing a book on Jewish refugee domestics.

Joy Damousi is Professor of History and Director of the Institute for Humanities and Social Sciences at the Australian Catholic University. She is President of the Australian Academy of the Humanities and a fellow of the Australian Academy of the Social Sciences. She has published widely on aspects of gender and women's history, memory and aftermaths of war, history of emotions, sound and war, and the history of migration and refugees. Her most recent book is *Memory and Migration in the Shadow of War: Australia's Greek Immigrants after World War II and the Greek Civil War* (2015).

Lisa Featherstone is an Australian historian, based at the University of Queensland. Her work focuses on sexuality, medicine and the law. She currently writes on sexual violence, including child sexual abuse and rape in marriage. She is the author of two monographs, *Let's Talk About Sex: Histories of Sexuality in Australia* and *Sex Crimes in the 1950s* (with Andy Kaldelfos). The latter was shortlisted for the NSW Premier's Prize in 2017. She has published extensively, including articles in *Gender & History, Women's History Review, Feminist Legal Studies, Australian Historical Studies* and the *Journal of the History of Sexuality*.

Katie Holmes is Professor of History and Director of La Trobe University's Centre for the study of the Inland. The interplay between an individual, his or her culture and environment has been central to her work and she has explored this in the context of environmental history, oral history, gender, women's diaries, gardens and mental illness. Her most recent work includes the co-authored *Mallee Country: Land, People, History* (2020); 'Does it matter if she cried? Recording emotion in the Australian Generations oral history project', *Oral History Review*, 44:1, 2017; and 'Talking about

Mental Illness: Life Histories and Mental Health in Modern Australia', *Australian Historical Studies*, 47: 1, 2016.

Hannah Loney is a Gilbert Postdoctoral Early Career Fellow in the School of Historical and Philosophical Studies at the University of Melbourne, Australia. Her research interests include women's history, twentieth-century Southeast Asian and Pacific history, transnational activism, histories of violence, oral history and international human rights. Hannah's book *In Women's Words: Violence and Everyday Life During the Indonesian Occupation of East Timor, 1975–1999* was published in 2018

Paula A. Michaels is an Associate Professor of History at Monash University. Her work centres on modern medicine and health, with a focus on the USSR in a transnational and comparative context. She is the author of two prizewinning books: *Curative Powers: Medicine and Empire in Stalin's Central Asia* (2003) and *Lamaze: An International History* (2014). Michaels also co-edited *Paths to Parenthood: Emotions on the Journey through Pregnancy, Childbirth, and Early Parenting* (with Renata Kokanovic and Kate Johnston-Ataata, 2018). She is currently working on a project on Soviet Cold War medical diplomacy.

Nathalie Huynh Chau Nguyen is an Associate Professor in History at Monash University. An Oxford graduate, she held four fellowships between 2005 and 2015, including two Australian Research Council Fellowships and a Visiting Fellowship at Oxford University. She is the author of four books, including 2010 Choice Outstanding Academic Title *Memory Is Another Country: Women of the Vietnamese Diaspora* (2009), and *South Vietnamese Soldiers: Memories of the Vietnam War and After* (2016). She is editor of *New Perceptions of the Vietnam War* (2015). Her latest grant is for an ARC Discovery Project on the refugee legacy for second-generation Vietnamese in Australia.

Rebecca Jo Plant, Associate Professor in History at the University of California, San Diego, is the author of *Mom: The Transformation of Motherhood in Modern America* and co-editor of *Maternalism Reconsidered: Motherhood, Welfare, and Social Policies in the Twentieth Century*. Along with Frances M. Clarke, she won the Letitia Woods Brown Memorial Prize and Berkshire Conference of Women Historians' Prize for best article for '"The Crowning Insult": Federal Segregation and the Gold Star Mother and Widow Pilgrimages of the Early 1930s' (*Journal of American History*). The two of them are currently completing a study on the problem of underage enlistment during the American Civil War.

Elizabeth Roberts-Pedersen is a Senior Lecturer in History at the University of Newcastle, Australia. She has published on several elements of the history of modern warfare, including international volunteering, discipline and military medicine. Her current project, funded by an Australian Research Council DECRA fellowship (2016–19), examines the effects of the Second World War on the theory and practice of psychiatry.

Martina Salvante is Assistant Professor of Twentieth-Century European History at the University of Nottingham, UK. Her research focuses on fascism and the interwar period with interests in gender and disability. Her latest publications include *La paternità nell'Italia fascista: simboli, esperienze e norme, 1922-1943* (2020) – an investigation of fatherhood under the fascist regime in Italy – and the two articles 'Introduction: Gender and Disability in the Two World Wars' and 'The Wounded Male Body: Masculinity and Disability in Wartime and Post-WWI Italy'.

Benjamin Twagira is an Assistant Professor of modern African history at Williams College, United States. His primary research interest is African social history with special emphasis on modern East Africa and twentieth-century urban Africa. Currently he is working on a book manuscript examining the social history of militarized Kampala, the capital of Uganda, between 1966 and 1986. His other research projects explore the intersections between postc-colonial military rule, gender and health and healing in urban East Africa. At Williams, he teaches survey courses on African history, as well as conducting thematic seminars in African history on health and healing, religion, the environment, urbanization and soldiering.

Christina Twomey is Professor of History at Monash University and a fellow of the Australian Academy of the Humanities and the Australian Academy of Social Sciences. She is a social and cultural historian with specific interest in humanitarianism, internment and imprisonment in wartime, photography and violence. She is the author of four books; her most recent book is *The Battle Within: POWs in Postwar Australia* (2018). She has also co-edited several collections, including *The Pacific War: Aftermaths, Remembrance and Culture* (with Ernest Koh, 2015) and *Detention Camps in Asia* (with Robert Cribb and Sandra Wilson, forthcoming with Brill).

ACKNOWLEDGEMENTS

The editors offer thanks to the Academy of the Social Sciences in Australia (ASSA) for its generous support of the workshop on gender and trauma in 2018, which served as the foundation for the present book. The Faculty of Arts at Monash University provided additional funding to support the travel of international participants.

1

Gender and Trauma since 1900

Paula A. Michaels and Christina Twomey

Pierre Aristide André Brouillet's 1887 painting, *Une leçon clinique à la Salpêtrière*, centres on Jean-Martin Charcot, whose work is widely seen as the starting point for our modern understanding of psychological trauma. It depicts Charcot demonstrating a hysterical fit induced by hypnosis to a lecture theatre of rapt, male physicians. Like those of Charcot's audience, the viewer's eyes gravitate to the patient, Marie 'Blanche' Wittmann. Unconscious and supported by Charcot's assistant, her white blouse and pale flesh contrast with the black sea of men's suits. Only one small detail betrays the psychological struggle raging within her limp body: a taut, flexed fist arches back sharply. Wittmann is portrayed here experiencing one of her fits, which included falls, violent convulsions, facial contortions and delirium.[1] After a childhood and early adulthood of physical and sexual abuse, Wittmann had come into the care of Charcot at his famed Paris hospital, Salpêtrière, where she became his star patient. Power in this image, as in real life, is drawn along gendered lines, though not always as clearly as they might initially appear. Wittmann's performance of hysteria was dissected and inscribed with meaning by men whose power over her lay in their medical gaze. Charcot owed his fame and fortune in large part to Wittmann and other women, whom he displayed to his colleagues to argue that hysteria was based in the nervous system, and not in the womb. In return, Wittmann received greater safety and security than she had previously known in her troubled life. Their relationship has been described as a 'partnership'.[2] Upon Charcot's death, Salpêtrière continued to be a haven for Wittmann, who worked as a photographic and radiological assistant; her attacks ceased (Figure 1.1).[3]

FIGURE 1.1 *André Brouillet, Une leçon clinique à la Salpêtrière, [A Clinical Lesson at the Salpêtrière], 1887.*

By theorizing that hysteria constituted a disorder of the nervous system, and not women's reproductive organs, Charcot opened the possibility that men, too, could suffer from this malady. His lectures sometimes presented cases of male hysterics, although the disorder continued to be associated primarily with women.[4] But if the image of Wittmann in *Une leçon clinique à la Salpêtrière* is the most iconic and enduring representation of female trauma, then it is surely the First World War combat veteran who stands as her male corollary and a 'central and recurring image of trauma'.[5] Popular culture and historical scholarship are replete with explorations of psychologically wounded soldiers who struggled to come to terms with the terrible things they endured and perpetrated at the front. Among the most well-known figures, immortalized in memoir, novels and film, are two poets – one seasoned, one a novice – and a psychiatrist, who converged at Craiglockhart War Hospital, near Edinburgh, during the First World War. Siegfried Sassoon took a public stand against the war; through the intercession of his friend and fellow poet Robert Graves, he avoided a military tribunal but found himself punished and discredited through institutionalization for shell shock at Craiglockhart. There he met aspiring poet Wilfred Owen, one of many young men battling wartime demons. From his work with men like Owen and Sassoon, Craiglockart psychiatrist W. H. R. Rivers began to formulate a theory of combat neurosis based on his interpretation of Sigmund Freud's writing.[6]

This twinned imagery of trauma – the female survivor of domestic violence and sexual assault, and the male combat veteran – weaves its way through the history of psychological suffering. Despite women's centrality to this history and the fact that they are more likely than men to suffer from trauma, women are marginalized in the research into, funding for, and popular perceptions of trauma.[7] The story of our modern conceptualization of trauma is typically told as a straight line from shell shock in the First World War, through combat neurosis in the Second World War, to Post-Traumatic Stress Disorder (PTSD), which psychiatrists formulated as a diagnostic category in the wake of the Vietnam War. Women are often erased entirely from this master narrative. Although scholars repeatedly point to the essential role feminist activists against domestic violence and sexual assault played in the formulation and acceptance of PTSD, women's place in this history is occluded in the collective consciousness by an overwhelming focus on combat veterans, almost all of whom are men.[8] Even studies that attend to how gender shapes trauma typically cordon off men's wartime stories from women's narratives, both in conflict zones and in peacetime.[9]

This book takes a step towards reconciling what has largely been two siloed conversations about the traumatic experiences of men and of women. Through eleven case studies drawn from both the Global North and South, and across the twentieth and twenty-first centuries, we examine trauma in war and peace with an eye towards the role of gender. The subjects include characters familiar in earlier literature on trauma – soldiers, prisoners of war, refugees, the victims of sexual offences – as well as those less often the focus of attention in such scholarship: humanitarians, domestic servants, birthing mothers, civilian witnesses to massacre, women who suffered from depression. How does putting these histories in dialogue shed light on the persistent marginalization of women in the master narrative of trauma? In juxtaposing histories around the globe, what can we learn about the sociocultural situatedness of gender and trauma? What change over time is evident, given transformations over the last century in women's political and social position? To explore these concerns, we must first clarify what we mean by trauma. We then briefly recount the medical and social history of trauma, with particular attention to how it intersects with gender. Finally, we articulate how the ensuing chapters speak to the need to bridge the scholarly divide between studies on male combat veterans and female civilians. A more holistic, inclusive approach refocuses attention on the common encounter with violence that underpins traumatic experience regardless of sex but is endemic to women's everyday lives.

What is trauma?

Because of the multiple and contentious ways that the term 'trauma' is used, it is necessary to define what we mean at the outset. Until the nineteenth century, the word referred solely to physical injury. Investigations in the budding fields of neurology and, later, psychiatry, stretched the definition to encompass, as literary scholar Cathy Caruth pithily puts it, 'a wound inflicted not upon the body, but upon the mind'.[10] Trauma is today understood typically to be the experience of a catastrophic, often sudden occurrence that overwhelms an individual's psychological capacity to process the event. Mental health professionals continue to seek clarity about who is at greatest risk and why. Psychiatrist Bessel A. van der Kolk and others argue that victims often experience feeling unable to respond to a life-threatening event with either fight or flight, and, instead, freeze in response, trapped in an unresolved, untenable psychic state. However, that the initial event – such as a serious car accident, sexual assault, natural disaster or combat – is experienced as life-threatening is a necessary, but not sufficient, explanation for trauma's lingering effects.[11]

In the aftermath of the event, sufferers of post-traumatic stress experience certain common symptoms, which can include

1. recurrent, involuntary and intrusive memories of the event;
2. recurrent distressing dreams;
3. dissociative reactions (e.g. flashbacks);
4. intense or prolonged psychological distress at exposure to internal or external cues that symbolize or resemble an aspect of the traumatic event and
5. marked physiological reactions to internal or external cues that symbolize or resemble an aspect of the traumatic event(s).[12]

Thus, a traumatic event (or the perception of it) inaugurates a vicious circle: the creation of a distressing memory, which in turn 'provokes the autonomous nervous system and the survival response (fight, flight, freeze), causing difficulty sleeping, irritability, an exaggerated startle reflex, hypervigilance, difficulty concentrating, and motor restlessness. The victim adapts to the distressful memory and consequent arousal through symptomatic avoidance and numbing'.[13]

The modern understanding of psychological trauma and its impact has changed over time. Over the last 150 years, many names have been used to describe this phenomenon: hysteria, shell shock, war neurosis, combat neurosis, traumatic neurosis, battle fatigue. Rebecca Jo Plant's chapter, for example, charts what was at stake in the approved nomenclature of psychological distress among US forces during the Second World War. Family members, military authorities and soldiers themselves challenged psychiatrists about terminology, such as 'psychoneurosis', that they perceived as encapsulating negative implications about masculinity, capability and integrity. The constellation of symptoms seen as indicative of the disorder, too, have undergone continual revision. Flashbacks, which are at present understood as a hallmark of PTSD, were virtually never reported among combat veterans of the First and Second World Wars. Even since PTSD's 1980 introduction into the psychiatric lexicon, some symptoms have fallen in and out of favour. A feeling of guilt was initially considered a possible indicator; it was removed from the list of symptoms in the 1987 revised edition of the DSM-III, only to be reinstated in the 2013 DSM-V.[14]

Variation over time calls into question whether the experience of trauma and its after-effects can be understood as transhistorical phenomena. The battlelines on this issue are drawn primarily along disciplinary boundaries. Mental health professionals are keen to find evidence of transhistoricity, while students of social sciences emphasize, instead, the ways that PTSD emerged in and was defined by the specific cultural context of the late twentieth-century United States. To see similarities with historical or literary figures of the past provides evidence to traumatologists that the disorder is not socially constructed, but, rather, went unrecognized by earlier societies. Psychiatrist Jonathan Shay is perhaps the most prominent popularizer of this idea, seeing in the stories of Achilles and Odysseus, for example, evidence of combat-related trauma.[15] Along with biological studies, such arguments buttress what medical professionals embrace as an 'objective validation' of PTSD's existence.[16] Even sceptics assert that the absence of such historical evidence does not attest to trauma being a construct, but, rather, a new disease, like AIDS.[17]

Social scientists argue that how we experience distressing events cannot be uncoupled from the sociocultural context in which they are lived. Context gives meaning to both how one experiences a distressing event psychically and how one's response is perceived and understood by society. In his path-breaking ethnography, Allan Young asserts that PTSD 'is not timeless, nor does it possess intrinsic unity. Rather, it is glued together by the practices, technologies, and narratives with which it is diagnosed, studied, treated, and represented and by various interests, institutions, and moral arguments that mobilized these efforts and resources'.[18] The position of Young and others is not that PTSD is not 'real', but, rather, that that reality manifests through practices that change over time and space. 'Heterogeneity' is at the heart of PTSD, serving as its 'unifying etiology' and from which derives an apparent universality.[19] Many different events can inspire traumatic memory and it can manifest in a range of behaviours. Under this umbrella emerges, in any given historical context, 'a distinctive *assemblage* . . . , colored by national medical traditions, institutional cultures, and popular attitudes'.[20]

In light of the expansive reach of our contemporary medical understanding of trauma and post-traumatic stress, attentiveness to cultural factors does not challenge the validity of the diagnosis. Several chapters in the collection, from a range of different cultural contexts, position themselves as a study of trauma despite the absence of the specific term from the narratives or interviews upon which they rely. Paula A. Michaels demonstrates how in the post-war Union of Soviet Socialist Republics women created narratives of suffering in childbirth, even without the language of trauma being available to them. Likewise, Nathalie Nguyen's analysis of Vietnamese women refugees' narratives and Benjamin Twagira's reading of women's experiences of militarization in post-independence Uganda identify civilian women's encounters with pirates and soldiers as traumatizing events. The threat of sexual violence often underpinned such incidents, but Nguyen also tracks the psychological cost of displacement, exposure to other forms of violence and the loss of family members at sea. A reliance on female narration of suffering and an attentiveness to the contours of experience allow for a more capacious understanding of events that have constituted or caused trauma, beyond the quintessential combat experience.

Some of the complexity in unravelling what scholars mean when they invoke the word 'trauma' to describe distressing events in different historical eras and cultural contexts lies in the slippage between two different, but related, usages. Didier Fassin and Richard Rechtman describe the clinical and colloquial uses of trauma as the 'genealogy of the medical category and of the moral norms', respectively.[21] These interrelated discourses shape the emergence, interpretation and popularization of medical knowledge. As the language of psychiatry becomes the vernacular, interest groups lean on medicine to buttress claims to victimhood. The legitimation of such claims offers both social validation and economic benefit through care and/or compensation for those who stake a claim. The chapters that follow explore both the intellectual/medical and the social/colloquial histories of trauma. Approaching trauma from the perspective of the social sciences, the authors recognize the flexibility and fluidity of the term 'trauma' and seek to ground it in local and national medical and cultural context.

A brief, gendered genealogy of trauma

As psychiatrist Judith Lewis Herman writes in her landmark work *Trauma and Recovery*, 'episodic amnesia' marks the history of psychological trauma.[22] It has had to be rediscovered (or, perhaps more accurately, reinvented) time and again in response to each new crisis. This pattern gives the history of trauma an fragmented quality. Herman identifies three crucial moments when trauma pushed its way into the popular consciousness: during the rise of attention to hysteria in mid- to late nineteenth-century France, shell shock in the United States and Great Britain in the First World War and PTSD during the Vietnam War and the second-wave feminist movement. Each of these turning points revisited and reimagined the origins and expression of psychological wounds, and each arose in close connection with the politics of its time. Hysteria or, as Charcot termed it, 'the Great Neurosis' emerged in concert with republican anticlericalism and the quest to shift authority over women's bodies and minds from the church to secular authorities.[23] What remained unchallenged, however, was patriarchal control.

Sigmund Freud's development of psychoanalysis grew directly out of the work of Charcot. Along with his mentor, Joseph Breuer, and Pierre Janet, he explored the psychological consequences of traumatic experiences. In the 1890s, he hypothesized that hysteria stemmed from childhood sexual abuse. He abandoned this 'seduction theory', however, when it became clear that to pursue this line of inquiry would be to lodge a serious accusation against seemingly respectable families in middle-class Vienna.[24] Unable or unwilling to believe that sexual abuse was so widespread, he explained away his patients' testimonies as fantasy, a belief that dominated psychiatry's response to claims of sexual abuse for the next three quarters of a century. And, of course, in assessing his female patients as unreliable narrators of their own affective and somatic experiences, Freud both leaned on and furthered the long-standing medical tradition of disempowering and delegitimizing women.[25]

Men, too, had not escaped the gaze of medical authorities. As already noted, Charcot expanded the definition of hysteria to encompass males. Nineteenth-century European men also began to be diagnosed with a new syndrome for a new, industrializing era: 'railway spine'. Sufferers showed no physical injury, but complained of aches and pains. Many found their claims dismissed as fabrications allegedly contrived in a quest for financial compensation.[26] These suspicions of male malingering informed the rise of the second intrusion of trauma into medical and public debate with the advent of shell shock during the First World War. Shell shock was understood as typically attributed to a weak nervous system; predisposition, not the horrors of war, accounted for mental breakdown. Running counter to prevailing notions of masculinity, such perceived frailty impugned men's virility and patriotism. Several contributions to this book, including those by Martina Salvante and Elizabeth Roberts-Pedersen, examine how the treatment of, and responses to, combat veterans blended predisposition theories, ideas about masculinity and understandings of psychological harm. The First World War, the Second World War and the Korean War each created a fresh wave of psychologically wounded warriors, but when the wars faded from headlines, 'capricious public interest' receded, and collective amnesia set in about soldiers' suffering.[27]

The 1970s ushered in a drive to redefine psychological trauma in a radically different way. Psychiatrists working with Vietnam veterans began to conceptualize men's mental health struggles in a new light, making connections between soldiers, Holocaust victims and survivors of the nuclear bombings in Hiroshima and Nagasaki. In its challenge to traditional gender roles, the feminist movement, too, influenced the perception and treatment of veterans' psychic wounds. Feminism offered a vocabulary for challenging soldiering as performative masculinity, a critique that proved potent in the context of an unpopular war. Arguing that 'hysteria [was] the combat neurosis of the sex war', feminists pressed psychiatrists for recognition of their own claims to victimhood.[28] Feminists sought to bring discussion of rape and childhood sexual abuse out from the shadows. Using the term 'rape trauma syndrome' to describe the psychological symptoms that many women experienced following sexual assault, Ann Burgess and Lynda Holstrom identified a symptomology close to that which was emerging from work with Vietnam veterans.[29] In pressing for frank examination of childhood sexual abuse, they denounced Freud's disavowal of seduction theory as a cowardly betrayal by Freud of his women patients.[30]

The unveiling of the PTSD diagnosis in the 1980 DSM-III marked a fundamental shift in the medical profession's conceptualization of trauma's causes. Victims' sources of suffering had until then been sited to some extent within themselves. Why did some, but not others, succumb to the shock of combat, rape, natural disaster or a catastrophic car accident? Prior to 1980, whatever the precipitating event, its psychological impact was attributed in part to the condition of the individual. Whether ascribed to a weak nervous system or an intrapsychic conflict traceable to early psychosexual development, a vulnerability predated the precipitating event and cast a pall of doubt over the sufferer. For their lack of resilience, victims of traumatic events were thus to some degree implicated in their ongoing struggles. PTSD offered two revolutionary claims: (1) that being traumatized by a sudden, terrible, overwhelming event was a normal reaction to abnormal circumstances and (2) that the event triggering the trauma became 'the sole etiological factor'.[31] No longer did something defined as insufficient or abnormal in the victim provide an explanation, in whole or in part, for post-traumatic stress.

PTSD, women and ordinary violence

Over the ensuing decades, this new understanding of post-traumatic suffering has spread from the medical community to society at large – first in the United States, then across the Global North. By the dawn of the twenty-first century, people in the Global South, too, had begun to invoke this standard, medicalized language of trauma to make their experiences intelligible to outside health professionals, journalists and aid workers.[32] Hannah Loney's chapter explores how East Timorese women engaged with the concept of trauma when recounting their experiences and memories of the Indonesian occupation of East Timor in the last quarter of the twentieth century. She provides a compelling example of how trauma had become 'a major signifier of our age'[33] that 'seems everywhere today',[34] 'the lingua franca of human suffering'.[35] With this popularization came concern that the ever-expanding inclusion of events defined as potentially traumatic seemed to dilute the meaningfulness and utility of the concept. As historian Ben Shephard put it, 'any unit of classification that simultaneously encompasses the experience of surviving Auschwitz and that of being told rude jokes at work must, by any reasonable lay standard, be a nonsense, a patent absurdity'.[36]

Shephard's critique raises several points that speak directly to the motivation behind this book. First, he implies that the suffering inflicted on someone by a rude (e.g. sexist, racist or classist) joke trivializes that of the Holocaust victim. But we ask: Can the definition of trauma be capacious without implying equivalence? Who benefits from narrowing the conceptualization of trauma? Would doing so perpetuate marginalization of those who, based on sex, race, class or other markers of difference, have historically suffered from the implicit and explicit biases in mental health discourse?[37] Jennifer Craig-Norton's chapter encapsulates these tensions. Focused on Jewish refugee domestics in Britain immediately prior to and during the Second World War, Craig-Norton examines the psychological cost of service for people whose class background made them unaccustomed to it, the particular vulnerability of women, and the difficultly for both groups of squaring their own suffering against the fate of those who perished or languished in European camps.

Shephard calls for 'dismantling the [conceptual] unity' of trauma as a way to accommodate a gradation of experiences, and in recent years psychologists have moved towards developing the vocabulary to do just that.[38] Sexism and other forms of prejudice may not create an imminent existential threat, but they are now identified as stressors that over time can lead to similar affective responses. Katie Holmes' chapter in this collection explores the accretion of women's everyday life experiences that could foment mental illness in late twentieth-century Australia, while simultaneously emphasizing the need to not overlook political and structural factors that often perpetuated their suffering. Mental health professionals now recognize both 'direct trauma' – the kind of shocking, overwhelming event typically associated with PTSD – and 'insidious trauma', which derives from low-grade, ongoing stressors over time, as potential sources for psychic wounds.[39] Highlighting the impact of insidious trauma, Herman proposes 'complex PTSD' as a distinct clinical diagnosis for those whose suffering derives from prolonged exposure to traumatic events, such as abuse and neglect in childhood.[40] Rather than rendering trauma and PTSD meaningless, these efforts to complicate our understanding make room for suffering that has to date largely been relegated to the periphery of medical and social discourse. Here, Lisa Featherstone's comparison of sexual assault criminal trials in the 1970s and 1980s demonstrates how criminal proceedings had long been impervious to the psychological harm to victims, and only in the 1980s began to acknowledge a growing body of work on the traumatizing effects of sexual violence.

Despite epistemological developments that seem to render the suffering of women and other disadvantaged groups more visible, the lion's share of attention and resources continues to flow towards male combat veterans. The very ubiquity of women's trauma and its horrific, but mundane, sources may play a role in the enduring marginalization of women's suffering. However terrible and traumatizing, the domestic and sexual violence at the heart of much of women's trauma lies within the spectrum of what anthropologists Jacky Bouju and Mirjam de Bruijn define as 'ordinary violence', that is 'violence experienced by ordinary people in their ordinary everyday lives'.[41] Nearly one in five women in the United States today are raped; the figure may be much higher, as research shows that as many as one-half of women who experience forced, unwanted sex never acknowledge it even to themselves as rape.[42] In the DSM, both combat and rape are listed as extraordinary events that could breach the psychic defences of any normal, healthy individual. But the sad truth is that, statistically speaking, rape is quotidian. Social and psychological pressure facilitates the problem by maintaining a 'zone of silence' around women's experiences of violence, which is then replicated in the sources on which researchers usually rely.[43]

These silences mean that women are rendered invisible to scholars not attentive to their presence and their experiences, with particularly vivid consequences when one looks at the question of violence in war. In an essay focused on research into psychological trauma and combat veterans in Asia, historian Mark Micale draws attention to the scholarship of Ben Zajicek, whose work investigates Soviet psychiatry during and after the Second World War. Micale is particularly struck by the value of Zajicek's case study for examining female combat veterans, who served in large numbers in the Red Army. Female Soviet veterans offer a unique data set, Micale argues, because 'in other nations, psychological trauma during times of war gets cast as a male psychopathology'.[44] Micale's comment is startling, because it reveals just how narrow and distorting the predominant view of war trauma is. Trauma as a consequence of war can be inscribed as a male affliction only if one focuses solely on combat soldiers. The fact that war is associated with male victimhood is not due to a lack of data on female soldiers, as Micale suggests, but to the blindness of some historians to women's presence and to the use of sexual violence as a weapon.

Female wartime psychiatric casualties were everywhere. Rape has been systematically used as a weapon of war throughout history. In the context of modern total war, the lines between front and rear dissolved. Along with men and children, women in the rear experienced bombings in London, Dresden, Hiroshima, and elsewhere that were no less frightening or deadly than what soldiers at the front endured. Women in many combatant nations were also present at or near the front lines as nurses, drivers and in other support capacities in both world wars. Facing charges of collaboration, they endured violent retribution after the Second World War.[45] Joy Damousi's contribution to this collection further suggests that a focus on female humanitarian workers also disrupts the tendency to view only male combat veterans as those potentially traumatized by working close to the front line.

By putting the experiences of women in peace and war alongside those of male combat soldiers, this book throws into sharp relief these distortions to the historical record. We also raise doubts about the extent to which PTSD marks a rupture with earlier conceptualizations with respect to gender.

Micale asserts that, in contrast to hysteria, 'no one claims that . . . PTSD [is a] male or female' malady.[46] It is clear from the ensuing chapters, however, that trauma is lived through gender in ways that change over time and place. Along with race, class, ability, sexual orientation and other markers of difference, gender conditions how trauma is experienced, made manifest and validated (or not) medically and socially. There can be no meaningful study of trauma without attending to gender.

Acknowledgements

An Aarhus University Visiting Research Grant supported the writing of Paula A. Michaels's contribution to this chapter.

Notes

1 Asti Hustvedt, *Medical Muses: Hysteria in Nineteenth-Century Paris* (London: Bloomsbury, 2012), 22.
2 Carlos S. Alvarado, 'Nineteenth-Century Hysteria and Hypnosis: A Historical Note on Blanche Wittmann', *Australian Journal of Clinical and Experimental Hypnosis* 37, no. 1 (2009): 30.
3 Wittmann endured a sad fate as an early assistant to Marie Curie. Radiation exposure led to cancer and amputations, though precisely what was amputated is disputed. See Alvarado, 'Nineteenth-Century Hysteria and Hypnosis', 25; J. van Gijn, 'In Defence of Charcot, Curie, and Wittmann', *The Lancet* 369, no. 9560 (2007): 462. On Charcot's work, see Georges Didi-Huberman, *The Invention of Hysteria: Charcot and the Photographic Iconography of the Salpêtrière*, trans. Alisa Hartz (Cambridge, MA: MIT Press, 2003). For a detailed analysis of Brouillet's painting, as well as a lithograph of it by Eugène Pirodon that hung above Sigmund Freud's famous couch in his London flat and a Freud Museum photographic postcard of the couch with the print in the background, see Forbes Morlock, 'The Very Picture of a Primal Scene: Une Leçon Clinique à La Salpêtrière', *Visual Resources* 23, nos. 1–2 (2007): 129–46. For a novel loosely based on Wittmann's life, see Per Olov Enquist, *Story of Blanche and Marie* (London: Vintage Books, 2007). A testament to the iconic quality of Brouillet's painting, the novel's cover features the image of Wittmann as he depicted her.
4 Mark S. Micale, *Hysterical Men: The Hidden History of Male Nervous Illness* (Cambridge, MA: Harvard University Press, 2009).
5 Cathy Caruth uses this phrase to describe all soldiers across the twentieth century. Cathy Caruth, *Unclaimed Experience: Trauma, Narrative, and History* (Baltimore, MD: Johns Hopkins University Press, 1996), 11.
6 On the development of British thinking on war neurosis, including its relationship to earlier notions of hysteria and railway spine, see Tracey

Loughran, *Shell-Shock and Medical Culture in First World War Britain* (Cambridge: Cambridge University Press, 2017). For a brief, well-illustrated treatment of Sassoon, Owen and Rivers' encounter at Craiglockhart, see Tracey Loughran, 'Shell Shock', *The British Library*, 7 November 2018, https://www.bl.uk/world-war-one/articles/shell-shock. This relationship is portrayed in the award-winning novel *Regeneration*, which was subsequently adapted to film. Pat Barker, *Regeneration* (London: Viking, 1991); Allan Scott, *Regeneration*, directed by Gilles MacKinnon (London: BBC Films, 1997).

7 Daniel N Ditlevsen and Ask Elklit, 'Gender, Trauma Type, and PTSD Prevalence: A Re-Analysis of 18 Nordic Convenience Samples', *Annals of General Psychiatry* 11, no. 1 (2012): 26; David J. Morris, *The Evil Hours: A Biography of Post-Traumatic Stress Disorder* (Boston, MA: Houghton Mifflin Harcourt, 2016), 15; Laurel B. Watson et al., 'The Influence of Multiple Oppressions on Women of Color's Experiences with Insidious Trauma', *Journal of Counseling Psychology* 63, no. 6 (2016): 656–67.

8 For studies that appropriately credit the role of women in advocacy for PTSD, see Judith Lewis Herman, *Trauma and Recovery* (New York: BasicBooks, 1992); Morris, *The Evil Hours*; Didier Fassin and Richard Rechtman, *The Empire of Trauma: An Inquiry into the Condition of Victimhood*, trans. Rachel Gomme (Princeton, NJ: Princeton University Press, 2009).

9 Psychiatrist Mardi J. Horowitz rightly notes that 'warfare stands out as a huge cause of PTSD in both military and civilian populations', and yet studies that address the psychological suffering of combat veterans virtually never make mention of these civilian casualties. Mardi J. Horowitz, 'Introduction', in *Essential Papers on Post Traumatic Stress Disorder*, ed. Mardi J. Horowitz (New York: New York University Press, 1999), 3. A striking exception to this pattern is Yasmin Saikia, 'War as History, Humanity in Violence: Women, Men, and Memories of 1971, East Pakistan/Bangladesh', in *Sexual Violence in Conflict Zones: From the Ancient World to the Era of Human Rights*, ed. Elizabeth D. Heineman (Philadelphia: University of Pennsylvania Press, 2011), 152–69.

10 Caruth, *Unclaimed Experience*, 3.

11 Bessel A. van der Kolk, *The Body Keeps the Score: Brain, Mind, and Body in the Healing of Trauma* (New York: Penguin Books, 2015); Peter A. Levine, *Waking the Tiger: Healing Trauma* (Berkeley, CA: North Atlantic Books, 1997).

12 'Trauma- and Stressor-Related Disorders', in *Diagnostic and Statistical Manual of Mental Disorders*, 5th edn, DSM Library (Washington, DC: American Psychiatric Association, 2013). https://doi.org/10.1176/appi.books.9780890425596.dsm07.

13 Allan Young and Naomi Breslau, 'What Is "PTSD"?: The Heterogeneity Thesis', in *Culture and PTSD: Trauma in Global and Historical Perspective*, ed. Devon E. Hinton and Byron J. Good (Philadelphia: University of Pennsylvania Press, 2016), 139.

14 E. Jones et al., 'Flashbacks and Post-Traumatic Stress Disorder: The Genesis of a 20th-Century Diagnosis', *The British Journal of Psychiatry*

182, no. 2 (2003): 158–63; Richard J. McNally, 'Is PTSD a Transhistorical Phenomenon?', in *Culture and PTSD*, 117–34.

15 Jonathan Shay, *Odysseus in America: Combat Trauma and the Trials of Homecoming* (New York: Scribner, 2002); Jonathan Shay, *Achilles in Vietnam Combat Trauma and the Undoing of Character* (New York: Scribner, 2005).

16 Rachel Yehuda and Alexander C. McFarlane, 'Introduction', in *Psychobiology of Post-Traumatic Stress Disorder*, ed. Rachel Yehuda and Alexander C. McFarlane (New York: New York Academy of Sciences, 1997), xv.

17 McNally, 'Is PTSD a Transhistorical Phenomenon?', 119.

18 Allan Young, *The Harmony of Illusions: Inventing Post-Traumatic Stress Disorder* (Princeton, NJ: Princeton University Press, 1997), 5.

19 Young and Breslau, 'What Is "PTSD"?', 135.

20 Young and Breslau, 'What Is "PTSD"?', 148. Emphasis in original.

21 Fassin and Rechtman, *Empire of Trauma*, 6.

22 Herman, *Trauma and Recovery*, 7.

23 Herman, *Trauma and Recovery*, 11.

24 Herman, *Trauma and Recovery*, 14.

25 For example, Barbara Ehrenreich and Deirdre English, *Complaints and Disorders: The Sexual Politics of Sickness* (Old Westbury, NY: The Feminist Press, 1975). The idea of a real event as the root cause of trauma did not completely disappear from psychiatric thinking after Freud. The work of both Otto Rank and Sandor Ferenczi sought to resurrect this strain, but its inroads were limited. Henri F. Ellenberger, *The Discovery of the Unconscious: The History and Evolution of Dynamic Psychiatry* (London: Fontana Press, 1994), 844–5; Judit Mészáros, *Ferenczi and Beyond: Exile of the Budapest School and Solidarity in the Psychoanalytic Movement during the Nazi Years* (London: Karnac Books, 2014), 212–13.

26 Ellenberger, *The Discovery of the Unconscious*, 438; Micale, *Hysterical Men*.

27 Morris, *The Evil Hours*, 102. See also Young and Breslau, 'What Is "PTSD"?', 148–9.

28 Herman, *Trauma and Recovery*, 32.

29 Ann Wolbert Burgess and Lynda Lytle Holmstrom, 'Rape Trauma Syndrome', *American Journal of Psychiatry* 131, no. 9 (1974): 981–6. See also Morris, *The Evil Hours*, 144–5; Herman, *Trauma and Recovery*, 29–31.

30 Fassin and Rechtman, *Empire of Trauma*, 80–4. The work of Robert Jay Lifton and Chaim Shatan, among others, played an important role in bringing these various threads together. See Robert Jay Lifton, *Death in Life: Survivors of Hiroshima* (New York: Random House, 1968); Robert Jay Lifton, *Home from the War: Vietnam Veterans, Neither Victims nor Executioners* (New York: Simon and Schuster, 1973); Chaim F. Shatan, 'Post-Vietnam Syndrome', *The New York Times*, 6 May 1972.

31 Fassin and Rechtman, *Empire of Trauma*, 84–7. The quote comes from p. 84.

32 See, for example, Ethan Watters, *Crazy Like Us: The Globalization of the Western Mind* (London: Robinson, 2010), 71–137.

33 Fassin and Rechtman, *Empire of Trauma*, xi.

34 Mark S. Micale, 'Toward A Global History of Trauma', in *Psychological Trauma and the Legacies of the First World War*, ed. Jason Crouthamel and Peter Leese (Basingstoke: Palgrave Macmillan, 2017), 289.

35 Ethan Watters, 'The Americanization of Mental Illness', *The New York Times*, 8 January 2010, sec. Magazine.

36 Ben Shephard, 'Risk Factors and PTSD: A Historian's Perspective', in *Posttraumatic Stress Disorder: Issues and Controversies*, ed. Gerald Rosen (Hoboken, NJ: John Wiley & Sons, 2004), 57.

37 Fassin and Rechtman, *Empire of Trauma*, 56. Fassin and Rechtman refer specifically to class and race; we add gender to their interpretation of the 'everyday mental health practice, forensic and colonial, that confronted trauma with a mix of scientific vulgate and prejudice'.

38 Shephard, 'Risk Factors and PTSD: A Historian's Perspective', 57.

39 Laura S. Brown, 'Treating the Effects of Psychological Trauma', in *Psychologists' Desk Reference*, ed. Gerald P. Koocher, John C. Norcross and Beverly A. Greens, 3rd edn (New York: Oxford University Press, 2013), 289–93.

40 Judith Lewis Herman, 'Complex PTSD: A Syndrome in Survivors of Prolonged and Repeated Trauma', *Journal of Traumatic Stress* 5, no. 3 (1992): 377–91; Evangelia Giourou et al., 'Complex Posttraumatic Stress Disorder: The Need to Consolidate a Distinct Clinical Syndrome or to Reevaluate Features of Psychiatric Disorders Following Interpersonal Trauma?', *World Journal of Psychiatry* 8, no. 1 (2018): 12–19.

41 Jacky Bouju and Mirjam de Bruijn, 'Introduction: Ordinary Violence in Africa', in *Ordinary Violence and Social Change in Africa*, ed. Jacky Bouju and Mirjam de Bruijn (Leiden: Brill, 2014), 3.

42 Michele C. Black et al., 'National Intimate Partner and Sexual Violence Survey: 2010 Summary Report' (Atlanta: National Center for Injury Prevention and Control of the Centers for Disease Control and Prevention, November 2011), 1, https://www.cdc.gov/ViolencePrevention/pdf/NISVS_Report 2010-a.pdf; Heather L. Littleton, Deborah L. Rhatigan and Danny Axsom, 'Unacknowledged Rape: How Much Do We Know About the Hidden Rape Victim?', *Journal of Aggression, Maltreatment & Trauma* 14, no. 4 (2007): 57–74.

43 Veena Das, *Life and Words: Violence and the Descent into the Ordinary* (Berkeley: University of California Press, 2007), 54. In her work on German women in the wake of the Second World War, historian Atina Grossman offers a provocative argument for how women break this zone of silence through the use of passive voice, humour and other discursive strategies. Atina Grossman, 'The "Big Rape": Sex and Sexual Violence, War, and Occupation in Post-World War II Memory and Imagination', in *Sexual Violence in Conflict Zones*, 137–51.

44 Micale, 'Toward A Global History of Trauma', 299.

45 On post-war retaliation against women, see, for example Megan Koreman, 'The Collaborator's Penance: The Local Purge, 1944-5', *Contemporary*

European History 6, no. 2 (1997): 177–92. The scholarly literature on rape traces back to Susan Brownmiller, *Against Our Will: Men, Women and Rape* (New York: Simon and Schuster, 1975). Events in Rwanda and in Bosnia in the 1990s catalyzed the growth of scholarship on the use of rape as a weapon of war. Significant recent works include Joanna Bourke, *Rape: A History from 1860 to the Present Day* (London: Virago, 2007); Sharon Block, *Rape and Sexual Power in Early America* (Chapel Hill: University of North Carolina Press, 2017); J. Robert Lilly, *Taken by Force: Rape and American GIs in Europe during World War II* (New York: Palgrave Macmillan, 2011); Miriam Gebhardt, *Crimes Unspoken: The Rape of German Women at the End of the Second World War* (Cambridge: Polity, 2017). For a survey of the main currents in the resultant literature, see Elizabeth D. Heineman, 'Introduction: The History of Sexual Violence in Conflict Zones', in *Sexual Violence in Conflict Zones*, 1–21. See also, Amy E. Randall, ed., *Genocide and Gender in the Twentieth Century: A Comparative Survey* (London; New York: Bloomsbury Academic, 2015), especially 1–34, 85–162.

46 Micale, *Hysterical Men*, 283.

Works cited

Alvarado, Carlos S. 'Nineteenth-Century Hysteria and Hypnosis: A Historical Note on Blanche Wittmann'. *Australian Journal of Clinical and Experimental Hypnosis* 37, no. 1 (2009): 21–36.

Barker, Pat. *Regeneration*. London: Viking, 1991.

Black, Michele C., Kathleen C. Basile, Matthew J. Breiding, Sharon G. Smith, Mikel L. Walters, Melissa T. Merrick, Jieru Chen and Mark R. Stevens. 'National Intimate Partner and Sexual Violence Survey: 2010 Summary Report'. Atlanta: National Center for Injury Prevention and Control of the Centers for Disease Control and Prevention, November 2011. https://www.cdc.gov/ViolencePrevention/pdf/NISVS_Report2010-a.pdf.

Block, Sharon. *Rape and Sexual Power in Early America*. Chapel Hill: University of North Carolina Press, 2017.

Bouju, Jacky and Mirjam de Bruijn. 'Introduction: Ordinary Violence in Africa', in *Ordinary Violence and Social Change in Africa*, edited by Jacky Bouju and Mirjam de Bruijn, 1–11. Leiden: Brill, 2014.

Bourke, Joanna. *Rape: A History from 1860 to the Present Day*. London: Virago, 2007.

Brown, Laura S. 'Treating the Effects of Psychological Trauma', in *Psychologists' Desk Reference*, edited by Gerald P. Koocher, John C. Norcross and Beverly A. Greens, 3rd edn, 289–93. New York: Oxford University Press, 2013.

Brownmiller, Susan. *Against Our Will: Men, Women and Rape*. New York: Simon and Schuster, 1975.

Burgess, Ann Wolbert and Lynda Lytle Holmstrom. 'Rape Trauma Syndrome'. *American Journal of Psychiatry* 131, no. 9 (1974): 981–6.

Caruth, Cathy. *Unclaimed Experience: Trauma, Narrative, and History*. Baltimore, MD: Johns Hopkins University Press, 1996.

Das, Veena. *Life and Words: Violence and the Descent into the Ordinary*. Berkeley: University of California Press, 2007.

Didi-Huberman, Georges. *The Invention of Hysteria: Charcot and the Photographic Iconography of the Salpêtrière*. Translated by Alisa Hartz. Cambridge, MA: MIT Press, 2003.

Ditlevsen, Daniel N. and Ask Elklit. 'Gender, Trauma Type, and PTSD Prevalence: A Re-Analysis of 18 Nordic Convenience Samples'. *Annals of General Psychiatry* 11, no. 1 (2012): 26.

Ehrenreich, Barbara and Deirdre English. *Complaints and Disorders: The Sexual Politics of Sickness*. Old Westbury, NY: The Feminist Press, 1975.

Ellenberger, Henri F. *The Discovery of the Unconscious: The History and Evolution of Dynamic Psychiatry*. London: Fontana Press, 1994.

Enquist, Per Olov. *Story of Blanche and Marie*. London: Vintage Books, 2007.

Fassin, Didier and Richard Rechtman. *The Empire of Trauma: An Inquiry into the Condition of Victimhood*. Translated by Rachel Gomme. Princeton, NJ: Princeton University Press, 2009.

Gebhardt, Miriam. *Crimes Unspoken: The Rape of German Women at the End of the Second World War*. Cambridge: Polity, 2017.

Gijn, J. van. 'In Defence of Charcot, Curie, and Wittmann'. *The Lancet* 369, no. 9560 (2007): 462.

Giourou, Evangelia, Maria Skokou, Stuart P. Andrew, Konstantina Alexopoulou, Philippos Gourzis and Eleni Jelastopulu. 'Complex Posttraumatic Stress Disorder: The Need to Consolidate a Distinct Clinical Syndrome or to Reevaluate Features of Psychiatric Disorders Following Interpersonal Trauma?' *World Journal of Psychiatry* 8, no. 1 (2018): 12–19.

Heineman, Elizabeth D., ed. *Sexual Violence in Conflict Zones: From the Ancient World to the Era of Human Rights*. Philadelphia: University of Pennsylvania Press, 2013.

Herman, Judith Lewis. 'Complex PTSD: A Syndrome in Survivors of Prolonged and Repeated Trauma'. *Journal of Traumatic Stress* 5, no. 3 (1992): 377–91.

Herman, Judith Lewis. *Trauma and Recovery*. New York: BasicBooks, 1992.

Horowitz, Mardi J. 'Introduction', in *Essential Papers on Post Traumatic Stress Disorder*, edited by Mardi J. Horowitz, 1–17. New York: New York University Press, 1999.

Hustvedt, Asti. *Medical Muses: Hysteria in Nineteenth-Century Paris*. London: Bloomsbury, 2012.

Jones, E., R. H. Vermaas, H. McCartney, C. Beech, I. Palmer, K. Hyams and S. Wessely. 'Flashbacks and Post-Traumatic Stress Disorder: The Genesis of a 20th-Century Diagnosis'. *The British Journal of Psychiatry* 182, no. 2 (2003): 158–63.

Kolk, Bessel A. van der. *The Body Keeps the Score: Brain, Mind, and Body in the Healing of Trauma*. New York: Penguin Books, 2015.

Koreman, Megan. 'The Collaborator's Penance: The Local Purge, 1944–5'. *Contemporary European History* 6, no. 2 (1997): 177–92.

Levine, Peter A. *Waking the Tiger: Healing Trauma*. Berkeley, CA: North Atlantic Books, 1997.

Lifton, Robert Jay. *Death in Life: Survivors of Hiroshima*. New York: Random House, 1968.

Lifton, Robert Jay. *Home from the War: Vietnam Veterans, Neither Victims nor Executioners*. New York: Simon and Schuster, 1973.
Lilly, J. Robert. *Taken by Force: Rape and American GIs in Europe during World War II*. New York: Palgrave Macmillan, 2011.
Littleton, Heather L., Deborah L. Rhatigan and Danny Axsom. 'Unacknowledged Rape: How Much Do We Know About the Hidden Rape Victim?'. *Journal of Aggression, Maltreatment & Trauma* 14, no. 4 (2007): 57–74.
Loughran, Tracey. 'Shell Shock'. *The British Library*, 7 November 2018. https://www.bl.uk/world-war-one/articles/shell-shock.
Loughran, Tracey. *Shell-Shock and Medical Culture in First World War Britain*. Cambridge: Cambridge University Press, 2017.
MacKinnon, Gilles, dir. *Regeneration*. London: BBC Films, 1997.
McNally, Richard J. 'Is PTSD a Transhistorical Phenomenon?', in *Culture and PTSD: Trauma in Global and Historical Perspective*, edited by Devon E. Hinton and Byron J. Good, 117–34. Philadelphia: University of Pennsylvania Press, 2016.
Mészáros, Judit. *Ferenczi and Beyond: Exile of the Budapest School and Solidarity in the Psychoanalytic Movement during the Nazi Years*. London: Karnac Books, 2014.
Micale, Mark S. *Hysterical Men: The Hidden History of Male Nervous Illness*. Cambridge, MA: Harvard University Press, 2009.
Micale, Mark S. 'Toward A Global History of Trauma', in *Psychological Trauma and the Legacies of the First World War*, edited by Jason Crouthamel and Peter Leese, 289–310. Basingstoke: Palgrave Macmillan, 2017.
Morlock, Forbes. 'The Very Picture of a Primal Scene: Une Leçon Clinique à La Salpêtrière'. *Visual Resources* 23, nos. 1–2 (2007): 129–46.
Morris, David J. *The Evil Hours: A Biography of Post-Traumatic Stress Disorder*. Boston, MA: Houghton Mifflin Harcourt, 2016.
Randall, Amy E., ed. *Genocide and Gender in the Twentieth Century: A Comparative Survey*. London and New York: Bloomsbury Academic, 2015.
Shatan, Chaim F. 'Post-Vietnam Syndrome'. *The New York Times*, 6 May 1972.
Shay, Jonathan. *Achilles in Vietnam Combat Trauma and the Undoing of Character*. New York: Scribner, 2005.
Shay, Jonathan. *Odysseus in America: Combat Trauma and the Trials of Homecoming*. New York: Scribner, 2002.
Shephard, Ben. 'Risk Factors and PTSD: A Historian's Perspective', in *Posttraumatic Stress Disorder: Issues and Controversies*, edited by Gerald Rosen, 39–61. Hoboken, NJ: John Wiley & Sons, 2004.
'Trauma- and Stressor-Related Disorders', in *Diagnostic and Statistical Manual of Mental Disorders*, 5th edn. DSM Library. Washington, DC: American Psychiatric Association, 2013.
Watson, Laurel B., Cirleen DeBlaere, Kimberly J. Langrehr, David G. Zelaya and Mirella J. Flores. 'The Influence of Multiple Oppressions on Women of Color's Experiences with Insidious Trauma'. *Journal of Counseling Psychology* 63, no. 6 (2016): 656–67.
Watters, Ethan. 'The Americanization of Mental Illness'. *The New York Times*, 8 January 2010, sec. Magazine.
Watters, Ethan. *Crazy Like Us: The Globalization of the Western Mind*. London: Robinson, 2010.

Yehuda, Rachel and Alexander C. McFarlane. 'Introduction', in *Psychobiology of Post-Traumatic Stress Disorder*, edited by Rachel Yehuda and Alexander C. McFarlane, xi–xv. New York: New York Academy of Sciences, 1997.

Young, Allan. *The Harmony of Illusions: Inventing Post-Traumatic Stress Disorder*. Princeton, NJ: Princeton University Press, 1997.

Young, Allan and Naomi Breslau. 'What Is "PTSD"?: The Heterogeneity Thesis', in *Culture and PTSD: Trauma in Global and Historical Perspective*, edited by Devon E. Hinton and Byron J. Good, 135–54. Philadelphia: University of Pennsylvania Press, 2016.

2

Trauma in post-First World War Italy

Experiences, erasures and denials

Martina Salvante

Beginning in the second half of the twentieth century, the concept of trauma was progressively employed to refer not only to physical but also to emotional or psychological wounds. As elaborated in this volume's introduction, anthropologists Didier Fassin and Richard Rechtman have argued that 'trauma has become a major signifier of our age. . . . It is the scar that a tragic event leaves on an individual victim or on a witness – sometimes even on the perpetrator'.[1] The analogy of the scar discloses the sensitive relation between the mind and the body, the psychological and the physical.[2] Nowadays the scope of trauma studies has extended so far that it covers a wide range of topics. This umbrella term encompasses physical and psychological damage, past disturbing experiences and their resurfacing in the present. The notion of trauma applies not only to individual symptoms of trauma-triggering events but also to the capacity of individual stories to contribute to a collective memory. In some cases, however, personal memories of trauma might be marginalized or forgotten in the official recollection of events. As a consequence, victims might seek to have their trauma recognized by contesting public memory.

This chapter addresses some of these issues, as it looks at the enduring impact and legacies of these 'scars' for both individuals and groups. Both real and symbolic wounds can have short-term or long-term legacies. The legacies and multifaceted nature of trauma are examined in this chapter, with particular attention devoted to post-First World War Italy. I focus on the cases of Italy's disabled veterans of the First World War and the crushing defeat that the Italian army suffered in October 1917 at Caporetto (present-day Kobarid, Slovenia). This disastrous battle was and still is tantamount to a national trauma, contributing to collective memory discourses of trauma in post-First World War Italy. Taking into account diverse aspects and meanings of trauma allows us to emphasize its associations with themes such as erasure and denial. I present here different cases and definitions of trauma in the First World War and subsequently reflect upon the long-term physical, political and economic effects of the conflict.

The chapter is divided into three sections: the first describes the role of military psychiatry in First World War Italy; the second section focuses on the entanglement of body and mind when considering trauma; and the third considers war pensions as instrumental to the politics of trauma and the 1917 Caporetto defeat as part of the collective memory of the conflict in Italy.

Psychiatry in the First World War

The role of the medical sciences in defining and healing psychological trauma during and after the First World War has been a central concern for historians.[3] Shell shock has also become more widely the emblematic condition of the Great War. Especially with regard to the British case, it has deeply informed our understanding of that conflict. As Jay Winter argues, shell shock 'turned from a diagnosis into a metaphor', referring not only to the disorders of soldiers but also to the damage inflicted by the war more broadly.[4] 'Shell shock came to signify a mixed bag of imperfectly understood but real disorders', while it also 'said something about the terrible newness of the war as a whole'.[5] If this term in Britain evolved into a metaphor, the same did not happen in other countries, where the terms *Kriegsneurosen*, *nevrosi di guerra*, *névrose traumatique* maintained their strictly medical meaning. The organization of psychiatric services differed from one national context to another, despite physician and psychiatric familiarity with the scholarly publications of adversaries, and the exchange of ideas and best practices with allies.[6]

In this section I describe, among other issues, how the concept of trauma was constructed in Italy. A brief account of the ways Italian psychiatry approached war neurosis – the term generally used in the country – follows. As in other belligerent countries, numerous soldiers contracted nervous diseases. Because of their increasing number, military and medical authorities resolved to set up a system of assistance addressing specifically those types of disorders.

Italy entered the Great War in May 1915, and the organization of a wartime psychiatric service was laid out in late summer that year on the initiative of illustrious civilian psychiatrists of the period, in particular, Augusto Tamburini, Leonardo Bianchi and Enrico Morselli.[7] The service provided each army corps with a skilled consultant, who had to respond to the requirements of both medicine and military discipline, to see to the rapid recovery of less serious cases and to arrange specialized wards near the front. In addition, two neuropsychiatric villages were put up immediately behind the front lines, precisely in Carnia and Cadore, to operate as 'miniature asylums'. In these structures, medics tended to cure the milder cases quickly, to identify the simulators and to send the most serious cases to hospitals or asylums in the rear. The inpatients were kept in strict isolation, carefully monitored by the military medical staff in charge of detecting any changes in their clinical condition or any potentially suspicious behaviour.[8]

The most severe or persistent cases could lead to committal for observation in the psychiatric wards of mental hospitals further from the front; after three months of observation and treatment without improvement, institutionalization became definitive.[9] Like in all belligerent countries, Italian psychiatrists (and health workers in general) played their nationalistic role in treating soldiers with disorders and releasing as many of them as possible back to the army for renewed service. Military medicine had, indeed, the purpose of maintaining the army's fighting strength. This objective, however, revealed the dual loyalty of care providers: 'military doctors had to consider not only the interests of individual soldiers-patients, but also – and primarily – the interests of the state and the military'.[10]

There are 40,000 men recorded as hospitalized for psychiatric reasons, while many more may have suffered a breakdown but did not receive any treatment. The relatively small number of men – less than 0.8 per cent of the more than five million serving in the Italian army – suggests the scale of the problem.[11] But the number may not reflect how many men suffered from psychological trauma as a consequence of war, as military authorities may have been reluctant to acknowledge signs of mental breakdown because they needed men for fighting. There may also have been resistance among servicemen to treatment, so as to avoid the stigma of mental illness.

The extensive mobilization of Italian psychiatry for the war effort did not result, however, in the development of original theoretical reflections about war pathologies. Rather, the theoretical models and therapies that had dominated pre-war psychiatry persisted during the conflict and psychiatrists 'continued to use traditional categories such as predisposition, heredity or degeneration'.[12] The dominant medical theory in Italy, as in other belligerent countries, maintained that war-related nervous and mental disorders affected predisposed individuals; combat circumstances triggered a latent constitutional weakness or inherent mental illness already present, lurking just below the surface.[13] In particular, Italian psychiatry was imbued with nineteenth-century paradigms revolving around the distinction between normal and anomalous types, incomplete development, hereditary defects or pathological degeneration. The Italian psychiatric culture was mainly based on a biological, strictly neuroanatomical, explanatory approach that had been largely shaped by Cesare Lombroso, the famed father of criminal anthropology.[14] As a consequence, mobilized psychiatrists tried in many cases to diminish the impact of the war on mental suffering, by attributing any psychological disorder to individual degeneration. For those who agreed with this approach, traumatized soldiers would sooner or later have manifested their mental disorders regardless of the conflict. It was almost unacceptable for Italian psychiatry to consider the causes of war neurosis as being purely emotive and therefore not measurable and not associated to a 'faulty' body/individual.[15]

Psychiatrists welcomed the war as an opportunity for sharpening observational tools, but the overwhelming number of soldiers led frequently to superficial diagnoses and inappropriate treatment. Moreover, doctors came into continual conflicts with military authorities, whose priority was to bring as many men as possible back into service. In an article on psychoneurosis published in 1920, psychiatrists Lionello De Lisi and Ezio Foscarini wrote that

> often in the haste of our work we were not able to do more than formulate, after the patient's recovery, a judgment drawn from moral rather than scientific criteria: a personal and unnecessary judgment for practical purposes given that the principal aim had been reached: to restore to or force upon an able man the ability to be a soldier.[16]

De Lisi and Foscarini capture the pressure under which wartime psychiatrists operated: to diagnose and treat soldiers without the luxury of time for observation in order to send them back to the front as promptly as possible. This approach compromised the medical foundation on which psychiatry sought to base its evaluation.

Class biases informed attitudes among both psychiatrists and officers towards soldiers who experienced mental health challenges in the course of the war. Bruna Bianchi emphasizes that the insistence of psychiatrists on the questions of predisposition or degeneration reflected and reinforced a feeling of diffidence, suspicion and disdain towards the soldiers who showed signs of mental and nervous disorders.[17] The military hierarchy nourished a sense of contempt and diffidence towards the rank-and-file soldiers, who were seen as weak, primitive, abnormal and also malingering. The majority of infantrymen came from rural and rather illiterate backgrounds and were often regarded by commentators as resigned, apolitical, ignorant and stoical, with an almost limitless capacity to endure suffering.

The Franciscan friar Agostino Gemelli, a chaplain, physician and psychologist, investigated the psychology of soldiers, examining their motivation, courage and psychological adaptation. As Director of the High Command's psychophysiological laboratory, he scrutinized the mindset of the airman and the common soldier.¹⁸ In his view, this latter juggled courage and fear by means of a sort of alienation, for which 'the soldier ceases to be "he"; his "I" is another; the life that he leads as a soldier is a parenthesis in his life; it is not "his" life but another life to which he attaches little importance, and so he lives outside himself'.¹⁹

Military authorities were interested in recovering soldiers as quickly as possible in order to send them back to the front line. As a consequence, psychiatrists sought to unmask the imposters, or identify the physical lesion that, according to their prevailing functionalist view, caused the trauma. Fakery became a sort of obsession for those psychiatrists who bitterly distrusted the soldiers who, in their view, were attempting to escape their patriotic duty. Strict medical observation, discipline and harsh treatment were the tools used to make those suspected of simulation confess their deception. Straightjackets and denunciation to the military justice system were other means employed against suspected simulators.

This nationalistic interpretation of mental disorders escalated in the last months of the conflict and, in particular, after the crushing October 1917 defeat of the Italian army at Caporetto.²⁰ As a consequence of that catastrophic event the psychiatric service was entirely restructured; hospitals and asylums in the northeast of Italy were evacuated after troops and refugees had fled the lands invaded by enemy armies. A new Psychiatric Centre for Preliminary Collection was established in Reggio Emilia in January 1918, at the dividing line between the war zone and the country. The new facility operated as a clearing house for soldiers with mental disorders coming from the entire war zone. After a strict observation, if declared fit they would be returned to the front; otherwise, they would be transferred to other institutions in the rear for treatment. The director of the new Centre was Placido Consiglio, a military psychiatrist who had already served during the Italo-Turkish war in 1911–12.²¹ The Psychiatric Centre for Preliminary Collection was permanently closed in March 1919: 11,000 soldiers passed through it in just over a year. In November 1918, 64 per cent of those observed in the Centre were deemed recovered and sent back to the war. The Centre was meant to 'fight against the simulator, the anomalous and the degenerate'. Its task was observation rather than treatment, forensic medicine rather than mental healthcare. The Centre was responsible for the provision of medico-legal reports and psychiatric capacity assessments.²² According to Placido Consiglio, the main characteristics of war neurosis were depression by heredity or predisposition, mental dissociation and hysteria. The weak, shy, unstable and emotive often escaped the demands of duty through illness or by feigning symptoms. The war acted purely as a trigger to a pre-existing disposition. In his view, the same disruptive characteristics could also increase criminality among the military, as, for example, in the case of defection.²³ Both criminal transgressions and psychiatric disorders were refracted through the lens of morality and degeneracy.

Trauma, army rank and discipline

Camp hospitals saw an increasing number of soldiers with serious and persistent illnesses, who had to be transferred to psychiatric wards in lunatic asylums in other parts of the country. Most of these patients exhibited mental confusion and depression. A letter from one Francesco, an officer candidate interned in the Treviso asylum, to a woman illustrates this affective state, when he writes: 'You always encourage me to hope, hope, hope. But I can't hope, I don't have the energy to hope, I wouldn't know what to hope for. [. . .] I am so much life-weary that my treatment here seems vain to me. Healing the dead is unnecessary'.[24]

Physical maladies often accentuated soldiers' disorientation, underscoring the entanglement of body and mind in trauma. For example, in the medical certifcate of a limbless soldier sent to the asylum in Cremona in October 1918, a doctor explained: 'He just recovered from a flu. Fought in the first battles of this war, when he was injured and his right leg was amputated. [. . .] He is delirious and has odd ideas about his leg growing back. He is impulsive and does not sleep. He considers himself dangerous for others' and his own safety'.[25] Despite his physical maladies, this man's phantom limb syndrome was, nonetheless, categorically regarded as a psychic disorder.[26]

Reigning ideas about class and gender informed how trauma was both experienced by soldiers and understood by psychiatrists. Rank-and-file soldiers' breakdowns frequently centred on anxiety about their families' material hardships. Correspondence suggests that these worries were often attributed to homesickness. In a letter addressed to his wife in broken Italian, a private from Southern Italy wrote while committed to the asylum in Cremona: 'Dear wife, I'm well and you? Tell me how you get something to eat since you have nothing. Who feeds our five children? Tell me if you can get up from bed and if you're feeling better. [. . .] We will all die without food'.[27] His inability as a husband and father to provide for his family's basic needs was a source of concern and was linked here to his sense of hopelessness.

Anxiety among officers expressed itself differently. They fretted about their failure to live up to wartime expectations of what they, as male citizens, owed the nation. These officers saw themselves as unworthy, for having disappointed themselves and their fatherland. Officers had a higher sense of duty and were often troubled by feelings of responsibility and dissimulation of any fears in front of their subordinates. In the medical record of a lieutenant treated at the asylum in Treviso, doctors reported that the man had 'been recalled because not able to endure the war toll, exhausted, depressed, and preoccupied with his inability to command his company'.[28] The disorder most commonly encountered by psychiatrists among officers in combat was neurasthenia, which Placido Consiglio attributed to 'their emotional temperament' or to the 'preceding weakness of their moral character'.[29]

Psychiatrists understood mental confusion as demonstrative of war neurosis. They argued that to cope with fear and pain, the soldiers repressed their thoughts; this repression, it was believed, manifested itself through a refusal to hear, see, speak or remember. Into the early 1920s, medical debates over organic versus psychic or emotional aetiology in the formation of psychoneurosis continued. The debate took place in the context of Italy's major specialist periodicals of the time, but was also part of a wider European reflection on this question.[30] Italian psychiatry remained anchored to the nineteenth-century paradigm of physical predisposition, thus rejecting the idea of war as a pathogenic event. War service was regarded as a patriotic duty for every 'normal' man and fear as an emotion that adult men could control. Italian psychiatrists tended to reduce psychic reactions to questions of moral strength and weakness, thus connecting the lack of willpower and self-control to hysteria. This latter, indeed, was the most common syndrome among hospitalized men in the ranks. The servicemen who presented signs of mental illness were seen as distancing themselves from traditional masculinity. Their supposed violation of the cultural codes of virility made them, in the eyes of psychiatrists or military hierarchies, potential malingerers.[31]

As historian Vanda Wilcox observes, mental breakdown was often seen as a form of desertion and therefore 'understood in a disciplinary rather than a medical framework, and men with nervous disorders were described as "degenerate" or "parasites"'.[32] Conflict and confusion between clinical and moral categories had an impact on medical diagnoses, as psychiatrists operated in their dual role of military officers and doctors in many cases. Hence, their therapeutic responses were often brutal and based on persuasion with the soldiers, because they were motivated by the urgency of the situation and by the tendency to deny the existence of real mental disorders.

Psychiatrists' harsh assessment and treatment, including electroshock therapy, of war-related psychological trauma influenced the post-war debate on war pensions. The interpretation of war neurosis as due to degeneration or organic defects often compromised veterans' pension claims, because their psychological disorders were not considered exclusively war-related or were believed to be curable. Those men were entitled to receive temporary allowances, but not long-term pensions. Of the over 40,000 acknowledged cases of nervous and mental illness during the war, only a small percentage was awarded a pension, while many of the 2,000 still seriously affected had not received any pension in 1926, as denounced by the *Opera nazionale per gli invalidi di guerra* (National Agency for the War Disabled).[33]

Historian Jay Winter warns scholars about the plausible underreporting and/or underestimation of psychiatric casualties, since, among others, 'those with physical wounds are rarely listed as having psychiatric disorders too', despite their comorbidity.[34] In her recent work on the facially disfigured,

Fiona Reid has underlined the importance of 'expanding the notion of trauma to include those traumatized by their wounds, as well as those directly traumatized by the war itself' to have 'a fuller, more complex picture of the post-war world and of the enduring impact of the conflict'.[35] Physically disabled veterans of wars past and present went through traumatic experiences, linked not only to the moment of their violent disablement but through the course of their medical treatment, rehabilitation, homecoming and readaptation to civilian life.

Even for soldiers who returned from the front with their bodies intact, reacclimating to civilian life proved a struggle. Although homecoming was a time about which soldiers had fantasized while on active service, the reality of their return often failed to align with their expectations. Sometimes they felt let down, even by those who were supposed to be intimates, such as relatives, fiancées and wives. For disabled veterans, too, broken promises and shattered dreams awaited many upon their return home. Returning disabled veterans had to contend with miserable episodes of refusal and abandonment. The Milan-based monthly *La stampella* (The crutch) reported news of the murder of a woman by an amputee veteran in September 1922.[36] The man had killed his fiancée, because she tried to break off their relationship under pressure from her family, which frowned on her engagement to a permanently disabled man. Furthermore, the journal occasionally reported on disabled veterans who committed suicide in the post-war years. These occurrences provide evidence of the ongoing emotional distress experienced by those returned from active service.

Homecoming was particularly charged with an intense anxiety for those who were returning to civilian life with a disability, as they attempted to take up previous affairs or jobs again and resume their pre-war social and family interactions. The letters addressed by many former patients to the director of a rehabilitation centre in Florence for those blinded in the war provide a picture of the different post-war destinies of the war disabled. They convey words of gratitude, dejection, requests for advice and for financial support.[37] Depressed and disheartened by his unemployment, for example, Vittorio wrote in 1925: 'I fought in two wars and tolerated serious hardships unlike modern heroes, but, at the end, all the blood that I shed brought me nothing. On the contrary, many others that are combatants only by name enjoy great benefits'.[38] In 1931, Vittorio's wife wrote to the director to solicit a job for her husband, who was becoming increasingly unhappy. Returning to work and being able to earn a living were individual and social expectations that disabled veterans faced and which were at the heart of their identity as men and, supposedly, family breadwinners. Despite living in an ultra-nationalist and warmongering regime like the fascist one in Italy, the ex-serviceman Vittorio felt left behind and expressed his frustration at the honours enjoyed by those who were combatants by name but not by nature.[39]

Collective memory and the politics of trauma

The rise of fascism to power in 1922 and the establishment of a dictatorship in 1925–6 increasingly promoted a clear-cut narrative of the First World War that erased the trauma and delegitimized the suffering of veterans. Remembrance and grief were replaced by triumphal narratives of war and sacrifice. Fascism celebrated the 1918 victory and used violence against those who were supposedly demeaning its significance: shirkers, pacifists, malingerers and political opponents were all identified as internal enemies and persecuted.

War pensions and the entitlement to benefits can be regarded as a window into the politics of trauma and notions of masculinity. In 1923, when Benito Mussolini's first government was in power, new legislation on war pensions was approved. It reduced the number of pension categories from ten to eight and also cut the number and types of potential beneficiaries in order to curtail the government expenditure on war pensions.[40] In particular, the new norm introduced a distinction between 'combatants' and 'non-combatants', so that special war pensions would be distributed exclusively to those who had 'actually and directly' taken part in combat operations. The law also called for the suspension or revocation of war pensions for those whose acts (such as desertion and self-harm) were considered to have damaged the military's prestige and reputation. The suspension and revocation came into force not only in cases where military courts had sentenced against felons but also when, more vaguely, 'desertion and self-harm had been otherwise verified' (art. 46). In all these cases, men and their families were left stigmatized and without a pension.

During the war, delaying returning from leave, failing to return, faking illness or committing self-harm had all been considered individual acts of 'flight from the war' and, as such, unmanly demonstrations of cowardice and fear. These crimes were harshly penalized with capital punishment or life imprisonment. Military discipline had been meted out, indeed, on extremely brutal lines during the war, particularly under the Chief of Staff of the Italian Army Luigi Cadorna.[41] Up to 750 capital sentences had been executed and dozens of summary executions had been practised on multiple occasions to make examples of those who had not complied with the strict military discipline (Table 2.1).[42]

In contrast to Great Britain, the Italian state to this day has still not pardoned those executed for desertion or cowardice.[43] Pressures from local communities, public commentators, ordinary citizens and historians led to the drafting of a decree on this matter in 2014, but despite the support of the president of the Republic, the Italian Parliament has as of 2020 not proceeded with final approval. Approved by the Chamber of Deputies on 21 May 2015, a draft law on the rehabilitation of the military personnel executed during the First World War was then subjected to scrutiny in the Senate for

TABLE 2.1 *Number of Executions per Offence Perpetrated*

Offence	Number of Executions
Desertion	391
Self-harm	5
Surrendering or disbanding	164
Indiscipline	154
Greed	2
Violence	12
Sexual offences	1
Espionage and treason	21
Total	750

more than a year.[44] Senators long debated whether to enact a rehabilitation or a pardon of those First World War servicemen, thus highlighting a certain cultural resistance to fully mend the memory of the men executed.[45] When an agreement on pardon seemed to have been reached, new general elections and the change of legislature halted the whole procedure.[46] This failed effort points to an enduring refusal to fully recognize the traumatic impact of the Great War on individuals and families, who were often haunted by feelings of shame. It also exposes the persistent stigma against those 'unmanly' men who failed the test of the warrior ideal. Historians, local communities and intellectuals, on the contrary, have largely contributed to raising the public awareness of those soldiers' destiny and prompting legislators to rehabilitate their memory.[47]

The defeat of Italian troops at Caporetto, too, endures in the collective memory. The breaching of Italian lines on 24 October 1917 and the invasion of large portions of Italy's north-eastern territories by enemy troops was a traumatic event for the country.[48] This battle would have meant total collapse, if Italian troops had not been able to establish a new defensive line along the Piave River. The joint Austro-Hungarian and German offensive resulted in the Italians falling back approximately 160 kilometres behind the original front line. Nationalists and military elites blamed the rout on the Left and its 'defeatist' propaganda among soldiers, many of whom had allegedly preferred to 'run away' rather than fighting against the enemy. In reality, many strategic and tactical errors, and an ill-equipped and poorly motivated army, contributed to the inability of Italian troops to withstand a well-planned enemy attack.[49] In the wake of the defeat, however, rank-and-file soldiers were executed by what were widely perceived by the Left to be incompetent and bloodthirsty generals keen to punish others for their own failures. In particular, they singled out Chief of Staff General Luigi Cadorna as responsible for the death of thousands of men, even decades after the end of the conflict.

Despite the recovery of the Italian army and its final victory over Austria-Hungary on 3 November 1918, the 1917 rout continued to haunt Italian memory. In post-war Italy, Caporetto remained a divisive event, often linked to defeatism and used as a propaganda tool by the rising fascist movement against so-called internal enemies.[50] In the late 1930s, Benito Mussolini's regime even erected an ossuary in Caporetto, where the corpses of about 7,000 soldiers were interred. The imposing shrine was meant to commemorate the sacrifice of the men who died in the conflict, but it also emphasized the significance of the victory in that highly contested border region. As the First World War became a cornerstone of fascist ideology and propaganda, the regime intended to use the newly constructed ossuaries, like the one in Caporetto, to cast the war as a triumph. Those monumental sites and the cult of the fallen soldiers that they promoted were meant to foster national cohesion under fascism and to serve as a call to arms for future wars.[51] Other memories or experiences of the conflict were thus marginalized, erased or denied as they were perceived by fascist authorities as non-conforming to its nationalistic, militaristic and imperialistic aspirations.

The seizure of power by the fascists in 1922 brought about major changes not only in the ways the war and the fallen were publicly remembered and commemorated but also in the ways private grief and mourning were experienced.[52] As historian Hanna Malone has emphasized with regard to the monumentalization of commemoration in the 1930s,

> the creation of the monuments marked the apex of a gradual process through which control over the fallen was passed to the military as an agent of the Fascist regime. [. . .] While previously remembrance of the fallen had been left to mourners, local councils, and veterans' groups, after 1928 both monuments and ceremonies commemorating the war dead were either prohibited or subject to state approval.[53]

Despite the erasure of physical and emotional pain from the national narrative and collective memory of the conflict under fascism, trauma never vanished from the lives of some veterans and their families. It resurfaced in the collective memory of the nation once the political conditions changed and historians turned their attention to the variety of individuals and groups who experienced the war both on the front line and behind the lines. It was only in the decades after the Second World War, for instance, that alternative stories of Caporetto found their way into public discourse and collective memory. The event continued to be a touchstone for Italian identity, as

FIGURE 2.1 *Mural (1969) memorializing Italian casualties from the Battle of Caporetto in Orgosolo, Sardinia. Photo by Grazia Cadeddu, 2019. Reproduced with permission.*

evidenced by Figure 2.1 which shows a 1969 graffiti listing the numbers of the dead, disabled, shot and missing among Italian soldiers. In particular, it blames Italian generals and, above all, General Cadorna, for both their decision to go to war and their harshness with the rank and file. This wall art demonstrates how Caporetto proved an enduring point of contention even decades after the event. The invasion's enduring meaning is also evident in the Italian expression 'una Caporetto', which indicates a downfall, much in the way 'Waterloo' in English can be used metaphorically to mean a decisive defeat in any sphere.

Conclusion

This chapter has focused on the multifaceted nature of trauma in Italy with regard to the experience of the First World War. In particular, it has looked at the enduring impact and legacies of that conflict for both individuals and local/national communities. It has also illustrated how psychiatrists in Italy addressed war-related psychological damage and how their theories were imbued with nineteenth-century medical paradigms, nationalism, an obsession with potential malingerers and gender stereotypes. Those doctors mainly continued to use pre-war categories such as predisposition, heredity and degeneration to diagnose servicemen's mental disorders, thus rejecting the idea of war as a pathogenic event. Their approach had repercussions not only on the treatment of the suffering men but also on their and their families' post-war destinies.

Servicemen who presented signs of mental illness were seen as violating culturally coded features of masculinity like bravery and patriotic sacrifice, and therefore, undeserving of any honours, benefits or public commemoration. The stigma attached to those 'unmanly' men who failed the test of the warrior ideal persisted at length, as also testified by the *damnatio memoriae* (condemnation of memory) inflicted upon the Italian servicemen who were executed or decimated for cowardice and desertion during the conflict. Personal memories of trauma have thus collided with official recollections of events, prompting the necessity for in-depth historical investigations into diverse memories of the Great War and into the significance of silence as 'the suppression of troubling images and events'.[54] Historians, indeed, still play a major part in recovering individual or collective traces of denial and erasure that have characterized the politics of remembering, forgetting or disavowing trauma in Italian society.

Notes

1 Didier Fassin and Richard Rechtman, *The Empire of Trauma: An Inquiry into the Condition of Victimhood*, trans. Rachel Gomme (Princeton, NJ; Oxford: Princeton University Press, 2009), xi.

2 See Dominick LaCapra, *Writing History, Writing Trauma* (Baltimore, MD: Johns Hopkins University Press, 2001), 42.

3 See Mark S. Micale and Paul Lerner, 'Trauma, Psychiatry, and History: A Conceptual and Historiographical Introduction', in *Traumatic Pasts: History,*

Psychiatry, and Trauma in the Modern Age, 1870-1930, ed. Paul Lerner and Mark S. Micale (Cambridge; New York: Cambridge University Press, 2001), 6–7. For the Italian case, see a recent book that presents a variety of case studies with regard to the idea of trauma, its diagnosis and treatment. Dario De Santis, ed., *Guerra e scienze della mente in Italia nella prima metà del novecento* (Canterano: Aracne editrice, 2020).

4   Jay M. Winter, 'Shell-Shock and the Cultural History of the Great War', *Journal of Contemporary History* 35, no. 1 (2000): 7; Jay M. Winter, 'Shell Shock', in *The Cambridge History of the First World War*, ed. Jay M. Winter, vol. 3: Civil Society (Cambridge: Cambridge University Press, 2014), 311.

5   Winter, 'Shell Shock', 317.

6   For example, *Atti della III Conferenza interalleata per l'assistenza agli invalidi di guerra (Roma, 12-17 ottobre 1919)* (Roma: Stab. Tip. La Rapida, 1919). Inter-allied conferences for the aftercare and professional re-education of disabled servicemen had been organized since 1917. See Gildas Brégain, 'Un problème national, interallié ou international? La difficile gestion transnationale des mutilés de guerre (1917-1923)', *Revue d'histoire de la protection sociale* 9, no. 1 (2016): 110–32.

7   Augusto Tamburini (1848–1919) is a key figure in Italian psychiatry. He directed the San Lazzaro asylum in Reggio Emilia from 1877 to 1907, turning it into a scientifically renowned institution. He also edited Italy's first journal of psychiatry, *Rivista sperimentale di freniatria*, in the period between 1877 and 1919. Leonardo Bianchi (1848–1927) was a neuropsychiatrist and politician, who supervised the organization of healthcare in Italy during the Great War (1916–17). Enrico Morselli (1852–1929) was professor of psychiatry at the Universities of Turin and Genoa. Interested also in psychology, social sciences and psychoanalysis, he founded and edited the journals *Rivista di filosofia scientifica* in 1881 and *Quaderni di psichiatria* in 1914.

8   Placido Consiglio, 'Un villagio neuro-psichiatrico in zona di guerra', *Rivista sperimentale di psichiatria* 42, no. 1 (1916–17): 175–82. See also Anna Grillini, 'Fast Therapy and Fast Recovery: The Role of Time for the Italian Neuropsychiatric Service in the War Zones', in *War Time: First World War Perspectives on Temporality*, ed. Louis Halewood, Adam Luptak and Hanna Smyth (London; New York: Routledge, 2018), 36–50.

9   Placido Consiglio, 'Il servizio neuropsichiatrico di guerra in Italia', in *Atti della III Conferenza interalleata per l'assistenza agli invalidi di guerra* (Roma: Tip. La Rapida, 1919), 499–510.

10 Leo van Bergen, 'Medicine and Medical Service', in *1914-1918 Online: International Encyclopaedia of the First World War*, ed. Ute Daniel et al. (Berlin: Freie Universität Berlin, 2014). DOI: 10.15463/ie1418.10221.

11 Numbers in Pierluigi Scolè, 'I morti', in *Dizionario storico della Prima guerra mondiale*, ed. Nicola Labanca (Roma-Bari: Laterza, 2014), 178–9, 187.

12 Vinzia Fiorino, 'First World War Neuroses in Italy: Emergency Management, Therapies and Some Reflections on Male Hysteria', in *Psychiatrie im Ersten Weltkrieg*, ed. Thomas Becker et al. (Konstanz: UVK Verlagsgesellschaft, 2018), 212. See also Bruna Bianchi, 'Psychiatrists, Soldiers, and Officers in

Italy during the Great War', in *Traumatic Pasts: History, Psychiatry, and Trauma in the Modern Age, 1870-1930*, ed. Paul Lerner and Mark S. Micale (Cambridge; New York: Cambridge University Press, 2001), 222–3.

13 Fiona Reid, 'War Psychiatry and Shell Shock (Version 2.0)', in *1914-1918 Online: International Encyclopedia of the First World War*, ed. Ute Daniel et al. (Berlin: Freie Universität Berlin, 11 December 2019). DOI: 10.15463/ie1418.10288/2.0.

14 Cesare Lombroso (1835–1909) was a physician and criminologist who founded the Italian School of Positivist Criminology. Lombroso believed criminals were destined to commit their crimes. See Mary Gibson, *Born to Crime: Cesare Lombroso and the Origins of Biological Criminology* (Westport, CT: Praeger, 2002). On the role played by Lombroso in the development of psychiatry in Italy, see Valeria Paola Babini, 'Looking Back: Italian Psychiatry from Its Origins to Law 180 of 1978', *The Journal of Nervous and Mental Disease* 202, no. 6 (2014): 428–31.

15 Recent studies and new primary sources, however, show that not all psychiatrists in Italy shared those traditional and functionalist views. See Dario De Santis, 'Introduzione. Una fucina di traumatizzati', in *Guerra e scienze della mente in Italia nella prima metà del novecento*, ed. Dario De Santis (Canterano: Aracne editrice, 2020), 17–36.

16 Lionello De Lisi and Ezio Foscarini, 'Psiconevrosi di guerra e piccolo cause emotive', *Note e Riviste di Psichiatria* 49 (1920): 14–15. Lionello de Lisi (1885–1957) became head of the Neuropsychiatric unit in Genoa in the late 1930s.

17 Bianchi, 'Psychiatrists, Soldiers, and Officers in Italy during the Great War', 229–30.

18 See Agostino Gemelli, *Il nostro soldato. Saggi di psicologia militare* (Milano: Treves, 1917). Gemelli (1878–1959) was born in Milan to a bourgeois family and went on to study philosophy, medicine and experimental psychology after having been ordained a priest in 1908. On Gemelli's researches and writings during the First World War, see Agostino Gemelli, *La filosofia del cannone e altri scritti di psicologia del soldato*, ed. Dario De Santis (Pisa: ETS, 2018). Gemelli founded the Università Cattolica del Sacro Cuore in Milan in 1921, where he also worked as professor of psychology and director of the Laboratory of Experimental Psychology.

19 Gemelli, *Il nostro soldato. Saggi di psicologia militare*, 103.

20 An Austro-Hungarian and German offensive broke into the Italian front lines at the end of October 1917, causing the retreat of Italian troops. Approximately 300,000 Italian soldiers were 'scattered' during the battle.

21 On Placido Consiglio (1877–1959) and the Centre, see Francesco Paolella, 'Un laboratorio di medicina politica. Placido Consiglio e il Centro psichiatrico militare di prima raccolta', in *Piccola patria, grande guerra. La prima guerra mondiale a Reggio Emilia*, ed. Marco Carrattieri and Alberto Ferraboschi (Bologna: CLUEB, 2008), 187–204; Andrea Scartabellati, 'Un Wanderer dell'anormalità? Un invito allo studio di Placido Consiglio (1877-1959)', *Rivista sperimentale di freniatria* 134 no. 3 (2010): 89–112.

22 Placido Consiglio, 'Il centro psichiatrico militare di 1a raccolta di Reggio Emilia', *Giornale di medicina militare*, no. 3 (1919): 340–55.

23 Placido Consiglio, 'Le psicosi, le nevrosi e la delinquenza militare in guerra', *Rivista sperimentale di freniatria e medicina legale delle alienazioni mentali*, nos. 3–4 (1923): 617–29.

24 Written in October 1916, the letter was kept by the doctors of the asylum to understand Francesco's psychological condition. It is published in Nicola Bettiol, *Feriti nell'anima: storie di soldati dai manicomi del Veneto, 1915-1918* (Treviso: Istresco, 2008), 84–5.

25 In Nicola Bettiol and Andrea Scartabellati, 'Destini della follia in guerra: vivere, sopravvivere e scrivere al S. Artemio di Treviso', in *Dalle trincee al manicomio: esperienza bellica e destino di matti e psichiatri nella Grande Guerra*, ed. Andrea Scartabellati (Torino: Marco Valerio, 2008), 167.

26 On phantom limb syndrome, see Gabriele Cipriani et al., 'The Phantom and the Supernumerary Phantom Limb: Historical Review and New Case', *Neuroscience Bulletin* 27, no. 6 (2011): 359–65.

27 In Bettiol and Scartabellati, 'Destini della follia in guerra', 208.

28 Mentioned in Bettiol, *Feriti nell'anima*, 322.

29 Placido Consiglio, 'Le anomalie del carattere dei militari in guerra', *Rivista sperimentale di freniatria* 42, no. 1 (1916–17): 139.

30 See, for example, Giacomo Pighini, 'Considerazioni patogeniche sulle psiconevrosi emotive osservate al fronte', *Il Policlinico* 24, no. 6 (1917): 243–68; Giuseppe Pellacani, 'Le neuropatie emotive e le psiconevrosi nei combattenti', *Rivista sperimentale di freniatria* 44, nos. 1–2 (1920): 1–65. See also Thomas Becker et al., eds., *Psychiatrie im Erstern Weltkrieg* (Konstanz: UVK Verlagsgesellschaft, 2018); Reid, 'War Psychiatry and Shell Shock'.

31 For some considerations on the gendering of hysterical traumatized soldiers as diagnosed by Italian psychiatrists, see Fiorino, 'First World War Neuroses in Italy: Emergency Management, Therapies and Some Reflections on Male Hysteria', 220–4. For a detailed account of these debates in other national contexts, see Paul F. Lerner, *Hysterical Men: War, Psychiatry, and the Politics of Trauma in Germany, 1890-1930* (Ithaca, NY: Cornell University Press, 2003); Tracey Loughran, *Shell-Shock and Medical Culture in First World War Britain* (Cambridge: Cambridge University Press, 2017).

32 Vanda Wilcox, *Morale and the Italian Army during the First World War* (Cambridge: Cambridge University Press, 2016), 193.

33 Opera nazionale per la protezione ed assistenza degli invalidi di guerra, *Per la tutela dei dementi di guerra* (Roma: Coop. Tip. Castaldi, 1926).

34 Winter, 'Shell Shock', 331.

35 Fiona Reid, 'Losing Face: Trauma and Maxillofacial Injury in the First World War', in *Psychological Trauma and the Legacies of the First World War*, ed. Peter Leese and Jason Crouthamel (Cham: Palgrave Macmillan/Springer International Publishing, 2017), 28.

36 *La stampella* was the bulletin of the Milanese branch of the *Associazione nazionale mutilati e invalidi di guerra* (ANMIG, National Association for the

War Disabled). This organization was established in Milan in April 1917 to advocate for those disabled in service to their country.

37 For more details on this institution and its beneficiaries, see Martina Salvante, '"Thanks to the Great War the Blind Gets the Recognition of His Ability to Act": The Rehabilitation of Blinded Servicemen in Florence', *First World War Studies* 6, no. 1 (2015): 21–35.

38 Archivio storico della Città di Firenze, Fondo Comitato ciechi di guerra, b. 248, P. Vittorio. The man had fought in the Italo-Turkish war in 1911–12 and in the First World War.

39 For some considerations on masculinity and disability in the Italian case, see Martina Salvante, 'The Wounded Male Body: Masculinity and Disability in Wartime and Post-WWI Italy', *Journal of Social History* 53, no. 3 (2020): 644–66.

40 Royal decree–law 12 July 1923, no. 1491.

41 On general Cadorna (1850–1928), see Mondini Marco, *Il capo: la grande guerra del generale Luigi Cadorna* (Bologna: Il Mulino, 2017). On military discipline in Italy, see Irene Guerrini and Marco Pluviano, 'Discipline and Military Justice in the Italian Army', in *Italy in the Era of the Great War*, ed. Vanda Wilcox (Leiden; Boston, MA: Brill, 2018), 80–98.

42 Enzo Forcella and Alberto Monticone, *Plotone d'esecuzione. I processi della prima guerra mondiale* (Bari: Laterza, 1968); Marco Pluviano and Irene Guerrini, *Le fucilazioni sommarie nella prima guerra mondiale* (Udine: Paolo Gaspari, 2004). For a comparative perspective, see Steven R. Welch, 'Military Justice', in *1914-1918 Online: International Encyclopaedia of the First World War*, ed. Ute Daniel et al. (Berlin: Freie Universität Berlin, 2014). https://encyclopedia.1914-1918-online.net/article/military_justice/2014-10-08.

43 All 306 British Empire Forces members who were executed for cowardice or desertion in the Great War were granted posthumous pardons in 2006.

44 Chamber of Deputies, 17th legislature, draft law A.C. N. 2741/XVII. Accessed 15 April 2020. https://www.camera.it/leg17/522?tema=disposizioni_concernenti_i_militari_fucilati_durante_la_prima_guerra_mondiale#il_contenuto_della_proposta_di_legge_a_c_2741__a.

45 Marco Pluviano, *Italie: Coup de force sur la rehabilitation des fusillés*, Observatoire du Centenaire, Université de Paris Sorbonne. Accessed 2 August 2019. https://www.pantheonsorbonne.fr/fileadmin/IGPS/observatoire-du-centenaire/Pluviano_-_rehabilitation_fusilles.pdf.

46 New draft laws (C. no. 1213 and S. no 991) were presented in September and December 2018.

47 Paolo Rumiz, 'L'ultima ferita della Grande guerra "L'Italia riabiliti i militari fucilati"', *la Repubblica*, 6 November 2014. https://www.repubblica.it/cronaca/2014/10/31/news/l_ultima_ferita_della_grande_guerra_l_italia_riabiliti_i_militari_fucilati-99937510/; Luciano Santin and Andrea Zannini, eds, *Fucilati per l'esempio: la giustizia militare nella Grande Guerra e il caso di Cercivento* (Udine: Forum, 2017); Irene Guerrini and Marco Pluviano, *Fucilati senza un processo: il 'Memoriale Tommasi' sulle esecuzioni sommarie nella Grande Guerra* (Udine: Gaspari, 2019).

48 Vanda Wilcox, 'The Catastrophe at Caporetto', *History Today*. Accessed 2 August 2019. https://www.historytoday.com/miscellanies/catastrophe-caporetto.

49 Giovanna Procacci, 'The Disaster of Caporetto', in *Disastro! Disasters in Italy since 1860: Culture, Politics, Society*, ed. John Dickie, John Foot and Frank M. Snowden (New York: Palgrave, 2002), 141–64.

50 Vanda Wilcox, 'From Heroic Defeat to Mutilated Victory: The Myth of Caporetto in Fascist Italy', in *Defeat and Memory: Cultural Histories of Military Defeat in the Modern Era*, ed. Jenny Macleod (Basingstoke; New York: Palgrave Macmillan, 2008), 46–60.

51 Daniele Pisani, 'From Italian Monuments to the Fallen of World War I to Fascist War Memorials', *RIHA Journal*. Accessed 17 April 2020. https://www.riha-journal.org/articles/2017/0150-0176-special-issue-war-graves/0165-pisani.

52 The fascist leader Benito Mussolini was appointed president of the Council of Ministers by King Victor Emmanuel III in October 1922 after having staged a coup, the so-called March on Rome. His rule turned dictatorial in the mid-1920s.

53 Hannah Malone, 'Legacies of Fascism: Architecture, Heritage and Memory in Contemporary Italy', *Modern Italy* 22, no. 4 (2017): 202.

54 Jay M. Winter, *War beyond Words: Languages of Remembrance from the Great War to the Present* (Cambridge: Cambridge University Press, 2018).

Works cited

Atti della III Conferenza interalleata per l'assistenza agli invalidi di guerra (Roma, 12–17 ottobre 1919). Roma: Stab. Tip. La Rapida, 1919.

Babini, Valeria Paola. 'Looking Back: Italian Psychiatry From Its Origins to Law 180 of 1978'. *The Journal of Nervous and Mental Disease* 202, no. 6 (June 2014): 428–31.

Becker, Thomas, Heiner Fangerau, Peter Fassl and Hans-Georg Hofer, eds. *Psychiatrie im Erstern Weltkrieg*. Konstanz: UVK Verlagsgesellschaft, 2018.

Bergen, Leo van. 'Medicine and Medical Service', in *1914–1918 Online: International Encyclopedia of the First World War*, edited by Ute Daniel, Peter Gatrell, Oliver Janz, Heather Jones, Jennifer Keene, Alan Kramer and Bill Nasson. Berlin: Freie Universität Berlin, 2014. DOI: 10.15463/ie1418.10221.

Bettiol, Nicola. 'Destini della follia in guerra: vivere, sopravvivere e scrivere al S. Artemio di Treviso', in *Dalle trincee al manicomio: Esperienza bellica e destino di matti e psichiatri nella Grande guerra*, edited by Andrea Scartabellati, 221–329. Torino: Marco Valerio, 2008.

Bettiol, Nicola. *Feriti nell'anima: storie di soldati dai manicomi del Veneto: 1915–1918*. Treviso: Istresco, 2008.

Bianchi, Bruna. 'Psychiatrists, Soldiers, and Officers in Italy during the Great War', in *Traumatic Pasts: History, Psychiatry, and Trauma in the Modern Age, 1870–1930*, edited by Mark S. Micale and Paul Frederick Lerner, 222–52. Cambridge; New York: Cambridge University Press, 2001.

Brégain, Gildas. 'Un problème national, interallié ou international ? La difficile gestion transnationale des mutilés de guerre (1917–1923)', 'A National, an Inter-Allied or an International Problem? The Difficult Transnational Management of Disabled War Veterans (1917–1923)'. *Revue d'histoire de la protection sociale* 9, no. 1 (2016): 110–32.

Cipriani, Gabriele, Lucia Picchi, Marcella Vedovello, Angelo Nuti and Mario Di Fiorino. 'The Phantom and the Supernumerary Phantom Limb: Historical Review and New Case'. *Neuroscience Bulletin* 27, no. 6 (December 2011): 359–65.

Consiglio, Placido. 'Il centro psichiatrico militare di 1a raccolta di Reggio Emilia'. *Giornale di medicina militare* 67, no. 3 (1919): 340–55.

Consiglio, Placido. 'Il servizio neuropsichiatrico di guerra in Italia', in *Atti della III Conferenza interalleata per l'assistenza agli invalidi di Guerra*, 499–510. Roma: Tip. La Rapida, 1919.

Consiglio, Placido, 'Le anomalie del carattere dei militari in guerra'. *Rivista sperimentale di freniatria* 42, no. 1 (1916–17): 131–72.

Consiglio, Placido. 'Le psicosi, le nevrosi e la delinquenza militare in guerra'. *Rivista sperimentale di freniatria e medicina legale delle alienazioni mentali* 47, nos. 3–4 (1923): 617–29.

Consiglio, Placido. 'Un villagio neuro-psichiatrico in zona di guerra'. *Rivista sperimentale di psichiatria* 42, no. 2 (1916–17): 175–82.

De Santis, Dario, ed. *Guerra e scienze della mente in Italia nella prima metà del novecento*. Canterano: Aracne editrice, 2020.

De Santis, Dario, ed. 'Introduzione. Una fucina di traumatizzati', in *Guerra e scienze della mente in Italia nella prima metà del novecento*, edited by Dario De Santis, 17–36. Canterano: Aracne editrice, 2020.

Delaporte, Sophie. 'Making Trauma Visible', in *Traumatic Memories of the Second World War and After*, edited by Peter Leese and Jason Crouthamel, 23–46. Cham: Palgrave Macmillan, 2016.

Fassin, Didier and Richard Rechtman. *The Empire of Trauma: An Inquiry into the Condition of Victimhood*. Translated by Rachel Gomme. Princeton, NJ; Oxford: Princeton University Press, 2009.

Fiorino, Vinzia. 'First World War Neuroses in Italy: Emergency Management, Therapies and Some Reflections on Male Hysteria', in *Psychiatrie im Ersten Weltkrieg*, edited by Thomas Becker, Heiner Fangerau, Peter Fassl and Hans-Georg Hofer, 211–26. Konstanz: UVK Verlagsgesellschaft, 2018.

Forcella, Enzo and Alberto Monticone. *Plotone d'esecuzione. I processi della prima guerra mondiale*. Bari: Laterza, 1968.

Gemelli, Agostino. *Il nostro soldato. Saggi di psicologia militare*. Milano: Treves, 1917.

Gemelli, Agostino. *La filosofia del cannone e altri scritti di psicologia del soldato*. Edited by Dario De Santis. Pisa: ETS, 2018.

Gibson, Mary. *Born to Crime: Cesare Lombroso and the Origins of Biological Criminology*. Westport, CT: Praeger, 2002.

Grillini, Anna. 'Fast Therapy and Fast Recovery: The Role of Time for the Italian Neuropsychiatric Service in the War Zones', in *War Time: First World War Perspectives on Temporality*, edited by Louis Halewood, Adam Luptak and Hanna Smyth, 36–50. London; New York: Routledge, 2018.

Guerrini, Irene and Marco Pluviano. 'Discipline and Military Justice in the Italian Army', in *Italy in the Era of the Great War*, edited by Vanda Wilcox, 80–98. Leiden; Boston, MA: Brill, 2018.

Guerrini, Irene and Marco Pluviano. *Fucilati senza un processo: il 'Memoriale Tommasi' sulle esecuzioni sommarie nella Grande Guerra*. Udine: Gaspari, 2019.

Jones, Edgar and Simon Wessely. *Shell Shock to PTSD: Military Psychiatry from 1900 to the Gulf War*. Hove; New York: Psychology Press, 2005.

LaCapra, Dominick. *Writing History, Writing Trauma*. Parallax. Baltimore, MD: Johns Hopkins University Press, 2001.

Lerner, Paul Frederick. *Hysterical Men: War, Psychiatry, and the Politics of Trauma in Germany, 1890-1930*. Ithaca, NY: Cornell University Press, 2003.

Loughran, Tracey. *Shell-Shock and Medical Culture in First World War Britain*. Cambridge: Cambridge University Press, 2017.

Malone, Hannah. 'Legacies of Fascism: Architecture, Heritage and Memory in Contemporary Italy'. *Modern Italy* 22, no. 4 (November 2017): 445–70.

Marco, Mondini. *Il capo: la grande guerra del generale Luigi Cadorna*. Bologna: Il Mulino, 2017.

Micale, Mark S. and Paul Lerner. 'Trauma, Psychiatry, and History: A Conceptual and Historiographical Introduction', in *Traumatic Pasts: History, Psychiatry, and Trauma in the Modern Age, 1870–1930*, edited by Paul Lerner and Mark S. Micale, 1–27. Cambridge; New York: Cambridge University Press, 2001.

Opera nazionale per la protezione ed assistenza degli invalidi di guerra. *Per La Tutela Dei Dementi Di Guerra*. Roma: Coop. Tip. Castaldi, 1926.

Paolella, Francesco. 'Un laboratorio di medicina politica. Placido Consiglio e il Centro psichitrico militare di prima raccolta', in *Piccola patria, Grande guerra. La prima guerra mondiale a Reggio Emilia*, edited by Marco Carrattieri and Alberto Ferraboschi, 187–204. Bologna: CLUEB, 2008.

Pellacani, Giuseppe. 'Le neuropatie emotive e le psiconevrosi nei combattenti'. *Rivista sperimentale di freniatria* 44, nos. 1–2 (1920): 1–65.

Pighini, Giacomo. 'Considerazioni patogeniche sulle psiconevrosi emotive osservate al fronte'. *Il Policlinico* 24, no. 6 (1917): 243–68.

Pisani, Daniele. 'From Italian Monuments to the Fallen of World War I to Fascist War Memorials'. *RIHA Journal*. Accessed 17 April 2020. https://www.riha-journal.org/articles/2017/0150-0176-special-issue-war-graves/0165-pisani.

Pluviano, Marco and Irene Guerrini. *Le fucilazioni sommarie nella prima guerra mondiale*. Udine: Paolo Gaspari, 2004.

Procacci, Giovanna. 'The Disaster of Caporetto', in *Disastro! Disasters in Italy since 1860: Culture, Politics, Society*, edited by John Dickie, John Foot and Frank M. Snowden, 141–64. New York: Palgrave, 2002.

Reid, Fiona. 'Losing Face: Trauma and Maxillofacial Injury in the First World War', in *Psychological Trauma and the Legacies of the First World War*, edited by Peter Leese and Jason Crouthamel, 25–47. Cham: Palgrave Macmillan/Springer International Publishing, 2017.

Reid, Fiona. 'War Psychiatry and Shell Shock', in *1914–1918 Online International Encyclopedia of the First World War*, edited by Ute Daniel, Peter Gatrell, Oliver Janz, Heather Jones, Jennifer Keene, Alan Kramer and Bill Nasson. Berlin: Freie Universität Berlin, 2019, DOI: 10.15463/ie1418.10288/2.0.

Rumiz, Paolo. 'L'ultima ferita della Grande guerra "L'Italia riabiliti i militari fucilati"'. la Repubblica, 6 November 2014. https://www.repubblica.it/cronaca /2014/10/31/news/l_ultima_ferita_della_grande_guerra_l_italia_riabiliti_i_mil itari_fucilati-99937510/.
Salvante, Martina. '"Thanks to the Great War the Blind Gets the Recognition of His Ability to Act": The Rehabilitation of Blinded Servicemen in Florence'. *First World War Studies* 6, no. 1 (2015): 21–35.
Salvante, Martina. 'The Wounded Male Body: Masculinity and Disability in Wartime and Post-WWI Italy'. *Journal of Social History* 53, no. 3 (2020): 644–66.
Santin, Luciano and Andrea Zannini, eds. *Fucilati per l'esempio: la giustizia militare nella Grande Guerra e il caso di Cerciuento*. Udine: Forum, 2017.
Scartabellati, Andrea. 'Un Wanderer dell'anormalità? Un invito allo studio di Placido Consiglio (1877–1959)'. *Rivista sperimentale di freniatria* 134, no. 3 (2010): 89–112.
Scolè, Pierluigi. 'I morti', in *Dizionario storico della prima guerra mondiale*, edited by Nicola Labanca. Roma-Bari: Laterza, 2014.
Welch, Steven R. 'Military Justice', in *1914–1918 Online: International Encyclopedia of the First World War*, edited by Ute Daniel, Peter Gatrell, Oliver Janz, Heather Jones, Jennifer Keene, Alan Kramer and Bill Nasson. Berlin: Freie Universität Berlin, 2014. DOI: 10.15463/ie1418.10393.
Wilcox, Vanda. 'The Catastrophe at Caporetto'. *History Today*. Accessed 2 August 2019. https://www.historytoday.com/miscellanies/catastrophe-caporetto.
Wilcox, Vanda. 'From Heroic Defeat to Mutilated Victory: The Myth of Caporetto in Fascist Italy', in *Defeat and Memory: Cultural Histories of Military Defeat in the Modern Era*, edited by Jenny Macleod, 46–60. Basingstoke; New York: Palgrave Macmillan, 2008.
Wilcox, Vanda. *Morale and the Italian Army during the First World War*. Cambridge Military Histories. Cambridge: Cambridge University Press, 2016.
Winter, Jay. 'Shell-Shock and the Cultural History of the Great War'. *Journal of Contemporary History* 35, no. 1 (2000): 7–11.
Winter, Jay M. 'Shell Shock', in *The Cambridge History of the First World War*, edited by Jay M. Winter, Vol. 3: Civil Society, 310–33. Cambridge: Cambridge University Press, 2014.
Winter, Jay M. *War beyond Words: Languages of Remembrance from the Great War to the Present*. Cambridge: Cambridge University Press, 2018.

3

Trauma, child refugees and humanitarians in the Spanish Civil War and the Second World War

A case study of Esme Odgers

Joy Damousi

In August 1939, Australian communist Esme Odgers was in charge of Spanish children who had been evacuated from war zones during the Spanish Civil War and were in holding centres under the care of the international organization, the Foster Parents Plan (hereafter, Plan). Eight groups of children – referred to as 'colonies' – were taken to Biarritz in France. Odgers wrote to Plan's head, Eric Muggeridge, describing the challenging work of caring for these children:

> Never have we worked so hard to get a colony organised as with this last lot of children that arrived from concentration centers. These youngsters have not had a proper bath nor a change of clothing for six months! All of them are covered with scabies from head to toe as a result of this filth. For the past six months they have been sleeping on the floor in cafes, barns, stables and deserted factories. Most of them suffer with bronchial coughs.[1]

Communicating with the children had been enormously difficult. As Odgers noted, 'we have tried to talk to them, but cannot hold their interest for any length of time. We have tried to kiss and pet the little ones, but so unused are they to affection, they pull away, not seeming to understand. They are extremely nervous, restless, wild and without discipline'. Odgers explained that she and her co-workers had tried to extract further information about where they had come from and what had happened to them. They had failed, and finally concluded that it was 'unwise to bring back recollections', as so 'unpleasant are their memories it brought on weeping. We shall, therefore, have to hold up the histories for the time being'. It would take 'gentle patience and loving care to bring these young ones back to life', Odgers predicted. The lack of feeling in the children she observed 'is something horrible', which was no doubt necessary to survive. She believed, however, that they were a wonderful group of children who would soon 'react well to their new surroundings'.[2] This direct confrontation with children who had been so affected by war deeply disturbed Odgers.

This chapter offers a distinctive perspective on gender and trauma by coupling these two concepts around humanitarian efforts in wartime. In making these connections, my point of departure is to focus on the experience of humanitarian workers on the front line of war activity. I am concerned with the enduring impact of witnessing traumatic events. This chapter looks at these issues in situ – that is, as events unfolded – and asks how to discuss trauma as it happens, rather than through the more familiar lens of memory, or oral history. In doing so, it takes us to the question of the archive and, more specifically, to letters as a site of recording emotional responses, to the use of language at the time and to the question of self-representation. I argue that the emotional labour that was so vital to organizations that dealt with refugee children has not been identified as a site of excessive stress, anguish, anxiety and depression. These encounters created great strain, diminishing the capacity to cope psychologically. I suggest that this is a form of war trauma that has largely been unacknowledged. Related to this focus on humanitarian workers is how women's experiences of war are often overshadowed by the highly visible and widely discussed experience of trauma by soldiers. Underlying many of these discussions is the assumption that wartime trauma is experienced typically in only one way by this group. A focus on women's humanitarian role challenges some of these parameters and allows for the meaning of trauma in war itself to be broadened, as well as highlighting the multiple ways it is manifested.

As noted in this book's introduction, scholarship on the psychological trauma of war remains disproportionately focused on men's experience of war as soldiers and the crisis in masculinity through war. This is especially the case with literature on the First World War, but it can also be said of work on the Second World War.[3] Drawing on oral histories and framed by memory studies, recent research has begun to consider how other groups have understood their trauma. The experiences of nurses, in particular, have been examined for how they negotiated the emotional challenges of war.[4] Literature exploring the obstacles facing humanitarian workers in recent conflicts is more extensive, drawing in contemporary and modern concepts of resilience and post-traumatic stress disorder (PTSD).[5] Histories of humanitarian workers have been studied largely through the perspectives of memory and the reconstruction of historical events but not explicitly as trauma; most of these works focus on wars in the latter half of the twentieth century.[6] While this chapter centres on a few dramatic months leading up to and immediately after the outbreak of the Second World War, its wider context includes the Spanish Civil War (1936–9). The psychological impact of civil wars is a burgeoning area of trauma studies, although this, too, remains understudied.[7]

How the experience of the front-line humanitarian on the ground is captured also draws us to the nexus between biography and humanitarianism. This chapter responds to the call to explore this connection more fully, through biographical approaches that capture humanitarianism 'in action'. Enrico Dal Lago and Kevin O'Sullivan argue for 'nuanced biographical studies' of less well-known humanitarian activists, including rank-and-file activists and their distinctive lived experiences.[8] By focusing on biography as a conceptual frame, we can also capture trauma on the ground, as a means of exploring the impact of war on an everyday level, and in so doing, further understand the multifaceted nature of trauma. While the biographical study of women as humanitarian workers, especially in the Spanish Civil War, has attracted a substantial scholarship, the psychological impact of their efforts remains underexamined. In broad terms, my aim is to explore how traumatic events can be forgotten if the parameters of understandings of trauma are set within a framework that erases women's experiences.

Taking Australian Esme Odgers (1910–?) as a case study, this chapter examines her correspondence for insights into the psychological consequences of humanitarian work. Odgers's activism has remained largely unexplored, garnering passing mentions of her efforts in the Spanish Civil War.[9] A careful analysis of her epistolary record, however, not only illuminates the uncommon life story of one individual but sheds light on the experiences of humanitarian aid workers more broadly. By refocusing our attention on affect, Odgers's story situates humanitarian workers in the broader story of war and trauma. Odgers's detailed, lengthy wartime letters offer insight into the material, social and psychological conditions under which humanitarian workers laboured. They suggest that such a vital activity was not only a varied experience but also a deeply traumatic one. The term 'trauma' has attracted a vast scholarship in history drawing on psychological and psychoanalytic models, as well as understandings shaped within social and cultural settings.[10] Within the context of this chapter, its meaning is embedded within a framework of the history of emotions, focusing on the emotional stress and strain associated with humanitarian work which also leads to anxiety, depression and an inability to cope psychologically under wartime conditions.

The Spanish Civil War

In the violent conflict between Republican rebels and Franco's forces, the Spanish Civil War created a significant refugee crisis.[11] It ushered in heightened interest in child refugees, as tens of thousands of Spanish Republican children were separated from their parents. Their dispersal between 1936 and 1939 made it a pan-European issue that led to the creation of transnational allegiances across several countries. By 1938, two million Republicans had fled. Seventy-eight thousand children had found refuge in France. An estimated 7,000 to 11,000 unaccompanied Spanish children were in French foster homes between 1937 and 1939. Evacuation abroad took place, including countries such as France, Belgium, England and the Soviet Union.[12]

One of the most notable campaigners for saving child refugees was Esme Odgers, an Australian communist and activist.[13] Born in 1910 in Tingha, New South Wales, she was the daughter of Cessnock coal miner Edwin Odgers. A member of the Communist Party of Australia, she travelled to Spain in 1936 to contribute to leftist international efforts to support the Republican fight to defeat Franco's fascist forces. Odgers joined several nurses and fellow communists from Australia and elsewhere to support these efforts. She began working for the National Joint Committee for Spanish Relief in London. In April 1937, the Committee merged with the Foster Parents Plan for Children in Spain to provide sponsorship of Spanish refugee children by parent sponsors in Britain.[14] It was here that Odgers met the journalist John Langdon-Davies and Eric Muggeridge, founder of the Plan. Odgers became actively and directly involved in Plan during the Spanish Civil War and the Second World War.[15] She ran three children's 'colonies' at Puigcerda, near the French border, looking after orphans who survived on donations from British and US supporters.[16] Odgers evacuated to France before the German invasion, settling in 1941 in Britain, where she continued her humanitarian efforts.[17] While in Britain, she had her first child, Eduardo, in September 1941 and married his father, Spaniard Jose G. Pablos, in January 1942. Esme, her husband and their son migrated to Venezuela in 1948, initially settling in Caracas, where Jose sought Venezuelan citizenship in January 1949.[18]

Glossy brochures produced by Plan to attract sponsors masked the harrowing and chaotic conditions of war that its workers endured. In early 1939, the bombing of Barcelona resulted in the mass migration of refugees. Plan moved children under its care from hostel to hostel in Biarritz in scenes that were dramatic, emotional and traumatic. Truckloads of these children passed refugees, some of whom attempted to board. Women pushed their children forward, hoping for their rescue, while the wounded begged for access to the vehicle to aid their journey. Muggeridge described the incident in February 1939 as one 'so gross in its terror or so mountainous in its tragedy'.[19] Merely keeping track of the children in their care proved challenging. Children evacuated from the towns of Siges and Sarria and Plan workers could not find them; the next day, they turned up in two trucks outside of Puigcerda.[20]

Plan relied on women's physical and emotional labour to drive and sustain its enterprise amid this chaos. The day-to-day activities overwhelmed Odgers, whose letters document the emotional and personal challenges before her. When asked for accounts and paperwork, Odgers replied with exasperation:

> I look at it from the point of view of suddenly being landed in France with close on 500 children. It would have been bad enough had we arrived in an organised fashion with unlimited supplies of money behind us. Instead we came willynilly – the children exhausted and ill, the colonies bare houses, no water in many of them, the children without clothes and shoes apart from what they arrived in the personnel distracted and unhappy because they knew not where their families were. . . . Under these conditions we could not go forward with high speed American efficiency and I confess that caring for the children came before . . . insisting that the committee should have its accounts.[21]

Odgers details her own emotional state while dealing with these pressures and deprivations of war. Through her letters, one sees a woman traumatized by witnessing death, displacement and dislocation of children. Her volatile emotions, which ranged from disappointment to excitement to exhilaration, had to be put aside in the face of the daily grind of humanitarian endeavour. At times, a profound sense of isolation drained her spirits, but not her resolve:

> I am lonely it is true, but not fed up. . . . Resentment boiled out from the eyes at the cruelties of the bombardments, of the pitiable sights of shattered youth, back from the trenches. . . . It is a tragedy too horrible to contemplate now, after two and a half years of sacrifice, there is the bitter hour of defeat for the Republicans. If at times I feel a little fed up because of the loneliness, it is soon dispelled in the warmth of the children's kisses, by the brightness of their faces in the classroom.[22]

Odgers's despair over the lost Republican cause is evident, but she seeks to console herself in her work with children. Tending to their needs appears therapeutic for her, as she tries to live with the horrors she has witnessed.

The experience of dealing with children presented several problems – not just material but also emotional through the housework required to sustain the colonies. In a letter to Muggeridge, Odgers outlined in detail the mundane nature of humanitarian work. In particular, the daily domestic drudgery of childcare was emotionally exhausting:

Here all is quiet and the only problems are the problems of the house. This one and that one didn't wash the children; the cook spoilt the soup, the children need a new set of underwear, more shoes are needed, school material – what do I know about the outside world? Listen to the radio yes, and hear the 'official' news. Quite alone and cut off from any kind of stimulating activities, and friends, which makes even the poorest existence brighter. . . . Yes I am despondent. . . . I feel I must make a grumble every [now] and then. Do you mind?[23]

Odgers hints at her mental state directly, characterizing herself as being 'despondent' – an affect suggestive of depression. Like her effort to focus on the children, her 'grumble' to Muggeridge offers respite and a release from these uncomfortable feelings.

Odgers's sacrifices did not go unrecognized, but the empathy of others gave her little comfort. A member of the American committee, Mildred Rackley, who served as an interpreter for the American Medical Bureau to Aid Spanish Democracy in Spain and helped to establish hospitals there in 1937–8, praised all that Odgers had done for the organization and what she had managed to achieve with the child refugees.[24] Writing to Odgers in March 1936, Rackley stated that

we have . . . admired you in your heroic work with the refugees. I went through an evacuation myself once – the evacuation of all the International Hospitals from the Central Zone in Spain, to Catalonia, and the responsibility . . . was almost too great for human endurance. You have gone through all that, to an intensified degree, with much more personal danger and horror.[25]

Despite such understanding of what she had been through, Odgers felt a sense of hopelessness over the human suffering that she continued to witness among the refugees in Biarritz. In March 1939, she wrote with profound sadness of

the awful tragedy that comes before my eyes every day of people without a country, without hope and a future stretching uncertain and unhappily before them. One of the girls working . . . has five brothers in prison (or perhaps shot), a husband prisoner or shot, and the 70 year old mother in jail – merely because she is the mother of 5 militant sons. . . . And on top of this there are the Austrians, the Czechs and the German refugees, not to give a thought to the thousands homeless and dying from hunger and epidemic in China. I need to get very drunk. . . . I cannot remember being so unhappy in my life.[26]

Perhaps the reference to drinking is just a glib joke, but it may also signal self-medication with alcohol. Her despair is certainly palpable and her need for escape is striking. In May 1939, in fact, it was with embarrassment, even shame, that she declared her need for time away.

> I am thinking of taking a holiday. It seems criminal to even think of such a thing at a time like this.... The last two years rest heavily on my shoulders.... The last three months in Spain were not easy and on top of that the evacuation and then organising the colonies without a rest in between.... I must rest very soon – for a fortnight only.[27]

Odgers continued to teeter emotionally between a sense of inspiration in a cause larger than herself and what today looks much like depression. She writes of feeling that she is 'living in an unreal world', in which she feels 'incredibly old, but a kind of external oldness – that one has never been young and never again will feel young'.[28] Her sentiments echo what American psychiatrist Robert Jay Lifton would decades later term 'psychic numbing', which describes the flat affect and detachment common among those suffering from what we now call PTSD.[29] In nearly the same breath that Odgers describes how 'the obstacles of war conditions ... saps one's strength', she insists that though 'it is a hard life you have chosen but so, oh so, very worthwhile despite all the appearances to the contrary'.[30] One wonders if it is the recipient of her letter that she is trying to persuade or herself, rallying against a decline into melancholia by reminding herself of the importance of this humanitarian work.

As the world plunged into the Second World War, Odgers remained determined to provide a haven for Spanish children. Writing in late 1939, she reflected on the continued importance of the task at hand, which she believed was to aid the children heal psychologically from the terrible experiences they had endured. She worried about their sense of alienation and loss of humanity after having 'been cut off from everything familiar to them, from the things that gave them consciousness of being human beings – love of parents, a continuity of existence no matter how poorly they lived'.[31] By March 1940, just two months before the Germans invaded France, the opportunity arose to go to the United States, but she hesitated to leave the children, who she was 'quite convinced' needed the care of a woman,

> no matter who the woman is – and even more so now that the war is on. Personally, I am emotionally tied to these dear people with whom I have lived in Spain and with whom I went through the evacuation and have lived with for the last year in France in circumstances so different to those in which we lived in Spain.[32]

The weight of her duties and her sense of obligation to the children is palpable when she writes that 'it is impossible to carry the whole of the work, particularly now with the greater difficulties caused by war.... For one person to do this job and then be a perfect liaison officer, is impossible'.[33] These strains would be further exacerbated by the onset of a global war.

The Second World War

As the Second World War progressed, Odgers became further distressed at what lay ahead for her and for the children under her care. At the war's outset, she felt desperate isolation, even as she also felt a connection with the tribulations of others thrown into this cataclysm. 'The emotional strain of life during these days is really terrible. . . . But how many people must be feeling as I do? And with the same sadness in their hearts that I have'. She lamented how war tears families apart, including her own. 'I think of my two dear brothers – such pals, such a joy to be with them – and now they are on the "verge" (only because Australia is so far away) of donning uniform and saying farewell to all that is familiar – to all that they love. . . . And my father who has already served three years in the Great war [sic], is still of the age to make him available for military service!' Odgers had witnessed with her own eyes how war was not a burden shouldered by men alone. Reflection on the suffering and vulnerability of her own family served to deepen 'my comprehension of the gap in the lives of our little ones, draws me closer to them'.[34] Her distress over world events and their implications for her own family fed her empathy for and connection to the children she served.

The outbreak of war in September 1939 led her mind to wander back to her earlier experiences in Spain. As war erupted, she asserted: 'I don't want to write about the war, I don't want to think about it – and yet my thoughts stray' to the war in Spain.[35] She revisited the trauma of what she witnessed there, asking Muggeridge how she could 'forget our terrible experiences during the evacuation?'[36] The Second World War was not a 'new war because it is surely a continuation of the Spanish war. Here we are in the midst of another bloody shambles'.[37] This new outbreak of hostilities, consuming new victims, stirred her feelings of compassion because of what she herself had lived through already. She felt a connection to Polish suffering at the time of the Nazi invasion, as 'thousands of Poles are passing through the same awful experience'.[38]

> And I turn on the radio to hear that the germans [sic] have machine gunned refugees leaving Warsaw . . . just as we were machine gunned during the evacuation. It seems to be a speciality if the german [sic] airmen – and no doubt many of the same ones who rained bombed [sic] on Barcelona are raining them in Varsovie at this moment.[39]

But, as previously, Odgers's empathy came bundled with a desire to numb herself to the never-ending grief. 'I could drink a bottle of catarro [beer] when I think of it, but there is so much to do, I am leaving that until after it is over'.[40] The oblivion promised by copious stiff drinks would have to wait for a time when her efforts to offer humanitarian aid were in less demand.

The situation of children who were evacuated from Paris was a great burden for her and her concern for them became stressful and unbearable. In anticipation of German invasion, 31,000 children were evacuated from Paris at the end of August 1939. Historian Laura Lee Downs estimates that by the first week of September, only 13 per cent of school children aged between three and fourteen years old remained in Paris and its environs. The evacuation of children featured centrally in the defence of the civilian population.[41] In December 1939, Odgers began to write about their fate. The strain of accepting new displaced children created even more pressure on her. It was difficult contemplating the predicament of Polish children, and possibly evacuating them from Hungary and Romania, as well as assisting Spanish children and then French children. Correspondence written by the children was strictly controlled, but occasionally the children broke the rules which was a great source of frustration for Odgers. But she was under no illusion about the children and wrote about them without sentimentality:

> It cannot be expected that all children we have are angels, and believe me, there are some 'toughies' among them. Some who even think that no gratitude is necessary to the foster parents for what they are doing for them, and an imposition would be regarded as a piece of good work instead of what it really would be – a cheap trick.[42]

Odgers also agonized about the Spanish children who had been repatriated, but who continued to write to their Foster Parents (FP). This tested Odgers. She told the children they could send letters to her and she would send them to the FPs. She understood why the children continued to write to their FPs. Given how desperate the situation was, 'they look round for someone to help them in their dilemma, and that someone is the strong, and everpresent, though never seen, foster parent. Someone who represents for them carefree existence and plenty'.[43] Odgers became increasingly strained by the future of the children for whom she had taken responsibility, and who were now heading into another war under even more desperate circumstances. The Spanish children who had returned to Spain were in renewed danger and she feared all her work would unravel:

> [now] they will receive . . . education so soaked with superstition and religious fanaticism that if all work . . . and all the dangers we have gone through to protect them, to re-establish mental discipline and open their minds, is . . . nullified . . . it will bring about a condition of restlessness, lawlessness and forlornness that will only make them more than ever a lost generation.[44]

Odgers reached a desperate breaking point, the emotional numbness and disassociation that is often a hallmark of PTSD: 'I am so tired I am a person without fellings [sic] – I just go on like a machine – afraid to stop otherwise I shall crumple into the dust – and I won't be able to do a Phoenix trick, either!'[45] She reassures Muggeridge that she will keep being positive and hopeful. She says she has two 'inspirations': '1. what I actually see taking place here in the colonies, the changes, the difference in bearing, the light dawning in the closed, but restless minds, of our children, and (2), the marvellous efforts you are making in America'.[46] Odgers looked positively on the United States, describing it as 'the hope of the world'.[47]

Another source of distress for Odgers was the reaction of some of the mothers to the evacuation of their children. While some mothers were relieved that Plan provided a haven for their children, not all mothers were prepared for the separation. The disputes that ensued between Esme and mothers of evacuated children were as distressing for her as they were for the women and children that Plan served. These conflicts point to the paternalism that invariably informed the acts of humanitarians in war. In one incident, Esme describes the stresses and demands of convincing one mother to keep her children in the colonies because they were safer there rather than outside the refuges. The mother had insisted that she wished the children to be with her, but Odgers was emphatic they were safer with her. She could understand that there was great anxiety now that France was at war, and that the children would 'again have to go through the horrible experiences they went through in Spain'.[48] But Odgers was determined to have the children return to her in France. She sought permission from the French authorities and crossed to Spain, where the mother had taken the children. Odgers could not fathom why they would not see common sense as their children were being cared for and attending school, but some mothers insisted on reclaiming their children.

> It all occupied nearly three days of my time, because the child, Africa, the eldest 16 years, cried and fainted and the other three wept and everyone else in the colony wept and I was the only one able to do anything. It was a horrible breakdown for the women in the colony, because the fears they have been harbouring that they, too, would have to return burst out at that point when they saw after all my efforts, the mother insisted on taking her children, and against the authority of the mother we cannot do anything.[49]

Even with such setbacks, Odgers was convinced of the good work that Plan was doing in evacuating children: 'we are bringing enlightenment into cloudy child minds – slowly but surely a little more wisdom is entering the world ... true, slowly and only a little, but we have an awful heritage to overcome ... and, the old saying can be employed – out of the acorn grew the oak'.[50]

As these actions demonstrate, determination and resolve were necessary qualities for humanitarians such as Odgers as she asserted herself in the most devastating circumstances. But doing this on her own was challenging. Odgers's isolation was a great strain for her, notwithstanding the daily activities that kept her active and busy.

> Somehow I feel alone and isolated today, with the world on my back; there is only one person who speaks my language in the colonies and he imperfectly. . . . Don't think I'm down hearted I am not but there is a devil of a lot of people in distress over in this part of the world; news from Spain does not improve . . . a new wave of persecutions are taking place, and the war takes a more formidable turns [sic], or so it seems.[51]

Her letters were also written with a stream of consciousness that revealed an increasing despondence, such as when she wrote, in November 1939, of the 'desolation and destitution for families and children who have to fight their own way through life or depend on charity and the consequent evils of inferiority complexes, . . . hardness and cynicism'.[52] She fretted about the long-term psychological consequences for children separated from their mothers at a tender age and who, by 1939, had been apart from them for three years. Many would never be reunited because of the war's high death toll.[53]

The war brought a new wave of child refugees, which heightened Odgers's anxiety and severely compromised her humanitarian efforts. How would they be expected to prioritize them? 'And now Polish children cry out in their misery to be helped. But can we do it? Our first duty is to the Spanish children – there is something special about them because their country put up a special fight'.[54] It was difficult for her to seek escape under these conditions. Reading offered some relief, including Alvah Bessie's *Men in Battle*, *Mortal Storm*, and the satirical *The Good Soldier Schweik*. But her craving for the pleasure of a social life is evident in her reminiscences of personal and material pleasures of the past:

> All this is a long way removed from your bridge parties, your golfing swimming and dances. . . . I have a great longing to slip into a willowy dress, slim around the waist and flaring out into endless mysterious folds, sip whiskey and soda from tall, thin glasses and with perhaps an audacious lady [carved] on them, and listen to soft sensuous music and dance to it and then stroll out on the balcony (of course there would have to be a moon and a tall male somewhere – but somewhere close!) and maybe I would like to have a fan that I could wave about gracefully as I talked mysteriously – you know – just like they do in the movies![55]

Such fantasies of another time and place sustained Odgers and provided her with emotional sustenance at a time when the deteriorating circumstances challenged her psychological resilience.

The prospect of taking children from other parts of Europe increasingly became an issue, even as there was still work to be done with Spanish children. In October 1939, Odgers asked Muggeridge about the future plans for war children and for the foster parent scheme, as well as the Spanish 'colonies', specifically. Odgers reiterated the importance of the work she was doing for the children, although she was constantly frustrated by the conditions. There was nothing 'exciting' about the work, 'it proceeds painfully as all newborn things are born in pain'.[56] Her vision was wider than just materially supporting the children. She sought to reinvent them and create new citizens: 'We have not only to smoothe [sic] out the ravages of the war years, we have to wipe out the heritage of the war years before the war, of reactionary Spain, of its deliberate policy of keeping it's [sic] people ignorant for political purposes'. In terms of children other than Spanish ones, Odgers believed that Plan could extend to Polish children, but the organization had limited capacity and this challenge would add to the strain under which she laboured.[57] Just two months after the Second World War erupted in Europe, in November 1939, she wrote to Muggeridge that

> sometimes I feel so alone and it is a great help to think of you in America (I mean the 'you' in the plural) working endlessly for us, and we are responding here with a jolly fine piece of work. No end of difficulties, of course, but that is due to the war, the fact that we are foreigners in a foreign country and looking after another lot of foreign children, but absolutely nothing is insoluble.[58]

As in much of Odgers's correspondence, one sees here her vacillation between despair and resilience.

Sponsorship had begun to dry up for Spanish children, compromising Odgers's ability to extend assistance to a growing circle of children. Plan began to develop a programme for all children displaced by war. To cope with the demand for help, Odgers suggested children be taken to the United States to ease the burden, even as she could not resist taking in more children.[59] The intensity of Odgers's work increased in December 1939, when Rita Alison from the Polish Relief Fund requested that she assist with Polish children who were to be evacuated from Hungary and Romania. Alison sought to house the children in the colonies she ran; Odgers obliged: 'Of course the saddest and most important phase of the relief work which must be done is in making arrangements for the children'.[60] In January 1940, the shifting circumstances of the Spanish children became very strenuous for her. Some children were being reclaimed by their parents, while others were not. As the war wore on, Spanish children were increasingly not the main focus of attention. By June 1940, her mental health was increasingly becoming fragile, tempered by her overwhelming sense of responsibility under increasingly stressful circumstances. The strain of living under war conditions and confronting tragedies in war pained Odgers. This experience appeared to be superficially and momentarily extinguished by a sense of purpose in her task of humanitarian aid. As the Second World War unleashed violence on civilians and Odgers's burdens escalated, the psychological cracks that had begun to emerge in her dealings with children during the Spanish Civil War developed into open traumatic wounds.

Conclusion

The work of implementing the child humanitarian scheme of Plan involved intense, emotional labour in caring for and managing children in wartime. Odgers's letters offer unique insight into the centrality of affect in humanitarian work – of the oscillating moods and temperaments, from the positivity to what was often a desperate despondency.

Unsurprisingly, Odgers never used the word 'trauma' in her correspondence. She spoke, instead, of distress, fear, mental exhaustion, anguish, emotional numbness, horror and the terror of violence. She endured terrible distress, watching the death and displacement of children and experiencing the bombardment of cities. She wrote about the pain of mothers reluctantly relinquishing their children to be taken to safe havens and the anguish of witnessing such acts. Odgers characterized the expression of emotions which articulated her distress and desolation as failure and defeat in the face of the challenges of war. Caring for children in the context of war was a specifically gendered exercise undertaken by women. It constituted a form of domesticated trauma, away from the front-line battles experienced by soldiers typically associated with war trauma, but a form of trauma nevertheless, embedded in the domestic task of caring for child victims during war.

Odgers's experience as recorded in her letters reflects a trauma specific to female humanitarian workers, such as Odgers, whose primary focus was rescuing children. While her efforts were lauded as heroic, such praise masked the emotional cost – a private, psychological strain that she never exposed publicly. This biographical study of a humanitarian whose history has not been fully explored before allows us to capture the complexity of trauma in war in real time. Her correspondence from the period offers a window into her psychological state at the time. Behind the shadows cast by war, her story and those of rank-and-file humanitarians deserve our attention for the light they shed on the everyday life in the trauma of war as experienced by women in pursuit of their humanitarian ideals.

Notes

1 Esme Odgers to Eric Muggeridge, 15 August 1939, box 81, folder 15, Records of Foster Parents Plan International, University of Rhode Island, Special

Collections and Archives, Kingston, Rhode Island (hereafter cited as FPPI, 81/15, URI).

2   Odgers to Muggeridge, 15 August 1939, FPPI, 81/15, URI.

3   Recent examples include Tracey Loughran, *Shell-Shock and Medical Culture in the First World War* (Cambridge: Cambridge University Press, 2017); Jason Crouthamel and Peter Leese, eds, *Psychological Trauma and the Legacies of the First World War* (Basingstoke: Palgrave Macmillan, 2017); Michael Roper, *The Secret Battle: Emotional Survival in the First World War* (Manchester: Manchester University Press, 2009); Fiona Reid, *Broken Men: Shell Shock, Treatment and Recovery in Britain, 1914-1930* (London: Continuum, 2010); Jessica Meyer, *Men of War: Masculinity and the First World War in Britain* (London: Palgrave Macmillan, 2009); Paul Lerner, *Hysterical Men: War, Psychiatry, and the Politics of Trauma in Germany, 1890-1930* (Ithaca, NY: Cornell University Press, 2003); Jason Crouthamel, *The Great War and German Memory: Society, Politics and Psychological Trauma, 1914-1945* (Exeter: University of Exeter Press, 2009). For the Second World War see Jason Crouthamel and Peter Leese, eds, *Traumatic Memories of the Second World War and After* (Basingstoke: Palgrave Macmillan, 2016); Daniel Chirot, Gi-Wook Shin and Daniel Sneider, eds, *Confronting Memories of World War II: European and Asian Legacies* (Seattle: University of Washington Press, 2014).

4   Christine E. Hallett, *Containing Trauma: Nursing Work in the First World War* (Manchester: Manchester University Press, 2009).

5   Ian Palmer, 'Psychological Aspects of Providing Medical Humanitarian Aid', *British Medical Journal* 331, no. 7509 (2005): 152–4; J. H. Berk, 'Trauma and Resilience during War: A Look at the Children and Humanitarian Aid Workers of Bosnia', *Psychoanalytic Review* 85, no. 4 (1998): 640–58; John H. Ehrenreich and Teri L. Elliot, 'Managing Stress in Humanitarian Aid: A Survey of Humanitarian Aid Agencies' Psychosocial Training and Support of Staff', *Peace and Conflict: Journal of Peace Psychology* 10, no. 1 (2004): 53–66; Lisa McKay, *Understanding and Coping with Traumatic Stress* (Pasadena, CA: Headington Institute, 2007); Barbara Cardozo et. al., 'Psychological Distress, Depression, Anxiety, and Burnout among International Humanitarian Aid Workers: A Longitudinal Study', *PLOS One* 7, no. 9 (2012): e44948; Ellen Connorton et al., 'Humanitarian Relief Workers and Trauma-related Mental Illness', *Epidemiologic Reviews* 34, no. 1 (2012): 145–55. It was not until the Geneva Convention of 1949 and the later Protocol of 1977 that the category of civilian non-combatant was identified, and the rights and obligations of non-combatants during conflict articulated. However, the Conventions did not require parties to guarantee the safety of humanitarian workers. https://ihldatabases.icrc.org/applic/ihl/ihl.nsf/1a13044f3bbb5b8ec12563fb0066f226/be7ceb034f2fc69dc12563cd0042bb17.

6   Bertrand Taithe and John Borton, 'History, Memory and "Lessons Learnt" for Humanitarianism', *European Review of History* 23, nos. 1–2 (2016): 210–24.

7   Recent works include Katherine O. Stafford, *Narrating War in Peace: The Spanish Civil War in the Transition and Today* (London: Palgrave Macmillan 2015).

8   Enrico Dal Lago and Kevin O'Sullivan, 'Prosopographies, Transnational Lives, and Multiple Identities and Global Humanitarianism', *Moving the Social:*

Journal of Social History and the History of Social Movements 57, no. 160 (2017): 175.
9 See, for example, Jim Fyrth and Sally Alexander, eds, *Women's Voices from the Spanish Civil War* (London: Lawrence and Wishart 1991); Amirah Inglis, *Australians in the Spanish Civil War* (Sydney: Allen and Unwin, 1987), 127–8.
10 For example, Michael S. Roth, *Memory, Trauma and History: Essays on Living with the Past* (New York: Columbia University Press, 2012); Cathy Caruth, *Unclaimed Experience: Trauma, Narrative and History* (Baltimore, MD: Johns Hopkins University Press, 1996); Dominick LaCapra, 'Trauma, History, Memory, Identity: What Remains?', *History and Theory* 55, no. 3 (2016): 375–400; Mark S. Micale and Paul Lerner, eds, *Traumatic Pasts: History, Psychiatry, and Trauma in the Modern Age, 1870-1930* (Cambridge: Cambridge University Press, 2001).
11 Peter Gatrell, *The Making of the Modern Refugee* (Oxford: Oxford University Press, 2013), 72–3.
12 Karl D. Qualls, *Stalin's Niños: Educating Spanish Civil War Refugees in the Soviet Union, 1937-1951* (Toronto: University of Toronto Press, 2020); Veronica Sierra Blas, 'Educating the communists of the Future: Notes on the Educational Life of the Spanish Children Evacuated to the USSR during the Spanish Civil War', *Paedagogica Historica: International Journal of the History of Education* 51, no. 4 (2015): 498; Dominique Marshall, 'International Child Saving', in *The Routledge History of Childhood in the Western World* , ed. Paula S. Fass (London: Routledge, 2013, 2015), 481.
13 *Workers' Weekly*, 20 June 1939.
14 Henry D. Molumphy, *For Common Decency: The History of Foster Parents Plan, 1937-1983* (Warwick, RI: Foster Parents International, 1984), 29–30; National Archives of Australia: A6126, Photocopies of microfilm copies of personal and subject files, 1920–60; 27, Esme Alice Odgers, Application for Passport, 1937; *Woman Today*, August 1937, 4; *Newcastle Morning Herald and Miners' Advocate*, 22 August 1941, 4.
15 *Woman Today*, August 1937, 4.
16 Mark Aarons, *The Family File* (Melbourne: Black Inc., 2015), 70.
17 *Townsville Daily Bulletin*, 26 February 1941, 10.
18 *Official Gazette of the United States of Venezuela*, 19 January 1949.
19 Molumphy, *For Common Decency*, 40.
20 Molumphy, *For Common Decency*, 40.
21 Odgers to Mildred Rackley, 2 May 1939, FPPI, 81/14.
22 Odgers to Edna Blue, 14 April 1939, FPPI, 81/14, URI.
23 Odgers to Muggeridge, 8 March 1939, FPPI, 81/14, URI.
24 Aeiwen D. Wetherby, *Private Aid, Political Activism: American Medical Relief to Spain and China, 1936-1949* (Columbia: University of Missouri Press, 2017), 97, 113. http://www.alba-valb.org/volunteers/mildred-rackley.
25 Mildred Rackley to Odgers, 7 March 1939, FPPI, 81/14, URI.
26 Odgers to Muggeridge, 8 March 1939, FPPI, 81/14, URI.

27 Odgers to [Rackley or Winfred], 4 May 1939, FPPI, 81/14, URI.
28 Odgers to Blue, 28 January 1940, FPPI, 81/17, URI.
29 Robert Jay Lifton, *Death in Life: Survivors of Hiroshima* (Chapel Hill: University of North Carolina Press, 1987).
30 Odgers to Blue, 28 January 1940, FPPI, 81/17, URI.
31 Odgers to Blue, 21 November 1939, FPPI, 81/16, URI.
32 Odgers to Blue, 23 March 1940, FPPI, 81/17, URI. Emphasis in original.
33 Odgers to Blue, 11 April 1940, FPPI, 81/17, URI.
34 Odgers to Muggeridge, 7 September 1939, FPPI, 81/15, URI.
35 Odgers to Muggeridge, 7 September 1939, FPPI, 81/15, URI.
36 Odgers to Muggeridge, 7 September 1939, FPPI, 81/15, URI.
37 Odgers to Muggeridge, 16 September 1939, FPPI, 81/15, URI.
38 Odgers to Muggeridge, 7 September 1939, FPPI, 81/15, URI.
39 Odgers to Muggeridge, 16 September 1939, FPPI, 81/15, URI.
40 Odgers to Walter, 12 September 1939, FPPI, 81/15, URI.
41 Laura Lee Downs, 'Au Revoir les Enfants: Wartime Evacuation and the Politics of Childhood in Britain and France, 1939-1940', *History Workshop Journal* 82, no. 1 (Autumn 2016): 121.
42 Odgers to Muggeridge, 19 December 1939, FPPI, 81/16, URI.
43 Odgers to Muggeridge, 19 December 1939, FPPI, 81/16, URI.
44 Odgers to Muggeridge, 19 December 1939, FPPI, 81/16, URI. Emphasis in original.
45 Odgers to Muggeridge, 19 December 1939, FPPI, 81/16, URI. Emphasis in original.
46 Odgers to Muggeridge, c. 28 November 1939, FPPI, 81/16, URI.
47 Odgers to Muggeridge, c. 28 November 1939, FPPI, 81/16, URI.
48 Odgers to Muggeridge, c. 28 November 1939, FPPI, 81/16, URI.
49 Odgers to Muggeridge, c. 28 November 1939, FPPI, 81/16, URI.
50 Odgers to Muggeridge, c. 28 November 1939, FPPI, 81/16, URI.
51 Odgers to Muggeridge, c. 28 November 1939, FPPI, 81/16, URI.
52 Odgers to Blue, 21 November 1939, FPPI, 81/16, URI.
53 Odgers to Blue, 21 November 1939, FPPI, 81/16, URI.
54 Odgers to Blue, 21 November 1939, FPPI, 81/16, URI.
55 Odgers to Blue, 21 November 1939, FPPI, 81/16, URI.
56 Odgers to Muggeridge, 6 October 1939, FPPI, 81/16, URI.
57 Odgers to Muggeridge, 6 October 1939; Odgers to Muggeridge, 15 November 1939, FPPI, 81/16, URI.
58 Odgers to Muggeridge, 20 November 1939, FPPI, 81/16, URI.
59 Odgers to Muggeridge, 22 November 1939, FPPI, 81/16, URI.
60 Rita Alison to Odgers, 6 December 1939, FPPI, 81/16, URI.

Works cited

Aarons, Mark. *The Family File*. Melbourne: Black Inc., 2015.
Berk, J. H. 'Trauma and Resilience during War: A Look at the Children and Humanitarian Aid Workers of Bosnia'. *Psychoanalytic Review* 85, no. 4 (1998): 640–58.
Blas, Veronica Sierra. 'Educating the communists of the Future: Notes on the Educational Life of the Spanish Children Evacuated to the USSR during the Spanish Civil War'. *Paedagogica Historica: International Journal of the History of Education* 51, no. 4 (2015): 496–519.
Cardozo, Barbara, Carol Gotway Crawford, Cynthia Eriksson, Julia Zhu, Miriam Sabin, Alastair Ager, David Foy, Leslie Snider, Willem Scholte, Reinhard Kaiser, Miranda Olff, Bas Rijnen and Winnifred Simon. 'Psychological Distress, Depression, Anxiety, and Burnout among International Humanitarian Aid Workers: A Longitudinal Study'. *PLOS One* 7, no. 9 (2012): e44948.
Caruth, Cathy. *Unclaimed Experience: Trauma, Narrative and History*. Baltimore, MD: Johns Hopkins University Press, 1996.
'Children's Republic', *Townsville Daily Bulletin*, 26 February 1941, 10.
Chirot, Daniel, Shin Gi-Wook and Sneider Daniel, eds. *Confronting Memories of World War II: European and Asian Legacies*. Seattle: University of Washington Press, 2014.
Connorton, Ellen, Melissa J. Perry, David Hemenway and Matthew Miller. 'Humanitarian Relief Workers and Trauma-related Mental Illness'. *Epidemiologic Reviews* 34, no. 1 (2012): 145–55.
Crouthamel, Jason. *The Great War and German Memory: Society, Politics and Psychological Trauma, 1914–1945*. Exeter: University of Exeter Press, 2009.
Crouthamel, Jason and Leese Peter, eds. *Psychological Trauma and the Legacies of the First World War*. Basingstoke: Palgrave Macmillan, 2017.
Crouthamel, Jason and Leese Peter, eds. *Traumatic Memories of the Second World War and After*. Basingstoke: Palgrave Macmillan, 2016.
Dal Lago, Enrico and O'Sullivan Kevin. 'Prosopographies, Transnational Lives, and Multiple Identities and Global Humanitarianism'. *Moving the Social: Journal of Social History and the History of Social Movements* 57, no. 160 (2017): 159–74.
Downs, Laura Lee. 'Au Revoir les Enfants: Wartime Evacuation and the Politics of Childhood in Britain and France, 1939–1940'. *History Workshop Journal* 82, no. 1 (Autumn 2016): 121–50.
Ehrenreich, John H. and Elliot Teri L. 'Managing Stress in Humanitarian Aid: A Survey of Humanitarian Aid Agencies' Psychosocial Training and Support of Staff'. *Peace and Conflict: Journal of Peace Psychology* 10, no. 1 (2004): 53–66.
Fyrth, Jim and Alexander Sally, eds. *Women's Voices from the Spanish Civil War*. London: Lawrence and Wishart 1991.
Gatrell, Peter. *The Making of the Modern Refugee*. Oxford: Oxford University Press, 2013.
Hallett, Christine E. *Containing Trauma: Nursing Work in the First World War*. Manchester: Manchester University Press, 2009.
Inglis, Amirah. *Australians in the Spanish Civil War*. Sydney: Allen and Unwin, 1987.

LaCapra, Dominick. 'Trauma, History, Memory, Identity: What Remains?'. *History and Theory* 55, no. 3 (2016): 375–400.

Lerner, Paul. *Hysterical Men: War, Psychiatry, and the Politics of Trauma in Germany, 1890-1930*. Ithaca, NY: Cornell University Press, 2003.

Lifton, Robert Jay. *Death in Life: Survivors of Hiroshima*. Chapel Hill: University of North Carolina Press, 1987.

Loughran, Tracey. *Shell-Shock and Medical Culture in the First World War*. Cambridge: Cambridge University Press, 2017.

Marshall, Dominique. 'International Child Saving', in *The Routledge History of Childhood in the Western World*, edited by Paula S. Fass, 469–90. London: Routledge, 2013/2015.

McKay, Lisa. *Understanding and Coping with Traumatic Stress*. Pasadena, CA: Headington Institute, 2007.

Meyer, Jessica. *Men of War: Masculinity and the First World War in Britain*. London: Palgrave Macmillan, 2009.

Micale, Mark S. and Lerner Paul, eds. *Traumatic Pasts: History, Psychiatry, and Trauma in the Modern Age, 1870–1930*. Cambridge: Cambridge University Press, 2001.

Molumphy, Henry D. *For Common Decency: The History of Foster Parents Plan, 1937–1983*. Warwick, RI: Foster Parents International, 1984.

'New Post for Esme Odgers: Five Children's Colonies', *Workers' Weekly*, 20 June 1939, 3.

Odgers, Esme. 'Children of Spain'. *Woman Today*, August 1937, 4.

Palmer, Ian. 'Psychological Aspects of Providing Medical Humanitarian Aid'. *British Medical Journal* 331, no. 7509 (2005): 152–4.

Personal and subject files, 1920–1960, A6126, National Archives of Australia, Canberra.

Qualls, Karl D. *Stalin's Niños: Educating Spanish Civil War Refugees in the Soviet Union, 1937–1951*. Toronto: University of Toronto Press, 2020.

Records of Foster Parents Plan International, Special Collections and Archives, University of Rhode Island, Kingston.

Reid, Fiona. *Broken Men: Shell Shock, Treatment and Recovery in Britain, 1914–1930*. London: Continuum, 2010.

Roper, Michael. *The Secret Battle: Emotional Survival in the First World War*. Manchester: Manchester University Press, 2009.

Roth, Michael S. *Memory, Trauma and History: Essays on Living with the Past*. New York: Columbia University Press, 2012.

Stafford, Katherine O. *Narrating War in Peace: The Spanish Civil War in the Transition and Today*. London: Palgrave Macmillan 2015.

Taithe, Bertrand and Borton John. 'History, Memory and "Lessons Learnt" for Humanitarianism'. *European Review of History* 23, nos. 1–2 (2016): 210–24.

Wetherby, Aeiwen D. *Private Aid, Political Activism: American Medical Relief to Spain and China, 1936–1949*. Columbia: University of Missouri Press, 2017.

4

Servitude, displacement and trauma

Jewish refugee domestics in Great Britain 1938–45

Jennifer Craig-Norton

Hildegard Hoffman was eighteen years old when she arrived in Great Britain from Leipzig, Germany, in the spring of 1938. Her mother had secured her a job with a Jewish doctor in London's East End and told her daughter 'a thousand times' that 'people are so kind to open their home to a refugee girl'. She had been looking after Jewish orphans in Leipzig after being forced out of school by a Nazi decree and was hired as a mother's helper by the London family who promised her a home and pocket money. Though she was 'absolutely devastated' to leave her parents, she entered her British employers' home thinking 'isn't it wonderful ... I'm going to meet everybody and that's going to be like my adopted family'.[1] Instead, she was excluded from family gatherings and expected, in addition to childcare, to keep the doctor's surgery clean, help in the kitchen, serve at the table and do 'the rough', as the daily scrubbing and whitening of the front steps was called.

The shock and dismay she had felt was undiminished fifty years later, when she gave her testimony. She recalled 'crying her eyes out' when she visited friends of her parents on her day off:

> I told them how awful it was and that I have to do something to go back home and they explained to me there was no such thing as going back

home – that I had to try everything to get my parents out but I can't go back home. . . . One of the most depressing things was since I was a little spoiled Jewish princess. . . . I had never done any real what I would call rough labour . . . and in those early morning hours with this menial horrible task to do. . . . I cried my eyes out every morning lying on my knees doing that.[2]

For Hoffman, who had enjoyed what she described as 'a fairy tale childhood' in an affluent family that employed a governess and two servants, the transition to exile was traumatic on many levels. She had lost her home and worked for employers she felt were uncaring, experiencing servitude as onerous and humiliating. She was also deeply fearful for her parents, whose rescue had become her responsibility. That task took on greater urgency after her father's arrest on Kristallnacht, the German Reich-wide pogrom on 9–10 November 1938 that targeted Jewish business and houses of worship for destruction and resulted in the arrest and incarceration of thousands of Jewish men.

Hoffman was one of over 20,000 Jewish refugees from Germany, Austria, Czechoslovakia and places of temporary refuge who came to the UK as live-in domestic servants in the late 1930s. In response to a widely perceived 'servant problem' in interwar Britain, which coincided in the late 1930s with the Jewish refugee crisis brought on by the increasing persecutions of the Hitler regime, the British government allowed large numbers of Jewish women, aged eighteen to forty-five, to apply for domestic service visas. This policy enabled thousands to escape, while helping to fill the demand for servants in British homes.[3] Like Hoffman, many were single young women from middle-class families whose lives had been upended by the exclusion of Jews from the economic, civic, social and educational life of Germany after the Nazi Party came to power in 1933. In their flight from fascism, these refugees' experiences were intertwined with the Holocaust; though personally spared its worst horrors, most left family behind in occupied lands and felt responsible for their fates.[4]

Nazi oppression precipitated their flight, but Jewish refugees from fascism occupy a liminal space in narratives of Holocaust victimhood as the 'lucky ones' who escaped and whose hardships would forever be measured, by themselves and by others, against the horrors faced by those who remained in German-controlled lands.[5] An outpouring of refugee testimony demonstrates, however, that though they found countries of refuge, their lives were not without pain. Like all Jewish refugees admitted to Great Britain in that period, domestics, who made up almost one-third of total arrivals, endured persecution, displacement and loss. However, some of their experiences were uniquely gender-inflected, an aspect of their lives that has barely registered in Holocaust and refugee scholarship.[6] The very work upon which the refugee domestics' emigration was predicated – as maids, cooks, nannies and butlers – was gendered in both its duties and its supervision.

Becoming a servant as the price of escape meant submersion within the private and dominantly feminine domestic spaces of British households, where gender norms defined labour roles and traditions of class dictated their daily lives.

Class issues affected the interactions of nearly all refugee domestics and their employers and shaped their responses to becoming live-in servants. Socio-economic changes in Britain and dissatisfaction with their treatment, lowly status and long hours drove many British working-class girls away from domestic service in the aftermath of the First World War, creating the 'servant crisis' that led to the refugee domestic visa programme. Social reformers and Parliamentary inquiries that documented working-class women's discontent with domestic service in the interwar period also showed that traditional attitudes among the servant-keeping classes, who expected the 'lower classes' to 'know their place' had not markedly altered in response to the shortage of servants.[7] Thus, most Jewish refugee domestics entered households with well-established class hierarchies to work for employers who had little experience dealing with servants who had not come from British working-class backgrounds and who were, by and large, inclined to hew to their traditional models of employer–servant relations. While popular culture has foregrounded a 'Downton Abbey' model of domestic service in grand houses with a large staff, in reality, the vast majority of residential servants were singly employed in middle-class homes, where they interacted intimately with their mistresses and other members of the household.[8] British literature of the late 1930s aimed at housewives suggested to its readers that, in hiring refugees, British women could obtain efficient maids while simultaneously doing 'a wonderful work of kindness' in relieving the suffering of persecuted Jewish girls.[9] There is evidence that some British families brought Jewish refugee domestics into their homes out of humanitarian motives, but testimonial accounts suggest that the majority of employers were primarily interested in simply acquiring servants, regardless of their circumstances or refugee status.

This chapter examines several distinct groups of Jewish refugee domestics, focusing on the intersection of gender and trauma as revealed in their life narrations and contemporaneous documentation. The largest cohort was single women, most of whom had been ill-prepared for roles as servants in their pre-emigration lives. Younger women comprised the majority of this group and their accounts of refugee life emphasize their inexperience and naivete, which left them vulnerable to exploitation, homesickness, loneliness and the unwanted sexual attention of males in the household (as, indeed, was also the case for young British-born maids). No better prepared to become servants than younger refugees, a much smaller group of older single women additionally suffered from the loss of their pre-emigration independence and autonomy and were often more burdened by the physical demands of the job.

Some refugee domestics were in the UK along with family members, and their experiences, while paralleling those of single women in many respects, also reflected the dynamics of these relationships. Mothers whose minor children had arrived separately on the movement now referred to as the Kindertransport – the scheme that brought about 10,000 unaccompanied, mostly Jewish children from Nazi-controlled and -occupied areas in Central Europe to Britain – comprise perhaps the greatest number among this subset of refugee domestics. Unable to live with their children while in service, many were forced to relinquish their maternal prerogatives to refugee agencies and foster caregivers. The relative few who took positions as married domestics confronted an upending of their normative roles. Men, whose traditional patriarchal positions as breadwinners and protectors had already been undercut by Nazi persecution that robbed them of their livelihoods, felt further diminished by undertaking unfamiliar domestic tasks for employers who, under different circumstances, might have been their social equals.

This chapter draws upon the accounts of refugee domestics and shows that their hardship and suffering did not end when they escaped Nazi control. A few of these accounts come from archival correspondence that preserves the contemporaneous voices of refugees and offers unique insights into their lives and feelings at the time, but most are derived from narratives recorded decades later. Like all such sources, these testimonies must be approached as constructed memories mediated by time, interviewer/interviewee relationships and other elements of their production; but their temporal distance from the events being recalled means that they are also capable of conveying, in ways that other sources are not, the long-lasting trauma of the refugee experience.[10] Utilizing these two types of sources, my analysis is divided into three sections: an examination of single Jewish women's experiences as refugee domestics; a contrasting look at the experiences of those who came with or were in Britain with family members; and an assessment of former refugees' narratives for evidence of trauma. These sources demonstrate that refugee domestics vividly recall the hardships and losses resulting from their persecution, exile and the difficult adjustments they were forced to make when they became servants. As they adapted to their new circumstances and reconciled themselves to their losses and tragedies, trauma manifested itself in psychological breakdown, maladaptation to post-refugee life and ongoing grief for families that they could not save from the Holocaust.

'I cried and cried and cried'

The majority of those who came to Britain as refugee domestics were single women whose lives had been, in some way or another, upended by the advent of Nazi rule in 1933. Of this group, those born between 1914 and 1921 made up the largest number. This younger generation of German Jews had been barred from attending university or pursuing professional careers from the earliest years of the Reich; similar curtailments affected young women in Austria after it was annexed in March 1938. Though excluded from many professions, these young women often trained in needlework trades or childcare, and most continued to live with their parents until their emigration. Many were only children, and most admitted to being unaccustomed to doing household work. They often described themselves as naive, making them especially vulnerable to financial, physical and sexual exploitation by their employers. Domestic service presented few physical challenges to these young women, but the loss of home, the jarring contrast with their former lives, the harsh treatment meted out by employers whom they had expected to be sympathetic and the separation from their families fed loneliness, depression, homesickness and despair.

Not all refugee domestics expected their British employers to be their adopted families, but most anticipated that their treatment by employers would mirror that of the maids, nannies and cooks who had worked for their parents. Former domestics' testimonies are rife with descriptions of 'perfect' childhoods peopled with devoted and well-treated servants. As Marione Silverman recalled, 'My mother never did very much work, we had a lady in the house – but she was not named a maid – she was like member of the family. She stood with us for all the years until she had to leave'.[11] Though likely idealized, such remembrances show that refugee domestics went to Britain with certain frameworks for understanding employer–servant relations, established by observing their mothers' dealings with staff whom they believed had been treated as family members. In British households, however, many felt as Herta Grove did when she asserted: 'I was a real maid. Not how our maids were in Germany'. In these refugees' recollections, the German maids of their childhoods had lived and eaten with the family and shared the household chores with their mothers; a 'real maid', by contrast, was one who shouldered the entire workload, lived and ate apart from the family, and whose employer–servant interactions were strictly businesslike.[12]

For young refugee maids, the greatest source of distress in domestic service was not the hard work, but the treatment they received from their mistresses. While it conformed to British standards of servant-keeping, refugees perceived this behaviour to be cold and indifferent. Believing, as Hildegard Hoffman had, that good-hearted British families were eager to ease their plight, most expected to be treated kindly. They thought that they would regard their mistresses as mother figures, as they imagined their German and Austrian maids had. The shattering of these expectations devastated many, including Susi Linton, who described herself as a 'spoiled, cherished, and protected' only child.

> 'Clean the steps, get the breakfast ready and start the washing'.... That's the way they talked to me. There was no personal contact, no sympathy, nothing, nothing ... two or three [other] ... refugee girls ... complained

the same as I did how badly treated they were. We got together on our day off . . . and stay[ed] all afternoon with a cup of coffee, crying . . . I didn't mind the work, but I did mind . . . the way I was treated.[13]

Linton articulates here one of the most common themes running through the narratives of refugee domestics – their employers' failure to see them as people, let alone as distressed refugees. As one woman sorrowfully noted, 'they had no feeling for me and could not sense who I was'.[14] She and others felt that their former identities, their suffering, even their very humanity, was invisible to their employers.

While younger women rarely mentioned falling ill or suffering injuries, older women often struggled with the arduous physical labour. Years in largely sedentary vocations had ill-prepared them for the physical demands of this work and many could not cope. The case files of one refugee agency hold numerous examples of former teachers and secretaries who lost their domestic service jobs and requested financial support because they had suffered knee and back injuries from heavy lifting and endless stair climbing, weight loss and chronic hand infections from harsh cleaning tasks, which rendered them unable to work.[15] With few resources, the loss of a job brought many such women to the brink of despair, as expressed by Emilia Elias, a former clothing designer who wrote to the refugee committee:

I lost my job after two weeks as a skullery [sic] maid and now I am out of work nearly 14 days. I try hard to find some, but it seems so hopeless. I would take any sort of rough work. . . . I owe . . . a week's lodging money and have not got a hot meal for 6 days. . . . I am ashamed to tell you these, but I am desperate, my shoes are gone, except my coat I have nothing to keep warm. I am on the edge of everything.[16]

Elias's physical as well as emotional well-being was tested by her failure to find work after she injured her foot, and her desolation can be heard in the plaintive phrase 'I am on the edge of everything'. The heavy physical demands of the job and the constant threat of losing one's position due to injury intensified the insecurities and anxieties of these women's refugee existence.

Some of the anguish evident in the accounts of refugee domestics arose from their being thrust into completely different cultural milieus and in the distressing contrast with their previous socio-economic class. Carola Domar recalled, 'I had to clean toilets, make beds, serve at the table, and here I was the daughter of a lawyer growing up the way I did – as a maid . . . that was extremely painful to me. I cried and cried and cried'.[17] Domar's words suggest that she perceived her work as beneath her; but it is also possible that Domar's grief emanated from fully realizing the impact of the losses wrought by her forced exile. Some, like Gertrude Buchler, who described being 'in a pretty desperate situation', believed that their employers' ignorance of their middle-class backgrounds accounted for their treatment as 'born maids'.[18] Others, such as Leopoldine Polly Zinram, felt that British families 'took us on realizing fully well that we were basically middle-class girls used to having maids around us', making their treatment as 'born maids' all the more painful.[19] There is evidence in the diaries that some British housewives kept for Mass-Observation, a social research organization founded in 1937, that though employers were aware of the middle-class origins of their refugee maids, they felt it impossible to treat them differently than their native-born servants, as their highest priority was maintaining their own position at the apex of household authority.[20]

In becoming refugee maids, older women experienced the same social and cultural dislocations as their younger counterparts, but the jarring contrast of their new lives with their previous identities as independent career women heightened their distress. When asked how difficult it had been to go 'from an office job to essentially a job as a maid', Ann Callman admitted to her interviewer that 'you had to swallow your pride quite a bit to do work which you at home had people who did it for you – it would take books to describe what pride I personally had to swallow'. She rose to the task, because it offered her an opportunity to bring out her twin sister, and, she hoped, her mother. She found the work physically debilitating and bitterly recalled that 'the adjustment which I had to do can't even be described in words. . . . I was continuously in tears'. She believed her employers 'thought that they were doing something for the Jews . . . showing me off as a refugee. I don't think it was kindness. It was more like "Here, I'm doing something for the poor refugee from Germany"'.[21] Many Jewish refugees of this period were similarly resentful about being 'shown off' by sponsors who sought community approbation; it especially rankled when they did not feel treated with sympathy or understanding.[22]

Even kind treatment by employers did not negate the disorienting effects of leaving a professional career for the life of a refugee domestic. Secondary school teacher Sophie Friedlander hoped to secure a similar position in Britain, but resentfully recalled that 'the only job that was offered to you was a domestic job'. She was hired by a professional couple who were genuinely interested in helping refugees, treated her as an equal and did not compel her to do maid work though they honoured their contract by paying her the standard servant wage.[23] Uncomfortable about this arrangement, she felt obligated to earn this money by taking on the unfamiliar and (to her) distasteful tasks of housecleaning and childcare. Acknowledging her good fortune, she noted that she 'couldn't have found a nicer family'; nevertheless, in exile she felt as though she 'was suddenly nobody'.[24] Like refugees and migrants in many places and eras, Friedlander was forced to abandon a professional avocation and take on menial work, which she experienced as an utter loss of identity. Unlike refugees in other milieus, however, Jewish refugee domestics were compelled to work as live-in maids as a condition of their escape, and once in Britain, strictly forbidden to take on any other work.²⁵ In describing feeling suddenly like 'nobody', Friedlander implicitly acknowledges the 'invisibility' of domestic servants in Britain, where class expectations and traditions usually segregated them from household life. Unacculturated to these norms, refugee domestics struggled to adjust.

Part of their invisibility as servants, and one of the most oft mentioned difficulties for refugee maids, was the social isolation of the job. Being relegated to the kitchen for meals, which is mentioned with startling frequency in refugees' testimonies, was a keenly felt exclusion. This practice, both in the loneliness it engendered and in its contrast with the experiences of their natal households, underscored their separation from home and family. Marion Friedlaender recalled that her employers

> were very nice people *but* – a servant is a servant. A maid is a maid. The food that was leftover at the table, I and the dog – Tinker was his name – was for us in the kitchen. . . . I sat in the kitchen crying, crying, crying and the dog was next to me putting his paws on me and licking my tears.²⁶

Carol Kutner did not even have the consolation of a dog to comfort her in a job in which she 'was not treated nice'. Kutner, who described herself as a sheltered only child, said of her mistress, 'I was treated as "I found somebody I can wash the floor with" – like that because I was utterly in her power – utterly'.²⁷ Kutner's recollection highlights how little agency many of these women felt in their positions as refugee maids. Language barriers, wartime anti-alien sentiments, employers' threats and the social isolation of a live-in servant's job all combined to create these feelings of insecurity, loneliness and despair.²⁸

In her comments, Carol Kutner acknowledged the fundamental power imbalance inherent in a master–servant relationship, which made them vulnerable to exploitation, including sexual molestation. Many testimonies contain mentions of unwanted sexual advances by male householders, though few were willing to discuss these incidents at length. Some made light of the episodes, or minimized them, suggesting the shame and embarrassment that was attached to such memories. Herta Graham, who took pains to say that her employers were 'kind' and allowed her to eat with them, confessed that when his wife was away, the master of the house sexually assaulted her, though she hastened to add that he had not wanted to rape her, but 'only to touch me'. Graham confessed later in her testimony that the assault was a traumatic experience, but de-emphasizing its severity may have helped her rationalize the decision not to report the incident and to remain in the family's employment, which she chose to do because it was a kosher home and, as an orthodox Jew, she was afraid she would not be able to find another position that allowed her to remain observant.²⁹ In their immediate responses and in the ways in which they reflected upon these incidents years later, Graham and others emphasized their limited choices, the paucity of support systems in exile, their feelings of powerlessness vis-à-vis their employers and the shame that such incidents and their memories evoked. These episodes also highlight one of the most obvious links between gender and trauma in these refugees' lives.

Whether young or older, single women confronted a myriad of challenges as refugee domestic servants. Coping with the bitter realities of exile and loss of home, fearing for families left behind and grappling with jobs for which they were often physically, emotionally and culturally unprepared, many of these women experienced loneliness, isolation, exploitation and despair. Thrust with little preparation into households whose servant-keeping practices were difficult to reconcile with those they recalled from their natal homes, refugee domestics faced difficult adjustments with limited agency, resources and options. The much smaller number of refugee domestics who arrived with or were joined by family members in Britain encountered similar difficulties, though sharing the refugee experience with relatives presented other challenges.

'I really cannot stand it . . . in Domestic, without a home and without my children'

The experiences of Jewish refugees who came to Britain on domestic visas with other family members – children, spouses, parents – varied according to the degree of dependency or burden-sharing that existed in their relationships with one another. Perhaps the largest number in this group were mothers who obtained domestic service visas as a strategy for reuniting with children they had sent ahead on Kindertransports – or planned to send for once established in the country of refuge. A smaller number came as domestic couples, usually as housekeeper and butler. Ranging in age from younger couples, including some with children, to those in their late forties and even early fifties, the male perspective within these family groups sets them apart from the larger cohort of Jewish refugee domestics.

The most obvious anxiety for mothers in domestic service was separation from and diminished control over their children's lives. Their first obstacle was arranging their own and their children's emigrations from their homelands. Once issued, domestic service visas were valid only for a short period, and if their children's emigration had not yet been arranged, mothers had to make an agonizing choice: leave first, and risk the unthinkable possibility that their children might not manage to join them, or delay their departure and possibly lose their visas. Two examples highlight this dilemma. After her visa arrived, Lisa Orchan, a widow stranded in Poland with her children, wrote to a London refugee committee pleading with them to arrange for the transport of her two children, as she was unwilling to take up her post and leave them behind. A place was found for her daughter Anna, but Lisa refused to abandon her youngest child, and both she and Leo were killed in the Shoah.[30] In contrast, Selma Weil left for Britain before her children, confident that she would be able to arrange for their emigration after she had established herself. Marianne and Robby Weil were in a children's home in Amsterdam awaiting transport to England when war broke out and, by a tragic twist of fate, were quarantined with chicken pox when the rest of the children in the home were hurriedly shipped to Britain. The Weil children were murdered in the Holocaust, leaving their mother to grieve the consequences of her decision to leave her children behind when she came to Britain as a maid.[31]

For most of those who managed to get both themselves and their children to Britain, hardships awaited. Employers refused to allow their servants' children to live in their homes, and most families were separated. Though they were more fortunate than those who were divided by war, these separations were nevertheless hard on refugees such as Tina Mandel, who had originally accepted a job that allowed her to keep her toddler with her, though in return for this concession she had to 'work hard without any payment'. Like many refugees, Mandel lost her job when Britain entered the war and sought help from a refugee committee. Taking their advice to place her child into a home and seek work, she wrote of the misery of separation from the child, 'who was my greatest and only joy in this wretched existence'.[32] Another young mother, Hilde Gerrard, was forced to put her twin toddlers in 'The Home for Friendless Children' while she worked as a domestic, and she saw them only on weekends. In a short memoir she wrote in the 1980s, she recalled hiding along the route the children took on their daily walk, 'just to see them trotting along . . . as the tears ran down my cheeks'.[33] Annaliese Goldschmidt also keenly felt the separation from her school-aged children, telling the refugee committee that had sponsored them that 'life is terribly hard for me and I cannot tell you how desperate I am . . . it is two years that I am separated from Hans and Marianne. . . . I really cannot stand it near so long in Domestic, without a home and without my children'.[34] A widow and formerly independent businesswoman, Goldschmidt was grudgingly allowed by her employers to have her children stay with her on school breaks, though she had to pay for their upkeep out of her meagre wages. Like other domestics, her desperation sprang from her limited agency and the restrictive circumstances under which she could have contact with her children.

Trapped in jobs they despised, and with few financial resources of their own, these women's maternal roles were almost entirely usurped by refugee committees. The West London Synagogue archives hold records of about twenty children whose mothers were in the UK as domestic servants, and inter-agency correspondence characterizes these mothers as bothersome, hysterical, overly involved and 'unhelpful'.[35] The widow Klara Wittman, whose children Fritz and Ilse were in Britain, was the subject of a great deal of correspondence, including an exchange between the chairmen of two refugee agencies involved in her children's care:

Both Fritz and his mother are very averse to being at a distance where they cannot see each other at frequent intervals.... [Q]uite clearly they feel they have the right to dictate while you pay. I pointed out that every second English boy had to be away from his mother while at school.... I rather fear that Mrs Wittman has not been a help to the child and it might be well to put out to her that as long as you are responsible for Fritz, your wishes must be obeyed.[36]

The letter exemplifies the refugee organizations' paternalistic belief that they knew what was best for these refugee children and that their financial beneficence entitled them to make all the decisions. Told that they had 'nothing to complain of' and that they were 'in far more fortunate circumstances than most refugees', such mothers were silenced by the imperatives of gratitude and indebtedness that are routinely imposed on refugees and immigrants in every era and culture.[37]

Married refugee domestics faced challenges to their normative relationships as they navigated their new roles as servants. Like older single women, older couples found it challenging to adapt to servant life after being forced to abandon their lives of middle-class autonomy. A childless couple in their early forties, Bronka Schneider and her husband Joseph struggled to adapt to work in the remote Scottish castle of their wealthy employers.[38] Joseph, in particular, found the going difficult. Though written from Bronka's perspective in a light-hearted style that minimized their hardships, her account makes clear that the mistress was impatient with Joseph's mistakes and that he felt demeaned by work he found dull. The book's editors reveal that Joseph himself later wrote that his job at the castle 'was to be the ghost'. This remark was perhaps a self-deprecating, humorous commentary on spooky British castles, but it can also be read as an acknowledgement of his own invisibility, inconsequence and emasculation as a servant.[39]

Perhaps the most well-known account of an unhappily situated older domestic couple is found in Lore Segal's lightly fictionalized 1964 memoir *Other People's Houses*. Segal, who came on a Kindertransport, describes the first day of her parents' lives as servants when her mother admired the drawing room piano, making a valiant attempt to establish 'that she too, had once been comfortably circumstanced' and that her husband, an accountant, had been professionally positioned on the same socio-economic level as their employer. The mistress did not acknowledge these remarks but only complained about having to wait eleven weeks for the couple's arrival. When informed by her new cook of the difficulties they encountered in escaping Germany, the mistress's 'eyes began to wander' with indifference.[40] Like many others, the Groszmanns had expected that employers who sought out refugee domestics would have some knowledge of or interest in the persecutions they had endured. They were disappointed to find that their employers saw them as no different from any other servants.

The adjustment to domestic service was painful for the Groszmanns. Mr Groszmann simply could not cope with the butler's task of serving at the table, and Segal wrote, 'my mother . . . wept bitterly for him, he looked so ridiculous'.[41] Her burden was increased when, in order to keep their jobs, Franzi Groszmann added his duties to her own chores of cooking and cleaning while he was relegated to the garden. Consistently attempting to bolster her husband, she asked her employer if he could not be addressed as Mr Groszmann instead of simply by his last name, but her mistress dismissed the request as inconceivable. Segal explores her own feelings of guilt about a father whose impotence and humiliation embarrassed her and portrays him as a pathetic figure who was routinely abased by the couple's various employers. Segal implies that the degradations of domestic work broke him completely, and he died before the war's close.[42]

It is difficult to draw conclusions about the suffering of married men who became domestics, for virtually every account is told from a female relative's perspective. These hint only obliquely at the ways in which men may have experienced their manual labour or their family's reduced financial circumstances as a humiliation. Testimony confirms that the psychological barriers to male domestic service and its perceived indignities were enough to inhibit some couples from using this path to escape the Reich. Older men with established careers and lives of material comfort were more reluctant to emigrate, let alone condition their exile on domestic work. While there is evidence in the accounts of those domestic couples and mothers of minor children that the shared experience brought them some measure of comfort, servitude challenged their relationships as they assumed unfamiliar roles, endured separations and coped with the consequences of exile.

Testimony and trauma

Refugees' testimonies speak of the hardship, resentment, depression and isolation that they experienced when forced to work as servants in order to escape from the German Reich, but they also document the traumas that were felt long after they had moved beyond their domestic service jobs. Later testimonies dwell on the loneliness, sexual abuse and loss of family members in the Holocaust, which caused the most enduring suffering. Interviewed when they were in their seventies and eighties, a surprising number of former refugees admit that they were only for the first time revealing their most upsetting experiences, which underscores the depth and durability of trauma's legacy.

Memories of desperate loneliness and sexual exploitation were often recalled with emotional intensity. When discussing her isolation and the sexual assault she endured when the mistress was out, Herta Graham assumed the voice of the vulnerable young woman she had been at the time as she recollected crawling under her bed each night and crying out 'Mummy why did you send me away?' Prior to her interview, she had rarely spoken about her refugee experiences, because, she said, 'You don't want to talk about nasty things'.[43] Carol Kutner also disclosed some traumatic episodes for the first time in her interview, including the revelation that, driven by loneliness, she engaged in relationships that she now regarded as shameful:

> I really still had nobody – I was totally alone and people will take advantage of other people when they are totally alone. There's things here that none of my family know ... so I don't know if I will ever tell. ... I look back, I say to myself how could I have been so gullible? I was being used left and right, but I was just happy for anybody who could give me some comfort.[44]

In his seminal examination of Holocaust survivor testimony, Lawrence Langer characterizes such revelations as 'humiliated memory', which 'represents pure misery, even decades after the events it narrates. Neither time nor amnesia soothes its gnawing'.[45] Even after the passage of fifty years, Kutner was still traumatized and unable to shed her shame for having sought comfort in relationships that she later saw as sexually and emotionally exploitative.

Testimony also reveals that one frequent manifestation of such trauma was the self-reported 'nervous breakdown'. Nelly Kuttner experienced this while in domestic service, after her employer spitefully forced her to perform a cleaning task in order to reclaim her luggage when she gave her notice. 'In that moment I was thinking from the Nazis I have escaped from lying down to wash the pavement and here I have to wash the floor. I took off my lovely silk stockings. I took off my silk dress, went up into the room and did the floor'.[46] This detailed, traumatic memory of complying with her mistress's demand links to her earlier trauma of public humiliation in the streets of Vienna, where wealthy Jews were forced to clean pavements while overseen by jeering crowds and Nazi authorities.[47] Soon after this incident Kuttner suffered what she called a 'nervous breakdown' and was unable to work for several months. A 1951 British study revealed that such trauma manifested for many in the post-war era, when refugees were twice as likely to be hospitalized for mental illness as native-born Britons.[48]

When describing the loss of their families, refugees' psychological distress is, not surprisingly, expressed most acutely. Like many others, Esther Clifford reported having a 'nervous breakdown' when confronted after the war with the news of her parents' deportation and deaths. Decades later she expressed pride in being able 'to pull out of the tragic situation of losing a family', but she also admitted 'no way that I pulled out completely ... there isn't a day that I don't think of them'.[49] This decades-long contestation with the past is echoed by Leopoldine Polly Zinram, who said of her mother's murder after deportation to Riga, 'it took me 40 years to face it fairly and squarely'.[50] Mementos that they show or talk about in their interviews, including photographs and final communications with their doomed parents, become focal points for the expression of trauma. One woman displayed her mother's visa rejection letter from the British Home Office; another spoke of the bunch of dried red roses she had kept for sixty years, the parting gift of her mother who was later murdered.[51] Others remain unable to share their trauma. Unable to speak to her children about her mother's deportation and murder in Riga, Alice Calder wrote a six-page memoir and gave it to them, instead. She admitted that her daughter 'would like . . . to talk about it. . . . [but] as you can see, I can't talk about it without crying [sobbing] and I don't want to do that'.[52] The pain engendered by the severing of mother–daughter bonds, in particular, stands out in these testimonies.

Losing their loved ones was one aspect of a complex web of trauma that refugee domestics experienced in the immediate and long-term aftermath of the Holocaust. The grief they felt about family members' deaths was complicated by feelings of guilt about their own survival and a reluctance to acknowledge the pain and hardship they themselves and others had endured as servants and refugees. When summing up her experiences, Herta Graham articulated these tensions: 'Of course, it wasn't a happy life for me . . . [but] I feel ashamed to say it wasn't a happy life compared to what other people went through'.[53] In framing her own suffering against the horrors of the Holocaust, Graham denies the validity of her own trauma, feeling shame in even naming it. For those refugees who tried and failed to bring their loved ones to Britain, these conflicted feelings are acute, even when they recognized their limited agency in effecting their families' rescues. Sadly, the very act of recording their memories further delegitimizes refugee domestics' suffering when interviewers express preferences for the stories of their lost family members over their own life narratives, as frequently occurs in these testimonies.[54] Finally, there is the silence about Jewish refugee domestics in scholarship on Britain and the Holocaust, especially in relation to other refugee groups, such as the Kindertransportees. Ironically, this lacuna mirrors the invisibility they felt as servants.

Those who came as refugee domestics suffered in similar ways to other Jewish refugees of the time: pre-emigration persecution and subsequent loss of home, culture, traditions, possessions, position, status, wealth and family. However, the particularities of refugee domestics' suffering were also explicitly gendered in many ways as they were compelled by the terms of their visas into a realm of (primarily) female subservience. For many, it meant engaging in arduous housekeeping tasks for the first time and being subjected to unwanted sexual attentions. Gender roles were challenged, as mothers were separated from their children and were compelled to relinquish maternal prerogatives. Men, too, confronted a loss of identity, as they entered a domestic sphere in a role that was foreign to them. Testimonies, most given decades later, attest to the outcomes of these experiences, including mental breakdowns and the long-term psychological suffering caused by their refugee status and the loss of their families in the Holocaust. Though they were themselves spared the horrors of the Holocaust, the evidence they left behind nevertheless attests to their trauma.

Notes

1. Hildegard Cohn Hoffmann, Interview 23246, 1999, Visual History Archive, USC Shoah Foundation, Los Angeles, CA (hereafter, VHA).
2. Hoffman, VHA.
3. For a more detailed discussion of refugees and 'the servant crisis', see Jennifer Craig-Norton, 'Refugees at the Margins: Jewish Domestics in Britain 1939-1945', *Shofar* 37, no. 3 (2019): 296–330 (296–301); Tony Kushner, 'An Alien Occupation – Jewish Refugees and Domestic Service in Britain, 1933-1948', in *Second Chance: Two Centuries of German-Speaking Jews in the United Kingdom*, ed. Julius Carlebach et al. (Tübingen: Mohr Siebeck, 1991), 553–7.
4. Deborah Dwork and Robert Jan van Pelt argue persuasively for the inclusion of refugees' experiences within narratives of the Holocaust. See their *Flight from the Reich: Refugee Jews 1933-1946* (New York: Norton, 2009), xii–xiii.
5. For former refugees' perspectives on this topic, see Letters to the Editor, *AJR Journal* 9, no. 2 (2009): 5.
6. Scholarship on women and the Holocaust has focused primarily on women in camps and ghettos. See, for example, Elizabeth Roberts Baer and Myrna Goldenberg, eds, *Experience and Expression: Women, the Nazis, and the Holocaust* (Detroit, MI: Wayne State University Press, 2003); Judith Tydor Baumel, *Double Jeopardy: Gender and the Holocaust* (London: Vallentine, Mitchell, 1998); Myrna Goldenberg and Amy H. Shapiro, eds, *Different Horrors/Same Hell: Gender and the Holocaust* (Seattle; London: University of Washington Press, 2013); Marlene Heinemann, *Gender and Destiny: Women Writers and the Holocaust* (New York: Greenwood Press, 1986).
7. For reports on the 'servant crisis', see Central Committee on Women's Training and Employment, *Second Interim Report* (London: HMSO, 1923); Gertrud Emmot, *Report of the Women's Advisory Committee of the Ministry of Reconstruction on the Domestic Servant Problem* (London: HMSO, 1919); Violet Firth, *The Psychology of the Servant Problem: A Study in Social Relationships* (London: C. W. Daniel, 1925); Celia Fremlin, *The Seven Chars of Chelsea* (London: n.p. 1940); Ministry of Labour, *Report to the Ministry of Labour on the Committee Appointed to Enquire into the Present Conditions as to the Supply of Female Domestic Servants* (London: HMSO, 1923). For contemporary studies of British domestic service, see Lucy Delap, *Knowing Their Place: Domestic Service in Twentieth-Century Britain* (New York: Oxford University Press, 2011) and Judy Giles, *The Parlour and the Suburb: Domestic Identities, Class, Femininity and Modernity* (Oxford: Berg, 2004).
8. Delap, *Knowing Their Place*, 5–6.
9. *Housewife*, February 1939, 28, quoted in Tony Kushner, *Journeys from the Abyss: The Holocaust and Forced Migration from the 1880s to the Present* (Liverpool: Liverpool University Press, 2016), 71, 147.

10 See Noah Shenker, *Reframing Holocaust Testimony* (Bloomington: Indiana University Press, 2015) for a critical analysis of Holocaust testimony gathering, its uses and limitations.
11 Marione Silverman, Interview 11859, 1996, VHA.
12 Herta Grove, Interview V.T/3152- 0.3/4025911, 2001, Yad Vashem, Jerusalem, Israel. While former domestics' recollections of German maids must be treated with some caution, it is true that Continental maids' living and working conditions differed significantly from those of British domestics. Generally, in German and Austrian cities, families lived with their maids in single-floor flats that had central heating and modern plumbing. This arrangement was in marked contrast to British homes with their narrow steep stairways, maids segregated in attics and basements, and servants' laborious tasks such as maintaining coal fires and emptying chamber pots.
13 Susi Linton, Interview 78, 2004, Refugee Voices, Association of Jewish Refugees (hereafter, AJR).
14 Herta Jacoby, 50.150*0020, 1977, Rosalyn Manowitz/Hebrew Tabernacle Congregation Collection (hereafter, HTCC), United States Holocaust Memorial Museum, Washington, DC (hereafter, USHMM).
15 Dr Merkin to Case Committee PJRF, 21 September 1943, University of Southampton Hartley Library (hereafter, USHL) MS183/569/602; Dr Merkin to Mr Gorowitz, 21 April 1942, USHL MS183/569/277; Ida Goldman to Mr Gorowitz, 5 January 1942, USHL MS183/213/2/702; Registration Card, September 3. 1940, USHL MS183/592/F2/576. The Polish Jewish Refugee Fund (PJRF) was a small voluntary agency formed to help the victims of the *Polenatkion* – the forced deportation of Polish Jews from the German Reich that had occurred on 29–30 October 1938. The PJRF operated under the umbrella of the Federation of Jewish Relief Organizations from offices in Soho Square, London, and offered modest financial and medical aid to those Jewish refugees of Polish citizenship, both adults and children, who had sought refuge in Britain. For the PJRF activities associated with the Kindertransport, see Jennifer Craig-Norton, *The Kindertransport: Contesting Memory* (Bloomington: Indiana University Press, 2019).
16 Emilia Elias to PJRF, 5 January 1940, USHL MS183/569/291.
17 Carola Domar, Interview 42125, 1998, VHA.
18 Buchler, VHA.
19 Leopoldine Polly Zinram, C410/039, 1989–91, Living Memory of the Jewish Community, British Library (hereafter, BL).
20 Tony Kushner, *Remembering Refugees: Then and Now* (Manchester: Manchester University Press, 2006), 127–9.
21 Ann and Lilo Callman, RG-50.150*0002, 1977–8, HTCC, USHMM. For an employer perspective on the subject of employing refugees as a humanitarian act, see Kushner, *Remembering Refugees*, 128.
22 See Craig-Norton, *The Kindertransport*, 107–9.
23 In order to protect the jobs of British domestics, employers were legally bound to pay their refugee servants the standard wage of 15 shillings per week,

though many accounts indicate that this dictate was widely abused and refugee servants were often underpaid or not paid at all. Fearful of recriminations or of being deported, few reported their underpayment to refugee committees or other authorities.

24 Sophie Friedlander, Interview 36225, 1997, VHA.
25 In general, refugees were freed from employment restrictions after Britain entered the war, but for some months, the authorities were ambivalent about allowing domestics to take on other jobs and most remained in domestic service until the end of 1940 or even later.
26 Marion Friedlaender, Interview 9904, 1996, VHA.
27 Carol Kutner, Interview 29005, 1997, VHA.
28 After war broke out, all aliens had to register with police and attend tribunals, which tested their loyalties and assigned classifications of friendly or enemy aliens. These classifications significantly affected aliens' lives in Britain, including decisions on internment, and tribunal judges carefully considered employers' recommendations. Some employers wielded this power over their refugee maids to threaten or otherwise compel their servants' compliance.
29 Graham, VHA. See also Marion Smith, Interview 102, 2005, AJR; Lisa Hoffman, Interview 598, 1985, Holocaust Video Testimonies, Yale Fortunoff Archive, New Haven, CT.
30 Lisa Orchan to Elsley Zeitlyn, 3 July 1939, USHL/MS/183/591/F3.
31 Papers related to Selma Weil and her children Marianne and Robby, 0.75/1576, Yad Vashem, Jerusalem, Israel.
32 Tina Mandel to Mr and Mrs Ginsburg, 20 November 1939, Mandel Family Papers 1938–49, MS650/MS62/15, Leo Baeck Institute Archives.
33 Hilde Gerrard, 'We Were Lucky', unpublished memoir 4011 (1984), 19, Wiener Holocaust Library, London, UK.
34 Annaliese Goldschmidt to Berniece d'Avigdor, 11 January 1941, 19 March 1941, USHL/MS140/A2049/94/6.
35 West London Synagogue to Bloomsbury House, 7 August 1941, USHL/MS140/A2049/94/6. See also USHL/MS140/A2049/96/8.
36 Mrs Malabre to Berniece d'Avigdor, 17 May 1941, 27 May 1941, USHL/MS140/A2049/94/16.
37 Cynthia Annersley to Mrs Malabre, 4 November 1940, USHL/MS140/A2049/94/16. See Craig-Norton, *The Kindertransport*, 53–4, 94–5, 100–1, 162, 322; Kushner, *Journeys*, 117, 122, 137–9, 151 for gratitude as a factor for Jewish refugees from Nazism, and Dina Nayeri, *The Ungrateful Refugee: What Immigrants Never Tell You* (Edinburgh: Cannongate, 2019) for a contemporary refugee's account of the traumas of being a refugee and the oppressive imperatives of gratitude.
38 Bronka Schneider, *Exile: A Memoir of 1939*, ed. Erika Bourguignon and Barbara Hill Rigney (Columbus: Ohio State University Press, 1998), 22.
39 Schneider, *Exile*, 124. This quote comes from a letter Joseph wrote many years later and is part of the memoir's epilogue, in which the editors of the memoir provide historical and other context about the Schneiders.

40 Lore Segal, *Other People's Houses*, 40th anniversary edn (New York: New Press, 2004), 83–4.
41 Segal, *Other People's Houses*, 78–82.
42 Segal, *Other People's Houses*, 120–43.
43 Graham, VHA.
44 Kutner, VHA.
45 Lawrence Langer, *Holocaust Testimonies: The Ruins of Memory* (New Haven, CT; London: Yale University Press, 1991), 77.
46 Nelly Kutner, EXS.1.RCGAES.3.KUT, 1995, Research Centre for German and Austrian Exile Studies, University of London.
47 For other examples of self-reported 'breakdowns', see Gerrard, 'We Were Lucky,' 16; Marianne Wall, Interview 43934, 1998, VHA; Marianne Rosson, Interview 47967, 1998, VHA.
48 Marion Berghahn, *German-Jewish Refugees in England: The Ambiguities of Assimilation* (London: St Martin's, 1984), 129. For testimonies of breakdowns later in life, see Susi Braun, Interview 78, 2004, AJR; Margaret Jones, Interview 43044, 1998, VHA; Margaret Hirschfield, Interview 20333, 1996, VHA.
49 Esther Clifford, Interview 22237, VHA, 1996.
50 Zinram, BL.
51 See Hoffman, VHA; Kuttner, VHA.
52 Alice Calder, RG-50.477.0549, 1990, Bay Area Holocaust Oral History Project, USHMM.
53 Graham, VHA.
54 See Craig-Norton, *Refugees at the Margins* for a discussion of this aspect of refugee domestics' testimonies. For a more general critique of interviewing techniques in Holocaust testimony, see Shenker, *Reframing Holocaust Testimony*.

Works cited

Baer, Elizabeth Roberts and Myrna Goldenberg, eds. *Experience and Expression: Women, the Nazis, and the Holocaust*. Detroit, MI: Wayne State University Press, 2003.

Baumel, Judith Tydor. *Double Jeopardy: Gender and the Holocaust*. London: Vallentine, Mitchell, 1998.

Bay Area Holocaust Oral History Project, United States Holocaust Memorial Museum, Washington, DC.

Berghahn, Marion. *German-Jewish Refugees in England: The Ambiguities of Assimilation*. London: St Martin's, 1984.

Central Committee on Women's Training and Employment. *Second Interim Report*. London: HMSO, 1923.

Craig-Norton, Jennifer. *The Kindertransport: Contesting Memory*. Bloomington: Indiana University Press, 2019.
Craig-Norton, Jennifer. 'Refugees at the Margins: Jewish Domestics in Britain 1939–1945'. *Shofar* 37, no. 3 (2019): 296–330.
Delap, Lucy. *Knowing Their Place: Domestic Service in Twentieth-Century Britain*. New York: Oxford University Press, 2011.
Dwork, Deborah and Robert Jan van Pelt. *Flight from the Reich: Refugee Jews 1933–1946*. New York: Norton, 2009.
Emmot, Gertrud. *Report of the Women's Advisory Committee of the Ministry of Reconstruction on the Domestic Servant Problem*. London: HMSO, 1919.
Firth, Violet. *The Psychology of the Servant Problem: A Study in Social Relationships*. London: C. W. Daniel, 1925.
Fremlin, Celia. *The Seven Chars of Chelsea*. London: n.p. 1940.
German and Austrian Exile Studies Centre, University of London.
Gerrard, Hilde. 'We Were Lucky'. Wiener Holocaust Library, University of London 4011, 1984.
Giles, Judy. *The Parlour and the Suburb: Domestic Identities, Class, Femininity and Modernity*. Oxford: Berg, 2004.
Goldenberg, Myrna and Amy H. Shapiro, eds. *Different Horrors/Same Hell: Gender and the Holocaust*. Seattle; London: University of Washington Press, 2013.
Grove, Herta. Interview V.T/3152- 0.3/4025911, 2001, Yad Vashem, Jerusalem, Israel.
Heinemann, Marlene. *Gender and Destiny: Women Writers and the Holocaust*. New York: Greenwood Press, 1986.
Holocaust Video Testimonies, Yale Fortunoff Library, New Haven, CT.
Kushner, Tony. 'An Alien Occupation – Jewish Refugees and Domestic Service in Britain, 1933–1948', in *Second Chance: Two Centuries of German-Speaking Jews in the United Kingdom*, edited by Werner Mosse, Julius Carlebach, Gerhard Hirschfeld, Aubrey Newman, Arnold Pauker and Peter Pulzer, 553–78. Tübingen: Mohr Siebeck, 1991.
Kushner, Tony. *Journeys from the Abyss: The Holocaust and Forced Migration from the 1880s to the Present*. Liverpool: Liverpool University Press, 2016.
Kushner, Tony. *Remembering Refugees: Then and Now*. Manchester: Manchester University Press, 2006.
Langer, Lawrence. *Holocaust Testimonies: The Ruins of Memory*. New Haven, CT; London: Yale University Press, 1991.
Living Memory of the Jewish Community, British Library, London.
Mandel family letters, 1938–1946: Letters and other documents concerning the experiences of Hermann and Tony Mandel, of Vienna, during the time of the Nazis, LBIJMB MSF 62/MS650 Leo Baeck Institute Archives, New York.
Ministry of Labour. *Report to the Ministry of Labour on the Committee Appointed to Enquire into the Present Conditions as to the Supply of Female Domestic Servants*. London: HMSO, 1923.
Nayeri, Dina. *The Ungrateful Refugee: What Immigrants Never Tell You*. Edinburgh: Cannongate, 2019.
Papers of the Polish Jewish Refugee Fund MS 190 AJ 390, The Papers of Rabbi Dr Solomon Schonfeld, MS183, The Papers of the West London Synagogue, MS140, University of Southampton Hartley Library, Southampton.

Papers related to Selma Weil and her children Marianne and Robby, 0.75/1576, Yad Vashem, Jerusalem.

Refugee Voices, Association of Jewish Refugees, London.

Rosalyn Manowitz/Hebrew Tabernacle Congregation Collection, United States Holocaust Memorial Museum, Washington, DC.

Schneider, Bronka. *Exile: A Memoir of 1939*. Edited by Erika Bourginon and Barbara Hill Rigney. Columbus: Ohio State University Press, 1998.

Segal, Lore. *Other People's Houses*, 40th anniversary edn. New York: New Press, 2004.

Shenker, Noah. *Reframing Holocaust Testimony*. Bloomington: Indiana University Press, 2015.

Visual History Archive, USC Shoah Foundation.

5

'Combat exhaustion' versus 'psychoneurosis'

American psychiatrists and the terminology of war trauma during the Second World War

Rebecca Jo Plant

In July 1944, several months after censors relaxed an official 'blackout' on all information related to military psychiatry and psychiatric casualties, the popular psychologist Henry Link charged military psychiatrists with 'literally *creating* mental cases ... at an appalling rate'. In an article published in the *American Mercury*, he described the more than 800,000 men rejected by Selective Service examiners on neuropsychiatric grounds – or in common parlance, 'NPs' – as 'in effect war casualties even though they have never been in uniform'. Because the stigma of mental disorder eroded men's self-respect and hampered their employment prospects, he alleged, psychiatric screening of potential recruits was creating a large pool of 'mental and emotional cripples'. In short, Link accused the nation's psychiatrists, armed with the 'heavy guns of psychiatric terminology', of waging what amounted to psychological warfare against the nation's own men.[1] After receiving 'hundreds of letters and clippings' in response, the *American Mercury* reported that few articles in its history had created 'so much discussion'.[2]

Psychiatrists viewed the accusation as damaging enough to require a response from the American Psychiatric Association. Penned by President Karl Bowman, the lengthy rebuttal lamented 'the gross misconception in the public mind regarding psychiatry' that Link's article both epitomized and fostered. 'The NP rating is a diagnostic rating, just as a heart murmur, or a tubercular condition are diagnostic ratings', he argued; the examining physician who detected a neuropsychiatric disorder simply identified a pre-existing problem, as when he diagnosed a case of undetected tuberculosis. According to Bowman, the real issue was not an abuse of psychiatric power but, rather, confusion regarding psychiatric *language*: 'The problem of the general misconception and mis-information regarding psychiatry is due to *terminology*. "Words that should serve as vehicles can end by jailing us!"'[3]

The *American Mercury* exchange was part of a broader debate over psychiatric terminology that came to a head in 1944–5 and threatened to derail the profession's progress towards establishing greater credibility as a medical specialty. To claim a central role in the war effort, psychiatrists clearly needed to defend the scientific legitimacy of their diagnostic language. Yet, because many in the military and the general public took a dim view of the profession, attempts to impose diagnostic labels threatened to backfire. By the time the *Mercury* exchange appeared, the War Department had, in effect, already pulled the plug on the psychiatric screening programme due to widespread concerns about the effects of psychiatric labelling.[4] Most psychiatrists had supported this move, recognizing that Selective Service physicians performed the most cursory of examinations, and that incautious use of psychiatric language only hindered their professional agenda. But when it came to discharging men already inducted into the Army, the stakes surrounding diagnostic prerogatives were higher, and psychiatrists proved more reluctant to cede ground.

Historians have typically viewed the Second World War as inaugurating a 'golden age' of psychiatry in the United States. This chapter tempers that assessment by showing how military imperatives and public opinion constrained psychiatric authority during the war, while exposing and exacerbating divisions within the profession itself. Proceeding chronologically, it unravels the protracted conflicts over psychiatric language and shows why different constituencies felt so invested in the terms used to describe soldiers' emotional and psychological woes. To capture these different viewpoints, it draws on a wide range of sources, including military psychiatrists' published writings and private correspondence, government documents, articles and letters-to-the-editor that appeared in the popular press, and publicly available transcripts of oral history interviews with veterans.

As these materials illustrate, wartime resistance to psychiatric authority centred on the term 'psychoneurosis', a diagnosis applied to men who broke down in training and seasoned soldiers alike.[5] Initially, psychiatrists attempted to alleviate concerns about the stigmatizing effects of psychiatric diagnosis through public education; like Karl Bowman in his *Mercury* rebuttal, they tried to convince Americans that psychiatric casualties were just like any other medical casualties. When these efforts largely failed, they yielded to pressure and in 1945 incorporated the colloquial yet widely used expression 'combat exhaustion' into their revised psychiatric nomenclature – a predecessor to the *Diagnostic Statistical Manual* (*DSM*), the so-called psychiatric Bible that identifies and classifies psychiatric illnesses – with the stipulation that it should be used only as a *temporary* diagnosis for select cases. They also committed to stop using the blanket term 'psychoneurosis' on medical records.[6] By adopting a diagnostic term that most considered unscientific, while relinquishing another that most considered legitimate, leading psychiatrists sought to defuse the public's and the military's frustration over their medical interventions.

Much of this frustration stemmed from the widely shared belief that psychiatric diagnoses emasculated generally healthy men while providing weak men with a medical rationalization for their failings. This chapter argues that psychiatrists' adoption of 'combat exhaustion' should be viewed as an attempt to shield proven combat veterans who succumbed to war trauma from being lumped together with 'true' psychoneurotics who never adjusted to military life. As Alan Derickson has shown, combat during the Second World War 'demanded of fighting men unprecedented levels of stamina and resiliency, levels which often exceeded the limits of human endurance'.[7] Under these conditions, ideals of manhood underwent a subtle redefinition; while daring displays of courage were still lauded, sheer stamina became the hallmark of the manly GI, valued even above the capacity for absolute emotional control. By agreeing to employ the diagnosis 'combat exhaustion' in select cases, psychiatrists aimed to rescue the manhood of soldiers who collapsed after sweating it out for many months, as opposed to those who broke down soon after coming under fire or, even worse, before ever being exposed to real danger.

The disputes surrounding psychiatric language and its effects on American manhood involved not only struggles between psychiatrists, the military and a sceptical public but also divisions within the profession itself. The Second World War is generally viewed as a primary catalyst for the dramatic rise of psychoanalysis within both psychiatry and the culture at large – a view borne out by the extraordinary surge in psychoanalytic training in the immediate post-war period.[8] The experiences of military psychiatrists, however, point to a more complicated story than narratives of psychoanalytic ascendancy would suggest. After all, the decision to bestow a medical imprimatur on the term 'combat exhaustion' represented a defeat for the psychoanalytically oriented branch of the profession. Psychiatrists M. Ralph Kaufman and Lindsay Beaton, for instance, strongly objected to the diagnosis 'combat fatigue' – often used interchangeably with 'combat exhaustion' – on the grounds that it had been adopted for reasons of 'expediency'.[9] Shifting the focus away from the tormented mind and towards the depleted body, the term suggested that what patients needed was not psychiatric or medical treatment, but simply rest, a good meal and a hot shower.

Did military psychiatrists' reluctant embrace of 'combat exhaustion' help to ease the difficulties that neuropsychiatric casualties faced upon their return to civilian society? This is a hard question to answer, but oral interviews with veterans suggest that the public interpreted it as primarily a mental and emotional condition, not a physical one, and that much of the stigma associated with 'psychoneurosis' carried over to the new term as well. What is clear is that the language of exhaustion and fatigue contributed to a broader understanding of war trauma that would be challenged down the road. It implied that neuropsychiatric casualties could be cured quickly and easily, primarily through rest, and that traumatic wartime experiences did not produce intractable mental disorders in previously healthy individuals. Some three decades later, the lack of terminology capable of explaining the delayed onset and chronic symptoms experienced by many Vietnam veterans would provoke another, even more protracted battle over what words to use when discussing the effects of war on men's minds.[10]

* * *

Historians agree that the Second World War constituted a watershed in the evolution of professional psychiatry in the United States.[11] The war served to accelerate and solidify developments that had been transforming the profession since before the First World War. Traditionally, psychiatrists had exercised their influence within the confines of public mental hospitals, where they treated the severely and chronically ill. Mental illness was conceived in largely somatic terms, as stemming from brain lesions and other physically identifiable sources. In the early twentieth century, the proliferation of smaller, more elite institutions and the gradual emergence of private practice singled a shift in the locus of psychiatric authority. The mental hygiene movement, founded in 1909 and oriented towards public education and the prevention of mental illness, also contributed to the extension of the psychiatric realm. It reflected the growing concern with less serious forms of mental disturbance – a trend bound up with the rise of psychodynamic paradigms, which emphasized the importance of life experiences, especially during childhood.[12]

The ascendancy of psychoanalysis was particularly significant, as it became the dominant psychiatric paradigm by the end of the Second World War. In the interwar period, American psychoanalysis transformed itself from an avant-garde cultural phenomenon, confined primarily to the East Coast, into a professionalized medical specialty. Two developments proved critical in promoting this transformation: the establishment of psychoanalytic institutes in the late 1920s and 1930s, and the American ban on lay analysis.[13] Beginning in the mid-1930s, this process of professionalization was both complicated and enhanced by an influx of refugee analysts fleeing Nazi persecution.[14] Although psychoanalysts remained a small and marginalized vanguard, they had firmly established the infrastructure that supported the profession's extraordinary post-war expansion by the time the United States entered the war.

This shift is readily apparent when comparing psychiatrists' activities in the First and Second World Wars. Psychiatric services in the First World War were comparatively limited. Screening occurred on a referral basis and focused on obvious neurological and physical defects. As a result, a mere 2 per cent of recruits were rejected on neuropsychiatric grounds. In contrast, all the Second World War recruits underwent in-person psychiatric screening at the local draft board and the Army induction centre. Examiners attempted to detect predisposition towards maladjustment, as well as identifying active neuroses and psychoses. But the shortage of medical examiners and the urgency of the moment meant that, in practice, these exams were cursory at best, often averaging just one or two minutes. Standards also varied widely, with African Americans and Native Americans subjected to disproportionately high rejection rates. Overall, 12 per cent of registrants, or over 1.8 million men, were rejected as 'unfit for military service' on neuropsychiatric grounds. In fact, NPs constituted the largest category – 38 per cent – of military rejections.[15]

The wartime mobilization accelerated developments in both psychiatry and psychoanalysis that ultimately drew the two professions into a closer relationship than they had previously shared. By late 1943, psychoanalysts had ascended to a number of key military posts, including the highest-ranking office in psychiatry – the directorship of the Neuropsychiatry Division of the Surgeon General's Office – which William Menninger (1899–1966) assumed in December 1943. The psychoanalysts who contributed to the war effort, however, represented a particular subset of the psychoanalytic movement. Almost all were American-born, and they tended to cultivate closer ties with psychiatrists receptive to psychoanalytic ideas than with émigré or refugee analysts. Indeed, while rhetorically promoting psychoanalysis, many also felt compelled to distance themselves from European-born analysts, whom they perceived as prone to infighting and overly invested in abstruse theoretical debates.[16] Portraying themselves as pragmatic and plainspoken, they claimed the mantle of 'psychodynamic psychiatrists', meaning that they adhered to a view of mental illness that stressed inner conflict, usually understood as the product of competing psychosexual drives, but one less doctrinaire and elaborately theorized than an orthodox Freudian approach.[17]

The diagnosis 'psychoneurosis' reveals military psychiatrists' indebtedness to Freud, who used the German term 'Neurosen' to describe psychological disorders that manifested unconscious conflicts. Even before the war, American interpretations of psychoanalysis typically downplayed Freud's emphasis on the central importance of repressed sexual desires, a tendency that became still more pronounced when numerous psychoanalysts and psychiatrists shifted their attention to military psychiatry. Menninger rather blandly defined psychoneuroses as 'a group of illnesses, subdivided into different types, all of which are characterized by a wide variety of physical and/or psychological symptoms in the absence of serious physical findings or organic changes'. Yet, his reliance on Freudian theory was evident not only in the words he used but also in his insistence that a 'major portion of our psyche is not accessible to our conscious make-up'.[18] The psychoneurotic soldier, he believed, fell victim to internal forces that lay beyond his conscious awareness, let alone control. Menninger's defence of the term 'psychoneurosis' was therefore bound up in his belief that the 'unconscious origin' of psychoneurotic disorders was 'a generally established scientific fact'.[19]

Despite these intellectual debts, Menninger and other leading military psychiatrists tended to distance themselves from psychoanalysis, fearing that it might cause War Department officials and those in the Surgeon General's Office to take their efforts less seriously. Most psychiatrists tried to present a united front in public, but skirmishes occurred behind the scenes. In late 1944, for example, the prominent Philadelphia psychiatrist Edward Strecker exerted his influence to stop distribution of a handbook intended for use in aviation medical training programmes. 'It is the prize damn foolishness of the season', Strecker wrote to Walter Jensen, a psychiatrist and air surgeon.[20] Jensen concurred, noting that John Murray, the director of psychiatry for the Army Air Force and a psychoanalyst who had trained in Vienna, was 'rather enthused about the psychoanalytical portion of it . . . in which naturally I did not agree'.[21] Air Surgeon Maj. Gen. David Grant spelled out his concerns about the same publication in greater detail. 'The paragraphs on "The Development of the Personality" present definite statements that oral and anal "zones of interest" are the main factors in the child's personality development', he complained. 'This is a theory, not a fact; and a theory that is questioned by many students of psychiatry as well as other physicians'. It was precisely 'such dogmatic expressions and highly questionable assumptions', Grant further cautioned, that had brought psychiatry 'into extreme discredit and suspicion among both scientific and lay persons'.[22]

Such disputes point to the central tenets that tended to distinguish the psychoanalytically trained from more mainstream psychiatrists. The former generally believed, as Leon Saul expressed it, that 'every war neurosis is a psychoneurosis, since the old unsolved conflicts of the past are stimulated by stress to assist in the production of a neurotic reaction'.[23] Whereas most military psychiatrists emphasized the *universal* and painfully *conscious* conflict between the impulse towards self-preservation and the desire to fulfil one's duties, psychoanalysts stressed the importance of *personally specific* and *unconscious* factors as well. As M. Ralph Kaufman, a psychoanalyst who served in the Pacific, argued in a co-authored paper, the 'faculty of the human mind which enables men to create phantasies in which the dangers and horrors of war are magnified endlessly' could be 'as significant as actual danger'.[24] Accordingly, psychoanalysts often favoured methods like narcosynthesis, in which sedated men were prompted to recall and articulate their traumatic experiences, over simple persuasion, sedation and rest.

In regard to diagnosis, psychiatrists who expressed deep scepticism of psychoanalysis tended to support calls for a revised diagnostic vocabulary and showed little hesitation about jettisoning the term 'psychoneurosis'. Psychiatrist Kenneth Appel, for example, argued in the summer of 1944 that there was 'tremendous need for more satisfactory psychiatric terminology'. He insisted that 'terminology should be simple and given in concepts and words with which physicians are already familiar'.[25] A *New York Times* editorial from August 1944 supported this view, claiming that it 'would be the easiest thing in the world for the Army doctors to invent a perfectly innocent and even pleasant' substitute for the unpopular term. 'A man discharged from military service on the ground, let us say, of "civilian orientation" would stand a much better chance of getting back his old job than if you call him a psychoneurotic'.[26] Most psychiatrists who had undergone psychoanalytic training, however, were very reluctant to abandon the term. Insisting that 'any stigma attached' to the term 'would carry over to any other word used in its place', William Menninger advocated for an approach based on public education rather than what he criticized as 'evasive terminology'.[27] In private correspondence, he voiced exasperation over the increasingly common charge that psychiatrists handicapped men by burdening them with stigmatizing diagnoses. 'We never know what these lay people expect us to do in the way of diagnosing', he sighed in May 1945. 'I suppose they want us to not call them [neuropsychiatric disorders] any name'.[28]

Yet, even Menninger conceded that public misconceptions surrounding psychoneurotic servicemen were rife. By 1944, the number of men rejected or discharged as 'psychoneurotic' had grown so large, he subsequently reflected, 'that "psychoneurosis" became a household word'.[29] This popular diffusion of psychiatric language seemed only to heighten the suspicion and prejudice that the men so labelled faced. The slang term 'psycho', for instance, coined in 1942 to refer to neuropsychiatric rejections or casualties, collapsed the categories of psychotic and neurotic into a single ominous entity. Dictionary definitions capture the confusion that prevailed: the *Cambridge Dictionary*, for instance, defines a 'psycho' not as a 'neurotic', but, rather, as a 'psychopath' or 'someone who is crazy and frightening'.[30] The rapid appropriation of this neologism by soldiers and civilians alike suggests that psychiatrists' frequently reiterated message – that psychoneuroses were relatively minor illnesses that affected normal people – was meeting with mixed reception at best.

Even as Army psychiatrists faced criticism from those who believed 'psychoneurosis' unfairly stigmatized men, they also had to contend with military men and their allies, who often argued the opposite – that the term was not stigmatizing enough. According to these critics, psychiatrists simply provided cover for men who lacked the will to tough it out. As an article in the *Christian Century* put it, '[A]n undisciplined boy with a spoiled-child complex, an aversion to Army life, a dislike for doing what he is told or a fear of personal injury, gets no help from having his tantrums or fears dignified into psychoneuroses and phobias and learning to talk about himself in psychiatric terms'.[31] Line officers in particular worried that recognition and diagnosis of psychiatric disorders had a demoralizing effect. All men who faced conditions ranging from unpleasant to gruelling longed for escape, they argued, and medical officers willing to provide a way out represented a serious threat to the conservation of manpower. Yet, many of these same officers hoped to shield soldiers who broke down after performing well in combat for a prolonged period from the stigma of psychiatric diagnosis.

Military psychiatrists countered challenges to their authority in two ways. First, they campaigned to impress upon the public that men discharged as 'psychoneurotic' suffered from real but relatively minor and very common disorders that often went undiagnosed in civilian life; such men were not insane, they argued, and most would be able to resume normal civilian lives with little difficulty. But with grave doubts about military psychiatry being voiced in the highest echelons of the US Army, they also agreed to compromise when it came to labelling the problems they identified. As early as the spring of 1943, General Omar Bradley ordered medical officers under his command to record only 'exhaustion' on the emergency medical tags of all suspected psychiatric cases; after seven days, if a man so tagged had not recovered, he would be evacuated further behind the lines and receive a proper diagnosis.[32] When the Surgeon General directed medical officers throughout the Army to adopt this approach in October 1943, he claimed that the diagnosis 'psychoneurosis' had proven problematic, because it suggested 'incurability' and 'war causation' and thereby 'interfered with recovery'.[33] In other words, he argued that diagnosis itself could affect patients' health: 'exhaustion' was designed not only to identify a condition but also to have a therapeutic effect.[34]

Meanwhile, the Surgeon General's Office tried to dispel confusion by clarifying the meaning of the term 'psychoneurosis'. In February 1944, the Office prepared a fact sheet on 'The Mental Health of U.S. Soldiers' designed to be released to women's organizations. 'Psychoneurotics comprise all but a few of this war's "battle fatigue" cases', the bulletin explained, 'and include men with no previous history of mental or nervous disorders'. Under the section heading, 'Kinds of Psychoneuroses', the terms 'Exhaustion and War Fatigue' were defined as interchangeable with 'nervous and mental disorders'. Interestingly, the category 'Traumatic War Neuroses' was said to apply only to '"normal men" . . . who crack under a strain or psychic shock (produced by combat conditions of extreme intensity)'. Thus, whereas the bulletin recognized the existence of a unique class of mental disorders specific to extreme combat situations, it continued to subsume such disorders under the general category 'psychoneurotic'.[35] But the impulse to separate out this group of victims from other, less credible and insufficiently masculine individuals is already apparent in the reference to 'normal men'. The problematic implication was that a predisposed individual, or one already known to suffer from neurotic conflict, could never be diagnosed with 'traumatic war neurosis', no matter the severity of what he endured.

The blackout on information regarding US psychiatric casualties ultimately prevented the release of this fact sheet, but the popular press began disseminating a similar message when censorship restrictions eased two months later.[36] In April 1944, an article in *Woman's Home Companion* noted that the term 'exhaustion' was used at the front 'for the sake of the man himself, of his people back home, and of the public', but stressed that 'psychoneurosis' was, in fact, the more accurate term, 'since peace or war, that's what it is'.[37] The following month, Surgeon General Maj. Gen. Norman T. Kirk issued a press release that stated,

All of us today have the opportunity – I would call it an obligation on the part of news writers – to explain the problem of psycho-neurosis to the American people. Through misunderstanding and lack of thinking, the term has come to mean to too many people a state of definite mental unbalance – that a person is crazy, as some like to put it.

In fact, the press release continued, every individual had a 'mental breaking point, just as he reaches a point where physical weariness overcomes him and he must sleep'. The soldier forced to continue beyond his breaking point became a 'psychoneurotic' casualty, but 'that does not mean that he is a permanent psychotic individual, a loss to the Army and a ward of government'.[38] In the wake of Kirk's call for a public relations intervention led by journalists, numerous articles appeared in the press reiterating the notion that everyone had a 'breaking point' and that psychoneurosis was a relatively benign and eminently curable disorder.[39]

These extensive efforts, however, did not succeed in reconciling the public to the term 'psychoneurosis' or allaying fears that soldiers diagnosed as such were being stigmatized. So in early 1945, leading civilian and military psychiatrists agreed to pursue another approach. In consultation with the Surgeon General's Office, they decided that the prefix 'psychoneurotic' should be excluded from military medical records. Instead, recorded diagnoses would describe specific types of reactions, such as 'anxiety reaction', 'phobic reaction', and 'psychogenic gastrointestinal reaction'. In addition, psychiatric diagnoses henceforth would require the evaluation of four factors: the type and severity of symptoms, the amount of precipitating stress, the degree of predisposition and the extent of incapacity. These guidelines provided the basic format for the Army nomenclature that was officially approved in October 1945.[40]

The revised nomenclature placed 'combat exhaustion' under the special category of 'transient personality reactions to acute or special stress'. Characterized as a reaction that could either prove fleeting and 'clear rapidly', or 'progress into one of the established neurotic reactions', the term was to be used only as a 'temporary diagnosis' for 'normal' persons exposed to severe physical or emotional stress. While acknowledging that 'the evaluation of unconscious internal conflicts' was necessary for the clinical evaluation and treatment of combat exhaustion, such considerations were not to play a role in diagnostic determinations. Instead, men would be temporarily diagnosed as suffering from combat exhaustion on the basis of external factors alone, with severe stress defined as that which would cause 'the average man' to 'develop disabling psychiatric symptoms when exposed to it'.[41] Thus, the psychoanalytic premise that all 'war neuroses' were, in fact, neuroses – understood primarily as expressions of intrapsychic conflict – was rejected so far as combat cases were concerned. Instead, a bifurcated understanding of wartime neuropsychiatric problems emerged that separated out 'normal' men who managed to fulfil their military duties for a respectable period from those who, due to 'immaturity' or a host of other psychoneurotic reactions, entirely failed to adjust to military life.

Despite the frequently reiterated caveat that 'every man has a breaking point', the terms 'combat exhaustion' and 'combat fatigue' attempted to reinscribe a sharp distinction between the 'normal' man and the predisposed, 'psychoneurotic' individual. Furthermore, the former was pronounced as eminently curable – and, as 'exhaustion' suggests – curable primarily through rest. An extreme expression of this view appears in the minutes of a January 1945 joint meeting of the Illinois Psychiatric Society and the Chicago Neurological Society. Outlining the criteria for diagnosing 'combat fatigue', one participant included 'recoverability' along with the standard emphasis on combat experience and lack of predisposition.[42] In doing so, he not only presumed that one could predict a patient's outcome at the time of diagnosis but also suggested that only those men who could regain their mental equilibrium deserved to be classified as victims of 'combat fatigue', regardless of the severity of trauma endured. This insistence on tightly linking the diagnosis 'combat fatigue' or 'combat exhaustion' to a positive prognosis points to a more widely shared tendency to deny the enduring effects of war. If psychiatrists and popular writers acknowledged that even the strongest man might break down, they also implied that war never led to chronic neuropsychiatric problems, except among those already predisposed.

Psychoanalysts and their allies conceded that terms like 'combat exhaustion' had 'considerable practical value in the military setting', as Kubie put it, but they worried about the 'danger of accepting this scientifically meaningless term as a conceptual basis for scientific investigation of the problem'.[43] They also insisted that 'true' exhaustion cases constituted a small percentage of neuropsychiatric discharges: 'the great majority' of those so diagnosed, according to Menninger, 'were primarily due to personality disturbances and were so treated'.[44] Moreover, even before the change to the nomenclature was approved, some critics echoed Menninger in predicting that the stigma associated with 'psychoneurosis' would be linked to 'combat exhaustion' as well. 'Many people use the term indiscriminately and confusion has arisen', two military psychiatrists complained, noting that people 'include in this group those cases which develop during the first few days of combat, and even others that have never experienced actual combat'. As a result, the 'usefulness of this terminology for distinguishing the more stable and willing from the unstable and unwilling personalities is thereby lost'.[45] In other words, men who had 'broken down under conditions of continuous long and severe stress' were still being lumped with psychoneurotics, but now under the rubric of 'combat exhaustion', which people began using to refer to all soldiers discharged on psychiatric grounds, regardless of combat experience, thereby rendering the term nonsensical.[46]

If the adoption of the terms 'combat exhaustion' or simply 'exhaustion' represented a compromise between psychoanalytic psychiatrists on the one hand, and the military and the public on the other, it was a compromise that satisfied no one. The attempt to shield combat veterans from a label that many found humiliating usurped psychiatrists' authority, forcing them to bend to the will of those outside the profession on the central issue of diagnostic terminology. But 'combat exhaustion' does not appear to have accomplished the task that it was set: separating out the real men from their failed counterparts. It was quickly understood to be a psychiatric diagnosis, one that many people used interchangeably with 'psychoneurosis'. This was true even in the case of a former medical officer, John Stamos, who treated neuropsychiatric casualties. 'They called it combat exhaustion', he told an interviewer a half-century after the war's end. 'I don't know what they call it today. But it could affect people who aren't even in combat'.[47] Stamos's recollections seem to confirm contemporary reports about conflicting uses of the term. If a man could be said to suffer from 'combat exhaustion' without ever coming under fire, the diagnosis evidently confused rather than clarified matters.

Veteran Francis Johnston, who served as a turret gunner during the war, resented this tendency to conflate the language of neurosis with that of exhaustion or fatigue. Unlike the rest of the Army, the Army Air Forces had used the diagnosis of 'operational fatigue' from the war's outset.[48] Yet, when Johnston returned home, he still felt that people regarded him as 'psycho-neurotic', or even worse, 'a psycho'. As he explained,

> At that time they were calling it 'psycho-neurosis' and, you know, they [said]: 'Oh, John got back to the States, and he's a psycho case', you know. Well, you don't know the circumstances until you go through it yourself. And he wasn't a psycho case; he was combat fatigued. So I never even went to look for jobs other than factory jobs because there they didn't ask any of that; they are just looking for bodies to work.

Saddled with what he believed to be a stigmatizing diagnosis, Johnston felt constrained in his employment options, even as the Veterans Administration (VA) almost immediately reduced his disability benefits. For decades thereafter, he continued to struggle, living 'like a hermit', and subjecting his wife to 'a lot of antics'.[49]

Then, sometime in the 1980s, a VA doctor 'brought this combat fatigue thing out of me', as Johnston put it. For the first time, he spoke to people about a traumatic memory of his guns failing as he tried to fire on a Japanese plane. 'I'm able to talk about it now like I'm telling you', he related to the interviewer in 1997. 'I could never do that before. But you could probably tell in my voice, it's changed right now, because this is what's happening. I take pills to calm me down. It's hard to get the air out'. At this point in their discussion, the interviewer abruptly shifted gears and asked a series of unrelated questions, perhaps wanting to spare Johnston further distress. But Johnston himself returned to the subject of his anxiety at the close of the interview, remarking that he would now need 'to sit down a while now and calm down'. The interviewer began to apologize, but Johnston waved him off. 'That's all right. That's part of my life', he stated. 'I've lived with that'.[50]

To this day, 'that' remains a problematic thing to name. Johnston's medical chart at the VA almost certainly indicated that he suffered not from 'combat exhaustion', 'combat fatigue' or 'operational fatigue', but from 'post-traumatic stress disorder' (PTSD), a diagnosis officially recognized only in 1980, when the American Psychiatric Association published *DSM-III*. This development, brought about in large part by pressure from veterans' groups, was bound up with broader changes that reshaped American society in the 1970s and 1980s. As psychological thinking went mainstream and feminism prompted a reassessment of gender norms, ideas about manhood evolved, granting men greater latitude to express a wider range of feelings, including those of vulnerability. For Johnston, these large-scale cultural and political changes translated into personal relief. Although he had been suffering from anxiety for years, he received treatment only after he encountered a doctor equipped with a term that allowed him or her to recognize, name and treat the thing that ailed him.

Conclusion

The battles over psychiatric terminology during the Second World War proved so protracted because of the multiple parties and the high stakes involved. The War Department needed to ensure that it received and retained men who could withstand military life, which meant having medical officers who would not allow soldiers to escape service through medical channels. Psychiatrists operating out of the Surgeon General's Office in Washington, D.C., had other preoccupations: they wanted to defend the legitimacy of the entire psychiatric enterprise – to convince the military, the federal government and society more broadly that their profession's expertise was necessary and valuable. This meant demonstrating the efficacy of treatment measures, defending how they conceptualized and categorized mental illness and countering public resistance by working to de-stigmatize mental illness. Because psychiatrists differed among themselves – with some perceiving war trauma largely as physical collapse due to exhaustion and extraordinary external stress, and others viewing it in more psychoanalytic terms – these were difficult ends to achieve. Finally, for men and their families, the overriding concern was recovery and reintegration, which meant mitigating the emasculating effects of psychiatric labelling, especially in regard to employment prospects.

With all these competing agendas, conflict over psychiatric terminology was inevitable. What should ultimately be privileged when determining how to refer to soldiers' psychological and emotional problems? Should it be concerns about the scientific integrity and consistency of psychiatric diagnoses? Should it be concerns about maintaining manpower at the front? Or should it be concerns about the potential difficulties that neuropsychiatric casualties might face upon their return? Line officers, psychiatrists, family members, and soldiers and veterans all acted according to their own particular interests, but no single group exerted sufficient power over the language of war trauma to control the outcome.

Over the next twenty-five years, psychiatrists would face less pushback than they experienced during the Second World War. With the 1952 publication of the first *DSM*, they replaced 'combat exhaustion' with another short-term diagnosis, 'gross stress reaction', which could be applied not only to soldiers but also to civilians who experienced traumatic events like natural disasters. In 1968, this substitute term was dropped from the revised *DSM-II*. The result was a vacuum that paved the way for a grassroots movement, led by Vietnam veterans and their advocates, which lobbied the American Psychiatric Association to introduce a new diagnosis, one that would acknowledge their suffering and allow them to seek treatment and recompense. The story of how PTSD became an official psychiatric diagnosis has been well told.[51] But as this chapter has shown, long before the 1970s, psychiatrists faced challenges from critics outside the profession who questioned their nomenclature and successfully advocated for change. The generation that helped to defeat the Nazis may have been more deferential to medical and psychiatric authority than those who came of age in the 1960s and 1970s, but when it came to diagnosing the nation's soldiers, they were not prepared to leave matters entirely to the experts.

Acknowledgements

The author thanks David Dawson, Rachel Klein, Jordan Mylet, and, especially, Frances M. Clarke and the editors of this volume for their helpful comments and suggestions on earlier versions of this article.

Notes

1 Henry C. Link, 'The Errors of Psychiatry', *American Mercury*, July 1944, 72–8.

2 Editors' note introducing Karl M. Bowman, 'Psychiatry at War: An Answer to "The Errors of Psychiatry"', *American Mercury*, September 1944, 336. Although Link's attack on psychiatry was clearly hyperbolic, it would be wrong to dismiss out of hand his claim that psychiatric labelling harmed men rejected for military service. In January 1943, the director of a clinic in Reading, Pennsylvania, communicated to the psychiatrist David M. Levy that they were now flooded with a new group of clients – 'people who have been drafted, diagnosed as psychiatric cases, and sent home'. The Army, he complained, 'has been telling these people what the psychiatric diagnosis was, for example, psychoneurosis, and for some reason or other this has been upsetting to the patients. Many of them went along for many years without being especially disturbed and became upset after they had heard their diagnosis discussed and after they were sent home unfit'. Paul Holmer to David Levy, 12 January 1943, folder 9 (Selective Service), box 18, David Levy Papers, Oskar Diethelm Library, Weill Medical College of Cornell University, New York, NY (hereafter, Levy Papers). David Levy communicated Holmer's concerns to Washington, and two months later the War Department issued a statement directing medical officers to 'use painstaking tact' when informing a man why it had been determined 'that he would be unable to adapt himself to the rigors of Army life'. The memo even suggested that 'any other suitable reason may be given'. Maj. Gen. J. A. Ulio, 5 March 1943, 'Rejection or discharged for Psychiatric Reasons', Memorandum No. W600-22-43, Adjutant General's Office, War Department, folder 9, box 18, Levy Papers.

3 Bowman, 'Psychiatry at War', 343. It is unclear whom Bowman is quoting here.

4 Beginning in April 1944, medical examiners were told that rejections on neuropsychiatric grounds should only be made in 'cases in which the history and examination clearly indicate the existence in the past and/or present of a personality disorder of partially or completely incapacitating degree'. For further discussion of this directive, Technical Medical Bulletin 33 (TB MED 33), see U.S. Army Medical Department, *Neuropsychiatry in World War II, vol. 1: Zone of Interior* (Washington, DC: Office of the Surgeon General, Department of the Army, 1966), 170. See also Naoke Wake's study of the architect of the wartime psychiatric screening programme, *Private Practices: Harry Stack Sullivan, Homosexuality, and American Liberalism* (Rutgers, NJ: Rutgers University Press, 2011); and Rebecca Schwartz Greene, 'The Role of the Psychiatrist in World War II' (PhD diss., Columbia University, 1977).

5 Scholars have not previously focused on the intense battle over psychiatric terminology during the Second World War, or the resonance and implications of the different terms used. See, for example, Allan V. Horwitz, *PTSD: A Short History* (Baltimore, MD: Johns Hopkins University Press, 2018), Kindle location 1320, which asserts that during the war, 'very general terms such as "combat neurosis", "combat exhaustion", and "war neurosis" replaced what

had previously been called "shell-shock". Just as the label "PTSD" would later do, each of these terms made an intrinsic connection between an external stressor and a resultant psychic disturbance'. But, in fact, the most common diagnosis for much of the war was 'psychoneurosis', which did not draw such a connection.

6   See chapter on 'Diagnostic Labels', in William C. Menninger, *Psychiatry in a Troubled World: Yesterday's War and Today's Challenge* (New York: MacMillan, 1948), 256–65.

7   Alan Derickson, '"No Such thing as a Night's Sleep": The Embattled Sleep of American Fighting Men from World War II to the Present', *Journal of Social History* 47, no. 1 (2013): 1–26 (quotations, 2–3). On the endurance model of manhood, see also Rebecca Jo Plant, 'Preventing the Inevitable: John W. Appel and the Problem of Psychiatric Casualties in the U.S. Army during World War II', in *Science and Emotions after 1945: A Transatlantic Perspective*, ed. Frank Biess and Daniel M. Gross (Chicago: University of Chicago Press, 2014), 209–38.

8   Nathan G. Hale, Jr, *The Rise and Crisis of Psychoanalysis in the United States: Freud and the Americans, 1917-1985* (Oxford: Oxford University Press, 1995), 211–14.

9   M. Ralph Kaufman and Lindsay H. Beaton, 'A Psychiatric Treatment Program in Combat', undated, folder 'Combat Neuroses', box 75, Lawrence Kubie Papers, Library of Congress, Washington, DC.

10 On the history of post-traumatic stress disorder (PTSD), see Wilbur Scott, 'PTSD in DSM-III: A Case in the Politics of Diagnosis and Disease', *Social Problems* 37, no. 3 (1990): 294–310; and Allan Young, *The Harmony of Illusions: Inventing Post-Traumatic Stress Disorder* (Princeton, NJ: Princeton University Press, 1995).

11 Important sources on US psychiatry during the Second World War include Ben Shephard, *A War of Nerves: Soldiers and Psychiatrists in the Twentieth Century* (Cambridge, MA: Harvard University Press, 2001), chs. 14–22; Greene, 'The Role of the Psychiatrist in World War II'; Gerald Grob, *From Asylum to Community: Mental Health Policy in Modern America* (Princeton, NJ: Princeton University Press, 1991), ch. 1; Ellen Herman, *The Romance of American Psychology: Political Culture in the Age of the Experts* (Berkeley: University of California Press, 1995), ch. 4; Hale, Jr, *The Rise and Crisis of Psychoanalysis in the United States*, ch. 11; Eva S. Moskowitz, *In Therapy We Trust: America's Obsession with Self-Fulfillment* (Baltimore, MD: Johns Hopkins University Press, 2001), ch. 4; Hans Pols, 'The Tunisian Campaign, War Neuroses, and the Reorientation of American Psychiatry during World War II', *Harvard Review of Psychiatry* 19, no. 6 (2011): 313–20; Josephine Callisen Bresnahan, 'Danger in Paradise: The Battle against Combat Fatigue in the Pacific War' (PhD diss., Harvard University, 1999); Ellen Dwyer, 'Psychiatry and Race During World War II', *Journal of the History of Medicine and Allied Sciences* 61, no. 2 (2005): 117–43; Ruth Leys, *Trauma: A Genealogy* (Chicago: University of Chicago Press, 2000), ch. 6; Christina S. Jarvis, '"If He Comes Home Nervous": U.S. World War II Neuropsychiatric Casualties and Postwar Masculinities', *Journal of Men's Studies* 17, no. 2 (2010): 97–115; and Alan Bérubé, *Coming Out*

Under Fire: The History of Gay Men and Women in World War II (New York: The Free Press, 1990), ch. 6.

12 For a general survey of these developments, see Gerald Grob, *Mental Illness and American Society, 1875-1940* (Princeton, NJ: Princeton University Press, 1983).

13 Hale, *The Rise and Crisis of Psychoanalysis in the United States*. See also Russell Jacoby, *The Repression of Psychoanalysis: Otto Fenichel and the Political Freudians* (Chicago: University of Chicago Press, 1983); Lawrence R. Samuel, *Shrink: A Cultural History of Psychoanalysis in America* (Lincoln: University of Nebraska Press, 2013); and Eli Zaretsky, *Secrets of the Soul: A Social and Cultural History of Psychoanalysis* (New York: Knopf, 2004).

14 For scholarship on the influence of refugee analysts, see Lewis Coser, *Refugee Scholars in America: Their Impact and Their Experiences* (New Haven, CT: Yale University Press, 1984), 42–82; Marie Jahoda, 'The Migration of Psychoanalysis: Its Impact on American Psychology', in *The Intellectual Migration: Europe and America, 1930-1960*, ed. Donald Fleming and Bernard Bailyn (Cambridge, MA: Harvard University Press, 1969), 420–62; Laura Fermi, *Illustrious Immigrants: The Intellectual Migration from Europe, 1930-1941* (Chicago: University of Chicago Press, 1968), 139–73; H. Stuart Hughes, *The Sea Change: The Migration of Social Thought, 1930-1965* (New York: Harper and Row, 1975), 189–239; and Martin Jay, *The Dialectical Imagination: A History of the Frankfurt School and the Institute for Social Research, 1923-1950* (Berkeley: University of California Press, 1973), 86–112.

15 Menninger, *Psychiatry in a Troubled World*, 341–2. The screening programmes in both world wars are discussed in Greene, 'The Role of the Psychiatrist in World War II'. For a more detailed discussion of statistics regarding neuropsychiatric rejections and casualties, see Herman, *The Romance of American Psychology*, 88–99.

16 For further discussion of the conflict between American and European-born psychoanalysts, see Rebecca Jo Plant, 'William Menninger and American Psychoanalysis, 1946-1984', *History of Psychiatry* 16, no. 2 (2005): 181–202.

17 Some psychoanalytically trained psychiatrists went so far as to deny a commitment to any particular theoretical framework, though such a perspective clearly informed their work. See, for example, Roy R. Grinker and John P. Spiegel, *War Neuroses in North Africa: The Tunisian Campaign, January-May 1943* (New York: Josiah Macy, Jr., Foundation, 1943). The authors use Freudian concepts like the ego and superego throughout, yet also claim, 'Our explanations, we feel, are based on observed phenomena; we have abstained from preconceived theories as much as possible' (298).

18 William C. Menninger, 'Psychoneurosis—A Summary for the Nurse', *American Journal of Nursing* 45, no. 5 (1945): 348–50.

19 U.S. Army Medical Department, *Neuropsychiatry in World War II, vol. 2: Overseas Theaters* (Washington, DC: Office of the Surgeon General, Department of the Army, 1973), 135.

20 Edward Strecker to Walter Jensen, 8 November 1944, folder 'Special Consultant, Secretary of War', box 'Misc.', Edward Strecker Papers, Institute of Pennsylvania Hospital, Philadelphia, PA (hereafter, Strecker Papers).

21 Jensen to Strecker, n.d., outside of folders, box 'Misc.', Strecker Papers.
22 David N. W. Grant to Eugene Reinart, 2 September 1944, folder 'Special Consultant, Secretary of War', box 'Misc.', Strecker Papers.
23 Leon J. Saul, 'Book review of Roy R. Grinker and John P. Spiegel's *Men Under Stress* (Philadelphia: Blakison, 1945)', *Psychosomatic Medicine* 8, no. 1 (1946): 69–71 (quotation, 69).
24 M. Ralph Kaufman and Lindsay H. Beaton, 'A Psychiatric Treatment Program in Combat', undated, folder 'Combat Neuroses', box 75, Kubie Papers.
25 Kenneth E. Appel, 'Report on Observations and Impressions on Visit as Psychiatric Consultant to Eighth Service Command Hospitals, June 20 to 27, 1944', folder 1348, box 110, Series 200, RG 1.1, Rockefeller Foundation Records, Projects, Rockefeller Archive Center, Tarrytown, NY.
26 'Topics of *The Times*', *New York Times*, 30 August 1944, 16.
27 Menninger, *Psychiatry in a Troubled World*, 260.
28 William C. Menninger to Edward Strecker, 24 May 1945, folder 'Special Consultant, Secretary of War', box 'Misc.', Strecker Papers.
29 Menninger, *Psychiatry in a Troubled World*, 259–60.
30 https://dictionary.cambridge.org/us/dictionary/english/psycho.
31 Quoted in 'Tantrum or Neurosis', *Time Magazine*, 7 August 1944, 30.
32 U.S. Army Medical Department, *Neuropsychiatry in World War II, vol. 2*, 9–12. This particular use of 'exhaustion' lacked a clear medical genealogy. The term 'neurasthenia', coined by neurologist George Beard in 1881, helped to popularize the concept of 'nervous exhaustion', but the diagnosis was widely discredited in the United States after the First World War, and according to Google Ngram, its use declined sharply thereafter. However, while there appears to be little direct connection between neurasthenia and combat exhaustion, the relationship between the two calls for more investigation. On the history of neurasthenia, see Marijke Gijswijt-Hofstra and Roy Porter, eds, *Cultures of Neurasthenia from Beard to the First World War* (Amsterdam: Editions Rodopi B.V., 2001); and David G. Schuster, *Neurasthenic Nation: America's Search for Health, Happiness, and Comfort, 1869-1920* (New Brunswick, NJ: Rutgers University Press, 2011).
33 *Neuropsychiatry in World War II, vol. 1*, 230.
34 Other sources also acknowledged that the terms like 'combat exhaustion' and 'combat fatigue' were expected to have therapeutic effects. For instance, a study of military psychiatry in the European Theater claimed that 'the term was coined and applied primarily for psychological reasons in an attempt to fix in the soldier's mind the idea that he could be cured simply by rest'. 'Combat Fatigue', Report of the General Board (Medical), United States Forces, European Theater, Study No. 91, 1945, Military History Institute, Carlisle, Pennsylvania. https://usacac.army.mil/sites/default/files/documents/carl/eto/eto-091.pdf.
35 War Department, Bureau of Public Relations, 'The Mental Health of U.S. Soldiers', 1944, Menninger Foundation Archives, Kansas Historical Society, Topeka.

36 Menninger discusses the fate of the fact sheet, as well as the changes in censorship policies, in U.S. Army Medical Department, *Neuropsychiatry in World War II*, vol. 1, 29–151.

37 Malcolm J. Farrell and Marie Beynon Ray, 'Will the Battle-Shocked Come Home Cured?' *Woman's Home Companion*, April 1944, 48–50.

38 Quoted in Bowman, 'Psychiatry at War', 340. Even this guidance, aimed at dispelling widespread misunderstanding, could be read as contributing to the confusion, since it seemed to suggest that a soldier suffering from psychoneurosis might be considered as temporarily psychotic.

39 See, for example, the account of a 'returned flier' in 'Give Us a Break!' *Woman's Home Companion*, October 1944, 27, 80–1. 'He fought for us till he could fight no more', the article explained. 'The army word for it was psychoneurosis'.

40 Menninger, *Psychiatry in a Troubled World*, 263–4.

41 The final nomenclature is reprinted in Menninger, *Psychiatry in a Troubled World*, Appendix B.

42 David Slight, 'Society Transactions: Illinois Psychiatric Society and the Chicago Neurological Society', *Archives of Neurology and Psychiatry* 55, no. 2 (1946): 151–2 (quotation, 151).

43 Byron Stookey, 'Society Transactions: New York Neurological Society and New York Academy of Medicine, Section of Neurology and Psychiatry', *Archives of Neurology and Psychiatry* 55, no. 2 (1946): 157–61 (quotation, 157).

44 Menninger, *Psychiatry in a Troubled World*, 141.

45 Roy L. Swank and Walter E. Marchand, 'Combat Neuroses: The Development of Combat Exhaustion', undated, box 1332, RG 112, Office of the Surgeon General/Army, National Archives and Records Administration II, College Park, Maryland. This report was later published as Swank and Marchand, 'Combat Neuroses: Development of Combat Exhaustion', *Archives of Neurology and Psychiatry* 55, no. 3 (1946): 236–47.

46 Even the Army's own magazine contributed to the muddle by equating psychoneurosis and combat exhaustion, as when it stated, 'A psychoneurotic GI (you may call him combat fatigued – it's the same thing) coming back from overseas isn't in a happy frame of mind'. Sgt. A. J. Auerbach, 'It's All in Your Mind', *Yank*, 14 December 1945, 31.

47 John A. Lupton, transcript of oral history interview with John J. Stamos, Illinois Supreme Historic Preservation Commission, 2010. https://illinoiscourthistory.files.wordpress.com/2014/11/justice-stamos-bio-abstract-and-complete-edited-transcript-final.pdf.

48 A restricted report by Maj. Donald W. Hastings, Capt. David G. Wright and Capt. Bernard C. Glueck, Army Air Forces, *Psychiatric Experiences of the Eighth Air Force: First Year of Combat, July 4, 1942-July 4, 1943* (New York: Josiah Macy, Jr., Foundation, August 1944), defined operational fatigue as 'a typical syndrome of breakdown occurring in essentially stable individuals, who by continued stress, harrowing experiences and physical fatigue develop an illness which is roughly half fatigue and half emotional illness' (34).

49 Transcript of oral history interview with John J. Stamos.
50 Mark Van Ells, transcript of oral history interview with Francis R. Johnston, Turret Gunner, Army Air Corps, World War II, 1997, Wisconsin Veteran Museum Center. https://www.wisvetsmuseum.com/wp-content/uploads/2017/03/Johnston-Francis-_OH621.pdf
51 Scott, 'PTSD in DSM-III'; Young, *The Harmony of Illusions*; and Horwitz, *PTSD*.

Works cited

Auerbach, Sgt. A. J. 'It's All in Your Mind'. *Yank*, 14 December 1945, 31.
Bérubé, Alan. *Coming Out Under Fire: The History of Gay Men and Women in World War II*. New York: The Free Press, 1990.
Bowman, Karl M. 'Psychiatry at War: An Answer to "The Errors of Psychiatry"'. *American Mercury*, September 1944, 336–43.
Bresnahan, Josephine Callisen. 'Danger in Paradise: The Battle against Combat Fatigue in the Pacific War'. PhD diss., Harvard University, 1999.
Coser, Lewis. *Refugee Scholars in America: Their Impact and Their Experiences*. New Haven, CT: Yale University Press, 1984.
Derickson, Alan. '"No Such thing as a Night's Sleep": The Embattled Sleep of American Fighting Men from World War II to the Present'. *Journal of Social History* 47, no. 1 (2013): 1–26.
Dwyer, Ellen. 'Psychiatry and Race During World War II'. *Journal of the History of Medicine and Allied Sciences* 61, no. 2 (2005): 117–43.
Ells, Mark Van. Transcript of oral history interview with Francis R. Johnston. Wisconsin Veteran Center, 1997.
Farrell, Malcolm J. and Marie Beynon Ray. 'Will the Battle-Shocked Come Home Cured?' *Woman's Home Companion*, April 1944, 48–50.
Fermi, Laura. *Illustrious Immigrants: The Intellectual Migration from Europe, 1930–1941*. Chicago: University of Chicago Press, 1968.
General Board (Medical), United States Forces, European Theater. 'Combat Fatigue', Study No. 91, 1945.
Gijswijt-Hofstra, Marijke and Roy Porter, eds. *Cultures of Neurasthenia from Beard to the First World War*. Amsterdam: Editions Rodopi B.V., 2001.
'Give Us a Break!' *Woman's Home Companion*, October 1944, 80–1.
Greene, Rebecca Schwartz. 'The Role of the Psychiatrist in World War II'. PhD diss., Columbia University, 1977.
Grinker, Roy R. and John P. Spiegel. *War Neuroses in North Africa: The Tunisian Campaign, January–May 1943*. New York: Josiah Macy, Jr., Foundation, 1943.
Grob, Gerald. *From Asylum to Community: Mental Health Policy in Modern America*. Princeton, NJ: Princeton University Press, 1991.
Grob, Gerald. *Mental Illness and American Society, 1875–1940*. Princeton, NJ: Princeton University Press, 1983.
Hale, Jr, Nathan G. *The Rise and Crisis of Psychoanalysis in the United States: Freud and the Americans, 1917–1985*. Oxford: Oxford University Press, 1995.
Hastings, Maj. Donald W., Capt. David G. Wright and Capt. Bernard C. Glueck. *Psychiatric Experiences of the Eighth Air Force: First Year of Combat, July 4, 1942–July 4, 1943*. New York: Josiah Macy, Jr., Foundation, 1944.

Herman, Ellen. *The Romance of American Psychology: Political Culture in the Age of the Experts*. Berkeley: University of California Press, 1995.

Horwitz, Allan V. *PTSD: A Short History*. Baltimore, MD: Johns Hopkins University Press, 2018.

Hughes, H. Stuart. *The Sea Change: The Migration of Social Thought, 1930–1965*. New York: Harper and Row, 1975.

Jacoby, Russell. *The Repression of Psychoanalysis: Otto Fenichel and the Political Freudians*. Chicago: University of Chicago Press, 1983.

Jahoda, Marie. 'The Migration of Psychoanalysis: Its Impact on American Psychology', in *The Intellectual Migration: Europe and America, 1930–1960*, edited by Donald Fleming and Bernard Bailyn, 420–62. Cambridge, MA: Harvard University Press, 1969.

Jarvis, Christina S. '"If He Comes Home Nervous": U.S. World War II Neuropsychiatric Casualties and Postwar Masculinities'. *Journal of Men's Studies* 17, no. 2 (2010): 97–115.

Jay, Martin. *The Dialectical Imagination: A History of the Frankfurt School and the Institute for Social Research, 1923–1950*. Berkeley: University of California Press, 1973.

Kubie, Lawrence. Papers. Library of Congress, Washington, DC.

Levy, David. Papers. Oskar Diethelm Library, Weill Medical College of Cornell University, New York, NY.

Leys, Ruth. *Trauma: A Genealogy*. Chicago: University of Chicago Press, 2000.

Link, Henry C. 'The Errors of Psychiatry'. *American Mercury*, July 1944, 72–8.

Lupton, John A. Transcript of oral history interview with John J. Stamos, Illinois Supreme Historic Preservation Commission, 2010.

Menninger Foundation Archives. Kansas Historical Society, Topeka.

Menninger, William C. *Psychiatry in a Troubled World: Yesterday's War and Today's Challenge*. New York: MacMillan, 1948.

Menninger, William C. 'Psychoneurosis—A Summary for the Nurse'. *American Journal of Nursing* 45, no. 5 (1945): 348–50.

Moskowitz, Eva S. *In Therapy We Trust: America's Obsession with Self-Fulfillment*. Baltimore, MD: Johns Hopkins University Press, 2001.

Plant, Rebecca Jo. 'Preventing the Inevitable: John W. Appel and the Problem of Psychiatric Casualties in the U.S. Army during World War II', in *Science and Emotions after 1945: A Transatlantic Perspective*, edited by Frank Biess and David M. Gross, 209–38. Chicago: University of Chicago Press, 2014.

Plant, Rebecca Jo. 'William Menninger and American Psychoanalysis, 1946–1984'. *History of Psychiatry* 16, no. 2 (June 2005): 181–202.

Pols, Hans. 'The Tunisian Campaign, War Neuroses, and the Reorientation of American Psychiatry during World War II'. *Harvard Review of Psychiatry* 19, no. 6 (2011): 313–20.

Rockefeller Foundation Records, Projects. Rockefeller Archive Center, Tarrytown, NY.

Samuel, Lawrence R. *Shrink: A Cultural History of Psychoanalysis in America*. Lincoln: University of Nebraska Press, 2013.

Saul, Leon J. 'Book review of Roy R. Grinker and John P. Spiegel's *Men Under Stress* (Philadelphia: Blakison, 1945)'. *Psychosomatic Medicine* 8, no. 1 (1946): 69–71.

Schuster, David G. *Neurasthenic Nation: America's Search for Health, Happiness, and Comfort, 1869–1920*. New Brunswick, NJ: Rutgers University Press, 2011.
Scott, Wilbur. 'PTSD in DSM-III: A Case in the Politics of Diagnosis and Disease'. *Social Problems* 37, no. 3 (1990): 294–310.
Shephard, Ben. *A War of Nerves: Soldiers and Psychiatrists in the Twentieth Century*. Cambridge, MA: Harvard University Press, 2001.
Slight, David. 'Society Transactions: Illinois Psychiatric Society and the Chicago Neurological Society'. *Archives of Neurology and Psychiatry* 55, no. 2 (1946): 151–2.
Stookey, Byron. 'Society Transactions: New York Neurological Society and New York Academy of Medicine, Section of Neurology and Psychiatry'. *Archives of Neurology and Psychiatry* 55, no. 2 (1946): 157–61.
Strecker, Edward. Papers. Institute of Pennsylvania Hospital, Philadelphia, PA.
Swank, Roy L. and Walter E. Marchand, 'Combat Neuroses: Development of Combat Exhaustion'. *Archives of Neurology and Psychiatry* 55, no. 3 (1946): 236–47.
'Tantrum or Neurosis'. *Time Magazine*, 7 August 1944, 30.
'Topics of *The Times*'. *New York Times*, 30 August 1944, 16.
U.S. Army Medical Department. *Neuropsychiatry in World War II, vol. 1: Zone of Interior*. Washington, DC: Office of the Surgeon General, Department of the Army, 1966.
Wake, Naoke. *Private Practices: Harry Stack Sullivan, Homosexuality, and American Liberalism*. Rutgers, NJ: Rutgers University Press, 2011.
Young, Allan. *The Harmony of Illusions: Inventing Post-Traumatic Stress Disorder*. Princeton, NJ: Princeton University Press, 1995.
Zaretsky, Eli. *Secrets of the Soul: A Social and Cultural History of Psychoanalysis*. New York: Knopf, 2004.

6

POWS into citizens

Repatriation, gender and the Civil Resettlement Units in Great Britain

Elizabeth Roberts-Pedersen

In the second half of the Second World War, the question of how best to manage the repatriation of the thousands of British prisoners of war (POWs) languishing in camps in Europe and the Far East grew in urgency for British repatriation authorities. The problem was not just one of logistics – the difficulties of corralling troop ships and planes – though the magnitude of the war and the disparate sites of fighting made that a factor, too.[1] British officials were also concerned with the psychological condition of the men they would retrieve. Commentary from the previous war suggested that captivity took a toll on even well-treated prisoners, with the resulting 'barbed wire syndrome' making men irritable, suspicious and slow to settle back into civilian life. With over 142,000 British personnel in German and Italian hands and around 50,000 prisoners of the Japanese, the scale of wartime captivity raised the stakes considerably as the end of the war approached.[2] How to avoid these tens of thousands of former POWs returning to Britain disaffected and adrift? Better still, how to bring these repatriated men into the full embrace of Britain's ambitious post-war settlement, with an emphasis on both the benefits and responsibilities of citizenship?[3]

One attempted answer to these questions was the Civil Resettlement Unit (CRU) scheme. Begun in March 1945 and running until 1947, this programme aimed to provide 'transitional' communities for former POWs to assist with their re-entry into civilian life. Twenty CRU facilities were established in stately homes across the country, on the understanding that the returned men would attend the unit closest to their civilian home. Each CRU housed up to 240 men for four weeks at a time.[4] Overseen by clinicians connected to the pioneering, psychoanalytically inclined Tavistock Clinic, whose director J. R. Rees was also Consultant Psychiatrist to the British Army, and staffed by a mixture of military personnel (including many women from the Auxiliary Territorial Service), social workers and vocational training officers, these residential units sought to 'readjust' repatriated men to the world outside the camp, enacting a kind of social therapy to turn the men from POWs into citizens.[5] The task of the CRUs was not just to assist the former prisoners with the practical elements of post-war life, such as employment and housing, but also to help them embrace their roles as breadwinning husbands and fathers in happy and emotionally stable families. To do this, the ex-POW who volunteered to attend a CRU at his first post-release Medical Board would be helped to '[relinquish] his dependence on the corporate life and corporate discipline of the Army' and gain 'self-confidence in his capacity to carry out civilian employment and domestic responsibilities'.[6] As one repatriation memorandum explained, the units were to provide 'a bridge between a past life in the Army and the POW camp, which has created difficulties varying for each individual, and a future in civil life'.[7] The CRUs aimed to enact repatriation in the most literal sense: the men were to be brought back to the civic life of the British nation by assuming the masculine duties of work, marriage and the stewardship of harmonious family life – rites of passage disrupted by captivity and the wartime presence of women in traditionally male occupations.[8]

This chapter argues that the rationale for and operations of the CRUs illuminate a number of key facets of the relationship between psychiatry, masculinity and the military during the Second World War. In a very practical sense, the CRUs exemplify the intersection of military aims and psychological expertise during the conflict, prefiguring the increasing alignment of psychological research with state ends in the early Cold War period.[9] In their clinical orientation and therapeutic practice, which in large part reflected the psychosocial and psychotherapeutic bent of the Tavistock Clinic, the CRUs also demonstrate the ways in which broadly psychodynamic theories of human functioning could shape conceptions of what it meant to be a male citizen in post-war Britain. In this way the CRU scheme paralleled other social policy initiatives of the period, such as family guidance, reforms to social housing and expanded access to education, that drew on psychosocial principles to foster emotional stability, economic participation and settled family life in post-war citizens.[10]

The aims and operations of the CRU scheme also suggest the importance of interrogating the applicability of a contested concept like 'trauma' within specific historical settings. As the introduction to this book asserts, humanistic and social scientific research demonstrates that trauma is not a timeless clinical entity, but, rather, a concept whose meaning shifts according to cultural, social and medical norms.[11] This view stresses that the current reigning paradigm of Post-Traumatic Stress Disorder (PTSD) is a comparatively recent invention, officially recognized only in 1980 and based, as Didier Fassin and Richard Rechtman argue, on the 'consecration of the event' as the singular cause of distress in traumatized patients.[12] This was not the situation in the Second World War. For CRU policymakers and clinicians, the POWs in their care were not regarded as axiomatically damaged by the difficult and often brutal experiences of captivity – even, as we will see, the maltreated former prisoners of the Japanese. Rather, in keeping with the general tenor of British wartime psychiatry, symptoms that in the present day might be interpreted as clear evidence of PTSD were more likely to be regarded as caused by pre-existing personality defects.[13] Returned prisoners were thought to suffer from disorders of 'adjustment' that inhibited their successful return to civilian life. The governing therapeutic concern was the degree to which the POW could be helped to surmount these impediments and reintegrate into society. 'Perhaps the best way to think of a repatriated prisoner-of-war', suggested a primer for the CRUs' vocational staff, 'is as a man who is going through a difficult period of mental readjustment while at the same time he is faced with many difficult practical problems'.[14] In this view, the real psychic danger lay not in the experience of the camps, but in the shock of coming home.

Two strands of theorizing underpinned the CRUs' focus on adjustment. The first derived from the First World War and the sparse medical literature on the psychological condition of British POWs imprisoned during that conflict. These accounts tended to emphasize the prisoners' apathy and irritability, as well as the absence of conventional shell shock symptoms such as tics, tremors and paralysed limbs. These men were not suffering from disorders of the battlefield, commentators reasoned, but from what became known as 'barbed wire disease', a separate disorder of captivity that made the men listless, impatient and distrustful of authority, and that in large part allegedly stemmed from boredom, injured pride and pre-existing tendencies towards nervousness and rumination.[15] Reports out of POW camps in Europe in the early years of the Second World War tended to reaffirm these views. Descriptions of the medical condition of several thousand Allied POWs repatriated from German and Italian camps as part of a prisoner swap in 1943 were particularly influential, solidifying a consensus in the War Office that, as in the last war, the primary problem of returned POWs would be their inevitable hostility towards military discipline, the demands of the workplace and the quotidian routines of family life.[16] In this view, actual experiences, such as the circumstances of capture or the harsh conditions within individual camps, counted less than the POW's attitude towards his imprisonment, which was, in turn, determined by the structure of his personality. As a repatriation planning memorandum from June 1945 put it, the clinical picture from the last war suggested that 'the effects of captivity depended more on subjective attitudes towards it than on exposure to peculiarly severe conditions'.[17] It followed that in the CRUs, the main therapeutic effort would be directed towards undoing the passivity and inertia captivity had instilled, rather than confronting any distressing experiences the men may have undergone.

The CRU pamphlet *Settling Down in Civvy Street*, issued by the War Office in May 1945, typified this approach. While it acknowledged to the returned prisoner that he would 'need time to find [his] feet again', it also reassured him that the war had imparted some important lessons, allowing him to see 'new countries and different people' and fostering 'a new outlook on civil life, a more developed outlook and, quite possibly, a better one than before'.[18] The pamphlet had virtually nothing to say about violence or hardship – a characteristic omission that not only diminished the privations faced by many British prisoners in the European camps but also elided the immense suffering of the POWs in the Far East (FEPOWs).[19] In part, this was a question of timing: the CRU scheme was formulated over the course of 1944 and early 1945, before the desperate situation of the prisoners of the Japanese became clear.[20] But given that the CRUs' clinical approach was predicated on the assumption that 'subjective attitudes' mattered more than 'severe conditions', confirmation of the brutal conditions in the Japanese camps might not have done much to alter the CRUs' therapeutic direction. Moreover, once former prisoners from the Far East did begin to arrive for treatment at the CRUs, they tended to be regarded as mentally stronger and more resilient than their European counterparts – a seeming anomaly repeated in much of the medical literature, and one that bolstered the CRUs' focus on the importance of personality over circumstance.[21]

For the clinicians of the CRUs, surviving the Japanese camps quickly became evidence of a man's intrinsic mental toughness. In No. 6 CRU, for example, where around one-fifth of the total patient cohort were FEPOWs, the medical officer reported that while the conditions in the Japanese camps were 'altogether more grim' than even the hardships of 1945 in the European camps, '[o]n the whole I have found that the Far Eastern repats have returned to normal life more quickly and more completely than the European repats'.[22] Hutchinson acknowledged that the FEPOWs' initial mental state may have been helped by the definitive end of the war and the certainty that they would not be redeployed to another theatre, an assurance not universally extended to the POWs repatriated from Europe.[23] But he also used vaguely social Darwinist language to present the former FEPOWs as innately resourceful and resilient, a position that implied the racial superiority of the surviving prisoners despite their suffering at the hands of an enemy now described as barbaric and cruel rather than weak and effeminate.[24] These men were characterized as 'more mentally alert' than their counterparts from the European camps, perhaps because 'life in captivity in the Far East was a struggle for existence in which only those who were prepared to use their wits, survived'.[25] An official report from Civil Resettlement Headquarters in December 1946 made an even starker distinction: in the Japanese camps '[o]nly the fittest survived', so that the prisoners who returned to Britain were physically, mentally and – perhaps – morally superior to both their dead comrades and their counterparts in the European camps. Whereas the prisoners from Europe had a propensity to become fixated on physical symptoms, the former FEPOWs viewed their own ailments – often more serious and aggravated by years of deprivation – with a degree of detachment. And while ex-FEPOWs might feel more guilt about being captured 'almost without a fight', and while their domestic problems could be more acute after years without contact with their families, their outlook was perceived as more realistic and empathetic. 'General reports tend to agree that the ex-Japanese Repatriate is a "better" man', the deputy assistant director of medical services argued. 'He has had a wider experience of physical suffering. He has more sympathy and understanding. Phantasies, although present, are less elaborate and detailed. . . . They show greater independence and improvisation. They have had to live by their wits, whereas the ex-European P.W. has had a battle of wits. Psychosomatic dysfunction is rarer'.[26] Like the sentiments expressed in the *Settling Down in Civvy Street* pamphlet, this emphasis on the clarifying, even transformative, effects of captivity suggests that policymakers and clinicians had a persistent wish to downplay the damage of captivity – not only to the returning prisoners but also, perhaps, to the repatriation bureaucracy itself. 'Adjusting' POWs to civilian life implied a short period of psychic recalibration. The fiscal commitment would be limited, and the man would return to his community as a productive wage-earning citizen. In such circumstances, the condition of former FEPOWs was necessarily interpreted in the most optimistic light, with behaviour that might now suggest dissociation or denial cast as hardiness or implacability. In his memoir *The Railway Man*, the former FEPOW Eric Lomax wrote that 'the deviousness, prevarication, and impassivity' that had been fundamental to his survival stayed with him long after the war, masking a deep and abiding unease that worsened over time.[27] The prevalence of FEPOWs in the PTSD literature suggests that his was far from an isolated experience, raising the possibility that the status of the FEPOWs as the CRUs' 'best' patients may have, in fact, inhibited some of the same prisoners' long-term recovery. As it was, the CRUs' focus on preparing men for the post-war world left little room for the contemplation of deeper distress.[28]

Alongside assumptions about the influence of pre-war personalities and the enervating, rather than brutalizing, experiences of captivity, the therapeutic approach of the CRUs was also influenced by wartime theorizing about the rehabilitative possibilities of communal settings. These developments were, in turn, part of a broader interest in 'the group' as an object of psychosocial study – a burgeoning area of research that inspired prescient minds in the Tavistock Clinic to establish the Tavistock Institute of Human Relations in 1946, with the CRU scheme positioned as one of its foundational projects.[29] The controversial wartime experiments at the Northfield Military Hospital, conducted in 1942 and 1943 by Tavistock clinicians Wilfred Bion and John Rickman and psychoanalyst S. H. Foulkes, are the most well-known attempts at rehabilitating wartime psychiatric casualties through a program of group therapy, communal activities and collective deliberation.[30] Around 100 POWs who had been repatriated during the 1943 prisoner swap and who had 'failed to adjust to life outside the Stalag' were patients at Northfield during this period, and were observed to be 'irritable, restless, depressed' and 'markedly resentful of everyone and everything' until they formed trusting relationships with the hospital staff.[31] This experience likely provided additional impetus for establishing the CRUs in early 1945.

CRU planners also drew on Northfield's therapeutic practices. Clinicians in both contexts were committed to re-establishing a collective ethos in men they regarded as isolated and preoccupied with personal problems. At Northfield, the communal life of the hospital was seen as a proxy for both the military and civil society, and participation in group activities was understood as a key means of reacclimatizing patients to their responsibilities to their units and society more broadly. A similar approach was envisaged for the CRUs, which ideally would combine communal social activities like dances and concerts with more focused therapeutic work in smaller group settings, including regular group discussions. In these sessions, steered but not dominated by a clinician, returned prisoners were to relearn personal and civic responsibility: how to articulate their thoughts and opinions, how to identify and solve problems and how to dissipate group tensions. According to a War Office memorandum outlining the practices and principles of the CRUs, one aim of group discussions was to help men 'resolve in public problems which may or may not affect them individually'.[32] That the men should perceive themselves as in charge of these processes was fundamental. The psychiatrist should not 'dogmatise or rule his patients', counselled one primer on group techniques; better to assume a '"passive" undidactic role, easing tensions and interpreting in a way determined by the emotional needs of the group'.[33]

In addition to its usefulness in modelling collective cohesion and morale, this kind of group therapy also served important practical ends. It was more cost-efficient than individualized therapy – an important consideration once it became clear that it would not be possible to provide 'whole-time psychiatric help' in each CRU.[34] Group discussion also averted some of the intensity of the conventional psychotherapeutic relationship, though clinicians were nevertheless warned to watch for evidence of strong 'transference', lest it 'cuts out the other members and so disintegrates the "group feeling"'.[35] Maintaining this group sentiment was paramount, as 'the relationships which are built up between the members are often more important than the topics which are usually discussed'. The staff should therefore resist the temptation to intervene, instead allowing the discussion to 'flow freely among a widening circle of members'. Successful groups were able to develop mechanisms of 'internal restraint', allowing them to avoid 'the more inflammatory subjects', and strengthening 'an internal discipline which controls any member who tends to be too talkative or too outspoken'.[36] This subordination of individual impulses to the collective good was central to the CRUs' reintegrative purpose, which was concerned not just with the prisoners' successful re-entry into civilian life but also the kind of responsible and participatory citizens they ought to become.

To this end, the CRUs were particularly concerned with preparing former prisoners for civilian employment. CRU planning documents framed employment as not only an economic necessity but a psychologically valuable one as well – a maxim woven into repatriation policy more broadly, as well as being a long-standing tenet of psychiatric therapy.[37] Since full employment was envisaged as a fundamental precept of the post-war economy, it was less a question of the men finding a job than choosing the right one.[38] While the focus was ostensibly on assisting men to make this decision, the former prisoners were also portrayed as unreliable arbiters of their own desires. Vocational officers assigned to the CRUs were warned that in the isolation of the camps the prisoners had created 'phantasies' about their post-war lives, including the type of work they might do upon their return. It was the role of the vocational staff to guide the former prisoner towards a job that would give him 'satisfaction and a sense of achievement from his work' and ensure 'a reasonable standard of living for himself and his family'.[39] At the same time, vocational staff were cautioned against appearing to override the men's own wishes, in much the same way as the CRU psychiatrists were counselled against dominating group discussions. Vocational officers were to 'continually stress' that 'the decision about his future employment rests with the repatriate himself' and that the staff were there merely to ensure 'a suitable frame of mind in which to approach that decision and the provision of adequate and realistic information on which to base it'.[40]

The CRU clinicians also regarded returned prisoners' decisions about employment as crucial for their future domestic lives. Indeed, in the pervading if contested ideas about masculinity and gender roles that characterized the period, themes of work and marriage were persistently intertwined. Men in the CRUs were preparing to re-enter a society in which wartime disruption had compounded shifts in the gender order begun two decades earlier. Between 1914 and 1945, mass wars, economic crises and other forms of sociopolitical upheaval fostered changes in the cultural prescriptions underwriting notions of masculinity and femininity, opening up opportunities to certain groups of women, while also destabilizing assumptions about men's rights, privileges and identities. Most notably, participation in wartime economies had profound ramifications for the economic independence and mobility of (white) middle-class women in urban areas. Their ability to delay marriage or reject it altogether, to pursue education and employment and, after 1928, to claim the rights of fully enfranchised citizens, elevated the civic visibility of British women. At the same time, war and economic uncertainty exposed gaps between masculine ideals of self-control and the unruly emotions those experiences evoked.[41] Just as the rates of shell shock in the British Army during the First World War cast doubt on the stability of men's emotional lives, the economic crises of the late 1920s and early 1930s underscored the fragility of the male breadwinner as a stable identity.[42] The mass mobilization required by the Second World War, and the widespread participation of British women in both the armed forces and the wartime economy, further compounded the uncertainties about men's automatic and exclusive access to paid work.[43] For the repatriated men in the CRUs and their clinicians, this context heightened both the importance of employment and its status and meaning in the public and domestic spheres.

For this reason, in the CRUs decisions about employment were inseparable from the health and stability of the families for which a newly employed repatriate would provide. CRU planners urged staff to recognize the difficulties resuming family life might present for the returned man: that it ran counter to the enforced passivity and all-male atmosphere of the camps; and, of course, that in the soldier's absence, loved ones on the home front had changed, too. 'Before the war, a normal family developed without the changes in its members being noticed to any great extent', explained one memorandum on these altered family dynamics. But newly reunited POW families 'find changes in one another for which they cannot account'. Nevertheless, '[t]he acceptance of those changes . . . has to be achieved as quickly and as easily as possible'.[44]

Reconstituting POW families also required that the CRUs took seriously the harmony of POW marriages. CRU planning documents and technical memoranda characterized these unions as relationships that ought to be sexually and emotionally satisfying for both parties once the initial period of adjustment was overcome. CRU policy therefore permitted men to visit their families regularly, and families were, in turn, encouraged to attend visitor days, with wives welcomed into group discussions on these occasions.[45] Such measures characterized a broader, state-sponsored approach to the strengthening of British marriages in the post-war period, heralding a shift from an interwar focus on sex education to an examination of the couple's 'shared emotional life'.[46] Here, again, wartime experience inspired post-war enterprises: the Tavistock Clinic became closely involved in this work via its Marital Unit, established in 1949. The ultimate aim of such therapeutic interventions, historian Teri Chettiar argues, was for spouses to achieve a complementary 'emotional maturity', which was understood in conventionally gendered terms: for men, their 'competence as breadwinners', and for women, 'their enthusiastic embrace of home-making and child-rearing'. Achieving emotional attunement within marriage was also a civic good, providing the best environment for the production of healthy and temperamentally sound children, who would go on to reproduce the virtues of their parents.[47]

Reconciling husbands and wives was also one iteration of a broader need to reacclimatize the repatriated men to female company.[48] In this regard, all women within the CRUs' orbit embodied therapeutic potential. The Auxiliary Territorial Service had been assigned to the CRUs largely for this purpose, and the female social workers who liaised with the POWs' families were cast as the men's sympathetic confessors, to whom the POW could 'unburden himself without the fear of loss of prestige' that marked his interactions with other men.[49] The wives of returned POWs also figured as curative agents, a post-war role not unfamiliar to the many wives and mothers designated as both heroes and villains in the psychic lives of their returned men.[50] The part of the POW wife was particularly exacting, requiring, as an article in *The Lancet* from May 1945 put it, 'more than usual insight and intelligence'.[51] It was not just that wives could not understand the men's experiences or that they represented the frivolity of the civilian world, but that their own experience of war work – in the services, or in industry – could be inimical to their husbands' self-conceptions. In one case, reported by a medical officer in No.1 CRU, a patient was so distressed by his wife's wartime successes, which he interpreted as a usurpation of his masculine privileges, that the marriage became unbearable. 'He was jealous of her, and of her opportunities, he was dissatisfied with himself and bad tempered', the doctor reported. 'As a result his wife received none of the well merited praise, on the contrary, he was in constant rebellion against what she had done for him'. Eventually they moved locations, starting a new life away from the wife's promising career and the home she had made during the war. This outcome was neither good nor just, the reporting doctor implied, but it was what had to be done to mollify a 'possessive, domineering, trouserful husband'. This kind of man 'is not easily changed', the officer conceded, 'and although I agree it would have been better for this man to have solved his trouble by relinquishing these rights of his . . . I do not think it was possible'. Instead, his wife had offered 'the supreme sacrifice, and I believe this will, in his eyes, be sufficient expiation of her crime against his self-esteem'.[52] Here the doctor clearly sympathized with the wife, but also understood that deferral to her difficult husband was the surest way of preserving the marriage – and, for the husband, the gender hierarchy it represented.

The overarching objective to save POW marriages is also evident in the close attention paid by CRU clinicians to a question of particular delicacy: how to best alleviate POWs' anxieties about their sexual potency. This appears to have been a widespread fear among men returning from captivity in both Europe and the Far East.[53] In the latter case the enormous physical toll of captivity and the prevalence of starvation and tropical diseases fostered the belief that many men would return to civilian life impotent or even sterile: the doctor in No.1 CRU claimed that '[a]bout 50% of [POWs] from the Far East have been told by [medical officers] that they may be sterile on return to civil life', though he was inclined to believe the number of cases of genuine sterility to be far less.[54] Isolating the source of these concerns among POWs in the European camps was more difficult, but it may have been linked to what some observers noted was a general waning of men's interest in sex as the deadening routines of camp life took hold and the men became fixated on food and news from home.[55] A confidential CRU memorandum of December 1945 titled 'Impotence in Repatriates' noted that '[t]he incidence of sexual impotence in repatriates is extremely high, and has been estimated at as much as 80%', though '[t]he number who consult the Medical Officer on this account is very much less'.[56] Few other issues got closer to the core of what it meant to be a man than the performance of virility, and it is not unreasonable to suspect that returning POWs might have been reticent to disclose such a problem, particularly younger men in the hothouse atmosphere of a CRU, where group discussions ruled the day.

Added to these cultural inhibitions was a degree of confusion about the causes and ultimate meaning of impotence. While by this period most doctors agreed that impotence was usually psychological in origin, there was nevertheless a brisk trade in physical interventions – '[r]est, drugs, diets, baths and douches' – that promised a swift and permanent cure.[57] On this score the official CRU advice was unequivocal: unless a returned POW was older or 'latently' homosexual, impotence was in the first instance ascribed to a crisis of self-confidence and therefore a symptom of incomplete post-war adjustment. That there was no apparent difference in prevalence between the POWs from Europe and the more physically compromised POWs from the Far East tended to support this interpretation, as did the fact that for the most part the men who did divulge their condition reported that they were able to achieve erections, just not sustain them.[58] For this reason clinicians were warned that it was important not to exacerbate the problem via elaborate therapeutics: '[t]he one and only treatment for impotence in the repatriate is reassurance'.[59] The use of 'tonics' was vehemently discouraged on these grounds, lest it imply that there was an intractable physical basis for the condition when this remedy inevitably failed.[60]

Eschewing physical causes and therapies in favour of psychological ones brought its own assumptions and consequences. Emphasizing the role of the 'severe emotional shock' of returning to civilian life, as well as the men's more specific worries (or guilt) about wartime infidelities, spread the causes of impotence beyond men's individual psyches in ways that complicated its resolution.[61] Unsurprisingly, clinicians regarded POW wives as having a crucial role in reassuring impotent men of their continuing patient affection, even if the wives were apt to be judged the ultimate cause of their husbands' affliction. At the same time, CRU advice counselled that wives' forbearance could persist only as long as the inherent fragility of the feminine constitution allowed. Reproducing the more slavish interpretations of Freud's ideas about female sexuality, the CRU memorandum warned that a married woman deprived of penetrative sex for too long would become a burden to her husband, impeding or even sabotaging his recovery.[62] Unlike marriages in which a 'potent man' married to a 'frigid woman' pursued 'his own solution' to the sexless union (presumably masturbation or extramarital sex), 'non-frigid' women married to impotent men were assumed incapable of finding satisfaction within or beyond the marital bed. The result was a 'sex-starved wife' whose pathologies transcended intellect and class: '[h]owever well-bred, highminded, religious or philosophical about it', the memorandum read, 'she generally becomes hard, cruel, callous, suspicious, restless, quarrelsome, intolerant, bickering, and never has any consideration for the husband'.[63] Such an unfortunate situation 'militates against a repatriate's returning potency', which was all the more reason for the CRUs to include POWs' sex lives in their therapeutic remit and solve the impotence problem alongside other adjustment issues. A similar rationale was evident in a contemporaneous CRU primer on premature ejaculation, which characterized the condition as 'a common cause of unhappiness in marital relations' and not, the document noted sternly, a sign of 'abounding virility' or 'super-abundant eroticism'. Here again, while the writer acknowledged the role of the Madonna/whore complex in 'splitting' men's attitudes towards women, they also emphasized that it was nevertheless the *wife's* role to 'bring affection, and understanding and patience to bear upon the problem'.[64] Like the woman with the successful wartime career who had ultimately deferred to the ego of her domineering repatriate husband, POW wives were expected to accommodate their returned husbands' sexual problems while containing their own sexual needs and desires (another kind of post-war austerity). In this way the CRUs' mantra of 'adjustment' was extended beyond the individual POW to his marriage as a whole, in a manner that resonated with post-war conceptions of marriage as complementary and companionate while still organized along conventional gender lines.

The characterization of POWs' impotence as a problem of psychosocial adjustment is indicative of the ways in which the clinicians of the CRUs regarded the project of POW repatriation more generally. The focus on mastering high emotion, on dispelling prison camp fantasies and on sending men back to civilian society with a clear sense of direction and realistic expectations was intended to facilitate the men's psychic return to their families and communities by way of appropriate employment and stable marriages. Achievement of these ends sought to reaffirm POWs' masculine identities within a post-war political order that asserted the importance of consensus, participation and cooperation in a vastly expanded welfare state. Therapeutic responses were therefore characterized as communal and integrative, a tendency evident not just in the group techniques of the CRUs but also in the expectation that wives would act as sympathetic therapeutic partners for their returned men. The logical culmination of these interventions was the production of uncomplaining workers and consumers, the upholding of conventional heterosexual partnerships and families, and the fostering of temperate citizens impervious to political extremes. In this sense the CRU scheme reflected the concerns of the early Cold War period as much as the anxieties of repatriation planners and military psychiatrists.

Finally, examining the attitudes of CRU clinicians towards the former POWs in their care demonstrates the importance of resisting transhistorical and transcultural approaches to trauma as a diagnostic category. Since the inclusion of PTSD in the DSM-III in 1980, psychic trauma has come to be understood as a disorder of universal application, the result of exposure to a catastrophic event that anyone, anywhere, at any time, would experience as profoundly damaging. Such assumptions are of little help in understanding or explaining the diagnostic and therapeutic practices of the past, when other cultural pressures and assumptions were at work. In the Second World War, the fundamental precepts of PTSD were reversed: events, even catastrophic ones, were not considered damaging in and of themselves; rather, it was men's maladaptive attitudes and responses that bred pathology. The CRUs' therapeutic programme can only be understood in this context. The aim was not the remediation of mental trauma, but the resumption of a civilian masculine identity, with the former prisoner discarding his experience of captivity in favour of full, mature participation in civic life. The purpose of the CRU scheme was neither to confront pain nor to deny it, but to render it an artefact of the camps and then to leave the camps behind.

Notes

1 On British demobilization and repatriation practices more generally, see Alan Allport, *Demobbed: Coming Home After World War Two* (New Haven, CT: Yale University Press, 2010). For instructive detail on the management of this difficult process in Europe, see S. P. Mackenzie, *The Colditz Myth: British and Commonwealth Prisoners of War in Nazi Germany* (Oxford: Oxford University Press, 2006), 384–96.

2 For these figures, see Clare Makepeace, *Captives of War: British Prisoners of War in Europe in the Second World War* (Cambridge: Cambridge University Press, 2017), 3, n. 3 and Felicia Yap, 'Prisoners of War and Civilian Internees of the Japanese in British Asia: The Similarities and Contrasts of Experience', *Journal of Contemporary History* 47, no. 2 (2012): 319.

3 For an overview of debates about the social democratic character of the postwar settlement and its eclipse from the 1970s onwards, see Emily Robinson, Camilla Schofield, Florence Sutcliffe-Braithwaite and Natalie Thomson, 'Telling Stories about Post-war Britain: Popular Individualism and the "Crisis" of the 1970s', *Twentieth Century British History* 28, no. 2 (2017): 268–304.

4 The formal CRU scheme had been preceded by a pilot programme, known as the 'No. 10 Special Reception and Training Unit', established in November 1944 on the outskirts of Derby. This experiment suggested important refinements, including serving the men at the table (queuing for food was 'far

too anxiety provoking') and in general avoiding anything that evoked the atmosphere of a wartime prison camp. The facility at Debry was not helped on this score by the fact that its buildings 'bore a certain resemblance to a stalag, particularly in the wintry weather'. See 'Civil Resettlement Planning Memoranda – V. An Outline of the Work of the Pilot Civil Resettlement Unit at Derby', April 1945, 1 and 6, Tavistock Institute of Human Relations, Civil Resettlement Units ([hereafter, TIHR, CRU]), SA/TIH/B/2/1/2/2/3, Wellcome Collection Archives and Manuscripts, London ([hereafter, WC). See also Ben Shephard, *A War of Nerves: Soldiers and Psychiatrists in the Twentieth Century* (Cambridge, MA: Harvard University Press, 2001), 314–17.

5   The Tavistock Clinic is the most prominent example of the interwar growth of psychotherapy services for voluntary patients. Opened in 1920, its therapeutic approach was eclectic but underscored by its founders' religious convictions. By the 1930s, however, it was more identifiably psychoanalytic. See Alastair Lockhart, 'The "Parson's Clinic": Religion and Psychology at the Interwar Tavistock Clinic', *History & Philosophy of Psychology* 12, no. 2 (2010): 11–23 and Mathew Thomson, *Psychological Subjects: Identity, Culture, and Health in Twentieth-Century Britain* (Oxford: Oxford University Press, 2006), 186–8. During the Second World War a strong working relationship developed between the Tavistock Clinic and the British Army, initially through personnel selection programmes: see Shephard, *War of Nerves*, 188–90.

6   See 'Appendix "A" – Technical Policy for Civil Resettlement', n.d., 1, in Director of Selection of Personnel to General Officers Commanding-in-Chief, Eastern, Northern, Scottish, Southern, Western and AA Commands and General Officers Commanding, London and Northern Ireland Districts, 20 February 1946 (hereafter 'Technical Policy for Civil Resettlement'), TIHR, CRU, SA/TIH/B/2/1/2/2/3, WC.

7   'Technical Policy for Civil Resettlement', n.d., 2, TIHR, CRU, SA/TIH/B/2/1/2/2/3, WC.

8   On the politics of gender and employment on the British home front, see Juliette Pattinson, '"Shirkers", "Scrimjacks" and "Scrimshanks"?: British Civilian Masculinity and Reserved Occupations, 1914–45', *Gender & History* 28, no. 3 (2016): 721–4.

9   This tendency is evident in both Britain and the United States: see Daniel Pick, *The Pursuit of the Nazi Mind: Hitler, Hess, and the Analysts* (Oxford: Oxford University Press, 2012); Peter Mandler, *Return from the Natives: How Margaret Mead Won the Second World War and Lost the Cold War* (New Haven, CT: Yale University Press, 2013); and Andrew Scull, 'The Mental Health Sector and the Social Sciences in Post-World War II USA. Part 1: Total War and Its Aftermath', *History of Psychiatry* 22, no. 1 (2011): 3–19 and 'The Mental Health Sector and the Social Sciences in Post-World War II USA. Part 2: The Impact of Federal Research Funding and the Drugs Revolution', *History of Psychiatry* 22, no. 3 (2011): 268–84.

10 These themes are explored in Michal Shapira, *The War Inside: Psychoanalysis, Total War, and the Making of the Democratic Self in Postwar Britain* (Cambridge: Cambridge University Press, 2013) and Thomson, *Psychological Subjects*, 209–49. For examples in the areas of housing and medical practice,

see Alistair Kefford, 'Housing the Citizen-Consumer in Post-war Britain: The Parker Morris Report, Affluence and the Even Briefer Life of Social Democracy', *Twentieth Century British History* 29, no. 2 (2018): 225–58 and Shaul Bar-Haim, '"The Drug Doctor": Michael Balint and the Revival of General Practice in Postwar Britain', *History Workshop Journal* 86 (2018): 114–32.

11 The standard account of the official recognition of PTSD is Allan Young, *The Harmony of Illusions: Inventing Post-Traumatic Stress Disorder* (Princeton, NJ: Princeton University Press, 1995). See also Ruth Leys, *Trauma: A Genealogy* (Chicago: University of Chicago Press, 2000) and Didier Fassin and Richard Rechtman, *The Empire of Trauma: An Inquiry into the Condition of Victimhood*, trans. Rachel Gomme (Princeton, NJ: Princeton University Press, 2009). For one challenge to the ubiquity of PTSD as a diagnostic category, see Kenneth MacLeish, 'On "moral injury": Psychic Fringes and War Violence', *History of the Human Sciences* 31, no. 2 (2018): 128–46.

12 Fassin and Rechtman, *Empire of Trauma*, 87.

13 Edgar Jones and Simon Wessely, 'British Prisoners-of-War: From Resilience to Psychological Vulnerability: Reality or Perception', *Twentieth Century British History* 21, no. 2 (2010): 173.

14 'The Vocational Staff and the Prisoner of War', n.d., 4, TIHR, CRU, SA/TIH/B/2/1/2/2/5, WC. The notion of 'adjustment' had some similarities with Adolf Meyer's influential, if at times notoriously opaque, theory of 'adaptation': see S. D. Lamb, *Pathologist of the Mind: Adolf Meyer and the Origins of American Psychiatry* (Baltimore, MD: Johns Hopkins University Press, 2014), 205–45.

15 Jones and Wessely, 'British Prisoners-of-War', 165–8.

16 Jones and Wessely, 'British Prisoners-of-War', 165–8.

17 Civil Resettlement Planning H.Q., 'Civil Resettlement Planning Memoranda – II. Recognition of the special problems of repatriation, and early military experiments in rehabilitation of repatriates', June 1945, 1, TIHR, CRU, SA/TIH/B/2/1/2/2/3, WC.

18 Civil Resettlement Units, *Settling Down in Civvy Street*, May 1945, 3, TIHR, CRU, SA/TIH/B/2/1/2/2/3, WC.

19 On the hardships suffered by British POWs in Europe, which varied according to rank and location, see Makepeace, *Captives of War*, 185, 187; and Mackenzie, *Colditz Myth*, 154–84.

20 If details about the conditions in the Japanese camps were vague, there was nevertheless a general sense that circumstances were quite dire and that, as one 1944 Directorate of Army Psychiatry memorandum stated, prisoners were 'likely to show gross physical as well as psychological symptoms on return': Directorate of Army Psychiatry, 'The Prisoner of War Comes Home', Technical Memorandum No.13, May 1944, 9, TIHR, CRU, SA/TIH/B/2/1/2/2/1, WC.

21 For this view of the FEPOWs see, Shephard, *War of Nerves*, 318–20 and Jones and Wessely, 'British Prisoners-of-War', 178–9.

22 Major R. W. Hutchinson, R. A. M. C., Officer i/m/c, No.6 C.R.U, 'A Comparison of Repatriates From Europe and the Far East', n.d., 1–3, TIHR, CRU, SA/TIH/B/2/1/2/1/3, WC.

23 Mackenzie, *Colditz Myth*, 396.

24 On the role of race hate in the Pacific theatre, see John W. Dower, *War Without Mercy: Race and Power in the Pacific War* (New York: Pantheon Books, 1993). On wartime captivity's upending of colonial racial hierarchies, see Agnieszka Sobocinska, '"The Language of Scars": Australian Prisoners of War and the Colonial Order', *History Australia* 7, no. 3 (2010): 58.1–58.19.

25 Major R. W. Hutchinson, R. A. M. C., Officer i/m/c, No.6 C.R.U, 'A Comparison of Repatriates From Europe and the Far East', n.d., 1, TIHR, CRU, SA/TIH/B/2/1/2/1/3, WC.

26 Deputy Assistant Director of Medical Services, Civil Resettlement Headquarters, 'The Medical and Psychological Aspects of Civil Resettlement – VI. The Difference in Mental Attitude between the ex-European and ex-Japanese Prisoners of War', 20 December 1946, 15, TIHR, CRU, SA/TIH/B/2/1/2/1/4, WC.

27 Eric Lomax, *The Railway Man* (London: Vintage, 1996), 183.

28 See Shephard, *War of Nerves*, 323; Christina Twomey, *The Battle Within: POWs in Postwar Australia* (Sydney: NewSouth Publishing, 2018), 223–4; and Gavan Daws, 'Ever After', in *Prisoners of the Japanese: POWs in World War II in the Pacific* (New York: Harper Perennial, 1994), 363–96. Examples of former POWs in the PTSD literature include Joan M. Cook, David S. Riggs, Richard Thompson, James C. Coyne and Javaid I. Sheikh, 'Posttraumatic Stress Disorder and Current Relationship Functioning among World War II Ex-Prisoners of War', *Journal of Family Psychology* 18, no. 1 (2004): 36–45 and Ian P. Burges Watson, 'Post-Traumatic Stress Disorder in Australian Prisoners of the Japanese: A Clinical Study', *Australian and New Zealand Journal of Psychiatry* 27, no. 1 (1993): 20–9.

29 The inaugural issues of the Tavistock Institute's journal *Human Relations* included two substantial articles on the CRUs: see Adam Curle, 'Transitional Communities and Social Re-connection: A Follow-Up Study of the Civil Resettlement of British Prisoners of War. Part I', *Human Relations* 1, no. 1 (1947): 42–68; and Adam Curle and E. L. Trist, 'Transitional Communities and Social Re-connection: A Follow-Up Study of the Civil Resettlement of British Prisoners of War. Part II', *Human Relations* 1, no. 2 (1947): 240–88. For an overview of how interest in 'the group' intensified after the war, see Pick, *Pursuit of the Nazi Mind*, 182–215.

30 For a thorough (if admiring) overview of the work at Northfield, see Tom Harrison, *Bion, Rickman, Foulkes and the Northfield Experiments: Advancing on a Different Front* (London: Jessica Kingsley Publishers, 2000). See also Nafiska Thalassis, 'Soldiers in Psychiatric Therapy: The Case of Northfield Military Hospital 1942–1946', *Social History of Medicine* 20, no. 2 (2007): 351–68 and Shephard, *War of Nerves*, 257–78. The psychiatrist Maxwell Jones also made a significant contribution to the theory and practice of therapeutic communities during the war years. However, Jones was attached the Maudsley Hospital (the great rival of the Tavistock Clinic) and therefore was not involved in Northfield or the CRUs, though his work with a POW unit at the Southern Hospital in Dartford operated on similar principles. See his accounts in Maxwell Jones, 'Rehabilitation of Forces Neurosis

Patients to Civilian Life', *British Medical Journal*, 6 April 1946, 533–5; and Maxwell Jones and J. M. Tanner, 'The Clinical Characteristics, Treatment, and Rehabilitation of Repatriated Prisoners of War with Neurosis', *Journal of Neurology, Neurosurgery and Psychiatry* 11, no. 1 (1948): 53–60.

31 See Harrison, *Northfield Experiments,* 192–3.

32 'Technical Policy for Civil Resettlement', n.d., 3, TIHR, CRU, SA/TIH/B/2/1/2/2/3, WC.

33 Capt. Millicent C. Dewar, 'Technique of Group Therapy', n.d., 2, TIHR, CRU, SA/TIH/B/2/1/2/2/2, WC.

34 'Technical Policy for Civil Resettlement', n.d., 3, TIHR, CRU, SA/TIH/B/2/1/2/2/3, WC.

35 Capt. Millicent C. Dewar, 'Technique of Group Therapy', n.d., 1, TIHR, CRU, SA/TIH/B/2/1/2/2/2, WC.

36 'Notes for Vocational Staff. No. 5 – Group Discussions', n.d., 1, TIHR, CRU, SA/TIH/B/2/1/2/2/5, WC.

37 See Directorate of Army Psychiatry, 'The Prisoner of War Comes Home', Technical Memorandum No. 13, May 1944, 8, TIHR, CRU, SA/TIH/B/2/1/2/2/1, WC; 'Technical Policy for Civil Resettlement', n.d., 4, TIHR, CRU, SA/TIH/B/2/1/2/2/3, WC. On the enduring importance of work to psychiatric therapy, see *Work, Psychiatry and Society, c.1750-2015*, ed. Waltraud Ernst (Manchester: Manchester University Press, 2016).

38 For an overview of the British wartime economy, see Stephen Broadberry and Peter Howlett, 'Blood, Sweat and Tears: British Mobilization for World War II', in *A World at Total War: Global Conflict and the Politics of Destruction, 1937–1945*, ed. Roger Chickering, Stig Förster and Bernd Greiner (Cambridge: Cambridge University Press, 2005), 157–76. See also Pattinson, 'British Civilian Masculinity', 720–4.

39 'Introductory Notes for Vocational Staff', n.d., 1, TIHR, CRU, SA/TIH/B/2/1/2/2/5, WC.

40 'Notes for Vocational Staff. No. 8 – Vocational Advice', n.d., 1, TIHR, CRU, SA/TIH/B/2/1/2/2/5, WC.

41 For a comprehensive overview of the forces shaping ideas about gender during this period, see Susan Kingsley Kent, *Gender and Power in Britain, 1640–1990* (London: Routledge, 2002), 271–310.

42 For studies of masculinity and emotion during the First World War, see Joanna Bourke, *Dismembering the Male: Men's Bodies, Britain, and the Great War* (Chicago: University of Chicago Press, 1996); Michael Roper, *The Secret Battle: Emotional Survival in the Great War* (Manchester: Manchester University Press, 2009); and Jessica Meyer, *Men of War: Masculinity and the First World War in Britain* (Basingstoke: Palgrave Macmillan, 2009). On the usefulness of the concept of a war-generated 'crisis of masculinity', see Mary Louise Roberts, 'Beyond "Crisis" in Understanding Gender Transformation', *Gender & History* 28, no. 2 (2016): 358–66. On the status of the breadwinner and the working patterns of women during the interwar period, see Kingsley Kent, *Gender and Power*, 302–3 and Jessica S. Bean, '"To help keep the

home going": Female Labour Supply in Interwar London', *Economic History Review* 68, no. 2 (2015): 441–70. Ben Griffin also notes the importance of work in sustaining masculine identities in specific historical contexts: 'Hegemonic Masculinity as a Historical Problem', *Gender & History* 30, no. 2 (2018): 377–400.

43 The participation of women in the wartime economy unsettled some returned POWs: Jones and Wessely, 'British Prisoners-of-War', 171.
44 'The Work of the Civil Liaison Office', n.d., 1, TIHR, CRU, SA/TIH/B/2/1/2/1/5, WC.
45 See 'Technical Policy for Civil Resettlement', n.d., 4, TIHR, CRU, SA/TIH/B/2/1/2/2/3, WC.
46 Teri Chettiar, '"More than a Contract"?: The Emergence of a State-Supported Marriage Welfare Service and the Politics of Emotional Life in Post-1945 Britain', *Journal of British Studies* 55, no. 3 (2016): 573.
47 Chettiar, '"More than a Contract"?', 578. Elsewhere Chettiar notes that this model of family-oriented therapy informed new treatment models for post-partum mental illness, with the Cassel Hospital adopting a therapeutic community model: 'Democratizing mental health: Motherhood, therapeutic community and the emergence of the psychiatric family at the Cassel Hospital in post-Second World War Britain', *History of the Human Sciences* 25, no. 5 (2012): 107–22.
48 The novelty and strangeness of encountering women after years of all-male company appears regularly in accounts of POWs' homecoming: see Mackenzie, *Colditz Myth,* 393 for one instance.
49 'The Work of the Social Service Officer', Address by Mrs A. D. Brown at C.R.H.Q., 10 February 1947, 2, TIHR, CRU, SA/TIH/B/2/1/2/1/5, WC.
50 See, for example, Rebecca Jo Plant, 'The Veteran, His Wife and Their Mothers: Prescriptions for Psychological Rehabilitation After World War II', in *Tales of the Great American Victory: World War II in Politics and Poetics*, ed. Diederik Oostdijk and Markha G. Valenta (Amsterdam: Vrije University Press, 2006), 3.
51 G. C. Pether, 'The Returned Prisoner-of-War', *The Lancet*, 5 May 1945, 572.
52 Major P. G. S. Johnson, R. A. M. C, Officer i/m/c, No.1 C.R.U., 'Family Guidance', n.d., 3, TIHR, CRU, SA/TIH/B/2/1/2/1/3, WC.
53 This was not confined to British POWs. Twomey notes that a number of Australian POWs in her study attributed their impotence to their POW experience, along with other sexual and marital difficulties: Twomey, *The Battle Within*, 135. See also Daws, *Prisoners of the Japanese*, 376.
54 Major P. G. S. Johnson, R. A. M. C, Officer i/m/c, No.1 C.R.U., 'Family Guidance', n.d., 4, TIHR, CRU, SA/TIH/B/2/1/2/1/3, WC.
55 See Shephard, *War of Nerves*, 316.
56 'Impotence in Repatriates', December 1945, 1, TIHR, CRU, SA/TIH/B/2/1/2/1/2, WC.
57 Angus McLaren, *Impotence: A Cultural History* (Chicago: University of Chicago Press, 2008), 182.

58 See 'Impotence in Repatriates', December 1945, 1, TIHR, CRU, SA/TIH/B/2/1/2/1/2, WC and 'The Medical and Psychological Aspects of Civil Resettlement: A Report by the Deputy Assistant Director of Medical Services, Civil Resettlement Headquarters', 20 December 1946, 14, TIHR, CRU, SA/TIH/B/2/1/2/1/4, WC.

59 'Impotence in Repatriates', December 1945, 5, TIHR, CRU. SA/TIH/B/2/1/2/1/2, WC.

60 'Impotence in Repatriates', December 1945, 4.

61 On the frequency of worries about infidelity in returning men, see Alfred Torrie, 'The Return of Odysseus: The Problem of Marital Infidelity for the Repatriate', *British Medical Journal*, 11 August 1945, 192; and 'Impotence in Repatriates', December 1945, 2, TIHR, CRU. SA/TIH/B/2/1/2/1/2, WC.

62 In particular, the interwar period saw increased emphasis on vaginal and not clitoral orgasms as the most mature form of female sexuality, a distinction fostered by Freud and his followers: see Alison M. Moore, 'Victorian Medicine Was Not Responsible for Repressing the Clitoris: Rethinking Homology in the Long History of Women's Genital Anatomy', *Signs: Journal of Women in Culture and Society* 44, no. 1 (2018): 53–81. This, in turn, increased the pressure on the man to 'perform': McLaren, *Impotence*, 172.

63 'Impotence in Repatriates', December 1945, 2, TIHR, CRU. SA/TIH/B/2/1/2/1/2, WC.

64 'A Common Cause of Unhappiness in Marital Relations – Ejaculatio Praecox', n.d., 1–3, TIHR, CRU, SA/TIH/B/2/1/2/1/2, WC. Premature ejaculation was once considered a form of impotence on the grounds that it inhibited the full enjoyment of intercourse: McLaren, *Impotence*, 89, 172. For a similar framing of wifely duties in the treatment of male alcoholics in the post-war decades, see Lori Rotskoff, *Love on the Rocks: Men, Women, and Alcohol in Post-World War II America* (Chapel Hill: The University of North Carolina Press, 2002), 149–93.

Works cited

Allport, Alan. *Demobbed: Coming Home After World War Two*. New Haven, CT: Yale University Press, 2010.

Bar-Haim, Shaul. '"The Drug Doctor": Michael Balint and the Revival of General Practice in Postwar Britain'. *History Workshop Journal* 86 (2018): 114–32.

Bean, Jessica S. '"To help keep the home going": Female Labour Supply in Interwar London'. *Economic History Review* 68, no. 2 (2015): 441–70.

Bourke, Joanna. *Dismembering the Male: Men's Bodies, Britain, and the Great War*. Chicago: University of Chicago Press, 1996.

Broadberry, Stephen and Peter Howlett. 'Blood, Sweat and Tears: British Mobilization for World War II', in *A World at Total War: Global Conflict and the Politics of Destruction, 1937–1945*, edited by Roger Chickering, Stig Förster and Bernd Greiner, 157–76. Cambridge: Cambridge University Press, 2005.

Burges Watson, Ian P. 'Post-Traumatic Stress Disorder in Australian Prisoners of the Japanese: A Clinical Study'. *Australian and New Zealand Journal of Psychiatry* 27, no. 1 (1993): 20–9.

Chettiar, Terri. 'Democratizing Mental Health: Motherhood, Therapeutic Community and the Emergence of the Psychiatric Family at the Cassel Hospital in Post-Second World War Britain'. *History of the Human Sciences* 25, no. 5 (2012): 107–22.

Chettiar, Terri. '"More than a Contract"?: The Emergence of a State-Supported Marriage Welfare Service and the Politics of Emotional Life in Post-1945 Britain'. *Journal of British Studies* 55, no. 3 (2016): 566–91.

Cook, Joan M., David S. Riggs, Richard Thompson, James C. Coyne and Javaid I. Sheikh. 'Posttraumatic Stress Disorder and Current Relationship Functioning among World War II Ex-Prisoners of War'. *Journal of Family Psychology* 18, no. 1 (2004): 36–45.

Curle, Adam. 'Transitional Communities and Social Re-connection: A Follow-Up Study of the Civil Resettlement of British Prisoners of War. Part I'. *Human Relations* 1, no. 1 (1947): 42–68.

Curle, Adam and E. L. Trist, 'Transitional Communities and Social Re-connection: A Follow-Up Study of the Civil Resettlement of British Prisoners of War. Part II'. *Human Relations* 1, no. 2 (1947): 240–88.

Daws, Gavan. *Prisoners of the Japanese: POWs in World War II in the Pacific*. New York: Harper Perennial, 1994.

Dower, John W. *War Without Mercy: Race and Power in the Pacific War*. New York: Pantheon Books, 1993.

Ernst, Waltraud, ed. *Work, Psychiatry and Society, c.1750–2015*. Manchester: Manchester University Press, 2016.

Fassin, Didier and Richard Rechtman. *The Empire of Trauma: An Inquiry into the Condition of Victimhood*, trans. Rachel Gomme. Princeton, NJ: Princeton University Press, 2009.

Griffin, Ben. 'Hegemonic Masculinity as a Historical Problem'. *Gender & History* 30, no. 2 (2018): 377–400.

Harrison, Tom. *Bion, Rickman, Foulkes and the Northfield Experiments: Advancing on a Different Front*. London: Jessica Kingsley Publishers, 2000.

Jones, Edgar and Simon Wessely. 'British Prisoners-of-War: From Resilience to Psychological Vulnerability: Reality or Perception'. *Twentieth Century British History* 21, no. 2 (2010): 163–83.

Jones, Maxwell. 'Rehabilitation of Forces Neurosis Patients to Civilian Life'. *British Medical Journal* 1, no. 4448 (6 April 1946): 533–5.

Jones, Maxwell and J. M. Tanner. 'The Clinical Characteristics, Treatment, and Rehabilitation of Repatriated Prisoners of War with Neurosis'. *Journal of Neurology, Neurosurgery and Psychiatry* 11, no. 1 (1948): 53–60.

Kefford, Alistair. 'Housing the Citizen-Consumer in Post-war Britain: The Parker Morris Report, Affluence and the Even Briefer Life of Social Democracy'. *Twentieth Century British History* 29, no. 2 (2018): 225–58.

Kingsley Kent, Susan. *Gender and Power in Britain, 1640–1990*. London: Routledge, 2002.

Lamb, S. D. *Pathologist of the Mind: Adolf Meyer and the Origins of American Psychiatry*. Baltimore, MD: Johns Hopkins University Press, 2014.

Leys, Ruth. *Trauma: A Genealogy*. Chicago: University of Chicago Press, 2000.

Lockhart, Alastair. 'The "Parson's Clinic": Religion and Psychology at the Interwar Tavistock Clinic'. *History & Philosophy of Psychology* 12, no. 2 (2010): 11–23.

Lomax, Eric. *The Railway Man*. London: Vintage, 1996.

Mackenzie, S. P. *The Colditz Myth: British and Commonwealth Prisoners of War in Nazi Germany*. Oxford: Oxford University Press, 2006.

MacLeish, Kenneth. 'On "moral injury": Psychic Fringes and War Violence'. *History of the Human Sciences* 31, no. 2 (2018): 128–46.

Makepeace, Clare. *Captives of War: British Prisoners of War in Europe in the Second World War*. Cambridge: Cambridge University Press, 2017.

Mandler, Peter. *Return from the Natives: How Margaret Mead Won the Second World War and Lost the Cold War*. New Haven, CT: Yale University Press, 2013.

McLaren, Angus. *Impotence: A Cultural History*. Chicago: University of Chicago Press, 2008.

Meyer, Jessica. *Men of War: Masculinity and the First World War in Britain*. Basingstoke: Palgrave Macmillan, 2009.

Moore, Alison M. 'Victorian Medicine Was Not Responsible for Repressing the Clitoris: Rethinking Homology in the Long History of Women's Genital Anatomy'. *Signs: Journal of Women in Culture and Society* 44, no. 1 (2018): 53–81.

Pattinson, Juliette. '"Shirkers", "Scrimjacks" and "Scrimshanks"?: British Civilian Masculinity and Reserved Occupations, 1914–45'. *Gender & History* 28, no. 3 (2016): 709–27.

Pether, G. C. 'The Returned Prisoner-of-War'. *The Lancet*, 5 May 1945, 571–2.

Pick, Daniel. *The Pursuit of the Nazi Mind: Hitler, Hess, and the Analysts*. Oxford: Oxford University Press, 2012.

Plant, Rebecca Jo. 'The Veteran, His Wife and Their Mothers: Prescriptions for Psychological Rehabilitation After World War II', in *Tales of the Great American Victory: World War II in Politics and* Poetics, edited by Diederik Oostdijk and Markha G. Valenta, 95–106. Amsterdam: Vrije University Press, 2006.

Roberts, Mary Louise. 'Beyond "Crisis" in Understanding Gender Transformation'. *Gender & History* 28, no. 2 (2016): 358–66.

Robinson, Emily, Camilla Schofield, Florence Sutcliffe-Braithwaite and Natalie Thomson. 'Telling Stories about Post-war Britain: Popular Individualism and the "Crisis" of the 1970s'. *Twentieth Century British History* 28, no. 2 (2017): 268–304.

Roper, Michael. *The Secret Battle: Emotional Survival in the Great War*. Manchester: Manchester University Press, 2009.

Rotskoff, Lori. *Love on the Rocks: Men, Women, and Alcohol in Post-World War II America*. Chapel Hill: The University of North Carolina Press, 2002.

Scull, Andrew. 'The Mental Health Sector and the Social Sciences in Post-World War II USA. Part 1: Total War and Its Aftermath'. *History of Psychiatry* 22, no. 1 (2011): 3–19.

Scull, Andrew. 'The Mental Health Sector and the Social Sciences in Post-World War II USA. Part 2: The Impact of Federal Research Funding and the Drugs Revolution'. *History of Psychiatry* 22, no. 3 (2011): 268–84.

Shapira, Michal. *The War Inside: Psychoanalysis, Total War, and the Making of the Democratic Self in Postwar Britain*. Cambridge: Cambridge University Press, 2013.

Shephard, Ben. *A War of Nerves: Soldiers and Psychiatrists in the Twentieth Century*. Cambridge, MA: Harvard University Press, 2001.

Sobocinska, Agnieszka. '"The Language of Scars": Australian Prisoners of War and the Colonial Order'. *History Australia* 7, no. 3 (2010): 58.1–58.19.

Tavistock Institute of Human Relations, Civil Resettlement Units, Wellcome Collection Archives and Manuscripts, London.

Thalassis, Nafiska. 'Soldiers in Psychiatric Therapy: The Case of Northfield Military Hospital 1942–1946'. *Social History of Medicine* 20, no. 2 (2007): 351–68.

Thomson, Mathew. *Psychological Subjects: Identity, Culture, and Health in Twentieth-Century Britain*. Oxford: Oxford University Press, 2006.

Torrie, Alfred. 'The Return of Odysseus: The Problem of Marital Infidelity for the Repatriate'. *British Medical Journal*, 11 August 1945, 192–3.

Twomey, Christina. *The Battle Within: POWs in Postwar Australia*. Sydney: NewSouth Publishing, 2018.

Yap, Felicia. 'Prisoners of War and Civilian Internees of the Japanese in British Asia: The Similarities and Contrasts of Experience'. *Journal of Contemporary History* 47, no. 2 (2012): 317–46.

Young, Allan. *The Harmony of Illusions: Inventing Post-Traumatic Stress Disorder*. Princeton, NJ: Princeton University Press, 1995.

7

Soviet maternity care and competing narratives of trauma

Paula A. Michaels

In 1970, the Soviet Union released a childbirth preparation film to ready mothers for the experience of birth. *To Mothers and Children* (*Materiam i detiam*) depicts clean, modern facilities and a polite, professional medical staff. With images of their attentive engagement in antenatal class, the film displays peoples from all corners of the USSR, from the Far North to Uzbekistan, readily identifiable thanks to their conspicuously native garb. The scenes cut between Soviet women labouring in maternity wards in eastern Ukraine's Kharkov (today, Kharkiv) and in Kamchatka, an isthmus between the Bering Sea and the Sea of Okhotsk in the Russian Far East. The narrator reminds viewers that 'there is no pain or agony. . . . This is a normal delivery', as experienced in every city, town and village across the USSR. After the baby is born, the physician holds him up and hands him to the mother, who coos, 'he's so cute'. 'Thank you', she says to her doctor, who skilfully managed her labour and delivery. The narrator stresses that the method was 'a result of the Soviet state's concern for the health and happiness of the individual'.[1]

This idealized depiction of the party and state's care for mothers fails to resonate with the common experiences of women in Soviet maternity wards as documented in other sources. To start with, most women were in the hands of midwives, not physicians. Few facilities, especially outside of Moscow, Leningrad and Kiev, offered the state-of-the-art care depicted in *Materiam i detiam*. Rather than being gentle and kind, medical workers had earned a reputation that ran the gamut from indifferent to gruff to outright incompetent. And not all mothers had normal deliveries; for those who experienced complications, labour and birth could prove not just frightening, but also life-threatening for themselves and their babies.

This chapter asks how psychological suffering in childbirth was understood in the post-war USSR. Childbirth provides a potent case study in gendered narratives of trauma, shedding light on the ways that experiences outside of military combat contributed to our contemporary understanding of trauma. Research today shows that as many as half of women worldwide experience birth as psychologically traumatic. Data from several developed countries suggests that up to 6 per cent of women from four to six weeks post-partum suffer from Post-Traumatic Stress Disorder (PTSD) and 30 per cent meet some of the criteria for PTSD. In developing countries, evidence suggests that the figures are as high or higher.[2] The ongoing battle to recognize and remediate traumatic birth makes it a useful window on trauma as a transhistorical, transcultural phenomenon.

The post-war USSR offers an intriguing and challenging site for exploring the question of gender and trauma across time and space. Whereas in the West in this period Freudian psychoanalysis reigned supreme, Freudianism had effectively been banned in the Soviet Union. How was traumatic birth explained without resort to Freudianism? Was traumatic birth even recognized? Did women see their births as traumatic? We do not have statistics about psychological trauma in birth in the USSR; in fact, it was only at the close of the 1990s that maternity care workers in the West began to apply the PTSD diagnosis to post-partum women, despite the fact that the PTSD diagnosis had entered the medical vocabulary in 1980. But despite this slow recognition of PTSD's applicability to childbirth, there is a pre-history of understanding birth trauma in the USSR that uses a different vocabulary to interpret the same or similar affective states.

I lean on an admittedly scant source base to reveal competing narratives of traumatic birth experiences. Generated by psychologists, medical narratives tell a story that places the onus for traumatic birth primarily on personal circumstances. In this version of birth trauma, women's experiences are deeply situational, stemming typically from immediate social and interpersonal factors. The work of psychologist I. Z. Vel'vovskii (1899–1981), in particular a 1963 book based on his doctoral thesis, forms the centrepiece of this analysis. Accessing women's experiences is considerably more challenging. Prudery meant that the kinds of birth stories published in Western women's magazines in the 1950s, 1960s and 1970s had no parallels in the USSR, while censorship in those decades made criticism of state care for mothers a difficult topic to broach. We can piece together some sense of women's experiences by casting a wide net for indirect evidence. Newspaper articles from the glasnost era (1985–91) offer some hints; from a somewhat later, but relatively freer time, these complaints and concerns are suggestive of women's experiences in earlier decades. Works of literature and film that appeared in the late 1980s and 1990s provide further evidence of what went on in Soviet maternity wards. Finally, recollections posted in the early-twenty-first century on social media give voice to how women remember their experiences with the passage of time.

Taken together, this varied source base offers a range of narrative perspectives, alternately overlapping and contradictory. I adopt the narratological approach that has in recent years deeply influenced not just scholarly analysis in the medical humanities, but also clinical practice. Whether relayed by psychologists, fiction writers, journalists or patients, stories of distressing birth experiences offer access to how women, their partners and clinicians make meaning of suffering. Fiction set in maternity wards might at first glance seem most clearly to be what can be called 'stories', but non-fiction narratives generated by doctors and patients are also stories. My analysis seeks to divest from medical narratives the privileged, imbalanced authority that contributes to the dominating power of biomedicine over women's bodies and lives.[3]

Context

Before proceeding to an analysis of what these diverse and divergent narratives can tell us about trauma and birth in the USSR, I set the stage with a brief explanation of terminology and of the broader social, political and economic context in which Soviet maternity practices and psychological theories unfolded.

My focus is on psychological, not physical trauma – though, often, pain and injury are closely correlated with psychological trauma. In the context of birth, the relationship between physical and psychic pain can be hazy and more indirect than one might expect. American midwifery researcher Penny Simkin observes that the 'definition of trauma comes very close to the definition of suffering'.[4] Pain differs from suffering in that the latter captures the affective quality that sometimes, though not always, accompanies pain. We suffer when pain becomes unbearable, not in the body, but in the mind. The relationship between pain and suffering is generally understood to be a direct one: the greater the pain, the greater the suffering. But childbirth poses a special case, as pain, as physician Eric Cassell puts it, 'can be extremely severe, and yet be considered uplifting'.[5] In short, not all pain is suffering and not all suffering is traumatic. At the same time, how we treat pain in childbirth is in part governed by our perception of the very specific cultural meaning of pain in this context – as either unnecessary, or meaningful and worthy of valourization.

There are those who are sceptical that a birth resulting in a healthy, living baby can, in fact, be traumatic. Harvard psychology professor and clinician Richard McNally lists it alongside watching violence on television, the extraction of a wisdom tooth and obnoxious jokes as stressors that are considered, in his view, absurdly, as possible triggers of PTSD.[6] I do not share his estimation of women's suffering in labour and birth, nor do the numerous medical researchers who have over the last two decades examined this issue. Suffice it to say that there is abundant clinical research from around the world demonstrating that a healthy, live birth can prove traumatizing, not only for the mother but also for the labouring woman's partner and for the medical staff.[7]

Rather than asking whether or not birth can even be traumatic, a more fruitful line of inquiry is to probe how stressors and their aftermath are, to invoke the work of Ivan Karp, 'culture bound syndromes'.[8] Can we speak about psychologically traumatic birth in the post-war USSR, despite the fact that it was never described as such? One encounters a vocabulary about disquiet, distress and disturbance. But even without the use of the word 'trauma', the sources depict responses that are recognizable as indicative of what we might today describe as signifiers of traumatic experiencing. Neither physicians nor their patients had today's vocabulary for it, nor a cultural context that would allow for open, clear, direct articulation of such feelings. But one senses something familiar, if shadowy in the sources.[9] I do, however, resist labelling it as trauma because most often it seems more precise to describe it as a 'distressing', rather than a 'traumatic', experience.

Soviet social, material and medical conditions created a unique context for maternity care. While it dominated psychiatric thinking in the West, Freudianism held no sway in the Soviet Union, where in the late 1920s it had been rejected. Marxists denounced Freudianism as anti-materialist, holding that theories concerning the ego and the id, the subconscious, penis envy, the Oedipus complex and the like were mere flights of Freud's imagination, without evidence generated by sound scientific method, and not demonstrable through the body's corporeal reality.[10]

Freudianism never disappeared completely from the Soviet scene, but Pavlovian physical psychology reigned. In the early years of the Cold War, Pavlovism – the wholesale, ideologically driven application of Pavlov's theories about the function and meaning of the nervous system to all manner of scientific endeavour – offered a home-grown alternative to science that originated in the capitalist West. That Pavlovism enjoyed the state's backing did not mean that it was without merit. In the arena of psychology, Pavlovian thinking made an important and enduring contribution, particularly regarding neuropsychology and the mind–body connection.[11] In the context of maternity care, Pavlovism was felt in an understanding of labour pain's origins and treatment as dependent on reflexes that were conditional and subject to reconditioning. In brief, like dogs trained over time to respond to a bell by salivating, women could be trained to respond to uterine sensations as benign indicators of labour's progress, rather than as painful stimuli.

Questions of maternity care, the physiology of labour and birth and obstetric pain management were subject to ideological concerns, but driven principally by real-world demands. Political and medical authorities alike sought to expand the quantity and quality of maternity care in an effort to encourage fecundity. As in the West, a post-war baby boom was on in the USSR, where it acquired a patina of urgency given the need for demographic recovery after the losses of the Second World War, during which twenty-six to twenty-eight million Soviet soldiers and civilians perished. The 1944 Family Law put in place state-sponsored financial support for unwed mothers. While, on the one hand, the 1944 law emphasized marriage, for example, by making divorce a more involved and expensive process, it also sought to destigmatize unwed motherhood through these state allowances. Further, it codified a woman's right to relinquish her child to a state institution for care without ceding her parental rights forever; the law left open women's ability to reclaim their children if and when they were better able to care for them. In this way, the state sought to encourage women not to seek abortions, which criminalization in 1936 had failed to extinguish.[12]

It was in this pro-natalist environment that obstetricians and psychologists articulated concern about the relationship between physical pain and emotional suffering in birth. Authorities expressed a belief that labour pain (or fear of it) had the potential to discourage women from having more children. Medical researchers sought to remove pain as a factor that tamped down the birth rate. There was considerable consensus that an increase in the use of nitrous oxide, used in Russian maternity care since the late-nineteenth century, would be the most efficient path to achieve this objective. However, this solution would have required considerable investment to increase production of nitrous oxide and of the machines that allowed for safe self-administration of it in combination with oxygen.[13] In the context of post-war fiscal constraints, the state was unwilling and probably unable to fund a dramatic increase in pharmacological obstetric pain medications. This neglect of women's pain and suffering in birth in subsequent decades came to look more like unmitigated indifference as state resources improved, but no significant investment in pharmaceutical production followed, right through to the USSR's 1991 demise.

The reasons for this inaction on the question of pain management in labour and birth are complex. Certainly, even in the relatively materially abundant 1960s and 1970s, the USSR had far more limited resources than, for example, the United States or Great Britain, to expend on the production and administration of pain relief in childbirth. There was also no grassroots consumer movement in the USSR to enable women to demand the kind and quality of maternity care they wanted and deserved. Whatever its shortcomings, capitalism afforded leverage to the consumer, particularly when mobilized in a mass action or social movement. Soviet women had no such influence. Moreover, a pervasive and deeply rooted indifference, including among many nurses and midwives, to women's suffering in birth, deflected attention from birth pain, which was typically dismissed as routine, universal, unavoidable, transitory and, ultimately, insignificant.

Medical Narratives of birth trauma

Almost alone among Soviet researchers in his concern with birth trauma, I. Z. Vel'vovskii built an international reputation through his work on psychoprophylaxis, a psychological approach to obstetric pain management.[14] His 1963 book offers about two dozen case histories that deal specifically with perinatal and post-partum distress, including instances of depression and psychosis. How was birth trauma understood in a context in which Freudianism was rejected? The answer is twofold. First, Vel'vovskii relies on the explanatory power of Pavlovian psychology, with its emphasis on the workings of the nervous system and the role of suggestion in the establishment of conditional response. Second, he underscores the social ills that in a Marxist world view are epiphenomenal manifestations of the economic substructure.

Of greatest importance to Vel'vovskii is the role played by the nervous system, specifically the balance of cortical and subcortical function. Women exhibit personality or 'character' types based not on early psychosexual development, as Freud and Helen Deutsch, his leading interpreter in the context of pregnancy and birth, would have it, but on the physical properties of their nervous system: its strength, balance and agility.[15] When Vel'vovskii describes thirty-year-old B as 'passive', he understands this as grounded in her neurological condition.[16] A certain character type might predispose a woman to a particular reaction to pain in labour or make her more susceptible to conditioning to alleviate her pain and suffering. Take, for example, the case of 26-year-old, first-time mother S, who, in Vel'vovskii's estimation, 'gave the impression of not being entirely normal' during her antenatal preparation and at the time of her admission to the maternity ward in labour.[17] Distrusting her evaluation of her own pain, Vel'vovskii asserted that her reaction to the pain outstripped the strength of her contractions. She became distressed and, according to Vel'vovskii, screamed, 'Give me anaesthesia! Give me a knife to cut myself. Give me a saw. I don't want to give birth'. Attempts to use hypnosis were unproductive. Sleeping pills and narcotics had no calming effect. She was so unmanageable and distressed that, with the goal of speeding labour and transferring her to a psychiatric facility immediately after birth, they administered two modest doses of an amphetamine. Immediately after the second dose 'she conducted herself absolutely calmly and with composure', birthed her baby vaginally, and, as Vel'vovskii put it, 'exhibited no further strangeness'.[18] He explained her behaviour neurologically through a process known as reciprocal induction, a Pavlovian term to describe overstimulation that led to cortical inhibition and uninhibited subcortical function.

Also in keeping with Pavlovian neuropsychology, Vel'vovskii stresses the role of suggestion. Words 'may serve to condition, provoke, and reinforce pain sensations in labour', Vel'vovskii observes, and, of course, many medical carers in the West would concur. To illustrate the power of suggestion to provoke trauma, take the example of first-time mother A, who never complained of pain but vomited every three to four contractions throughout labour and then at every one to two pushes during birth. Afterwards she stated that labour had been painless thanks to her effective employment of psychoprophylactic techniques, but 'the vomiting – that was the most horrible, as my mother told me'.[19] Her mother had told her that all the women in her family vomited during labour and birth and through the power of suggestion, in Vel'vovskii's estimation, these words had induced her own experience.

Vel'vovskii demonstrates attentiveness to the contribution of social factors to pain and suffering, pointing frequently to personal experiences – not in the deep recesses of early childhood as Freud or Deutsch would, but in the days, weeks, months and years right before pregnancy and birth. His team was optimistic about Ts's performance. He described her as 'extremely well prepared', and as giving 'the impression of a strong personality, very even-keeled and extraordinarily strong-willed in achieving her goal, easily able to suppress pain sensations'.[20] Understandably enough, Ts feared going into labour while defending her senior thesis. She could not put off the defence despite being heavily pregnant, because to delay graduation would complicate her housing situation for reasons that go unexplained. In fact, she went into labour on the eve of her defence, but allegedly, through the strength, balance and agility of her nervous system, succeeded in slowing the progress of labour. She claimed that she achieved this by trying 'not to pay attention to my sensations and to suppress them'.[21] By the time Ts arrived at the maternity clinic, she was already in a state of psychosis induced by 'extreme nervous exhaustion'.[22] In Ts's case we see how social considerations such as education and housing shaped her traumatic birth experience. A Marxist interpretation would stress how over time such social ills would wither away as true communism approached.

Women's counter-narratives

When we look beyond sources generated by medical professionals, it becomes evident that the conditions in Soviet maternity wards themselves contributed to women's emotional distress in labour and birth. Both social mores and state censorship precluded forthright discussions in the press or in the arts about this state of affairs at the time Vel'vovskii published his findings, but with M. S. Gorbachev at the helm of the Soviet state (1985–91), a more open atmosphere prevailed. During the period of glasnost, or 'openness', a number of women writers penned stories set in whole or in part in maternity wards to offer an alternative narrative about birth and trauma in the USSR. When put in dialogue with other sources, such as contemporaneous newspapers, it is clear that these stories are reflective of the reality of women's maternity care experiences, even if specific details or plot lines are fabricated. Taken together, these non-medical narratives attribute women's mental anguish to indifferent and even cruel treatment that compounded the fears they carried with them into their birthing experiences.

Formed in 1988, a women's writing group known as 'New Amazons' made the maternity ward a primary site for exploring women's roles and social position. The writing of Marina Palei, Irina Polianskaia, Natal'ia Sukhanova, Ludmila Petrushevaksia and others 'reveals', in the words of literary scholar Elizabeth Skomp, 'a wide range of attitudes toward maternity and women's reproductive potential and acts as perhaps the quintessential site of uniquely female experience'. Texts set in the maternity ward 'subvert traditionally venerated motherhood . . . , clashing sharply with traditionally held notions of the physically and morally ideal mother'.[23] These writers sought to demystify motherhood, including the physiological process of becoming a mother. Their stories present not radiant, voluptuous bodies, but battered, spent ones. Palei, for example, in 'Otdelenie propashchikh' (literally, 'The Losers' Ward', but published in translation as 'The Bloody Women's Ward'), describes women's suffering as 'read on their glistening bodies as if on a map: the mastitis scars on their sagging breasts, the Caesarean scars on their bellies, the drooping string-like veins on their ruined legs, the swollen stretch marks on their withered hips, flabby bellies folding like aprons or purses', from having given birth so many times.[24] These war-torn bodies offer, in Skomp's analysis 'a testament to pain women have suffered, name[ly] phenomena normal for any childbearing woman'.[25] Suffering in birth is revealed as a nearly universal marker of the female experience, a wound women carry around with them as casually and routinely as other signifiers of womanhood, like an apron or a purse. As one uncharacteristically humane physician observes in Sukhanova's 'Delos', 'surely there is nothing worse than childbirth'.[26] Birth is thus a typical, mundane, ubiquitous site of female suffering.

While some of women's suffering is presented as intrinsic to birth itself, the New Amazon stories also underscore how the physical space and the staff of the maternity ward offer no comfort in women's time of need. In 'Istoriia ozero Veselogo' ('How Lake Jolly Came About'; lit.: 'The Story of Lake Jolly'), for example, Nina Gorlanova describes the stench of bleach and urine overlaid with a waft of watermelon, which sent her protagonist Masha's head spinning. Dozens of mosquitos swarmed, while plaster 'hung in shreds from the ceiling'.[27] Palei's provincial obstetrics and gynaecology department reeks 'of ether and institutional soup'.[28] The grim atmosphere is ratcheted up in Elena Makarova's 'Na sokhranenii' ('For preservation'), which describes a morgue positioned directly under the maternity ward's window.[29] Pestilence and death haunt the space, hovering menacingly on the periphery of the altered consciousness of women in labour.

The New Amazons capture the indifference and sometimes outright cruelty to which Soviet women were subjected in maternity wards. Set in 1943, but originally published in 1981, Irina Grekova's 'Vdovii parokhod'

('Ship of Widows') describes how one new mother, loudly demanding that her baby be handed over to her right after birth, was told by a nurse, 'Shush! This isn't a marketplace. There's a hundred of you lying here and you're the only one making a fuss. We're all working here and you're squealing like a pig!'[30] When Makarova's pregnant protagonist in 'Na sokhranenii' arrives at the obstetrics/gynaecology ward, where women seeking abortion and giving birth await treatment side by side, the nurse who registers her barks questions at her and loses patience. When she answers that she does not know if she is Rhesus positive or negative, the nurse tells her, with no regard for how her words might fuel patient anxieties, 'that's bad. You should have figured that out before you got married'.[31] When Gorlanova's Masha in 'Istoriia ozero Veselogo' goes into hard labour, she shouts down the corridor to the midwife asleep at the desk for assistance. In response, the midwife 'opened her eyes wide for a second, and then, apparently deciding she was having a dream about a person on all fours, calmed down and went back to sleep'.[32] Masha crawls back into bed and gives birth alone, the midwife running in only at the cry of the newborn. She calls the doctor, who gripes that Masha was 'all torn up. [I'll] be sewing all night', and then scolds the exhausted Masha to 'make an effort!', presumably to deliver the placenta.[33] While the staff is reprimanded for their negligence, no medical personnel offer Masha any comfort or concern in this ordeal. Rather, they express irritation with her for getting them in trouble.[34]

While Masha's experience of unattended birth was an extreme case, Soviet women were, in a sense, alone even when in the company of others. The labouring woman was not allowed to have a partner, mother, sister or friend at her side for emotional support. While there was no law against it, both sensibilities and a lack of private rooms made it impossible in practice.[35] No nurse or midwife accompanied individual women during the course of their labours, checking on them only when faced with women's demands or pleas, or when they were ready to deliver (or, in Masha's case, not even then). As literary scholar Helena Goscilo observes, 'neither doctors nor personnel [in these stories] evince any sensitivity to the psychological effects of' women labouring and birthing in isolation; 'by and large the hospital cultivates not a bedside, but, rather, a broadside manner'.[36]

That women desire comfort and support during labour and birth is a nearly universal phenomenon, even if how it is expressed is historically and culturally context-sensitive; Soviet women were no exception. Some might argue that the USSR was a tough place, where gruff treatment from stony-faced workers, in the medical and other professions, was typical. It is fair to ask: Is it ahistorical to think that Soviet women would have desired or expected anything other than gruff treatment? Are these literary sources mere representations of a reality that to our eyes looks shocking, or are they a critique? In other words, if this was typical, did Soviet women think it acceptable? McNally rightly asserts that 'what counts as trauma varies as a function of context'.[37] Not only will different individuals react to stressors in different ways, but the perception of those events as stressors is also not transhistorical. He goes on to assert, more controversially, that 'perhaps one unfortunate consequence of the otherwise undeniable benefits of modernity is diminished resilience. Our relatively greater comfort, safety, health, and well-being may have rendered us more vulnerable to stressors far less toxic than the ones occurring' in earlier eras.[38] By logical extension, McNally might argue that Soviet women did not find these conditions distressing, let alone traumatic, as they were typical of the kind of behaviour and treatment to which they had been exposed all their lives and to which they were thus accustomed.

The weight of evidence, however, seems to categorically suggest otherwise. In the early 1980s, American sociologist Jean Ispa set out to study Soviet women's experiences of labour and birth in comparison to their American counterparts. There are limits to her study – she interviewed only twenty former Soviet citizens (and a similar sample of American women). All of her Soviet interlocutors were recent migrants, mostly Jewish; this is admittedly a small, unrepresentative sample of the general population. However, it does offer, like the writings of the New Amazons, access to patient perspectives that are silent in the medical literature. Ispa does not address traumatic birth explicitly, but she finds that

> it is a fair generalization that the Soviet women had more negative memories than American women. They enjoyed their pregnancies less, were less confident about the medical care available to them and their newborns, worried more about pain and possible fetal injuries during childbirth, felt less support from their husbands, worried more about their ability to produce milk, and disliked their hospital stays more.[39]

Particularly striking by comparison to American women was the level of fear about pain and fetal injury that Soviet women expressed. While fear in childbirth is a transhistorical, transcultural phenomenon, Ispa argues that her findings were not 'simply artifacts of tradition'.[40] These women may, in fact, have had more negative experiences and were more fearful than in prior decades, as the quality of Soviet medical care had perhaps declined since the 1950s, as evidenced by a rise in infant mortality from 1960 to 1975. Moreover, antenatal preparation classes that worked to alleviate some anxiety among American mothers at this time were rarely available and, when they were, put little emphasis on assuaging women's concerns. Knowing that pharmacological pain relief was rarely used, Soviet women awaited labour's onset with dread. Add to this the fact that, as Ispa writes, 'almost all of the women interviewed recalled impersonal, often gruff treatment by medical personnel, little medical attention during labor, and poor sanitation and food in the postnatal recovery room'.[41] The three women she interviewed who delivered second children in the United States after their emigration described the contrast as 'night and day'.[42] When Ispa's findings are taken together with the literary evidence, they challenge McNally's assertion that widespread distress cultivates resilience. Distressing experiences in birth in the USSR were common, may, indeed, have been traumatic for some women, and the ubiquity of these experiences did not diminish the trauma of them.

Just as the experience of emigration shapes women's reflections on birth in Ispa's study, so, too, the collapse of the USSR influences Soviet women's memory of this life-cycle event. The year 1991 constitutes a watershed, as Western ideas about both maternity care and trauma began to slowly reshape birth experiences within Russia. Russian women also learned about practices abroad through greater communication with émigré friends and family. Russian fathers, for example, for the first time became a more common, though not routine, sight in labour and delivery rooms, as both values changed and private rooms became more available. Private hospitals also put an emphasis on customer service and satisfaction that had been unknown in the Soviet period.[43] As the approach to care began to shift, some women were able to compare Soviet and post-Soviet experiences if they gave birth multiple times across the 1991 divide. Mothers saw their daughters receive a different kind of care in the post-Soviet era.

A 2009 thread on a Russian social media site invited women to offer their stories of Soviet maternity wards and garnered 165 responses, which provide a window on post-Soviet memories of pre-1991 birth. Having seen maternity wards represented in the Soviet media as warm, caring, supportive institutions, but hearing from women that they were treated poorly there, blogger 'germanych' invited his readers to share their stories.[44] Women remember their experiences with bitterness that seems barely diminished by the passage of time. Describing her experience giving birth in 1984 at the Leningrad Paediatric Institute, one mother posted that the staff treated patients

> horribly, they all spoke haughtily, they had no time for us. It was very cold, -25 degrees [Celsius; -13 Fahrenheit] outside. There was no hot water, they didn't allow us to have the kettles that relatives gave us. My mother gave me a box of sugar, and the whole ward used it secretly. There were 12 of us on the ward. No bathtub, the toilet was filthy. It's horrible to recall.[45]

Another woman, who gave birth in Yaroslavl in 1989, attested that when one woman in the same ward vomited during labour, the orderly 'shoved a rag in her face and yelled, "clean up after yourself!"'[46] One post stated that 'for men in the USSR there was the army, but for women there was the maternity ward and the abortion clinic'.[47] In likening the experience of women to that of soldiers, the commenter implies an equivalence between soldiering – to date, the most deeply probed site of trauma – and women's more universal, yet less acknowledged experiences in birth.

Men were aware of the torment to which their wives, sisters and daughters were subjected within the walls of the maternity homes. In the USSR's waning days, one V. Baskakov of Poltava oblast (Ukraine Soviet Socialist Republic) sent a question to *Argumenty i fakty*, a weekly tabloid known in the glasnost era for broaching intimate, taboo topics. 'There will soon be a big event in our family – we are having a baby', he wrote. 'But mixed with our great joy is unease – I'm very afraid to let my wife go to the maternity ward alone, having heard about the indifference and rudeness of the staff'.[48] Men's insight into women's suffering passed from generation to generation, as is evident when 'vladimirgin' wrote in 2009 that

> when my mother gave birth to my brother in 1984 . . . it was, in her telling, really horrible [*uzhas-uzhas*]. They only sort of, kind of began to do something when she began screaming that she herself is a doctor and she could find to whom exactly a complaint should be lodged with city health officials. If she had not shouted, there is no small chance that my brother would have been born dead (it was a complicated birth) :(((((.[49]

Capturing a sense of the unhealed wounds at the heart of the stories that mothers tell their sons and daughters, who are themselves becoming parents, a woman writing under the online identity of 'bormental r' laments: 'I pity the women of my generation, the poor girls of the 1970s, who could not even imagine' the kind of care that is available to women in the Global North.[50] Like the migrant women who first gave birth in the Union of Soviet Socialist Republics and then in the United States, the contrast set in sharp relief bormental r's feelings of what might best be described as grief over the suffering she had endured.

Conclusion

Certainly, as in the West, not all Soviet women had negative experiences. The same thread that offered the testimonials cited above had others, like one from 'phd_paul_lector', who wrote simply that 'Mama said that they treated her very well'.[51] Even for those who did not receive kindness and care from medical workers, camaraderie among women patients offered emotional support. Goscilo notes that

> official indifference to female psychology contrasts dramatically with the support and affirmation women generally find among their wardmates, even if the latter also prove a source of conflict and tension. Female bonding results in part from the extent to which life in the ward is laid bare for group consumption. Few, if any, secrets remain unguessed or

unrevealed. Furthermore, the leisurely, externally uneventful pace of hospital existence permits the exchange of biographies and confidences, which unites women through the revelation of hardships that seem less individual than endemic to their gender.[52]

The 1998 feature film *Happy Birthday* (dir. Larisa Sadylova) suggests that this is precisely how Soviet labour and lying-in is remembered.[53] The film is set in a small-town maternity home somewhere in the depths of Russia. Scenes of the maternity home's closure and relocation to a newer, more modern facility in the late 1990s bracket action that unfolds in flashback to an unspecified year during the Gorbachev era. Material conditions are poor, with the clinic looking virtually unchanged from the 1950s.[54] Medical staff are not outright abusive, though they lie to, mislead and are short-tempered with the labouring and new mothers. Most striking, however, is the humour and warmth evident among the patients. They share intimate stories and try to buck each other up as they face life's travails: absent or alcoholic fathers of their children; hostile in-laws; poverty; their own and their children's mental and physical impairments. The maternity ward is a respite, an oasis where the whirlwind of quotidian struggles pauses.

But the maternity hospital is no visit to the spa. If one does not assume that Soviet women were hardened to suffering simply by virtue of the fact that they had endured more than their fair share of it, then one sees considerable evidence that giving birth in the Union of Soviet Socialist Republics was for many women a deeply and unforgettably distressing experience. The support offered from one new mother to another proves noteworthy precisely because of its contrast to the treatment from medical staff at women's time of greatest need and vulnerability. That for some it rose to the threshold of what would today be diagnosable as PTSD is impossible to say for certain, but it need not meet that standard to merit acknowledgement and be understood as part of the gendered story of trauma, past and present. As commentator 'bad_muthafucka' wrote, 'the majority of medical personnel remain just the same' as in the Soviet era and thus it is a story of not only historical but contemporary concern.[55]

When looking at historical documentation and recollections of emotionally distressing and psychologically traumatizing birth experiences, the most obvious point of departure from today's understanding is the unwillingness to see birth itself as a source of trauma. In the 1960s, distress was seen through the lens of the medical profession as the consequence of either neurological predisposition or social strain. Later evidence, from the 1970s and 1980s, and from subsequent recollections, gives a view from below that points to the quality of care – or lack thereof – as a major, if not the major, source of suffering. When we strain to hear these voices, blame is clearly and unequivocally laid at the feet of those who were supposed to be caring professionals.

Notes

1 *Materiam i detiam* (Kievskaia kinostudiia nauchno-populiarnykh fil'mov, 1970).

2 Madeleine Simpson and Christine Catling, 'Understanding Psychological Traumatic Birth Experiences: A Literature Review', *Women and Birth* 29, no. 3 (2016): 203–4; Grace Zimmerman, 'Birth Trauma: Posttraumatic Stress Disorder After Childbirth', *International Journal of Childbirth Education* 28, no. 3 (2013): 61–6; and Tatiana Henriques et al., 'Postpartum Posttraumatic Stress Disorder in a Fetal High-Risk Maternity Hospital in the City of Rio de Janeiro, Brazil', *Cadernos De Saúde Pública* 31, no. 12 (2015): 2523–34.

3 On narratological approaches to medical humanities, see, for example, Rita Charon, *Narrative Medicine: Honoring the Stories of Illness* (New York: Oxford University Press, 2008); Rita Charon, *The Principles and Practice of Narrative Medicine* (New York: Oxford University Press, 2017); and Johanna Shapiro, 'Illness Narratives: Reliability, Authenticity and the Empathic Witness', *Medical Humanities* 37, no. 2 (2011): 68–72.

4 Penny Simkin, 'Pain, Suffering, and Trauma in Labor and Prevention of Subsequent Posttraumatic Stress Disorder', *The Journal of Perinatal Education* 20, no. 3 (2011): 167.

5 Eric J. Cassell, *The Nature of Suffering and the Goals of Medicine* (New York: Oxford University Press, 1994), 34.

6 Richard J. McNally, 'Is PTSD a Transhistorical Phenomenon?', in *Culture and PTSD: Trauma in Global and Historical Perspective*, ed. Devon E. Hinton and Byron J. Good (Philadelphia: University of Pennsylvania Press, 2016), 128.

7 Susan Ayers, 'Fear of Childbirth: Postnatal Post-Traumatic Stress Disorder and Midwifery Care', *Midwifery* 30, no. 2 (2014): 145–8; Cheryl Tatano Beck, 'Birth Trauma: In the Eye of the Beholder', *Nursing Research* 53, no. 1 (2004): 28–35; Debra K. Creedy, Ian M. Shochet and Jan Horsfall, 'Childbirth and the Development of Acute Trauma Symptoms: Incidence and Contributing Factors', *Birth* 27, no. 2 (2000): 104–11; Jenny Gamble and Debra Creedy, 'Psychological Trauma Symptoms of Operative Birth', *British Journal of Midwifery* 13, no. 4 (2005): 218–24; Henriques et al., 'Postpartum Posttraumatic Stress Disorder in a Fetal High-Risk Maternity Hospital in the City of Rio de Janeiro, Brazil'; Julia Leinweber et al., 'A Socioecological Model of Posttraumatic Stress among Australian Midwives', *Midwifery* 45 (2017): 7–13; J. H. Perlow et al., 'Birth Trauma: A Five-Year Review of Incidence and Associated Perinatal Factors', *The Journal of Reproductive Medicine* 41, no. 10 (1996): 754–60; J. L. Reynolds, 'Post-Traumatic Stress Disorder after Childbirth: The Phenomenon of Traumatic Birth', *Canadian Medical Association Journal* 156, no. 6 (1997): 831–5; Kayleigh Sheen, Helen Spiby and Pauline Slade, 'Exposure to Traumatic Perinatal Experiences and Posttraumatic Stress Symptoms in Midwives: Prevalence and Association with Burnout', *International Journal of Nursing Studies* 52 (2015): 578–87; Johanna E. Soet, Gregory A. Brack and Colleen DiIorio, 'Prevalence and Predictors of Women's Experience of Psychological Trauma During Childbirth', *Birth* 30, no. 1 (2003): 36–46; Tracey White et al., 'Postnatal

Depression and Post-traumatic Stress after Childbirth: Prevalence, Course and Co-occurrence', *Journal of Reproductive and Infant Psychology* 24, no. 2 (2006): 107–20; and Zimmerman, 'Birth Trauma'.

8   Ivan Karp, 'Deconstructing Culture-Bound Syndromes', *Social Science & Medicine* 21, no. 2 (1985): 221–8.

9   On the historical experience of traumatic birth primarily in the Anglo-American context, see Paula A. Michaels, 'Childbirth and Trauma, 1940s–1980s', *Journal of the History of Medicine and Allied Sciences* 73, no. 1 (2018): 52–72.

10 Martin Alan Miller, *Freud and the Bolsheviks: Psychoanalysis in Imperial Russia and the Soviet Union* (New Haven, CT: Yale University Press, 1998).

11 Ethan Pollock, *Stalin and the Soviet Science Wars* (Princeton, NJ: Princeton University Press, 2009). On the broader history of psychosomatic medicine, see Anne Harrington, *The Cure within: A History of Mind-Body Medicine* (New York; London: W.W. Norton, 2009). On Pavlov and his work, see Daniel Todes, *Ivan Pavlov: A Russian Life in Science* (New York: Oxford University Press, 2015).

12 Harold J. Berman, 'Soviet Family Law in the Light of Russian History and Marxist Theory', *Yale Law Journal* 56, no. 1 (1946): 26–57; Mie Nakachi, 'N. S. Khrushchev and the 1944 Soviet Family Law: Politics, Reproduction, and Language', *East European Politics & Societies* 20, no. 1 (2006): 40–68; and Mie Nakachi, 'Replacing the Dead: The Politics of Reproduction in the Postwar Soviet Union, 1944-1955' (PhD diss., University of Chicago, 2008).

13 Paula A. Michaels, *Lamaze: An International History* (New York: Oxford University Press, 2014), 27–33.

14 Michaels, *Lamaze*, 33ff.

15 Eric Shiraev, *Personality Theories: A Global View* (Los Angeles: Sage Publications, 2016), 177. See also, Helene Deutsch, *The Psychology of Women: A Psychoanalytic Interpretation*, 2 vols. (New York: Grune & Stratton, 1944).

16 I. Z. Vel'vovskii, *Sistema psikhoprofilakticheskogo obezbolivaniia rodov* (Moscow: Medgiz, 1963), 213. The initials used here to identify the case studies come from Vel'vovksii.

17 Vel'vovskii, *Sistema psikhoprofilakticheskogo obezbolivaniia rodov*, 229.

18 Vel'vovskii, *Sistema psikhoprofilakticheskogo obezbolivaniia rodov*, 229.

19 Vel'vovskii, *Sistema psikhoprofilakticheskogo obezbolivaniia rodov*, 233.

20 Vel'vovskii, *Sistema psikhoprofilakticheskogo obezbolivaniia rodov*, 231.

21 Vel'vovskii, *Sistema psikhoprofilakticheskogo obezbolivaniia rodov*, 231.

22 Vel'vovskii, *Sistema psikhoprofilakticheskogo obezbolivaniia rodov*, 231.

23 Elizabeth Skomp, 'Russian Women's Publishing at the Beginning of the 1990s: The Case of the New Amazons', *The Soviet and Post-Soviet Review* 33, no. 1 (2006): 93. See also, Jenny Kaminer, *Women with a Thirst for Destruction: The Bad Mother in Russian Culture* (Evanston, IL: Northwestern University Press, 2015). I am grateful to Beth Holmgren for suggesting to me the value of literary sources for the history of Soviet childbirth.

24 Marina Palei, 'The Bloody Women's Ward', in *Women's View*, vol. 3, Glas: New Russian Writing (Moscow: Glas, 1992), 84. An alternative translation into English is available in Marina Palei, 'The Losers' Division', trans. Jehanne Gheith, in *Lives in Transit: A Collection of Recent Russian Women's Writing*, ed. Helena Goscilo (Dana Point, CA: Ardis, 1995), 197. Still another version of this passage is found in Skomp, 'Russian Women's Publishing', 92.
25 Skomp, 'Russian Women's Publishing', 92.
26 Natalia Sukhanova, 'Delos', in *Zal ozhidaniia: rassakzy* (Moscow: Sovremennik, 1990), 17.
27 Nina Gorlanova, 'How Lake Jolly Came About', in *Nine of Russia's Foremost Women Writers*, trans. Jane Chamberlain, vol. 30, Glas: New Russian Writing (Moscow: Glas, 2003), 68.
28 Palei, 'The Bloody Women's Ward', 74.
29 Elena Makarova, 'Na sokhranenii', in *Otkrytyi final: povesti* (Moscow: Sovetskii pisatel', 1989), 61.
30 Cited in Helena Goscilo, *Dehexing Sex: Russian Womanhood During and After Glasnost* (Ann Arbor: University of Michigan Press, 1996), 125.
31 Makarova, 'Na sokhranenii', 60.
32 Gorlanova, 'How Lake Jolly Came About', 76.
33 Gorlanova, 'How Lake Jolly Came About', 76.
34 Gorlanova, 'How Lake Jolly Came About', 79–80.
35 Iurii Feklistov, 'Rozhaem vmeste', *Ogonek*, May 1989, 32.
36 Goscilo, *Dehexing Sex*, 125.
37 McNally, 'Is PTSD a Transhistorical Phenomenon?', 129.
38 McNally, 'Is PTSD a Transhistorical Phenomenon?', 129.
39 Jean Ispa, 'Soviet and American Childbearing Experiences and Attitudes: A Comparison', *Slavic Review* 42, no. 1 (1983): 9.
40 Ispa, 'Soviet and American Childbearing Experiences and Attitudes', 9.
41 Ispa, 'Soviet and American Childbearing Experiences and Attitudes', 9.
42 Ispa, 'Soviet and American Childbearing Experiences and Attitudes', 9.
43 Michele Rivkin-Fish, *Women's Health in Post-Soviet Russia: The Politics of Intervention* (Bloomington: Indiana University Press, 2005).
44 Germanych, 'Vopros k zhenskoi auditorii', LiveJournal, *1965* (blog), 20 May 2009. https://germanych.livejournal.com/138984.html.
45 madlesha, comment on Germanych, 'Vopros k zhenskoi auditorii'.
46 greenbat, comment on Germanych, 'Vopros k zhenskoi auditorii'.
47 nnagina, comment on Germanych, 'Vopros k zhenskoi auditorii'.
48 V. Baskakov, 'Vopros-otvet', *Argumenty i fakty*, 19 September 1991, 7.
49 vladimirgin, comment on Germanych, 'Vopros k zhenskoi auditorii'.
50 bormental r, comment on Germanych, 'Vopros k zhenskoi auditorii'.
51 phd_paul_lector, comment on Germanych, 'Vopros k zhenskoi auditorii'.

52 Goscilo, *Dehexing Sex*, 125–6.
53 *S dnem rozhdeniia!*, directed by Larisa Sadilova (Moscow: Gosudarstvennyi komitet Rossiiskoi Federatsii po kinomatografii; Regional'nyi obshchestvenii fond podderzhki kino, 1998).
54 See, for example, *Chelovek rodilsia* (Moscow: Mosfilm, 1956).
55 bad_muthafucka, comment on Germanych, 'Vopros k zhenskoi auditorii'.

Works cited

Ayers, Susan. 'Fear of Childbirth, Postnatal Post-Traumatic Stress Disorder and Midwifery Care'. *Midwifery* 30, no. 2 (2014): 145–8.
bad_muthafucka. Comment on Germanych, 'Vopros k zhenskoi auditoria'. LiveJournal. *1965* (blog), 20 May 2009. https://germanych.livejournal.com/138984.html.
Baskakov, V. 'Vopros-otvet'. *Argumenty i fakty*, 19 September 1991, 7.
Beck, Cheryl Tatano. 'Birth Trauma: In the Eye of the Beholder'. *Nursing Research* 53, no. 1 (2004): 28–35.
Berman, Harold J. 'Soviet Family Law in the Light of Russian History and Marxist Theory'. *Yale Law Journal* 56, no. 1 (1946): 26–57.
bormental r. Comment on Germanych, 'Vopros k zhenskoi auditoria'. LiveJournal. *1965* (blog), 20 May 20, 2009. https://germanych.livejournal.com/138984.html.
Cassell, Eric J. *The Nature of Suffering and the Goals of Medicine*. New York: Oxford University Press, 1994.
Charon, Rita. *Narrative Medicine: Honoring the Stories of Illness*. New York: Oxford University Press, 2008.
Charon, Rita. *The Principles and Practice of Narrative Medicine*. New York: Oxford University Press, 2017.
Creedy, Debra K., Ian M. Shochet and Jan Horsfall. 'Childbirth and the Development of Acute Trauma Symptoms: Incidence and Contributing Factors'. *Birth* 27, no. 2 (2000): 104–11.
Deutsch, Helene. *The Psychology of Women: A Psychoanalytic Interpretation*. 2 vols. New York: Grune & Stratton, 1944.
Feklistov, Iurii. 'Rozhaem vmeste'. *Ogonek*, May 1989, 32–3.
Foucault, Michel. *The History of Sexuality*. Translated by Robert Hurley. New York: Pantheon, 1978.
Gamble, Jenny and Debra Creedy. 'Psychological Trauma Symptoms of Operative Birth'. *British Journal of Midwifery* 13, no. 4 (2005): 218–24.
Germanych. 'Vopros k zhenskoi auditorii'. LiveJournal. *1965* (blog), 20 May 2009. https://germanych.livejournal.com/138984.html.
Gorlanova, Nina. 'How Lake Jolly Came About', in *Nine of Russia's Foremost Women Writers*, translated by Jane Chamberlain, 30:67–90. Glas: New Russian Writing. Moscow: Glas, 2003.
Goscilo, Helena. *Dehexing Sex: Russian Womanhood During and After Glasnost*. Ann Arbor: University of Michigan Press, 1996.
greenbat. Comment on Germanych, 'Vopros k zhenskoi auditorii'. LiveJournal. *1965* (blog), 20 May 2009. https://germanych.livejournal.com/138984.html.

Harrington, Anne. *The Cure Within: A History of Mind-Body Medicine*. New York; London: W.W. Norton, 2009.
Henriques, Tatiana, Claudia Leite de Moraes, Michael E. Reichenheim, Gustavo Lobato de Azevedo, Evandro Silva Freire Coutinho and Ivan Luiz de Vasconcellos Figueira. 'Postpartum Posttraumatic Stress Disorder in a Fetal High-Risk Maternity Hospital in the City of Rio de Janeiro, Brazil'. *Cadernos De Saúde Pública* 31, no. 12 (2015): 2523–34.
Ispa, Jean. 'Soviet and American Childbearing Experiences and Attitudes: A Comparison'. *Slavic Review* 42, no. 1 (1983): 1–13.
Kaminer, Jenny. *Women with a Thirst for Destruction: The Bad Mother in Russian Culture*. Evanston, IL: Northwestern University Press, 2015.
Karp, Ivan. 'Deconstructing Culture-Bound Syndromes'. *Social Science & Medicine* 21, no. 2 (1985): 221–8.
Leinweber, Julia, Debra K. Creedy, Heather Rowe and Jenny Gamble. 'A Socioecological Model of Posttraumatic Stress among Australian Midwives'. *Midwifery* 45 (2017): 7–13.
madlesha. Comment on Germanych, 'Vopros k zhenskoi auditorii'. LiveJournal. *1965* (blog), 20 May 2009. https://germanych.livejournal.com/138984.html.
Makarova, Elena. 'Na sokhranenii', in *Otkrytyi final: povesti*, 58–126. Moscow: Sovetskii pisatel', 1989.
Materiam i detiam. Kievskaia kinostudiia nauchno-populiarnykh fil'mov, 1970.
McNally, Richard J. 'Is PTSD a Transhistorical Phenomenon?', in *Culture and PTSD: Trauma in Global and Historical Perspective*, edited by Devon E. Hinton and Byron J. Good, 117–34. Philadelphia: University of Pennsylvania Press, 2016.
Michaels, Paula A. 'Childbirth and Trauma, 1940s–1980s'. *Journal of the History of Medicine and Allied Sciences* 73, no. 1 (2018): 52–72.
Michaels, Paula A. *Lamaze: An International History*. New York: Oxford University Press, 2014.
Miller, Martin Alan. *Freud and the Bolsheviks: Psychoanalysis in Imperial Russia and the Soviet Union*. New Haven, CT: Yale University Press, 1998.
Morris, David J. *The Evil Hours: A Biography of Post-Traumatic Stress Disorder*. Boston, MA: Houghton Mifflin Harcourt, 2016.
Nakachi, Mie. 'N. S. Khrushchev and the 1944 Soviet Family Law: Politics, Reproduction, and Language'. *East European Politics & Societies* 20, no. 1 (2006): 40–68.
Nakachi, Mie. 'Replacing the Dead: The Politics of Reproduction in the Postwar Soviet Union, 1944–1955'. PhD diss., University of Chicago, 2008.
nnagina. Comment on Germanych, 'Vopros k zhenskoi auditorii'. LiveJournal. *1965* (blog), 20 May 2009. https://germanych.livejournal.com/138984.html.
Ordynskii, Vasilii, dir. *Chelovek rodilsia*. Moscow: Mosfilm Studios, 1956.
Palei, Marina. 'The Bloody Women's Ward', in *Women's View*, 3:74–93. Glas: New Russian Writing. Moscow: Glas, 1992.
Palei, Marina. 'The Losers' Division', in *Lives in Transit: A Collection of Recent Russian Women's Writings*, edited by Helena Goscilo, translated by Jehanne Gheith, 191–202. Dana Point, CA: Ardis, 1995.
Perlow, J. H., T. Wigton, J. Hart, H. T. Strassner, M. P. Nageotte and B. M. Wolk. 'Birth Trauma: A Five-Year Review of Incidence and Associated Perinatal Factors'. *The Journal of Reproductive Medicine* 41, no. 10 (1996): 754–60.

phd_paul_lector. Comment on Germanych, 'Vopros k zhenskoi auditorii'. LiveJournal. *1965* (blog), 20 May 2009. https://germanych.livejournal.com/138984.html.
Pollock, Ethan. *Stalin and the Soviet Science Wars*. Princeton, NJ: Princeton University Press, 2009.
Reynolds, J. L. 'Post-Traumatic Stress Disorder after Childbirth: The Phenomenon of Traumatic Birth'. *Canadian Medical Association Journal* 156, no. 6 (1997): 831–5.
Rivkin-Fish, Michele. *Women's Health in Post-Soviet Russia: The Politics of Intervention*. Bloomington: Indiana University Press, 2005.
Sadilova, Larisa, dir. *S dnem rozhdeniia!*. Moscow: Gosudarstvennyi komitet Rossiiskoi Federatsii po kinomatografii; Regional'nyi obshchestvenii fond podderzhki kino, 1998.
Shapiro, Johanna. 'Illness Narratives: Reliability, Authenticity and the Empathic Witness'. *Medical Humanities* 37, no. 2 (2011): 68–72.
Sheen, Kayleigh, Helen Spiby and Pauline Slade. 'Exposure to Traumatic Perinatal Experiences and Posttraumatic Stress Symptoms in Midwives: Prevalence and Association with Burnout'. *International Journal of Nursing Studies* 52 (2015): 578–87.
Shepherd, Ben. 'Risk Factors and PTSD: A Historian's Perspective', in *Posttraumatic Stress Disorder: Issues and Controversies*, edited by Gerald M. Rosen, 39–61. Chichester: Wiley, 2004.
Shiraev, Eric. *Personality Theories: A Global View*. Los Angeles: Sage Publications, 2016.
Simkin, Penny. 'Pain, Suffering, and Trauma in Labor and Prevention of Subsequent Posttraumatic Stress Disorder'. *The Journal of Perinatal Education* 20, no. 3 (2011): 166–76.
Simpson, Madeleine and Christine Catling. 'Understanding Psychological Traumatic Birth Experiences: A Literature Review'. *Women and Birth* 29, no. 3 (2016): 203–7.
Skomp, Elizabeth. 'Russian Women's Publishing at the Beginning of the 1990s: The Case of the New Amazons'. *The Soviet and Post-Soviet Review* 33, no. 1 (2006): 85–98.
Soet, Johanna E., Gregory A. Brack and Colleen DiIorio. 'Prevalence and Predictors of Women's Experience of Psychological Trauma During Childbirth'. *Birth* 30, no. 1 (2003): 36–46.
Sukhanova, Natalia. 'Delos', in *Zal ozhidaniia: rassakzy*, 3–28. Moscow: Sovremennik, 1990. https://www.worldcat.org/title/zal-ozhidaniia-rasskazy/oclc/976452738&referer=brief_results.
Todes, Daniel P. *Ivan Pavlov: A Russian Life in Science*. Oxford: Oxford University Press, 2015.
Vel'vovskii, I. Z. *Sistema psikhoprofilakticheskogo obezbolivaniia rodov*. Moscow: Medgiz, 1963.
vladimirgin. Comment on Germanych, 'Vopros k zhenskoi auditorii'. LiveJournal. *1965* (blog), 20 May 2009. https://germanych.livejournal.com/138984.html.
Watters, Ethan. 'Suffering Differently'. *The New York Times*, 12 August 2007, sec. Magazine. https://www.nytimes.com/2007/08/12/magazine/12wwln-idealab-t.html.

White, Tracey, Stephen Matthey, Kim Boyd and Bryanne Barnett. 'Postnatal Depression and Post-traumatic Stress after Childbirth: Prevalence, Course and Co-occurrence'. *Journal of Reproductive and Infant Psychology* 24, no. 2 (2006): 107–20.

Zimmerman, Grace. 'Birth Trauma: Posttraumatic Stress Disorder After Childbirth'. *International Journal of Childbirth Education* 28, no. 3 (2013): 61–6.

8

Trauma and sexual violence

Narratives and cases in late twentieth-century Australia

Lisa Featherstone

In the late 1970s, a sports coach sexually assaulted four boys in regional Australia. He abused the boys, aged between eight and eleven years old, when they were under his supervision at various sporting events. The case went to court in 1980, with the perpetrator pleading guilty to four counts of indecent assault, although at trial the judge intimated that at least some of the instances could have met the standard for the more serious charge of sodomy.[1] Justice Herron focused on two key issues at the sentencing. First was the character of the offender. The judge noted that he had 'hitherto been a person of good character', and cited references from members of the community and his employer. This was typical of many sentencing hearings in this period – the 'good bloke defence' emphasized the citizenship of men, especially those who held a public position, and performed voluntary or paid work in community organizations.[2] In this case, it also went in his favour that the perpetrator was seen as 'contrite' and had pleaded guilty, which meant that the boys did not need to face a public trial.[3] Second, the judge focused on the broader community, noting that his primary concern was 'to protect the public, in particular, young children' and to give assurance to parents that the law would shelter *all* children.[4] Here the emphasis was again on the public face of offending – the need to be seen to do justice and to prevent further future crimes, rather than addressing the private pain or suffering of the individual victims.

At this sentencing hearing, and many others like it, the physical and mental plight of the four children was all but invisible. Any psychological damage to the boys was not mentioned at all in the court. By 1980, this was perhaps unusual, for it had become more common across the late 1970s for judges to quietly note the potential for psychological harm to children who had been sexually assaulted.[5] Even so, a child's ordeal was never central to the courtroom process, and sometimes, as in this case, could be overlooked altogether. Within a trial or sentencing hearing, trauma was a marginal consideration: thinking about psychological damage to the child was not the core business of the court.

This chapter investigates how concepts of trauma were utilized and practised in the theatre of the law. Beginning with a brief, contextual overview of ideas about sexual offending in the 1970s and 1980s in Australia, the chapter then offers a critique of contemporary social and medical understandings of trauma, drawing on medical and psychological literatures to show how ideas of harm shifted across the second half of the twentieth century. Finally, I look more closely at the ways that concepts of trauma and psychological distress manifested in the courtroom during trials for sexual offending. I am concerned not only with the aetiologies of trauma in a disease model but also with the analysis of ways this played out beyond the medical text. Though expressed clearly in this period in writings about sexual abuse, I argue that the idea of psychological trauma was slow to filter into the courtroom. Responses to ideas of trauma and psychological harm were shifting, but only gradually, and there remained a variety of ways that broad concepts of trauma were explored in the courtroom, from clear articulations, to muddy references, to outright ignoring it as a possibility. By investigating multiple forms of offending, change over time and different forms of prosecution, it becomes clear that ideas of trauma and sexual violence were complex and under negotiation across this period. Comparing trials from 1970 and 1980 – before and after the substantial impact of second-wave feminism, medical debates and sociopolitical tussles over legal reform – renders visible the ways that attitudes towards trauma shifted in response to these transformations.

The cases considered here are drawn from a database of sexual offences developed by Andy Kaladelfos and myself, created by research in the Supreme Court and Quarter Sessions records in New South Wales, Australia's largest jurisdiction. From 610 transcripts from the era under investigation here, I chose fifteen cases that engaged specifically, often deeply, with concepts of physical and psychological trauma.[6] These transcripts highlight multiple, often fragmented, attitudes to a victim's psychological harm, and allow close examination into the ways that trauma was understood and imagined in the workings of the court. The transcripts give access to the words spoken during the court process, including the voices of the complainant, the judge, lawyers, police officers, doctors, psychiatrists and, sometimes, the offender. The transcripts do not reveal body language, tone or reception but, despite this limitation, they offer a unique view into the courtroom and its machinations.[7] Here, I draw upon these sources to consider the ways 'trauma' was utilized – conceptually and pragmatically – by the law.

The 1970s and 1980s were a period of unparalleled change in social, political and legal attitudes towards sexual violence in Australia. Second-wave feminism drew attention to a range of women's issues, offering powerful critiques of domestic violence and rape.[8] Led by South Australia, socially progressive states began to consider law reform around sexual crimes, including the decriminalization of homosexuality, and the redefinition of rape. Across all Australian jurisdictions – in some more slowly than others – there was substantial change to the way sexual assault was understood as a crime, including the extension of rape to include acts beyond penile-vaginal penetration; new protections for complainants on the stand in an attempt to halt the re-traumatization of the victim; and the criminalization of rape in marriage.[9] These transformations were significant and pervasive, impacting on the public debates around sexual violence, as well as the policing and prosecution of sexual offences.

Trauma and sexual offences

Twin goals drove law reform: a desire for social and political change, and the hope of protecting victims from further harm and trauma. Yet, this application of ideas about trauma to sexual offending was relatively new. Medical concepts of psychological disturbance had formed slowly from the Victorian period, strengthened by theories about psychological harm and neurosis that had developed during and after the First World War.[10] Understandings of wartime psychological suffering were gendered, with a model of aetiology and treatment that did not extend to women and children, or even to men who did not serve.[11] Following British traditions, Australian doctors focused largely on somatic and anatomical explanations of disease, and the alienist – as psychiatrists were then known – remained a lowly form of medical practitioner largely confined to asylums. While the United States embraced psychiatry and psychoanalysis – and psychiatry was enshrined in the American criminal justice system with the medicalization of sexual offending in the interwar years[12] – in Australia, psychiatry was still establishing itself as a specialty, and psychoanalysis lay on the very fringes of the profession.[13] Thus psychiatric thinking about mental harm was not authoritative in Australia.

The broader invisibility of psychological trauma was replicated in instances of sexual assault. In the mid-twentieth century, medical care of both adult and child victims focused on penetration and subsequent physical injuries, such as bleeding or sexually transmitted disease, or the social impact, such as teenage pregnancy.[14] There was no discussion of psychological harm from sexual violence in contemporary medical journals, and psychiatry had yet to make a significant impact in the courtroom, with doctors in the 1950s regularly ignored and even disparaged while giving testimony.[15]

New understandings of trauma and sexual assault emerged slowly from the 1970s, including the important feminist intervention that rapists were motivated by power and violence, rather than by sex. This reframed sexual assault as an issue of masculine authority. Increasingly, feminist writers and activists spoke personally and politically about the impact of this sexual violence on women. Discussions about child sexual abuse were often initiated by feminist activists, rather than by social workers and health professionals involved in the new and emerging debates over child physical abuse and neglect. Working in rape crisis centres and women's refuges, feminists saw that adult women who had been abused as children suffered after-effects for decades. Feminists developed a narrative of ongoing trauma that continued well after the initial assault.[16] This powerful and pervasive commentary on the previously hidden harms of sexual offences was widely taken up in the mainstream media. From the late 1970s onwards, newspapers, women's magazines and journals, all featured articles on the trauma of rape, and focused increasingly on the psychological (rather than physical) harm from sexual abuse of children.[17]

The new ideas of trauma from sexual assault were – in theory – not necessarily gendered. Medical texts referred to the 'child', and in discussions about the psychological impact of trauma, gender was not necessarily discussed. However, evolving theories tended to highlight the trauma in the sexual assault of women and girls, rather than men and boys, for several reasons. First, feminist activists and scholars were central to writings about sexual violence in this time period, with women's liberationists focusing on male sexual assault of women and girls. With this centering of women by women, few male victims sought help at rape crisis centres or in government-run facilities.[18] Second, psychologists and family therapists working in a Freudian framework tended to highlight the importance of family violence against daughters, drawing on a legacy of psychoanalytic theories of the Oedipal Complex. In clinical care, too, these groups tended to treat women and girls, and wrote up case studies which focused on female victimization, especially within the family.[19] Third, females made up the majority of complainants in criminal trials, among both adults and children. Though Australia's Royal Commission into Institutional Responses to Child Sexual Abuse (2013–17) has uncovered a long history of sexual abuse against boys, most criminal trials involved sexual assault in non-institutional settings, and girls did make up the majority of victims. Ideologically, this divide served to frame ideas of trauma, vulnerability and compensation along gendered lines, with girls and women seen as most at risk of harm, though there was some acknowledgement that male children, if not adult men, could face trauma from sexual abuse.

Medicine, sexual assault and trauma

In Australia, a few articles on child sexual abuse began to appear in the *Medical Journal of Australia (MJA)* and other specialist journals in the mid-1970s, as part of a new interest in child abuse and neglect and to educate professionals working in the field. 'Rape trauma syndrome' had emerged in the international medical literature from the early 1970s.[20]

Medical studies in Australia tended to suggest that child sexual abuse was uncommon, and certainly far less a problem than physical abuse or neglect.[21] In these early works, there was scant medical discussion of the *trauma* of child sexual abuse. In 1978, child psychiatrist H. M. Connell authored an article in the *MJA* that was the only in-depth consideration of trauma and sexual assault over the decade.[22] Connell contextualized sexual abuse within other forms of abuse, neglect and familial dysfunction: where the mother was a sex worker, for instance, or when divorce had occurred.[23]

Connell's article reflects a tendency for children's emotional responses to be linked to family dysfunction, rather than to abuse.[24] Although the term 'trauma' is not used, Connell notes a potential for psychological harm as a consequence of abuse. First, he mentions that a treating doctor must be cognizant of 'psychological adjustment' after sexual abuse. He stresses that children must be told the assault was not their fault, but also warns against any excessive seclusion or pandering; the child was to return to normal activities as soon as possible. Second, Connell acknowledges that while 'most children survive this type of attack surprisingly well', there may be 'symptoms of anxiety' that persist after the first few weeks. For these children, he recommends a referral to a child psychiatric service. Connell suggests that a child's distress could be magnified by the parental responses to abuse, including 'blaming the child', which was 'not uncommon'. Yet, this was not necessarily tied to an idea of trauma from the abuse, or anything resembling what would later be called post-traumatic stress disorder. Instead, any distress a child might feel is seen as a function of poor management by families and healthcare professionals.

Influenced by a range of socio-medical issues, the medical literature in the 1980s encompassed changing ideas about trauma. Though there had been mixed responses to the psychological suffering felt by veterans from the conflict in Vietnam – and many veterans were accused of malingering – in an age of increasingly mixed media, it was difficult to ignore their distress.[25] Further, as Elizabeth Roberts-Pedersen notes, Australians were exposed to a range of other shocking public events across the 1970s and 1980s, such as the Granville rail disaster and the Ash Wednesday bushfires, and physicians examined men and women's individual and community responses to trauma and crisis.[26] These events coincided with new psychiatric theories, particularly the introduction of PTSD in the 1980 edition of the American Psychiatric Association's Diagnostic and Statistical Manual of Mental

Disorders, popularly known as the DSM-III. PTSD was understood to be a response to a significant and unusual trigger, a 'psychologically traumatic' life event that is 'generally outside the range of usual human experience', such as rape, assault, combat, natural disasters, accidents and torture.[27]

The new understanding of trauma would take time to filter into broader medical, social and legal practice. Even so, there was an intensified medical focus on some forms of sexual violence, in particular child sexual abuse. The 1980s saw a substantial rise in the number of *MJA* articles on child sexual abuse and, to a much lesser degree, sexual assault of adult women. This new literature did not necessarily name PTSD as a potential diagnosis, but authors explored psychological harm from sexual violence, and the mainstream media echoed these emerging concerns.[28] For example, in a 1985 article on child sexual abuse in the *Women's Day*, Dr Ferry Grunseit, head of the child abuse unit at Sydney's Royal Alexandra Hospital for Children, claimed that 'for the child [abuse] is always a terrible event and all the children become severely emotionally disturbed. With the best of care they may later survive psychologically, but many bear scars for life'.[29]

By the mid-1980s, both the medical and popular literature asserted that the true harm of sexual assault was psychological, and that trauma could be long-lasting with manifest impacts on all aspects of a child or woman's life. Over less than a decade it became hard to imagine sexual assault, especially of children, without considering the psychological impact in the short and long term. Nonetheless, these shifts were slow to infiltrate into the court, where the focus often remained on physical trauma and social issues including pregnancy and family breakdown.

Trauma in court

An individual's trauma was not the court's core business. Though feminists had clearly articulated the links between rape, violence and the trauma which ensued, feminist thinking did not intrude upon the courtroom. This reflected the function of the court: a trial or sentencing hearing focused on the accused, with the aim to establish whether the accused was guilty, and if so, to develop an appropriate response (a warning, monitoring, rehabilitation or punishment). The court attempted to ameliorate the complainant's injury in terms of an offender's punishment and, ultimately, protection of society from future harm. Psychological damage to the complainant could thus be rendered invisible. For example, in a 1970 sentencing hearing, a prisoner pleaded guilty to six charges of indecent assault on three girls aged eight to ten. Despite the guilty plea to sexual assault, the police witness told the court that the children had not been harmed. The police officer testified that the girls had afterwards shown precocious knowledge of sexual acts and sexualized language, but when pressed by the defence, the officer agreed that no harm had been done to them.[30] Harm was imagined in this instance in terms of penetrative sex only, and in particular the loss of virginity. The idea of harm did not include any aspects of psychological damage.

Harm continued to be imagined through the prism of physical violence, across the next decade. In July 1979, a twelve-year-old girl had truanted from school, and visited several pinball parlours around Sydney, ending up at the flat of a number of young men. Two men had sex with her; and the matter went to court in 1980. The original charges of rape were downgraded to carnal knowledge, and the men pleaded guilty, while one of the men also pleaded guilty to assault occasioning actual bodily harm from having punched the girl. Despite the guilty pleas, at sentencing Justice Cross spoke at length about the behaviour of the complainant, who had drunk wine, smoked marijuana, danced, done back-flips, and lain in bed semi-naked with another man. Despite her age, the girl was seen to act in adult ways, and thus was expected to be able to make mature decisions. Indeed, Justice Cross saw the punch laid by one offender as more serious than the non-consensual sex, asserting that

> the Courts cannot condone intercourse with girls so young that their consent is no defence to a charge of carnal knowledge. But it seems to me that if ever a girl went out of her way to put herself at risk, this girl did. The really serious aspect is perhaps not so much the intercourse as the blow to her head.[31]

The offender who had beaten the girl was given a custodial sentence, while the other, who was not seen as having been physically violent, was granted a good behaviour bond.[32]

In the 1970s, older ideas about the nature of harm coexisted in the courtroom with nascent connections between sexual assault and trauma, leading to tentative discussions of harm that went beyond the physical. Even at the start of the decade – before feminism's peak in Australia – one encounters acknowledgement of victims' fears and longer-term anxiety, often driven by the female victims themselves. In 1970, for example, a young schoolteacher was physically and sexually assaulted by two men. She was violently beaten, and the men had attempted to rape her. At trial, the Crown Prosecutor showed photographs of her face and leg, asking her to explain the consequences of the assault. She replied that she had been 'terribly nervous' since the assault, and had suffered from numbness of her face, which had required surgery. Here, the victim gives equal weight to physical and mental trauma. Her view of the assault highlights her psychological distress, in ways not seen in trials in the mid-century period.[33]

In another 1970 trial, the Crown Prosecutor wanted to present evidence of psychological harm to the complainant, who was the subject of an alleged gang rape by a group of 'bikies', one of whom stood accused of rape and indecent assault. After the alleged assault, the complainant had suffered a breakdown and entered a psychiatric facility. Witnesses who saw her just after the attack reported that she exhibited a flat affect and was non-responsive. The Crown claimed her shock and mental collapse was evidence that she had not consented to group sex. Further, he argued that her treatment in hospital was evidence of 'injury', and hence should be admitted, just as evidence of physical trauma would be admitted. The defence claimed evidence of psychological trauma was prejudicial to his client: after all, she may have been unstable before the sex. The question really became: Could it be proved that her breakdown was caused by rape? In this trial, the judge allowed psychiatric testimony of both a doctor and a nurse from a psychiatric clinic.[34]

Despite the embryonic acknowledgement of the potential for psychological harm evidenced in victim's statements, prosecution strategies and, sometimes, judges' actions, psychological harm remained underappreciated. In a 1970 sentencing hearing when the accused man had pleaded guilty to rape, the judge suggested that it went in the prisoner's favour that 'you did not cause the woman any physical injury of any consequence, although you handled her somewhat roughly before she recognised the futility of struggling further'.[35] The judge ignored psychological trauma, and trivialized the physical violation of the rape.

Other cases demonstrated the possibility of imagining psychological harm, but only for certain victims. Judges sometimes commented that women who were not virgins suffered less as a result of sexual assault than chaste women. In the sentencing at one rape case in 1970, for example, the judge suggested that, while the victim may have been 'terrified' at the time of the assault, she was 'not subjected to suffer the same traumatic after-effects that some more innocent girl might have suffered'.[36] Such attitudes allowed psychological harm to be reframed in moral terms, with trauma imagined as mediated not only by a woman's sexual experience but also by factors such as her mental health history, class and race.[37]

Trauma could also be obscured when the complainant was a child. Children and youths were regularly presented as willing participants – even instigators – of sexual activity, though they were well under the legal age of consent. In 1970, for example, a young man pleaded guilty to the indecent assault of three girls aged six, eight and nine years. At the sentencing, defence counsel raised the issue of consent with the police officer giving testimony:

> Q. In respect to these girls, I appreciate they were very young and, perhaps, were not capable of consenting or objecting too much, but in fact they did not object to this behaviour.
> A. That is correct.[38]

Legally, the charge of indecent assault on a female under the age of sixteen did not concern consent. The only question for the court was the victim's age and proven sexual activity. Defence lawyers nonetheless raised the issue of consent in an attempt to mitigate the crime, and to reduce any sentence. The emphasis on a child's consent, however, also minimized the victim's trauma and psychological harm.

In the early 1970s, the clearest articulation of psychological harm occurred in cases when the sexual assault was considered particularly deviant. In one hearing that shocked courtroom officials, a prisoner had pleaded guilty to six charges of indecent assault on three girls under the age of ten. He had shown the children print pornography, including images of bestiality. Judge Brennan expressed his concern at the sentencing:

> It is not physical harm that is done to a little girl like this; it is the psychological harm. If, in effect, her introduction to sex is something that is nauseating and disgusting and repellent, then you put a warp into her which should never be . . . such conduct as yours is one of the worst things that can be done by human beings to other human beings.[39]

But it was largely in cases of extreme pathology on the part of the offender that the issue of psychological trauma to the child was consistently mentioned. Ironically, it was the accused's actions, not the victim's feelings or responses, that defined trauma in these instances.

By 1980, in line with the changing socio-medical attitudes towards trauma, there was an emerging acknowledgement of the victim's psychological experience, though a victim-focus remained peripheral to the court. One example, with adult female complainants, illustrates many of the complexities. In 1980, the New South Wales Supreme Court found one man guilty of five counts of rape, and two counts of intent to rape, in separate instances on different women. In each case, he had broken into the home of the adult female victim when she was alone, or with small children. He entered a guilty plea on all charges, though he did not acknowledge one charge of anal rape, which the prosecutors later dropped.[40] During the sentencing hearing, the judge called for short explanations of each of the assaults from the police, giving details of the time, place and a summary of the attack itself. The women had all been threatened, and when a child was in the next room, the offender had warned he would harm, kill, or, in one case, rape the child. Most of the women had not been beaten, though one woman's attempt to fight off her attacker had led to him beating her about the head. As the police officers went through the cases, they generally made brief note of the psychological impact of the assault. The court was told that one woman, for instance, 'was not physically injured as a result of this assault. However, she did suffer severe mental stress for some time after'. Another woman had to be hospitalized for her physical assault and mental distress, while a third was hospitalized for five weeks for medical treatment for her psychological trauma. In all but one of the seven charges, the police briefly mentioned the psychological harm to the victim; the judge also mentioned the mental stress to the women when summing up.[41] Even so, the evidence of trauma was always minimal in the scheme of the sentencing hearing. Despite the guilty plea, defence counsel actively aimed to limit the court's reflection on women's ongoing psychological trauma, to minimize the impact on the offender's sentence.[42]

Across the decade, other trials showed only rudimentary ideas about harm, or, at worst, an open resistance to the possibility of trauma. Court psychiatrists could reduce complex cases of familial sexual assault to a simplistic model where family reintegration – rather than the welfare of the victim – was the priority.[43] For example, in one case in 1980, a stepfather pleaded guilty to carnal knowledge and indecent assault of his stepdaughter, aged nine. It was a complicated case: the offender had been sexually abused as a child, and had a long history of sexual issues, including incest and bestiality. He had long suffered from nervousness and anxiety, for which he had been treated on and off for years. He explained to the judge that he had turned to his stepdaughter after his wife lost interest in sex.[44] As one psychiatrist noted, the offender had a high sex drive, and he did not necessarily control it: it would be difficult to guarantee that he would not re-offend. But a second psychiatrist told the court that the best option would be family re-unification, suggesting that the family enter therapy to control the sexual excesses and abuse of power of a confirmed sexual abuser. While the judge sentenced the prisoner to gaol, the case illustrates a psychiatric model focused less on child victims than on compelling families to conform to social norms even when the breakdown of the family unit is beyond question.

Compensating for trauma

Perhaps the one instance where trauma and harm were clearly and powerfully articulated inside the courtroom was in court proceedings for compensation. In 1967, New South Wales introduced laws that allowed crime victims to seek compensation from an attacker. This was part of a broader attempt to better support survivors and acknowledge their often considerable injuries. While the laws were most often used for violent street crime, under the legislation both adult and child complainants could seek compensation for sexual assault.[45] In the sample of New South Wales cases, the complainants were, overwhelmingly, adult women.[46] This gender imbalance perhaps reflects the realities of the compensation process, which required a courtroom attestation of physical and mental harm. Male victims may not have been willing or able to endure so publicly casting themselves as victims, given the social norms about male physical prowess and virility. Economic factors may also have shaped the gender distribution of complainants, as women's lower pay and reduced career opportunities may have created financial strains that forced women to court.

This sample suggests that, once the decision was made to seek compensation, cases were likely to be successful. Sometimes monetary compensation was granted even in cases where the defendant had been found not guilty beyond reasonable doubt. In these instances, the judge was provided with, or called for, additional information that had not been admissible at trial. The burden of proof was thus lower in compensation claims than in the criminal court.

As with all courtroom interactions, the court and judiciary retained strict protocols concerning evidence from the complainant, and the 'performance' of the hearing remained (ideally) formal and unemotional. Issues of economic value, such as hospital costs and lost wages, predominated, but the process allowed for testimony, however fragmented, of a victim's experience in her or his own voice. The victim's testimony was buttressed by the provision of medical evidence. The claimant used testimony from a psychiatrist or psychologist to assert a claim to trauma on medical grounds. It also provided an opportunity to reiterate the various forms of harm to the complainant, this time in the authoritative language of medico-legal terminology.

In 1970, for instance, a male offender was brought to court for a sentencing hearing and a compensation claim. He had pleaded guilty to the rape of an adult woman, having broken into her home, threatened her with a knife, and raped her. The judge sentenced the offender to eight years, with no chance of parole for four years. In her compensation claim, the complainant was asked to give a few details of the impact of the crime. She focused on the costs of medical bills. She had contracted a sexually transmitted disease from the assault which required treatment, and a visit to a psychiatrist.[47] The complainant had no report from the psychiatrist, as he demanded full payment of the $40 consultation fee before he would consider writing a report, which would cost a further $20. In this period before Medicaid or Medicare, there would be no government assistance for the complainant and she could not afford these bills.

When the judge questioned her on the opinion of the psychiatrist, she replied, 'He said that I was in a shocking state; that I just had to try and forget it, and I just cannot'.[48] There was no detailed examination of her mental trauma or psychological outcomes, the complainant herself was not questioned in any detail and no psychiatric report was requested. The judge acknowledged her 'injury' and 'loss', directing payment of $600, of which $80 was for medical bills and the rest for her 'injury' suffered from the assault. In 1970, even in a claim for compensation, the specifics of her trauma and psychological state were never clearly delineated. Harm could be acknowledged, but not fully investigated, and there was little acknowledgement of the serious trauma from sexual assault.

Within a decade, however, the discussion in the court over compensation allowed for a more thorough dialogue over a victim's trauma. In a case in the Supreme Court in 1980, a young woman sought compensation from her stepfather, who had been found guilty of her rape in 1976, when she was fifteen years old. The Crown first called psychiatrist Sheila Metcalf, who had seen the complainant on two occasions in 1979–80. Dr Metcalf gave evidence that the complainant's condition had 'deteriorated' during this time, and 'that she was physically more depressed and had become more aware of her suffering and of her difficulties'. Dr Metcalf suggested the depression was a 'direct result' of the sexual assault. The attack itself was complicated by her familial situation, as her mother had rejected her after the rape, and she had moved in with her grandparents, who were able to give her only limited financial support. The doctor revealed that the victim had attempted suicide on more than one occasion, and feared her attacker would seek her out on his release.

The judge questioned the psychiatrist on the complainant's ability to work, and to enter into marriage in the future. He also asked her about the need for treatment: How much therapy would the victim require to improve her depression? Though the complainant did not give evidence in person in the court, the judge clearly had access to her records and the details from the trial. At the judgement, he quoted at great length from the psychiatric reports submitted by Dr Metcalf, and gave his own interpretation of her suffering, her inability to work and her need for psychiatric therapy. He granted her the full $10,000 available under New South Wales law, stating that he could not provide further support for therapy, as he had already granted her the maximum payable in compensation for her injury. This case shows the way that, by 1980, the suffering and trauma of familial sexual violence was more fully understood both in theory and practice, and within the lesser evidentiary requirements of the compensation claim, trauma could be acknowledged and interpreted to gain an outcome favourable to the victim.

By the mid-to-late 1980s, such testimony followed a well-worn path, and began in some ways to resemble what would later become formal, written victim impact statements (which are presented after a conviction and before the sentencing).[49] In one rape case, heard in 1985, a man pleaded guilty to a sexual assault on a young woman, who made a claim for compensation. The complainant gave distressing evidence that she had been unable to work since the sexual assault. She had been a well-known, well-paid model, with advertising contracts to major clients and covers on prominent women's magazines. During her modelling career, she earned over $700 a week; now she was looking for work as a waitress, with a wage of only about $220 per week. Her claim over lost earnings was, however, complicated by a leg injury unrelated to the sexual assault, which had also prevented her from working. Yet she argued that as her leg mended, she could not return to modelling, as she was haunted by memories of the event, and uneasy with men. Her dread prevented her from working with photographers and their assistants: 'being in the situation with someone that I don't know it is a bit frightening to me now'.[50]

The victim also noted a number of other psychological impacts, including severe insomnia and significant familial breakdown after the assault. The offender had previously been her mother's boyfriend, and her mother had chosen to maintain a friendship with him, rather than with her daughter. The estrangement from her mother also meant the victim was not allowed to see her younger brother. Her emotional suffering can be glimpsed when she testified that that her mother 'obviously cares for him more than me'. As well as her oral testimony, she had also provided a written affidavit, where she detailed her experiences of being 'extremely upset', 'nervous', 'cried', 'suffered' and 'distressed'.

Psychiatrist Dr Keith Mayne provided a report to the judge, stating that the victim had suffered a 'moderately severe reactive depressive illness' after the attack, and that 'for several months she was distressed and rarely went out of the house', while suffering from insomnia that required taking sleeping tablets. Mayne concluded that her depression had lifted a little, but that, fearing another assault, she remained 'nervous and anxious'. Subsequent reports confirmed her continuing mental health struggles, with Dr Mayne asserting that 'he would not expect her to be fit for work for some considerable time'. In response, the judge awarded the survivor $17,385 in damages: $5,000 for lost income; $12,000 to compensate for her 'psychiatric condition'; and $385 for the costs of her affidavit. Though PTSD was never mentioned, her trauma was acknowledged, and there was some limited movement towards reparation.

Conclusions: Trauma and violence

This chapter has charted changing attitudes towards trauma and sexual offending from the 1970s into the 1980s. Beginning with an overview of social and medical thinking about trauma, it shows that this era saw growing interest in the concept of trauma. By highlighting the tightening definition of trauma, showing the new medical conceptualization of trauma and the concomitant increased public awareness through feminist and media agitation, I demonstrate that trauma and harm became integrated into understandings of sexual assault in the 1970s and 1980s. This was undoubtedly a period of rapid escalation in knowledge about trauma and gendered violence.

It is not, however, a simple, triumphalist history of progress. These ideas were slow to filter through to the courtroom. In trials and sentencing hearings, ideas of trauma to the complainant were rarely broached, and when they were raised there was a certain ambivalence. Sometimes, trauma was acknowledged; at other times it was overlooked or minimized through discussions of the complainant's own actions. A victim's trauma was articulated only in compensation claims, which were a small part of the court's business. In the main, trauma was overlooked, even in cases in which it might seem most obvious, such as those involving the sexual assault of children. Further, victims were given little opportunity to articulate their own trauma in the courtroom. Their voices are all but absent. Despite substantial shifts in the theorization and medicalization of trauma and sexual violence in this time period, the court response lagged considerably.

Notes

1. State Records New South Wales (hereafter, NSW): Court Reporting Branch; NRS 2713, Criminal Transcripts, District Court, *R v Appin*, 1980 (hereafter 'Criminal Transcripts'). All witnesses, aside from state officials, have been given pseudonyms or rendered nameless.
2. On the 'good guy', see Jane Gilmore, *Fixed It: Violence and the Representation of Women in the Media* (Sydney: Viking, 2019), 111–17.
3. Criminal Transcripts, District Court, *R v Appin*, 1980.
4. Criminal Transcripts, District Court, *R v Appin*, 1980.
5. See Lisa Featherstone, '"Children in a terrible state": Understandings of Trauma and Child Sexual Assault in 1970s and 1980s Australia', *Journal of Australian Studies* 42, no. 2 (2018): 164–76.
6. Other cases did deal with trauma, at least in comparison with research undergone on similar transcripts from New South Wales in the 1950s. See Lisa Featherstone and Andy Kaladelfos, *Sex Crimes in the Fifties* (Melbourne: Melbourne University Publishing, 2015), 15–16.
7. For more information on the collection of trial transcripts, see Featherstone and Kaladelfos, *Sex Crimes in the Fifties*, 8–10.
8. Susan Brownmiller, *Against Our Will: Men, Women, and Rape* (New York: Simon and Schuster, 1975); and Robin Morgan, *Going Too Far* (New York: Vintage, 1978). In Australia, see among others, 'Rape Crisis', *Vashti's Voice*, March 1974, 1; and 'Women Against Rape', *Sydney Women's Liberation Newsletter*, May 1976, 8.
9. Gail Mason, 'Reforming the Law of Rape: Incursions into the Masculinist Sanctum', in *Sex, Power and Justice: Historical Perspectives on Law in Australia*, ed. Diane Kirkby (Melbourne: Oxford University Press, 1990), 50–69; Lisa Featherstone, '"That's what being a woman is for": Opposition to Marital Rape Law Reform in Late Twentieth Century Australia', *Gender and History* 29, no. 1 (2017): 87–103; and Deidre O'Connor, 'Rape Law Reform– The Australian Experience Part 1', *Criminal Law Journal* 1 (1977): 305–19.
10. On pre-First World War theories, see Mark S. Micale and Paul Lerner, eds, *Traumatic Pasts: History, Psychiatry, and Trauma in the Modern Age, 1870– 1920* (Cambridge: Cambridge University Press, 2001) and Effie Karageorgos, 'Mental Illness, Masculinity, and the Australian Soldier: Military Psychiatry from South Africa to the First World War', *Health and History* 20, no. 2 (2018): 10–29. On the meanings of shell shock in the First World War, see George Mosse, 'Shell-Shock as a Social Disease', *Journal of Contemporary History* 35, no. 1 (2000): 101–8; and Jay Winter, 'Shell Shock and the Cultural History of the Great War', *Journal of Contemporary History* 35, no. 1 (2000): 7–11. On Australia, see Stephen Garton, 'Freud versus the Rat: Understanding

Shell Shock in World War I', *Australian Cultural History* 16–17 (1997–8): 45–59; and Joanna Bourke, 'Shell Shock and Australian Soldiers in the Great War', *Sabretache* 36, no. 3 (1995): 3–10.

11 Joseph Pugliese, 'The Gendered Figuring of the Dysfunctional Serviceman in the Discourses of Military Psychiatry', in *Gender and War: Australians at War in the Twentieth Century*, ed. Joy Damousi and Marilyn Lake (Cambridge: Cambridge University Press, 1995), 162–77.

12 George Chauncey, 'The Postwar Sex Crime Panic', in *True Stories from the American Past*, ed. William Graebner (New York: McGraw-Hill, 1993), 160–78; and Estelle Freedman, '"Uncontrolled Desires": The Response to the Sexual Psychopath, 1920–1960', in *Passion and Power: Sexuality in History*, ed. K. Peiss and C. Simmons (Philadelphia, PA: Temple University Press, 1989), 199–225.

13 See Stephen Garton, 'The Rise of the Therapeutic State: Psychiatry and the System of Criminal Jurisdiction in New South Wales, 1890-1940', *Australian Journal of Politics and History* 32, no. 3 (1986): 378–88; Stephen Garton, 'The Melancholy Years: Psychiatry in New South Wales, 1900–1940', in *Australian Welfare History: Critical Essays,* ed. Richard Kennedy (Melbourne: Macmillan, 1982), 138–66; and Joy Damousi, *Freud in the Antipodes: A Cultural History of Psychoanalysis in Australia* (Sydney: UNSW Press, 2005), 26–35.

14 Featherstone and Kaladelfos, *Sex Crimes*, 14.

15 Featherstone and Kaladelfos, *Sex Crimes*, 191–212.

16 Cathy Waldby, *Breaking the Silence: A Report based upon the Findings of the Women Against Incest Phone-in Survey* (Sydney: Women Against Incest, 1985), 4; and 'Sexual Abuse of Children', *WEL-Informed*, August 1978, 6.

17 See, for example, Anne Summers, 'How Women Are Trained', *National Times*, 29 November 1976, 6; Rosemary Munday, 'Rape The Victims', *Australian Women's Weekly* (hereafter, *AWW*), 3 May 1978, 18; Jaqueline Rees, 'Researching the Hidden Crime of Family Violence', *AWW*, 13 December 1978, 21; 'Judge: Parents must be Alert', *West Australian*, 18 October 1980; 'Sexual Abuse of Children "Prevalent"', *Courier Mail*, 17 October 1980; Derryn Hinch, 'Saving 2,000 Youngsters', *The Sun-Herald* 21 July 1985; 'It's Evil', *The Sun*, 5 July 1985; 'Teacher Admits to 2000 Sex Attacks', *Daily Mirror*, 5 July 1985; 'Incest – the Hidden Crime You Want Brought into the Open', *AWW*, 30 April 1980, 16–25; 'Sexual Abuse: Could Your Child be a Victim?' *Woman's Day*, 2 December 1985; and 'Silence on Child Abuse Alleged', *Sydney Morning Herald*, 25 September 1980.

18 Nascent men's rights groups were quick to suggest that men were excluded from the counselling and help available at feminist rape crisis centres. See Elizabeth Evatt, Felix Arnott and Anne Deveson, *Royal Commission on Human Relationships: Final Report*, Vol. 5 (Canberra: Australian Government Publishing Service, 1977), 185; and Elizabeth Evatt, *Royal Commission on Human Relationships: Official Transcript of Proceedings*, Vol. 1 (Sydney: Sydney Commonwealth Reporting Service, 1974–6), 444.

19 R. W. Medlicott, 'Parent-Child Incest', *Australian and New Zealand Journal of Psychiatry* 1, no. 4 (1967): 180; NSW, *Report of the NSW Child Sexual*

Assault Task Force (Sydney: Government Printer, 1985), 19; Beth Pengally, 'A Feminist Critique of the Idea of Incest as a Product of the Dysfunctional Family', in *Incest and the Community: Australian Perspectives*, ed. Penelope Hetherington (Perth: University of Western Australia, 1991), 184–97; and Family Law Council, *Child Sexual Abuse Report September 1988* (Canberra: Commonwealth Government, 1988), 12–13.

20. A. W. Burgess and L. L. Holmstrom, 'Rape-Trauma Syndrome', *The American Journal of Psychiatry* 131, no. 9 (1974): 981–6.
21. M. G. Ryan, A. A. Davis and R. K. Oates, 'One Hundred and Eighty-Seven Cases of Child Abuse and Neglect', *Medical Journal Australia* (hereafter, *MJA*) 2, no. 19 (1977): 623–8.
22. HM Connell, 'The Wider Spectrum of Child Abuse', *MJA* 2, no. 8 (1978): 391–2.
23. Connell, 'The Wider Spectrum', 392.
24. Connell, 'The Wider Spectrum, 392; Connell, 'Incest: A Family Problem', *MJA* 2, no. 8 (1978): 362; and Gordon Parker, 'Incest', *MJA* 1, no. 13 (1974): 490.
25. For complex readings of Vietnam veterans and responses to trauma, see Stephen Garton, *The Cost of War: Australians Return* (Melbourne: Oxford University Press, 1996), 229–54; and Christina Twomey, 'Trauma and the Reinvigoration of Anzac: An Argument', *History Australia* 10, no. 3 (2013): 85–105.
26. Elizabeth Roberts-Pedersen, 'Introduction: Trauma and Its Histories in Australia', *Health and History* 20, no. 2 (2018): 2.
27. *Diagnostic and Statistical Manual of Mental Disorders, Third Volume* (hereafter, *DSM-III*) (Washington, DC: American Psychiatric Association, 1980), third printing 1987, 36. See also Matthew J. Friedman, 'PTSD History and Overview'. https://www.ptsd.va.gov/professional/treat/essentials/history_ptsd.asp.
28. Ferry Grunseit, 'Child Abuse', *MJA* 2, no. 11 (1983): 527; Robert Adler, 'Doctors and the Sexually Abused Child', *MJA* 145, no. 7 (1986): 305; and Helen R. Winefield and Sally N. Castell-McGregor, 'Experiences and Views of General Practitioners', *MJA* 145, no. 7 (1986): 312.
29. 'Sexual Abuse: Could Your Child be a Victim?' *Woman's Day*, 2 December 1985.
30. Criminal Transcripts, Quarter Sessions, *R v Danes*, 1970.
31. Criminal Transcripts, Supreme Court, *R v T Rainweather and Richardson*, 1980.
32. Criminal Transcripts, Supreme Court, *R v Rainweather and Richardson*, 1980.
33. Criminal Transcripts, Quarter Sessions, *R v Giblin and Smith*, 1970.
34. Criminal Transcripts, Supreme Court, *R v Leverson*, 1970.
35. Criminal Transcripts, Supreme Court, *R v Eliopoulos*, 1970.
36. Criminal Transcripts, Supreme Court, *R v Patrickson*, 1970.
37. See discussions on the 'ideal' victim, Susan Estrich, *Real Rape: How the Legal System Victimizes Women Who Say No* (Cambridge, MA: Harvard University Press, 1987); and Kim Stevenson, 'Unequivocal Victims: The Historical Roots

of the Mystification of the Female Complainant in Rape Cases', *Feminist Legal Studies* 8, no. 3 (2000): 343–66.
38   Criminal Transcripts, Quarter Sessions, *R v Reed*, 1970.
39   Criminal Transcripts, Quarter Sessions, *R v Davies*, 1970.
40   Criminal Transcripts, Supreme Court, *R v West*, 1980.
41   Criminal Transcripts, Supreme Court, *R v West*, 1980.
42   Criminal Transcripts, Supreme Court, *R v West*, 1980.
43   Pengally, 'A Feminist Critique', 184–97.
44   Criminal Transcripts, Supreme Court, *R v Esposito*, 1980.
45   Duncan Chappell, 'Compensating Australian Victims of Crime', *Australian Law Journal* 41 (1967): 3–11.
46   This is an incomplete sample of transcripts; it may be that some compensation claims were not recorded and archived.
47   Criminal Transcripts, Supreme Court, *R v Jewett*, 1970.
48   Criminal Transcripts, Supreme Court, *R v Jewett*, 1970.
49   In New South Wales, victim impact statements were introduced in 1999.
50   Criminal Transcripts, Supreme Court, *R v Castlemaine*, 1985.

Works cited

'A Justifiable Risk?' *WEL-informed*, September 1979.
Adler, Robert. 'Doctors and the Sexually Abused Child'. *Medical Journal of Australia* 145, no. 7 (1986): 305.
American Psychiatric Association. *Diagnostic and Statistical Manual of Mental Disorders, Third Volume*. Washington, DC: American Psychiatric Association, third printing 1987.
Bourke, Joanna. 'Shell Shock and Australian Soldiers in the Great War'. *Sabretache* 36, no. 3 (1995): 3–10.
Brownmiller, Susan. *Against Our Will: Men, Women, and Rape*. New York: Simon and Schuster, 1975.
Burgess, A. W. and L. L. Holmstrom, 'Rape-trauma Syndrome'. *The American Journal of Psychiatry* 131, no. 9 (1974): 981–6.
Chappell, Duncan. 'Compensating Australian Victims of Crime'. *Australian Law Journal* 41 (1967): 3–11.
Chauncey, George. 'The Postwar Sex Crime Panic', in *True Stories from the American Past*, edited by William Graebner, 160–78. New York: McGraw-Hill, 1993.
Connell, H. M. 'Incest: A Family Problem'. *Medical Journal of Australia* 2, no. 8 (1978): 362.
Connell, H. M. 'The Wider Spectrum of Child Abuse'. *Medical Journal of Australia* 2, no. 8 (1978): 391–2.
Damousi, Joy. *Freud in the Antipodes: A Cultural History of Psychoanalysis in Australia*. Sydney: UNSW Press, 2005.
Estrich, Susan. *Real Rape: How the Legal System Victimizes Women Who Say No*. Cambridge, MA: Harvard University Press, 1987.

Evatt, Elizabeth. *Royal Commission on Human Relationships: Official Transcript of Proceedings*, Vol. 1. Sydney: Sydney Commonwealth Reporting Service, 1974–6.

Evatt, Felix Arnott and Anne Deveson. *Royal Commission on Human Relationships: Final Report*, Vol. 5. Canberra: Australian Government Publishing Service, 1977.

Family Law Council. *Child Sexual Abuse Report September 1988*. Canberra: Commonwealth Government, 1988.

Featherstone, Lisa. '"Children in a terrible state": Understandings of Trauma and Child Sexual Assault in 1970s and 1980s Australia'. *Journal of Australian Studies* 42, no. 2 (2018): 164–76.

Featherstone, Lisa. '"That's what being a woman is for": Opposition to Marital Rape Law Reform in Late Twentieth Century Australia'. *Gender and History* 29, no. 1 (2017): 87–103.

Featherstone, Lisa and Andy Kaladelfos. *Sex Crimes in the Fifties*. Melbourne: Melbourne University Publishing, 2015.

Freedman, Estelle. '"Uncontrolled Desires": The Response to the Sexual Psychopath, 1920–1960', in *Passion and Power: Sexuality in History*, edited by K. Peiss and C. Simmons, 199–225. Philadelphia, PA: Temple University Press, 1989.

Friedman, Matthew J. 'PTSD History and Overview'. https://www.ptsd.va.gov/professional/treat/essentials/history_ptsd.asp.

Garton, Stephen. *The Cost of War: Australians Return*. Melbourne: Oxford University Press, 1996.

Garton, Stephen. 'Freud and the Psychiatrists: The Australian Debate 1900 to 1940', in *Intellectual Movements and Australian Society*, edited by Brian Head and James Walter, 170–87. Melbourne: Oxford University Press, 1988.

Garton, Stephen. 'Freud versus the Rat: Understanding Shell Shock in World War I'. *Australian Cultural History* 16–17 (1997–98): 45–59.

Garton, Stephen. 'The Melancholy Years: Psychiatry in New South Wales, 1900–1940', in *Australian Welfare History: Critical Essays*, edited by Richard Kennedy, 138–66. Melbourne: Macmillan, 1982.

Garton, Stephen. 'The Rise of the Therapeutic State: Psychiatry and the System of Criminal Jurisdiction in New South Wales, 1890–1940'. *Australian Journal of Politics and History* 32, no. 3 (1986): 378–88.

Gilmore, Jane. *Fixed It: Violence and the Representation of Women in the Media*. Sydney: Viking, 2019.

Grunseit, Ferry. 'Child Abuse'. *Medical Journal of Australia* 2, no. 11 (1983): 527–8.

Hinch, Derryn. 'Saving 2,000 Youngsters'. *The Sun-Herald*, 21 July 1985.

'Incest – the Hidden Crime You want Brought into the Open'. *Australian Women's Weekly*, 30 April 1980.

'It's Evil'. *The Sun*, 5 July 1985.

'Judge: Parents must be Alert'. *West Australian*, 18 October 1980.

Karageorgos, Effie. 'Mental Illness, Masculinity, and the Australian Soldier: Military Psychiatry from South Africa to the First World War'. *Health and History* 20, no. 2 (2018): 10–29.

Mason, Gail. 'Reforming the Law of Rape: Incursions into the Masculinist Sanctum', in *Sex, Power and Justice: Historical Perspectives on Law in Australia*, edited by Diane Kirkby, 50–69. Melbourne: Oxford University Press, 1990.

Medlicott, R. W. 'Parent-Child Incest'. *Australian and New Zealand Journal of Psychiatry* 1, no. 4 (1967): 180–7.

Micale, Mark S. and Paul Lerner, eds. *Traumatic Pasts: History, Psychiatry, and Trauma in the Modern Age, 1870–1920*. Cambridge: Cambridge University Press, 2001.
Morgan, Robin. *Going Too Far*. New York: Vintage, 1978.
Mosse, George. 'Shell-Shock as a Social Disease'. *Journal of Contemporary History* 35, no. 1 (2000): 101–8.
Munday, Rosemary. 'Rape the Victims'. *Australian Women's Weekly*, 3 May 1978.
New South Wales. *Report of the NSW Child Sexual Assault Task Force*. Sydney: Government Printer, 1985.
O'Connor, Deidre. 'Rape Law Reform – The Australian Experience Part 1'. *Criminal Law Journal* 1 (1977): 305–19.
Parker, Gordon. 'Incest'. *Medical Journal of Australia* 1, no. 13 (1974): 488–90.
Pengally, Beth. 'A Feminist Critique of the Idea of Incest as a Product of the Dysfunctional Family', in *Incest and the Community: Australian Perspectives*, edited by Penelope Hetherington, 184–97. Perth: University of Western Australia, 1991.
Pugliese, Joseph. 'The Gendered Figuring of the Dysfunctional Serviceman in the Discourses of Military Psychiatry', in *Gender and War: Australians at War in the Twentieth Century*, edited by Joy Damousi and Marilyn Lake, 162–77. Cambridge: Cambridge University Press, 1995.
'Rape Crisis'. *Vashti's Voice*, March 1974.
Rees, Jaqueline. 'Researching the Hidden Crime of Family Violence'. *Australian Women's Weekly*, 13 December 1978.
Roberts-Pedersen, Elizabeth. 'Introduction: Trauma and Its Histories in Australia'. *Health and History* 20, no. 2 (2018): 1–9.
Ryan, M. G., A. A. Davis and R. K. Oates, 'One Hundred and Eighty-Seven Cases of Child Abuse and Neglect'. *Medical Journal Australia* 2, no. 19 (1977): 623–8.
'Sexual Abuse: Could Your Child be a Victim?' *Woman's Day*, 2 December 1985.
'Sexual Abuse of Children'. *WEL-Informed*, August 1978.
'Sexual Abuse of Children "Prevalent"'. *Courier Mail*, 17 October 1980.
'Silence on Child Abuse Alleged'. *Sydney Morning Herald*, 25 September 1980.
State Records New South Wales, Court Reporting Branch; NRS 2713, Criminal Transcripts.
Stevenson, Kim. 'Unequivocal Victims: The Historical Roots of the Mystification of the Female Complainant in Rape Cases'. *Feminist Legal Studies* 8, no. 3 (2000): 343–66.
Summers, Anne. 'How Women Are Trained'. *National Times*, 29 November 1976.
'Teacher Admits to 2000 Sex Attacks'. *Daily Mirror*, 5 July 1985.
Twomey, Christina. 'Trauma and the Reinvigoration of Anzac: An Argument'. *History Australia* 10, no. 3 (2013): 85–105.
Waldby, Cathy. *Breaking the Silence: A Report Based Upon the Findings of the Women Against Incest Phone-in Survey*. Sydney: Women Against Incest, 1985.
Winefield, Helen R. and Sally N. Castell-McGregor. 'Experiences and Views of General Practitioners'. *Medical Journal of Australia* 145, no. 7 (1986): 311–13.
Winter, Jay. 'Shell Shock and the Cultural History of the Great War'. *Journal of Contemporary History* 35, no. 1 (2000): 7–11.
'Women against Rape'. *Sydney Women's Liberation Newsletter*, May 1976.

9

Embodied, psychological and gendered trauma in militarized Kampala (Uganda)

Benjamin Twagira

Gendered trauma provides an important lens through which to explore militarized histories. Not only is militarization a traumatic experience because the process rapidly transforms people's daily lives; it often also goes hand in hand with significant violence. This chapter considers gendered trauma in Uganda between 1966 and 1986, a period that was characterized by hyper-militarization. Drawing from oral histories of people who lived in the Kampala neighbourhood of Mengo, I explore the embodied and psychological impact of militarization. Both women and men feared bodily harm; women especially lived with the very real fear of being sexually assaulted. The interviews I conducted highlight how Kampalans dealt with militarization's long-lasting impact on the body, people's discomfort with changing norms around gender and the ongoing challenges of processing memories from this time. Like other authors who have contributed to this collection I conceive of 'trauma' broadly as a narrative of human suffering. I will show that gender was central to how Kampalans and Ugandans experienced and now narrate the degradations and suffering wrought by militarized violence.

In post-colonial Africa, militarism has been gendered in particular ways. Amina Mama and Margo Okazawa-Rey have noted how the military regimes that dominated the post-colonial scene on the continent were driven by 'restorative masculinity', suggesting that gendered trauma is a deeply ingrained aspect of militarization.[1] Writing about Idi Amin's regime in Uganda, Alicia Decker similarly observed that gendered imagery and discourses suffused the entire state apparatus.[2] While centring gender as a mechanism for narrating violence against communities, I bear in mind the role of culture in guiding how societies process traumatic experiences. As Christopher Taylor has noted, living through a violent experience can lead to 'ethno-maladies' resembling a well-known category such as post-traumatic syndrome disorder (PTSD).[3] Even as I follow in the footsteps of other scholars across the globe who have long observed that the phenomena of militarism and militarization possess a strong gender component, the narrative of trauma as gendered still roots this analysis in the local context of the patrilineal social structures specific to central and southern Uganda.[4]

Of blood, body parts and psychosis: Traumatic narratives in post-colonial Uganda

On that day I was not on duty and I heard just people saying that they saw a body in a sack somewhere, and later on they said it was Kay Amin who was cut. But on that day I was not on duty, so I did not know [how she died].[5]

When Amin came to power in the 1970s, we were new to Mengo. We would see a [sedan] car that visited our neighbours regularly. We quickly found out that it was because that family's daughter had married a soldier. We never met this soldier, but we heard that he worked in the General Service Unit or the State Research Bureau.[6] When Uganda experienced economic hardship and everyday commodities became scarce this car would bring to this family food and other goods that were not otherwise available to other citizens. The car would pull up, and soldiers would pull open the [trunk] and it would be full of stuff that were scarce at the time, such as cooking oil, soap, salt, and even rice. There is one day I remember vividly; in September 1977, the same car pulled up and the men went straight inside. They looked like they were in a rush, and then we saw blood dripping from the trunk of the car.[7]

These quotations from Kampalans are drawn from two major sources of testimony about this period in Ugandan history. The first vignette is from one of several testimonies contained in the *Report of the Commission of Inquiry into Violations of Human Rights: Verbatim Record of the Proceedings* (1995). The commission was established in 1987 by the government under President Yoweri Museveni, who came to power in 1986 after a five-year military rebellion. The commission was the new government's attempt to address the violence that had plagued the country since the mid-1960s. The second account is from my own interviews conducted between 2013 and 2014 (and on a follow-up research trip in summer 2016). Demonstrating how Ugandans utilized tropes of gendered trauma to characterize their experiences living under militarization, these interviews form the primary source base for this chapter. No doubt the interviewees' willingness to speak was due in part to the passing of time, and the commission that the government had set up, together with other activities Museveni's government undertook to separate itself from the previous regimes that ruled Uganda until 1986. A new generation of young people, who came of age after 1986, was also seeking to learn about these experiences, and often young people listened in during interviews with those who lived through militarization or who had memories of the era obtained from relatives. Finally, and importantly, my fieldwork coincided with political developments that made the 1970s especially relevant in popular discussions of Ugandan politics. Idi Amin's son, Hussein Lumumba Amin was in the news and about to run for political office. In a widely publicized and contentious event, Uganda hosted Israeli prime minister Benjamin Netanyahu to commemorate the fortieth anniversary of the 'raid on Entebbe'. All of this led to public interest in – and, indeed, desire to share experiences about – the post-colonial period preceding 1986, making it an opportune moment to collect oral histories of the era of militarization.

Oral history has been an indispensable methodology since the founding of the field of African history.[8] Histories of militarization and violence are especially reliant on this approach. The military destroyed documents about its activities, and any spared documents were often looted in the chaos that followed the fall of governments.[9] Luise White warns of the danger of taking as historical fact stories that circulated about soldiers in several versions, for example, as rumour and gossip. Instead, she suggests reading these stories as 'drawn from a store of historical allusions that have been kept alive and given new and renewed meanings by the gossip and arguments of diverse social groups'.[10] Ugandans used the powerful visual images of blood and body parts – bodies in sacks and in car boots – to formulate arguments about militarization. Not only did these stories emphasize that trauma is itself gendered, they also circulated throughout the neighbourhood to warn people of soldiers who could cut off women's body parts and who were dangerous as in-laws. Such stories also emphasized – and even exaggerated – the notion that soldiers degraded men as men.

The Ugandan army in Kampala

Prior to independence from Britain in 1962, men from the north dominated the Ugandan army. During the late nineteenth- and throughout the first quarter of the twentieth century, colonial governments drew their military and law enforcement officers from societies they had labelled martial and warlike. Despite this belief in military prowess, British colonial officials sought out men from decentralized societies that were likely to follow orders. The colonial government preferred to recruit from northern Luo societies, and set physical requirements, such as a minimum height of 5 feet 8 inches (173 centimetres), unlikely to be met by southern Bantu societies.[11] As a consequence, northerners comprised 61 per cent of the Ugandan army after independence.[12]

Despite northern dominance of the army and the police force, the centre of the colonial government and economic heart of the Ugandan Protectorate were located in the southern kingdom of Buganda.[13] Since the late nineteenth century, Mengo had been the seat of the Buganda kingdom.[14] The city of Kampala emerged from this early urban centre. In 1900, the kingdom's representatives negotiated an arrangement with British colonial agents to preserve the kingdom within the new Ugandan Protectorate. Throughout the colonial period, Africans were the primary residents of the Mengo neighbourhood, and the kingdom remained the main authority governing them. While the capital of the Ugandan Protectorate was based in Entebbe, about 35 kilometres away, Kampala was its commercial centre. After independence in 1962, the capital was transferred to Kampala.

The post-independence arrangement, whereby Buganda remained a semi-autonomous entity within the new nation of Uganda, led to conflict between the kingdom and the new central government. In May 1966, President Milton Obote ordered an attack on the kingdom and dissolved all of Uganda's traditional monarchies.[15] The king of Buganda fled the country, and shortly thereafter the government turned several of the kingdom's spaces located in the Mengo neighbourhood into military installations. The imposing administration building that once acted as the kingdom's parliament became the headquarters of the army (Republic House). The enormous palace and the Ministry of Public Works building became an army barracks and shop. From the mid-1960s, Mengo was always overflowing with military personnel, since it served as both their place of work and residence.

The main challenge to Obote's power originated from the Kampala area, and he trusted soldiers from his northern home region to manage this problem. Even after independence, most high-ranking officers were northerners, as were most members of the ruling party and its leadership. The few southern soldiers in the military were likely to be based in upcountry barracks. Fears that the exiled king continued to be popular led the army in the city to continually target urban men for arrests and other forms of abuse. Furthermore, military leaders and soldiers were not equipped to understand the complex sociological makeup of urban society.

Successive governments faced constant armed rebellion, which meant that Kampala was in a state of constant warfare, and dangerous, for most of the next two decades. The soldiers stationed there initially defended Obote's government, as Uganda transitioned to a highly authoritarian state. Later, the army enforced the dictatorship of Idi Amin after he mounted a successful coup against Obote in 1971. When the forces loyal to Obote fought and overthrew Idi Amin in 1979, the army maintained the same urban bases in

Mengo until the late 1990s, when the government under President Yoweri Kaguta Museveni finally removed them.[16]

Women, militarization and gendered trauma

In recounting the daily trauma of living alongside the military, Kampalans rooted their memories in specific historical, social, cultural and highly gendered contexts. Though they lived through traumatic experiences as individual women and men, socially and culturally familiar tropes dominated narratives of these experiences. Individual encounters with soldiers could result in bodily harm, but such incidents also circulated as narratives and acted as a warning to others.

As a result of violent incidents – either actual or rumoured – Kampalan women emphasized both mental and bodily preparation as they carried out everyday life with soldiers as their neighbours. For example, Julian Namusisi worked in the Katwe neighbourhood and on her way home she had to regularly walk past groups of soldiers. She enacted for me how while going home in the night, she pretended to be a *musambwa*, a word used to mean a spirit medium. In other words, she would stiffly walk in a straight line and not respond to anyone who spoke to her. 'These soldiers did not understand Buganda culture, and they thought spirit mediums came out in the night and walked among us'.[17] Others recalled the era of militarization in quite visceral terms. For example, when referring to the constant anticipation of an attack, women especially used the phrase *okusika ediiba* (We tightened our skin) emphasizing the psychological terror of living in a militarized neighbourhood. *Okusika ediiba* can be best interpreted as an ongoing state of terrorizing dread. Interviewees repeatedly stated that fear continued to haunt them. For example, rumours about soldiers cutting people piece by piece, starting with the ears, until they died, made Rita Nakitende's family flee their home for about a week. For Kampalans, this constant anticipation that they would be physically tortured, with the fear that went along with it, was deeply traumatizing.

The potential for violence was a particular cause of concern, and caution was often expressed through nicknames given to soldiers who acted impetuously and who could physically assault innocent civilians or even murder. One military officer was named after Uganda's major psychiatric hospital, *Butabika*, because his violence was notable for its extreme cruelty and indiscriminate nature.[18] In contrast, those who were likely to commit sexual assault were spoken about in whispers and hushed tones. Compounding women's anxiety, sexual assault victims could not go to the police or any other authority, since the neighbourhood was under military occupation. The nearest police station was about a little more than two miles away, and even then soldiers were above police jurisdiction.

Moreover, it was common for soldiers to force women prisoners to have sex with them in exchange for their release. Interviewees told me that women were often arrested for flimsy or invented reasons. In the late 1970s, Joyce Mugenyi, a trader in the Mengo market, was arrested for allegedly selling rotten goods. She knew her arrest was based on false pretences, since the soldier who picked her up did not give her any further information about the charge. She was taken to the Lubiri (palace) barracks and put into a cell with other female prisoners. She discovered that one of the two guards, Rony, frequented her market stand and was friendly to her. He informed her that the arresting soldier was not a good man (he was 'bad' – meaning that he was known to rape prisoners). Some soldiers brought women into these cells and then later in the night picked these women up and raped them. Joyce spent two nights in the cell in Lubiri barracks, and Rony hid her during the night. When the arresting soldier came for her, Rony and the other guard told him an officer had picked her up.[19] On the third day, the arresting soldier gave up and released Joyce. Other female interviewees also testified that women who rejected advances from soldiers were often arrested on trumped up charges.[20] In multiple interviews, women emphasized 'bad' soldiers. 'Whenever new soldiers came to the city [through regular rotations] friendly soldiers told us who was "bad" in this group so we know who to avoid'.[21]

Elsewhere I demonstrate how women in militarized Kampala played a more elevated role than men, especially as the faces of homesteads. They emerged as protectors of family property, and of members of households, especially men.[22] Nonetheless, fears of being sexually abused also guided how they protected themselves, their daughters and other relatives, and their belongings. Scholars of warfare have documented the ways in which rape has been used as a weapon of war.[23] As Helen Moffett has suggested, rape is also 'a narrative of social control'.[24] Listening to Kampalans describe the processes they went through to protect themselves and their loved ones, and the lives they led during this period, one understands that sexual violence, including rape, was a form of social control. More significantly, however, these examples demonstrate how bodily and psychological trauma were intertwined.

Indeed, rumours circulated in the Mengo neighbourhood that if an urban man was found in the company of any woman – be it a daughter, sister, wife or girlfriend – soldiers would abuse the woman or girl simply for being with a potential rebel. These rumours varied significantly from terrible acts of sexual violence to the most horrific and unimaginable acts. This is why men went into hiding as soon as they heard the oft high-pitched call 'Abasajja baabo bazze' (there they come; the men have come). Richard Kigozi recalled that sometimes these neighbourhood announcements turned out to be false alarms. 'Regardless of whether soldiers were indeed approaching and whether their intention was to dishonour us by raping women did not matter; we just scattered and ran into hiding'.[25] Thus, men feared inciting sexual attacks on wives, daughters and other relatives residing with them, and lamented the psychological trauma caused by this experience.

Kampala women did, in fact, walk a 'fine line' when they interacted with the military. Physical harm was a daily source of anxiety for women. They also feared breaching new and shifting laws. Sexual assault was widely used as a pretext for punishment and retaliation against women throughout the era of militarization. For example, Alicia Decker details how national policies that targeted women's morality often resulted in rape as punishment for those women who allegedly transgressed the moral line.[26] In Mengo, morality campaigns took effect shortly after the soldiers moved into the neighbourhood. Examples include the ban on miniskirts and regulations targeting alcohol drinking. Soldiers bore responsibility for enforcing such campaigns and had the licence to sexually assault transgressors.[27]

Both existing and proposed policies had a significant impact on how all urban women lived their everyday lives. Moreover, these policies – whether implemented or not – created an ongoing fear of violation for women. For example, when Idi Amin's government debated whether to expel single women from the city as a policy to curb prostitution, women quickly modified their homes and even looks to give a different impression. In preparation for any number of soldiers approaching a homestead, single women, especially, hurriedly created evidence either that they were married or that they were older than they actually were. Interviewees told me that when women heard that a soldier or soldiers were approaching their home, they would display men's clothes in a prominent location before they even knew the soldiers' objective.[28] Grace Nakawanga, who was single and lived in Mengo by herself at the time, purchased some men's clothing, which she hung by the door. 'If the [soldiers] came to check they would discover that I am married and leave without bothering me'.[29] Others displayed male relatives' clothes they might have had in their possession. All in all, these burdensome policies had a long-lasting impact on the women, especially as they created an atmosphere of fear of bodily harm.

Gendered violence can also be discerned when we consider the experiences of very young women and girls in militarized Kampala. Even being a school-age young woman communicated to the soldiers that 'you were available', and women informants used this characterization more broadly to imply a continuum from sexual violence to courtship and marriage. Women of all ages were preoccupied by the fear of sexual violence. 'It was important [for us] to make a statement to them that we are not available'.[30] At the same time that men were vulnerable, women who were younger felt protected if they had a man living with them. 'The moment we heard that soldiers were doing that with young women I asked a male relative to come and stay with me here. His clothes were displayed so that if you stepped into our house, you saw them before you saw mine'.[31]

Reporting sexual assault was difficult for women in militarized Kampala. To report any violation would bring shame to themselves and to their families while there was nothing anybody could do to the soldier or soldiers in question. In Mengo, the nearest police station, the Old Kampala Police Station, was three to four miles (4.8 to 6.4 kilometres) away. Many Mengo residents noted that this police station responded to their cases only if it did not involve soldiers. Rita Sanyu confirmed, 'If you told them that I am reporting a case involving a soldier, they told you we cannot help you. Go talk to the military. They are above us'.[32] Many feared that reporting such incidents might lead to retaliatory rapes. Married women hesitated to report such cases because they feared that their husbands would not agree that it was assault, and if a husband interpreted the rape as consensual sex, he could end the marriage. A Mengo resident described such a situation that occurred between a neighbour's wife and an army soldier:

> A high-ranking officer came to the home of our neighbour and point-blank told him that he was in love with his wife. 'You and me love the same woman'. Can you imagine someone telling you that they love your wife, in your own home? The officer then drove away leaving everyone in shock. . . . A few days later when the husband was at work and the woman was at home, the soldier came back and took the wife away. He brought her back another day later. The husband was enraged. He accused his wife of cooking up a plan to sleep with two men. She denied it and was just ashamed. The husband did not know what to do. He took his wife to her home village (divorced her) and also fled Kampala, fearing the army officer.[33]

As this example makes clear, soldiers embedded in neighbourhoods and vested with almost unchecked power threatened family stability. The man who narrated this and other, similar stories intended to demonstrate how soldiers disrespected and abused the honour of urban men. From their perspective, rape perverted the meanings of marriage and threatened men's masculinity. More crucially, these stories demonstrate the dilemmas that female victims faced, with significant social ramifications.[34] Not only was a woman physically harmed, but it was also a deeply psychologically torturing experience for her. Her experience explains why women often did not share assaults by soldiers. The fact that her husband 'sent her to her home village' was an outcome that many married women must have worked hard to avoid by not reporting incidents to their husbands or others.

The frequent incidence of sexual assault also raised ethical and moral questions about marriages between Mengo women and the soldiers. Some interviewees readily admitted that a daughter or relative was abducted and forced into a marriage. For example, Sifa Sentamu's neighbours knew that her daughter was married to a soldier, but what they did not know was that she had initially been kidnapped. On the surface, Sifa's daughter looked happy in her marriage with the soldier with whom she had three children while he was stationed in Mengo. Sifa recalled how some people were even jealous of their family because they had access to consumer goods that were largely unavailable during the economic crisis under Idi Amin's government:

> Our neighbours were envious of us. Every week our [son]-in-law would send bars of soap, packets of sugar, rice, and so on. A car would park by our door and his escorts would offload [commodities] as our neighbours looked on. We tried to share but you cannot satisfy everyone's need. People were gossiping about us. As a mother I could not even talk to my friends about how my daughter came to marry this soldier. I told my daughter to be strong.[35]

The situation that Sifa's family found themselves in demonstrates another element of these marriages. Soldiers – especially those in Idi Amin's army – had access to goods that were scarce, and there was social pressure on the women married to them to share the goods with neighbours. The pressure also played a role in making women continue to live with their likely kidnappers. Unlike Sifa's daughter, there were some Kampala women who married soldiers willingly. Many women described how military men often made better husbands than urban civilian men. For example, some interviewees pointed out how military husbands were good providers to both the wife and family and often gave the wife more independence than other men did. Still, the family and social complications surrounding rape meant that some women either stayed with their rapists or kept quiet about incidents of sexual assault.

For Ganda traditionalists and monarchists, who constituted many of the residents of the Mengo neighbourhood, marriage to a northerner, especially one connected to the government, symbolized betrayal. While some women broke the social code of not marrying anybody connected to the Milton Obote regime, others exercised their personal freedoms and entered into relationships with soldiers or northern men. However, these marriages often entailed scorn and shame for these women and their families. When the topic of marriage to soldiers or politicians associated with the expulsion of the king came up, Kampalans pointed to the example of the wife of Milton Obote himself, Miria Kalule Obote, who was a Ganda woman with family in Kampala. Informants emphasized to me how Miria traumatized and caused an irreparable psychological effect on her family. Normally having a daughter who marries a person of high profile, such as the president, entails significant intangible and tangible benefits, including economically. Yet, Miria's father is remembered for having ridden a 'poor man's bicycle' even as his daughter was married to the president of the republic. According to Kampalans' account about this marriage, Miria's father declined to take any bridewealth from Obote, and refused to accept an offer of a vehicle to drive him around from the president. According to Kampalans, 'he rode his bicycle around like a madman because of his daughter's marriage' to an avowed enemy of Buganda.[36]

Kampalan women paid attention to the image – both real and metaphorical – that they projected. Mothers dressed their young daughters in a way to even hide that they were girls. They picked family clothing based on the criteria of disguising children: they dressed pubescent girls as young boys and teenage girls to look like older and married women. As Jaja Kezia described the extraordinary anxiety mothers felt about their children, she turned and looked in the direction where a now older daughter Rita Namusisi was sitting, and said: 'This one was the most difficult child to disguise. I remember when the soldiers became really bad; she was just beginning to go through puberty, and we kept hearing the bad things that were happening to children of that age'. Then Kezia observed that

> Rita was the most difficult to dress. No matter how you disguised her she looked like a girl. She had a beautiful face with a skin that clearly looked like a beautiful girl, and spoke like a young woman. I made her put on a [cap], boy pants and baggy T-shirts and sternly warned her never to say one word to strangers, because if she ever spoke she sounded older than she really was.[37]

Thus, women were constantly anxious about what type of body they and their daughters projected through voice and shape. Rita, listening to her mother talk about her childhood, jokingly observed: 'I was a beautiful girl and my mother turned me into an ugly boy'.

Masculinity and narratives of gendered trauma in Kampala

Masculine authority, once invested in rulers of the kingdom, transferred to the army after 1966. The southern men who saw themselves as representatives of Ugandan national prestige and cosmopolitanism now transferred their energies to political activism, at odds with the northern-dominated army that controlled their daily lives. The rivalry between the two groups of men, exacerbated by the displacement of one by the other, sat at the heart of the trauma, bodily and psychological, experienced by men in Kampala.

Kampalan men's memories of urban militarization centre around this sentiment of vulnerability to soldiers, which shaped a traumatic response. In order to appreciate its resonance, one has to consider both Uganda's colonial histories and Buganda's recent past. It is possible that the colonial reliance on 'martial races' from the northern Luo for military recruitment engrained a sense of emasculation for southern (and, in this case especially, Ganda) men.[38] At the same time, the fact that the Ganda were perceived as the urban and even 'modern' ethnic group in the Protectorate led to resentment among other men, especially northerners. As a result of these potent tensions,

Kampalan men knew that an encounter with the army in their homes would likely end in violence if a husband was present, as opposed to when the army found a woman alone. The soldiers, who often walked in groups of three to five when going on urban missions, also feared that the civilian men they encountered had military training and would attack them.[39]

Urban men remembered their interactions with members of the military stationed in their neighbourhoods as being especially fraught at the household level. In a patrilineal culture, one function of the head of a household in the region is to receive and host guests who visit a homestead. The militarization of the city challenged this gendered source of respectability. Soldiers made incursions into the civilian population and homesteads for several reasons: they came to patrol neighbourhoods, loot, enforce the draconian laws, spy on the population or cause other forms of trouble. The presence of civilian men turned these encounters into a dangerous mix. Many of my interviewees felt that 'men have their ways that challenged the soldiers'.[40] They repeated this sentiment over and over to highlight the vulnerability and powerlessness that urban men felt in homestead encounters. Kampalan men lamented that the arrival of soldiers in their neighbourhoods eroded their masculinity.

Kampalans heard and shared stories about how soldiers emasculated the men in general, but even more so especially in their homesteads. Over time, a perception and consensus emerged that when soldiers 'visited' homes, it was better for the men not to be present. During the day women and younger children stood outside watching every direction and if soldiers appeared they would run and inform the men of their household to run. For example, one Mengo resident, David Sebugwawo, recalled how women homestead watchers would tell their husbands, sons, fathers, brothers or brothers-in-law with urgency 'There they are! The men have come!' and then added disbelievingly, 'it was as if they were the men and we were not'.[41]

One way of attacking men's honour and 'making men suffer' was to show them that they could not protect 'their women'.[42] Soldiers interpreted men's presence as a challenge to the soldiers' manhood and authority, and as a result, the soldiers allegedly punished the men by raping 'their women'. In one such story from Mengo, the husband was ordered to sit with his young children and watch the soldiers as they raped his wife. That night he hanged himself. The shame, according to many accounts, overwhelmed him. How could he face his family and the wider community the next day? A man whose honour had been abused in this way was better off dead. In accounts like this one little is said about the women victims. The vulnerability and psychological torture of the men, on the other hand, is highlighted. 'We were hearing that the soldiers will rape your wife in your presence just to make you suffer. We would therefore hide from the soldiers, to make sure that they do not humiliate us'.[43] Such incidents show both how soldiers attacked urban men's masculine honour and how a socially constructed sense of vulnerability emerged during this period. As a result, these men would understandably flee their homes in order to escape being humiliated.

Soldiers humiliated and abused men's honour as a way of attacking urban men *as men*. 'Abuse of one's honour' was a recurring theme during my interviews with both women and men in Mengo. Interviewees used the word *okujooga* to describe what the soldiers did to them. For example, an interviewee would say: 'Abo abasajjabatujooga', meaning 'those men abused our honour'. Many of the men of Kampala were middle-class, husbands, urban, cosmopolitan and held well-known social positions, which gave them a presumed respectability.[44] But when the soldiers entered their neighbourhood, they set about showing urban men that they could not take this respectability for granted any more. Thus, when interviewees told me that soldiers abused urban men's honour (*kujooga*) they meant that the soldiers denied urban men's claim – or right – to respectability.[45]

Abuse of men's honour was a systemic political approach. Soldiers at roadblocks stripped men of their ties and working jackets, asking them 'Onafikiri wewe ni raisi Obote?' (Do you think you are President Obote?), implying that certain embodied displays of urban masculinity belonged only to the head of state. The presence of soldiers in the city exacerbated existing tensions rooted in class. Certain cosmopolitan and professional attire marked men as completely urban and possessing a desired status, differentiating them from other men, such as rural, urban poor or even members of the military. Soldiers were rejecting this cosmopolitan claim to masculinity. Furthermore, Idi Amin enjoyed humiliating men, a point made by Henry Kyemba, a former minister in Amin's government who fled the country and published a memoir about his experience of working for the dictator. Kyemba vividly describes how a group of men were forced to kneel before President Amin, as a way of humiliating them.[46]

When urban men were required to kneel at roadblocks or in other encounters with soldiers, it was especially humiliating because of the significant gender and class implications that kneeling before someone implies in the region. In Buganda, for example, as an obligatory sign of respect, women and girls kneel when greeting or serving men, and junior women do so for senior women.[47] Men prostrated only before the king, which in part made public displays of men kneeling for either Idi Amin or the soldiers an act of expropriating legitimate power. When the Amin regime was toppled in 1979, a local monthly magazine celebrated the departure of his soldiers emphasizing how Idi Amin and his military abused people's honour.[48] President Amin also humiliated African leaders with whom he disagreed, often by attacking their manhood. For example, after a fallout with the Zambian president, Kenneth Kaunda, Amin insulted him by calling the Zambian head of state a woman 'who cannot satisfy her man'.[49] While Idi Amin saw himself in opposition to the Western man and to African leaders, the soldiers saw themselves in opposition to the urban man: the perceived household head, potential rebel and member of the political opposition. One of the men's responses was to constantly be on the lookout and to flee their homes.

The psychological impact of such humiliation was deep and led to men further second-guessing their actions in order to feel safe. For example, male household heads ceded power to their wives or other women in the urban household. In addition to running away when soldiers approached, men also avoided responding to a knock at the door. Whenever someone knocked, at night or during the day, the wife would be the one responsible for opening the door, and the men would stand on alert, ready to run. John Kizito lived near the road that soldiers frequently used as they left or went to the so-called army shop station. He worked at a woodwork shop as a carpenter in Katwe, a bustling part of Kampala about four miles from his home. He recalled how he preferred being at work rather than at his home, where he was always fearful that soldiers might come to the house. Whenever soldiers came, John's wife would give him the time to dress, and then, as if to reveal a long-held secret, he added: 'I had my spot [in the house] that was kept secret. Maybe my wife knew about it, but nobody else'.[50] John would stand in this spot and listen as his wife greeted the stranger at the door. If it sounded serious, if the soldiers were looking for men or they wanted to search the house for contraband or rebels, for example, John would slip out of the house through the back door. Others climbed into the attic and hid there. To do so they contorted their bodies to spread their legs to fit in a tight space between the ceiling and the roof. Over and over again men left their wives, mothers, sisters and sisters-in-law to negotiate with the military. In recounting such incidents, Kampalan men emphasized the feeling that militarization robbed them of their manhood.

Male interviewees described with sadness how they lost control of their households because of the military presence. Zakariya Mukiibi was a teacher at the Catholic high school in the Rubaga neighbourhood throughout this period and still lives in the rectangular shaped house that was built in the early 1960s. The house's main door faces other old homes in the neighbourhood. Today when he sits by his door he has the vantage point of identifying anyone approaching his part of the neighbourhood through a long winding passageway between the concrete walls of other buildings. He remembered that during the era of militarization, 'my wife sat here', indicating the cemented veranda, and 'I would be sitting back there', pointing behind a curtain that separates the living room and the rooms beyond.[51] His wife would warn him whenever she saw the soldiers approaching, and Zakariya would exit through a back door. He described to me that he thought women were better with soldiers than men. He lowered his body, nearly on all fours but certainly with his knees fully on the ground to demonstrate how women would genuflect to the soldiers, something men could not do, he explained. 'If you as a man were stopped and changed the posture of your body, for example trying to beg, they would hit you with the butt of the gun, and say, "*wacha matatizo wewe* [don't you dare make trouble"]'. Men also viewed this necessity to genuflect or behave weakly in the presence of soldiers as emasculating.[52] Women in Mengo, on the other hand, were culturally required to lower their bodies while greeting men or older women. Ordinarily, this position was and remains a marker of women's weak social status, but in militarized Kampala, it sometimes became an asset they used to protect themselves and loved ones.[53] Kampalans repeatedly used bodily gestures to demonstrate how they could survive encounters with soldiers.

Men in militarized Kampala were in a quandary. On Mengo and Kampala streets, they had to look and act a certain way in order to survive everyday encounters with the soldiers. Certain self-representations that people had long associated with urban masculinity made men military targets. In interviews, men described the kind of man who did not threaten the soldiers. They were inarticulate, timid and visibly rural. Men described how they made themselves look dirty in order not to attract attention: 'I always put dirt on my shoes on purpose, and kept my *kiwi* [shoe polish] and a brush at work', remembered Benon Semambo. Benon recalled how he and other urban men disguised themselves to project a certain look on Kampala streets, but such disguises were either difficult to pull off or too humiliating in homesteads.[54]

The very way that Kampalans explained the removal of the king and Bugandan royal institutions from Mengo emphasized the psychological trauma that it caused to an entire urban community. 'Removing the king from our kingdom', many Baganda repeatedly claimed, 'is like removing a person's head. That person is no longer a real human being. We need our king to feel like we are full humans'.[55] This sentiment confirms that the removal of the king was generally traumatizing. Above all, the removal of the king was a gendered act because the king was thought of as the husband of all women of the land and as the father of all men and women in Buganda. His title was *sabasajja* [the father of fathers]. In essence, he was the husband of all of Buganda. The removal of the king was such a political sticking point that when Idi Amin came to power, he returned the body of the king, who had died in exile in 1969, to the country for official burial.

Both bodily and psychological trauma characterized family relationships at the household level as well. For example, Julius Kitende noted that his father drank more alcohol and became abusive during military rule. Perhaps Julius' experience and observation that his father drank more during this time was a result of the emergence of the *'the beer of the beds'* – a new kind of premises that replaced public bars for Kampalans. With the entry of soldiers into urban neighbourhoods, bars became dangerous as they turned into sites of abuses by soldiers. The new premises were homes where customers drank alcohol and stayed overnight and walked home in the morning. While these home-based bars saved Kampalans from likely violent encounters with soldiers in the night, they also encouraged unmitigated consumption of alcohol. In another example, Samson Semambo's aunt did not have children of her own. As a result, she had made him her heir, and had already given him a plot of land, even as a teen. During this period, he noticed that she was changing. Her moods became volatile. She began to tell him that she regretted giving him the plot. More troubling for Samson, however, was that she began to physically abuse the children who lived with her, including him, by regularly beating them. Samson's theory is that the presence of soldiers, and their abuses, changed something in his elderly aunt. Prior to this, she had been sweet and non-violent. 'She had never lifted her finger as a reaction to what we did. She had never beaten us before until after the king was expelled'. Yet, after 1966, she began rethinking her will and who ought to inherit her property and began doubting if her 'son' should be the one to inherit the property. It is no wonder then that Kampalans connect militarization to significant psychological impact on them and their families. While some of these impacts are hard to confirm, like the changes in Samson's aunt, others can be directly linked to the military presence. The drinking premises were clearly spaces where men went to relax and recuperate their masculinity without the fear of being abused by soldiers. Yet, the practice of drinking all night also led to conflict at the household level.[56]

Conclusion

Local conditions, context, beliefs, social structures and values are essential to understand how trauma manifests itself. Even though there is no exact word for trauma in Luganda or other languages spoken in Kampala, I chose to analyse my interviewees' stories as narratives of trauma. When asked about their experiences of militarization, Kampala's women and men narrated this history as one that led to a great deal of bodily harm and ongoing psychological trauma. Moreover, they emphasized that militarization targeted men as men and women as women. For the men, emasculation caused psychological torture and trauma. Women, in contrast, were more likely to be distressed by the constant anticipation, which led to the changing of their looks and identities in the hope of living through an encounter. Both the women and men described these psychological traumas as embodied experiences. In many ways this is why the rumours and gossip about military encounters were so visceral in their narration and tended to emphasize bodily harm and bodily reaction. Stated that way, rumour and gossip acted not only as a narrative of ongoing suffering but also as a necessary warning to the urban public. Rumours that circulated included those about soldiers who arrived with blood dripping from their cars; soldiers who made fathers watch as their wives and daughters were raped; or soldiers who forced men to greet them by taking the posture that is culturally expected of the women. Many Kampalans cited such stories to explain why they ran into hiding. Gendered trauma is therefore a useful tool for capturing the experience and narrative of extreme suffering.

Acknowledgements

I thank Laura Ann Twagira, Susan E. Gagliardi and the anonymous reviewer for their insightful comments.

Notes

1. Amina Mama and Margo Okazawa-Rey, 'Editorial: Militarism, Conflict and Women's Activism', *Feminist Africa*, no. 10 (2008): 1–8.
2. Alicia C. Decker, *In Idi Amin's Shadow: Women, Gender, and Militarism in Uganda* (Athens: Ohio University Press, 2014), 10.
3. Christopher C. Taylor, 'Ihahamuka—PTSD in Post-Genocidal Rwanda: Culture, Continuity and Change in Rwandan Therapeutics', in *African Medical Pluralism*, ed. William C. Olsen and Carolyn Sargent (Bloomington: Indiana University Press, 2017), 170–84.
4. See Decker, *In Idi Amin's Shadow*; and Cynthia Enloe, *Maneuvers: The International Politics of Militarizing Women's Lives* (Los Angeles: University of California Press, 2000).
5. For examples of violations, abuses and assassinations that the military orchestrated not only in Kampala but also across the country, see the report by a commission set up by Yoweri Museveni's government after 1986. The testimonies from this commission exist in a fifteen-volume report: Republic of Uganda, *Report of the Commission of Inquiry into Violations of Human Rights: Verbatim Record of Proceedings* (Kampala: The Government of Uganda, 1995), Volume 4, 3566.
6. These are institutions that were notorious and infamous for violence in post-colonial Uganda.
7. Interview by author with Sara Chope in Mengo, Kampala, Uganda, 12 September 2014.
8. Jan Vansina, *Oral Tradition as History* (1965; repr. Madison: University of Wisconsin Press, 1985); Luise White, *Speaking with Vampires: Rumor and History in Colonial Africa* (Berkeley: University of California Press, 2000); and Luise S. White, Stephan Miescher and David William Cohen, eds, *African Words, African Voices: Critical Practices in Oral History* (Bloomington: Indiana University Press, 2001).
9. Decker, *In Idi Amin's Shadow*, 175.
10. See White, *Speaking with Vampires*, 82.
11. David Killingray, *Fighting for Britain: African Soldiers in the Second World War* (Rochester, NY: James Currey, 2010), 40–2.
12. Amii Omara-Otunnu, *Politics and the Military in Uganda (1890-1985)* (New York: St. Martin's Press, 1987).
13. Buganda refers to the territory where the people collectively called Baganda live; one person from Buganda is Muganda. The adjective Ganda is used as

a reference for everything *of* Buganda, such as a Ganda woman or man, or Ganda culture.

14 Richard Reid and Henri Medard, 'Merchants, Missions and the Remaking of the Urban Environment in Buganda, C. 1840-90', in *Africa's Urban Past*, ed. David M. Anderson and Richard Rathbone (Portsmouth, NH: Heinemann, 2000), 98–108.

15 Uganda as an entity came into being in the late nineteenth century when British colonial agents brought together disparate societies, some of which had centralized kingdom institutions. The colonial government did not displace these kingdoms after conquest, but, rather, worked through them to administer the territory, in what was called 'indirect rule'. By 1966, when the then post-independence government abolished traditional monarchies, Buganda Kingdom was one of a handful of kingdoms in the country. Others included Bunyoro, Ankole and Toro kingdoms.

16 For examples of violations, abuses and assassinations that the military orchestrated not only in Kampala but also across the country, see the report by a commission set up by Yoweri Museveni's government after 1986. The testimonies from this commission exist in a fifteen-volume report: Republic of Uganda, *Report of the Commission of Inquiry into Violations of Human Rights: Verbatim Record of Proceedings*.

17 Interview by author with Julia Namusisi, in Nakulabye, Kampala, Uganda, 20 September 2014.

18 Interview by author with Rita Sanyu, in Mengo, Kampala, Uganda, 25 April 2014.

19 Interview by author with Joyce Mugenyi, in Nansana, Kampala, Uganda, 24 March 2014.

20 This was still going on even in the 1990s. See 'Soldiers Named in Sex Scandal with Suspects', *The Monitor*, 5 December 2001, n.p.

21 See interview with Joyce Mugenyi.

22 See Benjamin Twagira, '"The Men Have Come": Gender and Militarisation in Kampala, 1966-86', *Gender & History* 28, no. 3 (2016): 813–32.

23 Lisa F. Jackson (dir.), 'The Greatest Silence: Rape in the Congo', 1:16 (Women Make Movies, 2008). See also Alexandra Stiglmayer, *Mass Rape: The War against Women in Bosnia-Herzegovina* (Lincoln: University of Nebraska Press, 1994); and Yasmin Saikia, *Women, War, and the Making of Bangladesh: Remembering 1971* (Durham, NC: Duke University Press, 2011).

24 Helen Moffett, '"These Women, They Force Us to Rape Them": Rape as Narrative of Social Control in Post-Apartheid South Africa', *Journal of Southern African Studies* 32, no. 1 (2015): 129–44.

25 Interview by author with Richard Kigozi, in Mengo, Kampala, Uganda, 13 May 2014.

26 Decker, *In Idi Amin's Shadow*, 136.

27 My interviewees constantly mentioned fashion as a frequent pretext for rape. See also Grace Bantebya-Kyomuhendo and Marjorie Keniston McIntosh,

Women, Work and Domestic Virtue in Uganda, 1900-2003 (Athens: Ohio University Press, 2006), 163; and Decker, *In Idi Amin's Shadow*, 72–3.

28 Interview by author with Nakato Kimuli, in Mengo, Kampala, Uganda, 20 April 2014. Interview by author with Sylvia Mutebi, in Mengo, Kampala, Uganda, 4 February 2014. Interview by author with Grace Namutebi, in Mengo, Kampala, Uganda, 15 February 2014.

29 Interview by author with Grace Nakawanga, in Mengo, Kampala, Uganda, 3 May 2014.

30 Interview by author with Judith Nandawula, in Mengo, Kampala, Uganda, 16 May 2014.

31 Interview by author with Judith Nandawula, in Mengo, Kampala, Uganda, 16 May 2014.

32 Interview by author with Rita Sanyu, in Mengo, Kampala, Uganda, 21 April 2014.

33 Interview by author with David Jingo, in Mengo, Kampala, Uganda, 25 May 2014.

34 For more examples, see Benjamin Twagira, '*Bajeemi* Urbanites: Roots of Social Resilience in Militarized Kampala, Ca. 1966-1986' (PhD dissertation, Boston University, 2017).

35 Interview by author with Sifa Sentamu, in Nakulaybe, Kampala, Uganda, 12 May 2014.

36 Interview by author with Mary Kezia, in Mengo, Kampala, Uganda, 21 September 2014.

37 Interview by author with Jaja Kezia, in Mengo, Kampala, Uganda, 21 September 2014.

38 Omara-Otunnu, *Politics and the Military in Uganda*, 32.

39 Indeed, several veterans of the Second World War had played a public role at the kingdom.

40 Interview by author with Ekiriya Kolya, in Mengo, Kampala, Uganda, 12 September 2014.

41 Interview by author with Damian Sebugwawo, in Mengo, Kampala, Uganda, 10 September 2014. See also interview by author with Dan Kato, in Mengo, Kampala, Uganda, 2 September 2014.

42 Interview by author with Damian Sebugwawo, in Mengo, Kampala, Uganda, 10 September 2014. See also interview by author with Dan Kato, in Mengo, Kampala, Uganda, 2 September 2014.

43 Interview by author with Daniel Mpima, in Nakulabye, Kampala, Uganda, 14 September 2014.

44 Among these men were chiefs, clan leaders, princes and others who held other royal titles.

45 For local conceptions of honour, see John Iliffe, *Honour in African History* (Cambridge: Cambridge University Press, 2005).

46 Henry Kyemba, *A State of Blood: The Inside Story of Idi Amin* (New York: Grosset & Dunlap, 1977), 91. Decker also provides examples of Amin

emasculating his perceived enemies, particularly other heads of state. For instance, see Decker, *In Idi Amin's Shadow*, 97.
47 Christine Obbo, *African Women: Their Struggle for Economic Independence* (London: Zed Press, 1980), 45; and Sylvia Nannyonga-Tamusuza, *Baakisimba: Music, Dance and Gender of the Baganda People of Bugand*a (Pittsburgh, PA: University of Pittsburgh Press, 1999).
48 See letter in Musizi, July 1979. For a discussion of honour in African societies, see Iliffe, *Honour in African History*.
49 Kyemba, *A State of Blood*, 246. Idi Amin made similarly emasculating comments about Tanzanian president Julius Nyerere. See also Decker, *In Idi Amin's Shadow*, 152–3.
50 Interview by author with John Kizito, in Nakulabye, Kampala, Uganda, 21 June 2014.
51 Interview by author with Zakariya Mukiibi, in Mengo, Kampala, Uganda, 12 October 2014.
52 Interview by author with Zakariya Mukiibi, in Mengo, Kampala, Uganda, 12 October 2014. Also, interview by author with David Mugenyi, in Mengo, Kampala, Uganda, 2 March 2014.
53 Godfrey B. Asiimwe, 'Household Gender and Resource Relations: Women in the Marketing of Income Generating Crops in Uganda', *Eastern Africa Social Science Research Review* 26, no. 2 (2010): 45; Obbo, *African Women*.
54 Interview by author with Benon Semambo in Nakulabye, Kampala, Uganda, 7 June 2014.
55 Interview by author with Amos Kato, in Nakulabye, Kampala, Uganda, 9 October 2014. See also, Ekiriya Kolya, 20 September 2014.
56 See Interview by author with Julius Kitende in Katwe, Kampala, Uganda, 9 September 2014.

Works cited

Asiimwe, Godfrey B. 'Household Gender and Resource Relations: Women in the Marketing of Income Generating Crops in Uganda'. *Eastern Africa Social Science Research Review* 26, no. 2 (2010): 1–30.
Bantebya-Kyomuhendo, Grace and Marjorie Keniston McIntosh. *Women, Work and Domestic Virtue in Uganda, 1900–2003*. Athens: Ohio University Press, 2006.
Bezzoli, Belinda. 'Memory, Forgetting, and the Alexandra Rebellion of 1986', in *States of Violence: Politics, Youth, and Memory in Contemporary Africa*, edited by Edna G. Bay and Donald L. Donham, 179–214. Charlottesville: University of Virginia Press, 2007.
Decker, Alicia C. *In Idi Amin's Shadow: Women, Gender, and Militarism in Uganda*. Athens: Ohio University Press, 2014.
Enloe, Cynthia. *Maneuvers: The International Politics of Militarizing Women's Lives*. Los Angeles: University of California Press, 2000.

Hinton, Devon E. and Athanase Hagengimana. '"Ihahamuka": A Rwandan Syndrome of Response to the Genocide: Blocked Flow, Spirit Assault, and Shortness of Breath', in *Culture and Panic Disorder*, edited by Byron Good and Devon Byron, 205–29. Palo Alto, CA: Stanford University Press, 2009.

Iliffe, John. *Honour in African History*. Cambridge: Cambridge University Press, 2005.

Killingray, David. *Fighting for Britain: African Soldiers in the Second World War*. Rochester, NJ: James Currey, 2010.

Kyemba, Henry. *A State of Blood: The inside Story of Idi Amin*. New York: Grosset & Dunlap, 1977.

Mama, Amina and Margo Okazawa-Rey. 'Editorial: Militarism, Conflict and Women's Activism'. *Feminist Africa* 10, no. 1 (2008): 1–8.

Moffett, Helen. '"These Women, They Force Us to Rape Them": Rape as Narrative of Social Control in Post-Apartheid South Africa'. *Journal of Southern African Studies* 32, no. 1 (2015): 129–44.

Musisi, Nakanyike B. 'Gender and the Cultural Construction of "Bad Women" in the Development of Kampala-Kibuga, 1900–1962', in *"Wicked" Women and the Reconfiguration of Gender in Africa*, edited by Dorothy Louise Hodgson and Sheryl McCurdy, 171–87. Portsmouth, NH: Heinemann, 2001.

Nannyonga-Tamusuza, Sylvia. *Baakisimba: Music, Dance and Gender of the Baganda People of Buganda*. Pittsburgh, PA: University of Pittsburgh Press, 1999.

Obbo, Christine. *African Women: Their Struggle for Economic Independence*. London: Zed Press, 1980.

Omara-Otunnu, Amii. *Politics and the Military in Uganda (1890–1985)*. New York: St. Martin's Press, 1987.

Reid, Richard and Henri Medard. 'Merchants, Missions and the Remaking of the Urban Environment in Buganda, C. 1840–90', in *Africa's Urban Past*, edited by David M. Anderson and Richard Rathbone, 98–108. Portsmouth, NH: Heinemann, 2000.

Republic of Uganda. *Report of the Commission of Inquiry into Violations of Human Rights: Verbatim Record of Proceedings*. Kampala: The Government of Uganda, 1995.

Saikia, Yasmin. *Women, War, and the Making of Bangladesh: Remembering 1971*. Durham, NC: Duke University Press, 2011.

'Soldiers Named in Sex Scandal with Suspects'. *The Monitor*, 5 December 2001, n.p.

Southall, Aidan William and Peter C. W. Gutkind. *Townsmen in the Making: Kampala and Its Suburbs*. Kampala: East African Institute of Social Research, 1953.

Stiglmayer, Alexandra. *Mass Rape: The War against Women in Bosnia-Herzegovina*. Lincoln: University of Nebraska Press, 1994.

Taylor, Christopher C. 'Ihahamuka—PTSD in Post-Genocidal Rwanda: Culture, Continuity and Change in Rwandan Therapeutics', in *African Medical Pluralism*, edited by William C. Olsen and Carolyn Sargent, 170–84. Bloomington: Indiana University Press, 2017.

Twagira, Benjamin. '*Bajeemi* Urbanites: Roots of Social Resilience in Militarized Kampala, Ca. 1966–1986'. PhD diss., Boston University, 2018.

Twagira, Benjamin. '"The Men Have Come": Gender and Militarisation in Kampala, 1966-86'. *Gender & History* 28, no. 3 (2016): 813–32.

Vansina, Jan. *Oral Tradition as History*. 1965; repr. Madison: University of Wisconsin Press, 1985.

White, Luise. *Speaking with Vampires: Rumor and History in Colonial Africa*. Berkeley: University of California Press, 2000.

White, Luise S., Stephan Miescher and David William Cohen, eds. *African Words, African Voices: Critical Practices in Oral History*. Bloomington: Indiana University Press, 2001.

10

'The missing ones'

Vietnamese diasporic memory and women's narratives of loss

Nathalie Huynh Chau Nguyen

Lending our visit a melancholic note, it was raining heavily the day in July 2016 that we saw the former refugee camp of Pulau Galang in the Riau Archipelago of Indonesia.[1] The view from the coach was of large stretches of encroaching greenery and occasional glimpses of dilapidated wooden buildings behind high strands of grass. This vast camp had once housed thousands of Vietnamese refugees, but apart from a few buildings and places of worship, most of the site was reverting to trees and grasses. Of the extended network of refugee camps that sprang up throughout Southeast Asia and Hong Kong in response to the post-1975 Vietnamese diaspora, the former camp of Pulau Galang is the only one to have been preserved. It is a site of pilgrimage for Vietnamese survivors and their families. One of the most moving sites was the camp cemetery, which contained several tombstones bearing handwritten inscriptions. One monument which we could not see, however, was the Vietnamese refugee memorial that was unveiled at the site in 2005, and subsequently destroyed at the request of the Vietnamese government.

The fall of Saigon on 30 April 1975, and the communist takeover of South Vietnam signalled the end of the Vietnam War and the prelude to one of the most significant diasporas of the late twentieth century. The Vietnamese who fled their country after 1975 were subjected to widespread state repression and events of mass trauma in post-war communist Vietnam, including the internment of 1 million people in re-education camps, the forced de-urbanization of another 1 million souls to New Economic Zones in rural areas, restriction on free speech and movement, and discrimination directed against three specific groups in society: those associated with the former South Vietnamese government, ethnic Chinese and Amerasians.[2] The scale of the post-war Vietnamese exodus was unprecedented, as was the international response, which involved two major United Nations conferences convened in Geneva, in 1979 and 1989, to deal with the Indochinese refugee crisis, and the resettlement of Vietnamese in fifty countries worldwide.[3]

Many Vietnamese refugees have remained silent about their past and about the experience of forced migration. Behind this reticence lies the vast quiet of the missing and the dead of the exodus. More than 2 million Vietnamese left their homeland in the two decades following the end of the war. The number of refugee deaths remains unknown, but estimates range from 100,000 to more than 1 million.[4] Refugees died of thirst or starvation, drowned in rough waters or perished at the hands of pirates. Others died when their boat was pushed back out to sea by hostile state officials. On 22 November 1978, for example, after twice being turned away by Malaysian authorities, a refugee boat with 254 people aboard sank at the mouth of the Trengganu river.[5] While a few dozen survived by swimming ashore, over 200 men, women, and children drowned within sight of 'hundreds of spectators, including cameramen'.[6] Many Vietnamese asylum seekers did not even reach the open waters, drowning, instead, in rivers while attempting to reach the sea. Those who lived in riverine and coastal communities in southern Vietnam remember seeing countless corpses drifting by or washed up on riverbanks and beaches in the post-war years.[7] Women and children were often among the first to drown when boats capsized.[8] As most bodies lacked any form of identification, their relatives could not be notified and victims' remains were buried in unmarked graves.[9]

The massive death toll of the exodus and the absence in many cases of human remains have led to specific forms of mourning and remembrance in the Vietnamese diaspora. For the families of the missing, the loss of their loved ones 'is described as ambiguous and unresolved – a liminal space "between life and death"'.[10] There are no bodies to identify and grieve over, and decades later there is still no resolution to families' search for answers. While most of those who vanished did so at sea, others went missing on overland escape routes to neighbouring countries.[11] This chapter will explore, first, the memorialization of the Vietnamese exodus in the form of monuments unveiled at the sites of two former refugee camps in Malaysia and Indonesia; and, second, the personal narratives of Vietnamese refugee women, and their accounts of those who disappeared during their escape from Vietnam. Refugee memorials and the narratives of refugee women constitute different means of memorializing the Vietnamese refugee experience. They are juxtaposed here because they share the following factors: first, they bring into the public domain the private grief of those who have lost loved ones; and, second, they manifest the mourning of the Vietnamese diaspora in a transnational context. Both give form to the memory of the missing and the dead of the Vietnamese exodus, and provide an avenue for potential healing. Refugee memorials constitute a site of mourning and a physical space where relatives can lay flowers or offerings, and women's articulation of their trauma story 'becomes a testimony, a publicly accessible "ritual of healing" that inscribes the victim into a sympathetic discourse-community and inaugurates the possibility of psychological reintegration'.[12] Both, however, are tenuous and fragile. The Vietnamese refugee memorials in Malaysia and Indonesia existed only briefly before being destroyed at the insistence of the Hanoi government, while the voices of Vietnamese refugee women rarely feature in national histories and have limited exposure in the public domain. Both encompass the articulation of individual, familial and communal losses for the Vietnamese diaspora. The interweaving of these two forms of mourning points not only to the strength of the emotions associated with great trauma but also to the difficulty and precariousness of refugee memorialization. The narratives of Vietnamese women are valuable because women are traditionally seen as keepers and transmitters of culture.[13] In the context of forced migration from Vietnam, women provide gendered interpretations of refugee trajectories because they were subjected not only to violence but also to rape and abduction in pirate attacks on refugee boats. The three women whose personal accounts are related here were interviewed during oral history projects conducted in Australia between 2005 and 2010.[14] Their experience of trauma arose not from a single event, but as 'the outcome of a constellation of life experiences' encompassing conditions in post-war Vietnam, family separation and the escape journey, as well as its aftermath.[15] All three escaped from Vietnam by boat in the 1970s and 1980s, and all lost family members at sea. Thirty to forty years later, the fate of these missing family members is still unknown. Enquiries with the United Nations High Commissioner for Refugees (UNHCR), International Red Cross, International Red Crescent and the Catholic Church have yielded no results. How have women reflected on the disappearance of loved ones? What form do their memories take? How have they dealt with ambiguous loss? The women's narratives elucidate the ways in which, as individuals and as members of the Vietnamese diaspora, they have remembered the refugee experience, the extent of trauma suffered and the scale of loss after 1975.

Memorials

The fate of two refugee memorials serves as a metaphor for the impermanence of refugee history. Funded through the transnational efforts of the Vietnamese diaspora, the memorials were raised on the sites of two former refugee camps in 2005: Pulau Bidong in Malaysia and Pulau Galang in Indonesia.[16] As Quan Tue Tran notes, the history of these memorials shows 'diasporic Vietnamese as historical agents that actively define their past, present, and future by asserting and defending very specific claims on the multiple geographies they have traversed'.[17] Both memorials bore the same commemorative inscription:

> In commemoration of the hundreds of thousands of Vietnamese people who perished on the way to freedom (1975-1996). Though they died of hunger or thirst, of being raped, of exhaustion or of any other cause, we pray that they now enjoy lasting peace. Their sacrifice will never be forgotten.[18]

Of the large network of camps that housed Vietnamese refugees from 1975 to 2000, most have been dismantled, and only one, Camp Vietnam on the Indonesian island of Galang, has been preserved as an 80-hectare site containing a small museum, places of worship and a cemetery. Representatives from Vietnamese communities in Australia, Canada, the United States, Great Britain, France and Denmark attended the unveiling of the memorial on 24 March 2005.[19] Local authorities welcomed the returning refugees: 'You are not the boat people of the past. We salute you. We hope that you will return to visit this island'.[20] Designed by the Melbourne-based Archive of Vietnamese Boat People and carved by Indonesian stonecutters, the memorial resembled an oversized tombstone.[21]

Hanoi, however, complained that the memorials 'denigrated the dignity of Vietnam'.[22] Barely three months later, the Indonesian and Malaysian governments yielded to pressure from the Vietnamese government, and ordered the destruction of the memorials. The local authorities in Galang demolished the memorial's inscription in late May 2005, but, interestingly, they left the frame in place, suggesting ambivalence about the directives they had received. Local authorities in Malaysia delayed destroying the Bidong memorial.[23] The partial destruction of the Galang memorial and impending dismantling of the Bidong memorial led to numerous protests by Vietnamese communities in the United States, France and Australia. Quynh Dao from the Australia–Vietnam Human Rights Committee, wrote the following letter to the *Jakarta Post*:

> Please do not give in to the Vietnamese communists. They deny the living even the right to commemorate deceased relatives, friends and compatriots. They deny the dead the right to be remembered. They deny the Indonesian people the right to commemorate a great deed of humanity.[24]

While the Bidong memorial was destroyed to its foundation in October 2005, the Indonesians responded by adding a replacement plaque to the Galang memorial. By 2007, that replacement had disappeared and the remains of the memorial were destroyed to its foundation by the Indonesian authorities. By 2008, even the foundation had been removed.[25] All traces of the memorial, like the one in Malaysia, have been erased.

While the physical evidence of the Vietnamese refugee memorials in Galang and Bidong have disappeared, the connotations of their brief existence endure in refugee memory, photographic archives and writings. The Vietnamese state succeeded in its demand that the refugee memorials in two neighbouring Southeast Asian states be removed, but it could not exert the same influence on the major resettlement countries. A clear legacy of the former Galang and Bidong memorials, for example, is the Vietnamese refugee memorial raised in 2008 in the Melbourne suburb of Footscray by the Vietnamese-Australian Community in Victoria. Just as the earlier monuments had acknowledged the humanitarian efforts of Indonesia and Malaysia, respectively, as well as those of international agencies, on behalf of Vietnamese refugees, this monument acknowledges Australian and international humanitarian efforts to settle Vietnamese refugees, and its commemorative inscription hews closely to the wording of the vanished Southeast Asian memorials.[26] There may be few tangible remnants of the Vietnamese refugee experience throughout Southeast Asia, but its memorialization persists in a range of cultural forms in wider transnational contexts.

The brief history of the memorials illustrates the ways in which Vietnamese diasporic communities rallied in their efforts to memorialize the Vietnamese exodus and remember their missing and their dead. The two short-lived memorials on Pulau Galang and Pulau Bidong were the result of communal and transnational efforts including cooperative fund-raising by Buddhist and Catholic leaders as well as ordinary members of Vietnamese communities in Australia, North America and Europe. The memorials gave physical shape to the refugee movement and its death toll over the two decades following the end of the Vietnam War. They constituted a political reminder of post-war state repression in Vietnam, postulated a rationale for the mass departures and signified a place of remembrance and of mourning for survivors and their families. The location of the memorials on the site of two former refugee camps that had housed hundreds of thousands of Vietnamese provided not only a physical marker of loss, and a link between past events and current memory, but also an additional reminder of the scale of this forced migration.

The obliteration of the Galang and Bidong memorials reflects the Vietnamese state's attempts to suppress refugee remembrance beyond the borders of Vietnam, and echoes the destruction of memorials of the former South Vietnam after the end of the war in 1975, including the Mourning Soldier by sculptor Nguyen Thanh Thu, and the razing of South Vietnamese military cemeteries. 'Southern dead', writes Hue-Tam Ho Tai, 'absent from national commemoration, often go unmentioned in the collective narrative of their extended families. Condemned to the shadows, they refuse, however, to remain unmourned'.[27] The Vietnamese state's erasure of South Vietnamese war dead, and its subsequent efforts to silence commemorations of the Vietnamese refugee tragedy evince its reluctance, like other communist states, to admit to human rights violations or to engage in truth and reconciliation. Vietnamese diasporic memory has a particular role to play in preserving refugee histories and resisting the state version of history. Memorialization of the South Vietnamese past and the Vietnamese exodus can at present occur only overseas among Vietnamese diasporic communities while its manifestations – as the fate of the Galang and Bidong memorials attests to – can be transient and tenuous, and subject to the interests of other states.

Narratives

While memorials are one means of giving form to remembrance, the personal testimony of survivors is another means of doing so. The following three oral narratives by Vietnamese refugee women were recorded in Australia in 2005, and provide detailed accounts of losses at sea, either witnessed or retold. Two of the women escaped by boat in 1978, while the third did so in 1988. All lost close family members during the exodus. Embedded within their life histories as survivors are their memories of loved ones who disappeared at sea.

The first narrative is that of my sister-in-law, Dzung.[28] In 1980, she escaped from Vietnam as an unaccompanied minor at the age of ten. While her life story is a remarkable account of survival at sea, and the rescue of the fifty-six refugee men, women and children on her boat by the German mercy ship *Cap Anamur*, it also contains the story of five family members lost at sea in 1978: two sisters, her older brother, and two nieces. Most of the family photographs, along with the family book, were burnt during the North Vietnamese invasion of South Vietnam in 1975, but among the few surviving photographs is a beautiful one of her sister Hoa, taken in Saigon in 1970. Eight years later, Hoa disappeared at sea with her two daughters, aged seven and three, along with Hoa and Dzung's only brother Chuong, their sister Tuyet, and the 200 other people on their boat. Their escape from Vietnam was 'government-sponsored'. In 1978–9, the Vietnamese government was involved with various overseas crime syndicates in organizing the trafficking of refugees, charging them an average of $US 2,000 in gold and confiscating their houses and goods.[29] It was a convenient way for authorities to dispose of political and ethnic undesirables, while profiting financially in the process. Refugees were supposed to be guaranteed a safe passage, but the reality for many was 'a one-way ticket to a watery grave'.[30]

Two months after Hoa and the others disappeared at sea, sponsorship papers arrived from her husband in the United States. He had been a South Vietnamese Marine and had left with the Americans in 1975. He had arranged for Hoa and her entire family to leave Vietnam on a US ship in the final days of the war. Hoa, however, opted to stay with her parents because her father chose not to leave his country. The entire family, including children and grandchildren, were trapped in Saigon when the war ended. Three years later, Hoa's parents made the fateful decision to pay for the 'semi-official' departure of three children and two granddaughters from Vietnam. Dzung notes:

> we never heard from them again. We tried the Red Cross and the Catholic Church. Even my brother-in-law in America tried everything, but we never heard from them. Up to this day, we don't know whether they are still alive somewhere, or whether they actually died. We still don't know yet.

For ten years, Hoa's husband waited and hoped for news of his missing wife and daughters, but her family eventually told him to move on with his life. He married again, but remains haunted by the loss of Hoa and their two daughters. Even now, Dzung and her surviving siblings still refer to those who disappeared in 1978 as 'the missing ones'.[31] They refuse to acknowledge that their loved ones have died. When my book *Memory Is Another Country* was published in 2009,[32] my sister-in-law told me that she was glad to see her sister Hoa's photograph in it, as a reader might recognize Hoa, and the family would finally have news of her. After forty years, she still clings to the hope that her siblings and nieces may have somehow survived with an injury or memory loss, and that they are alive somewhere. For Dzung, the process of reconstructing her family history, telling the story of her missing siblings and nieces and providing the few existing photographs is an act of memory, a means of giving tangible form to the remembrance of loved ones. It also underlines a continued process of grieving.

The second narrative is that of Phuong.[33] Born in 1963, Phuong escaped from Vietnam in 1988 with her two sons, aged seven and six. Hers is a shocking story. Her reconstruction of events moves away from the boat journey before circling around and returning to a pirate attack, and her last sight of her sons and the 100 other people on the boat who drowned when they were pushed overboard by the pirates. She remembers that after three days at sea, her vessel encountered pirates. They searched the passengers one by one, repeatedly, in the hopes of finding gold:

> As the pirates wanted us to come out of the hold, I had to put my son onto the deck first. While I was still in the hold, they threw my child away. Yes . . . threw . . . into the sea. I did not see this. When I put my older son onto the deck, he saw this and he cried: 'Mum, they threw my younger brother away'. I went up on deck. I didn't see him either. I only saw many men in the water clinging to the boat's stern. The pirates forced the men to jump into the sea. People tried to cling to the stern but the pirates forced their hands open and pushed them away. Then they took the women onto the pirate ships, four women to each ship. I asked to

keep my son with me. But they refused and hit me with a large piece of wood. I was dragged onto the pirate ship.

As they approached Thailand, Phuong asked the pirates to let her jump into the sea as she had been repeatedly raped and 'could not bear it any longer'. The pirates gave her and three other women plastic cans, and the four women floated at sea 'from nine o'clock in the morning to twelve o'clock at night' before being rescued by a Thai fishing boat. The horror of floating at sea for hours and in the dark still haunts her. Her narrative points to the intense and recurring imagery of traumatic memory. She states, 'I can't forget that experience. The memory of it still obsesses me'. As Cathy Caruth writes, 'to be traumatized is precisely to be possessed by an image or event'.[34] Phuong was not only subjected to the violence of rape but also witnessed the violence meted out to others, including to her own children. Phuong's younger son disappeared overboard, and she never saw her older son again, despite numerous enquiries to international aid agencies.

The last narrative is that of Anh, who was born in 1943, the eldest of four siblings.[35] Her sisters Nga and Suong escaped with their brother Kiet in 1978; Kiet died during that journey. Their boat was approximately 24 metres long and held 124 people. Most were hidden in secret compartments under the deck. The men and women were in separate compartments. When the water pump broke down, the boat captain encouraged the young men to bail the water out of by hand. Kiet took his turn and fell overboard around two in the morning, while both of his sisters were asleep. His younger sister Suong remembers that he died on the eighth day out and that they reached the refugee camp sixteen days later. Anh heard the news of Kiet's death just a few days before she herself escaped from Vietnam with her two young children in October 1978. She relates:

> It took me a long time to accept that my brother had died, that he was no longer alive. We hoped that he would come back and see us. I knew on one level that he had died but I still hoped that he may have somehow survived.
>
> From time to time, I think about Kiet, and I see him as a young man.
>
> Normally I don't dream much, but I saw him once in a dream a long time ago, more than twenty years ago, I just saw him in a normal family setting here in Australia, as if he hadn't died and that he was here in Australia, like Nga or Suong, that he was here.

Anh's narrative is quiet and contained. She states that she has learned to deal with events in a restrained manner. As she notes,

> I don't respond much to emotion. I don't seem to get angry, and when good things happen, I don't react much either. I have always been like

that. When we were young, we were taught that as a girl, you shouldn't show much emotion. We can't shout when we're happy, we can't cry much, we're supposed to be calm and well-behaved, and I've been like that all my life.

I don't think ahead. It's part of the way I look at things. If something is bad, I don't see it as being bad forever, if something is good, I take it easy, slowly. I see it as a coping mechanism.

Anh's calm and measured words may be a specific response to trauma, a 'management strategy adopted by survivors to enable them to speak, without which words would be drowned by emotion'.[36] However, Anh is also aware that she has internalized the cultural lessons from her past and her Vietnamese upbringing. Vietnamese women were traditionally brought up to abide by the Three Obediences (to father, husband and son), and the Four Virtues: Right Occupation, Right Speech, Right Appearance and Right Conduct.[37] They were instructed to be modest, hardworking and quiet, and not to indulge in unseemly displays of emotion. In Anh's case, this restraint on her emotions has enabled her to deal with successive losses in her life: the death of her mother from tuberculosis, the collapse of her country in 1975, the disappearance of her brother Kiet at sea, the death of her father in Vietnam, and, last, the death of her sister Nga of cancer in Australia. She puts emotion aside. As she says, 'It's there. I don't push it behind, I don't take it out, it's just there. I just feel I don't have much time to think a lot'. She made the gesture of a box or coffer next to her while she was speaking, in this way identifying not only a place for her emotions but also a survival strategy for validating those emotions while also containing them. This restraint has granted her the fortitude to bear many reverses in her life.

The women's narratives convey distinctive ways of dealing with grief and ambiguous loss. Pauline Boss and Janet Yeats define ambiguous loss as 'a loss that remains unclear and without resolution. It has no close or finality because the loss is ongoing'.[38] They suggest, furthermore, that ambiguous loss 'represents a category of loss and grief that is frequently disenfranchised' because 'society seems to deny mourners their rights to grieve long term'.[39] For Dzung, conveying her story and that of her siblings, is a means of not only communicating her family history but also disseminating it in a wider forum in the hope that news of these missing siblings and nieces – even decades after their disappearance – will somehow come to light. Her negotiation of these losses conveys a tension between grief and hope: grief for the lives lost, and hope that there will be a resolution to the family's continuing search for answers. Her narrative illustrates, in the words of political scientist Jenny Edkins, 'families' insistence on the irreplaceable, grievable lives of their lost relatives'.[40] Phuong's narrative bears the hallmarks of post-traumatic stress disorder (PTSD), with obsessive recurring images and a fractured life history that returns repeatedly to her experience of greatest trauma. Anh's recollections reveal that, like Dzung, she clung to the hope that her brother had survived falling overboard. Her dream image of her brother as a young man in Australia underlines the pathos of a life unlived, unfulfilled and prematurely obliterated. Her way of coping with grief and the absence of loved ones is by keeping her emotions at bay. While she is aware that this means that there are no great joys as well as no great sorrows in her life, this is the way that she has dealt with overwhelming loss. Her story contains several layers of silence and grief.

Conclusion

The narratives of these three women take place against a background of contested histories and realities, and highlight two central themes. The first is the gap between the state version of events – imposed in this case outside of the borders of Vietnam in the form of the destruction of refugee memorials in Indonesia and Malaysia – and the lived experience of Vietnamese refugees. The Vietnamese state insisted in a forty-page English-language publication in 1979 that the departures of so-called refugees from Vietnam were due to economic, not political factors.[41] Their reframing of the unfolding refugee crisis seeks to negate state-perpetrated violence in post-war Vietnam, including internment without trial, forced displacement and forced labour, and to undermine the reasons why Vietnamese were leaving their country in such large numbers. Vietnamese diasporic identity, in counterpoint, is built on a defining narrative of escape by sea, and a 'collective memory of persecution, trauma and loss'.[42]

The focus on refugee memorials and on women's articulation of the refugee experience is significant because both have largely been silenced in the public sphere. The Bidong and Galang memorials to Vietnamese refugees were destroyed at the insistence of the Hanoi government. As to women's experiences, the narratives of Dzung, Phuong and Anh have three features in common: first, their awareness of the lack of visibility of Vietnamese women's voices; second, their willingness to participate in a project on Vietnamese women remembering and narrating refugee pasts – a project led by a Vietnamese female academic and including Vietnamese female interviewers; and third, the fact that their contributions form part of a wider project on Vietnamese diasporic remembrance. The missing memorials and the women's voices attest to the persistence of refugee memory and the enduring nature of grief, even in the face of official erasure and lack of exposure.

While the narratives of these three women relate different responses to the refugee experience and to ambiguous loss, all were transmitted through oral histories, and conveyed to me, in Edkins's words, as 'an encircling of the trauma, a refusal to forget the lessons, an insistence on the acknowledgement that, however impossible to understand, what happened happened'.[43] As boat people and as survivors, the women bear witness to large-scale events in history and the physical dangers and vicissitudes of their own journeys as well as the personal grief of losing family members during the exodus. Their narratives constitute a tribute to the missing, resist the Vietnamese state's attempts to remove the missing from history and make a significant contribution to a collective diasporic history.

As a researcher, I need to acknowledge my own part in diasporic memory work. My background as a child refugee situates me in an intergenerational dialogue between those Vietnamese (mostly first generation) who experienced the boat journey and the refugee camps directly and those who were either born overseas or were too young to have a direct recollection of the post-war exodus. An academic seeking to record the voices of Vietnamese refugee women and to communicate them to a wider audience, I provide my own interpretation of women's memories and stories. Just as the women's narratives are shaped by their past experience as well as current circumstances, my articulation of their stories is shaped by my own lens as a Vietnamese-Australian researcher. As noted by Marita Eastmond, 'the nature of the enquiry as well as the personal experience and cultural assumptions of the researcher are all filters through which the story is sifted and represented as text'.[44] For women to agree to tell their stories was a gesture of trust, and I am aware that this trust was engendered by their knowledge of my own background. The women's narratives, and the textual form through which I am conveying their words, form part of a living and evolving archive of refugee memories.

While memorials and personal testimony give shape to refugee remembrance, diasporic cultural production constitutes another means of doing so. All three forms of expression signify active resistance to the Vietnamese state's recasting of history. As noted by psychologist Marco Gemignani, 'the strategic use of history permits reinterpretations and relocations of traumatic memory as well as the formation of self-healing narratives that reframe refugee identities in the light of ethnic history and shared experience'.[45] The controversies over the Galang and Bidong refugee memorials, and the contestations between official state narratives and refugee narratives, provide a political backdrop to the ongoing memory work of the Vietnamese diaspora.

This process of memorialization extends into the second generation while modes of production vary from oral histories and archives in national collections to scholarly, literary and artistic outputs. Vietnamese-Australian artist Phuong Ngo's exhibition *Article 14.1*, first performed in Melbourne in 2014, specifically references the Universal Declaration of Human Rights according to which 'everyone has the right to seek and to enjoy in other countries asylum from persecution'.[46] Ngo's artwork involves his subsisting for ten days on the rations his parents survived on during their boat journey from Vietnam in 1982. Visitors to the exhibition can fold paper boats while listening to first-hand refugee accounts. Ngo is a second-generation Vietnamese-Australian. His artistic endeavours convey his individual reflections on and his translation of his parents' refugee background and family history. The memory work of the younger generations of Vietnamese overseas has the added advantage of greater accessibility, linguistically and artistically, to the host society. Their cultural production extends diasporic interpretations and reconstructions of the Vietnamese past and its symbolism in the present to wider international and multicultural audiences.

Notes

1 The author visited the site with a group of students from Monash University as part of a third-year course that she was teaching on 'In the Footsteps of Refugees' in July 2016.

2 See Jacqueline Desbarats, 'Human Rights: Two Steps Forward, One Step Back?' in *Vietnam Today: Assessing the New Trends*, ed. Thai Quang Trung (New York: Crane Russak, 1990), 47–64; Linda Hitchcox, *Vietnamese Refugees in Southeast Asian Camps* (Basingstoke: Macmillan in association with St. Antony's College, Oxford, 1990), 37–68; James M. Freeman and Nguyen Dinh Huu, *Voices from the Camps: Vietnamese Children Seeking Asylum* (Seattle: University of Washington Press, 2003), 7; Kieu-Linh Caroline Valverde, 'From Dust to Gold: The Vietnamese Amerasian Experience', in *Racially Mixed People in America*, ed. P. P. Maria Root (Newbury Park, CA: Sage Publications, 1992), 144–61; Steven DeBonis, *Children of the Enemy: Oral Histories of Vietnamese Amerasians and Their Mothers* (Jefferson, NC: McFarland, 1995); and Robert S. McKelvey, *The Dust of Life: America's Children Abandoned in Vietnam* (Seattle: University of Washington Press, 1999).

3 W. Courtland Robinson, *Terms of Refuge: The Indochinese Exodus and the International Response* (London: Zed Books, 1998), 127.

4 While there were 839,228 Vietnamese arrivals in UNHCR camps between 1975 and 1997, to this number must be added the 134,000 who were evacuated to the United States in 1975, the 263,000 who fled to the People's Republic of China in 1978/79, and the 623,509 who left under the Orderly Departure Program. The total comes to 1.9 million. See Robinson, *Terms of Refuge*, 272 and 294–5. When we include estimated refugee deaths, the figure comes to well over 2 million. On estimates of refugee deaths, see Keith St. Cartmail, *Exodus Indochina* (Auckland: Heinemann, 1983), 8, 12 and 227; Hitchcox, *Vietnamese Refugees*, 85; Robinson, *Terms of Refuge*, 59; Mary Terrell Cargill and Jade Quang Huynh, *Voices of Vietnamese Boat People: Nineteen Narratives of Escape and Survival* (Jefferson, NC: McFarland, 2000), 4; and Nathalie Huynh Chau Nguyen, *Voyage of Hope: Vietnamese Australian Women's Narratives* (Altona, CA: Common Ground Publishing, 2005), 16–17.

5 St. Cartmail, *Exodus*, 223.

6 St. Cartmail, *Exodus*, 223.

7 See Nguyen, *Voyage of Hope*, 16.

8. Phung, interview with the author, Melbourne, Victoria, 7 December 2006. Phung is identified by one name for privacy reasons. Phung is from the coastal city of Vung Tau, and relates that in the late 1970s and early 1980s, she saw bodies washed up on local beaches 'nearly every week' and that most were those of women and children 'because women didn't know how to swim'.
9. Nguyen, *Voyage of Hope*, 16.
10. Sarah Wayland, Myfanwy Maple, Kathy McKay and Geoffrey Glassock, 'Holding on to Hope: A Review of the Literature Exploring Missing Persons, Hope and Ambiguous Loss', *Death Studies* 40, no. 1 (2015): 55.
11. While the majority of refugees from Vietnam were boat refugees, approximately 5 per cent were land refugees. See Robinson, *Terms of Refuge*, 295.
12. Suzette A. Henke, *Shattered Subjects: Trauma and Testimony in Women's Life-Writing* (New York: St Martin's Press, 1998), xviii.
13. Kumari Jayawardena, *Feminism and Nationalism in the Third World* (London: Zed Books, 1986), 257.
14. The women were interviewed as part of two projects: a small project at the Australian-Vietnamese Women's Welfare Association funded by a 2004 Victorian Multicultural Commission grant and a large project on *Vietnamese Women: Voices and Narratives of the Diaspora* funded by the Australian Research Council in 2005–10.
15. Selma Leydesdorff, Graham Dawson, Natasha Burchardt and T. G. Ashplant, 'Introduction', in *Trauma and Life Stories: International Perspectives*, ed. Kim Lacy Rogers, Selma Leydesdorff and Graham Dawson (London: Routledge), 2.
16. See Quan Tue Tran, 'Remembering the Boat People Exodus: A Tale of Two Memorials', *The Journal of Vietnamese Studies* 7, no. 3 (2012): 80–121. Tran provides a detailed history of the refugee memorials in Bidong and Galang.
17. Tran, 'Remembering', 82.
18. The inscription was signed 'Overseas Vietnamese Communities 2005'. See Fadli, 'Vietnam Boat People's Plaque Torn Down', *The Jakarta Post*, 20 June 2005. https://www.vnbp.org/vietnamese/memorial/baochi/newspaper01.htm; and Tran, 'Remembering', 90.
19. See Fadli, 'Vietnam Boat People' and Tran, 'Remembering', 82.
20. Tran, 'Remembering', 87.
21. Tran, 'Remembering', 90, 91–2.
22. Peter Wilmoth, 'Boat People Condemn Loss of Monument', *The Age*, 26 June 2006. https://www.vnbp.org/vietnamese/memorial/baochi/1119321940275.pdf.
23. Tran, 'Remembering', 102.
24. Quynh Dao, quoted in Ashley Carruthers and Boitran Huynh-Beattie, 'Dark Tourism, Diasporic Memory and Disappeared History', in *The Chinese/Vietnamese Diaspora*, ed. Chan Yuk Wah (London: Taylor and Francis, 2012), 151.
25. Tran, 'Remembering', 103–7.

26 The right-side inscription reads: 'In commemoration of the hundreds and thousands of Vietnamese people who perished in pursuit of freedom (1975–1996). Whatever the cause might be: hunger or thirst, wreckages or pirates, sickness or exhaustion, we all pray that they may now rest in peace. Their sacrifice will never be forgotten', signed 'The Vietnamese-Australian Community in Victoria 2008'. See http://monumentaustralia.org.au/themes/government/oppression/display/31332-vietnamese-refugees.

27 Hue-Tam Ho Tai, 'Faces of Remembrance and Forgetting', in *The Country of Memory: Remaking the Past in Late Socialist Vietnam*, ed. Hue-Tam Ho Tai (Berkeley: University of California Press, 2001), 191.

28 Dzung, interview with the author, Melbourne, Victoria, 13 June 2005. Dzung is identified by one name for privacy reasons.

29 See Robinson, *Terms of Refuge*, 28.

30 St. Cartmail, *Exodus*, 26.

31 Dzung, conversation with the author, Melbourne, Victoria, 16 March 2019.

32 See Nathalie Huynh Chau Nguyen, *Memory Is Another Country: Women of the Vietnamese Diaspora* (Santa Barbara, CA: Praeger, 2009), 12–13 and 89.

33 Phuong, interview with Thao Ha, Richmond, Victoria, 11 October 2004,. Phuong is identified by one name for privacy reasons.

34 Cathy Caruth, 'Introduction', in *Trauma: Explorations in Memory*, ed. Cathy Caruth (Baltimore, MD: The Johns Hopkins University Press, 1995), 4–5.

35 Anh, interview with the author, Footscray, Victoria, 11 and 28 June 2005. Anh is identified by one name for privacy reasons.

36 Ruth Wajnryb, *The Silence: How Tragedy Shapes Talk* (Crows Nest: Allen & Unwin, 2001), 223.

37 See, for example, Cam Nguyen, 'East, West, and Vietnamese Women', *The Journal of Vietnamese Studies* 5 (1992): 46.

38 Pauline Boss and Janet R. Yeats, 'Ambiguous Loss: A Complicated Type of Grief When Loved Ones Disappear', *Bereavement Care* 33, no. 2 (2014): 63.

39 Boss and Yeats, 'Ambiguous Loss', 66.

40 Jenny Edkins, *Missing: Persons and Politics* (Ithaca, NY: Cornell University Press, 2011), xii.

41 Tran, 'Remembering', 94.

42 Carruthers and Huynh-Beattie, 'Dark Tourism', 148.

43 Edkins, *Missing*, 4.

44 Marita Eastmond, 'Stories as Lived Experience: Narratives in Forced Migration Research', *Journal of Refugee Studies* 20, no. 2 (2007): 249.

45 Marco Gemignani, 'The Past Is Past: The Use of Memories and Self-Healing Narratives in Refugees from the Former Yugoslavia', *Journal of Refugee Studies* 24, no. 1 (2011): 132.

46 See Debbie Cuthbertson, 'Artist Phuong Ngo Revisits His Family's Life as Boat People', *Sydney Morning Herald*, 3 May 2014. https://www.smh.com.au/entertainment/art-and-design/artist-phuong-ngo-revisits-his-familys-life-as-boat-people-20140502-37n4t.html.

Works cited

Boss, Pauline and Janet R. Yeats. 'Ambiguous Loss: A Complicated Type of Grief When Loved Ones Disappear'. *Bereavement Care* 33, no. 2 (2014): 63–9.

Cargill, Mary Terrell and Jade Quang Huynh. *Voices of Vietnamese Boat People: Nineteen Narratives of Escape and Survival*. Jefferson, NC: McFarland, 2000.

Carruthers, Ashley and Boitran Huynh-Beattie. 'Dark Tourism, Diasporic Memory and Disappeared History', in *The Chinese/Vietnamese Diaspora*, edited by Chan Yuk Wah, 147–60. London: Taylor and Francis, 2012.

Caruth, Cathy. 'Introduction', in *Trauma: Explorations in Memory*, edited by Cathy Caruth, 3–12. Baltimore, MD: The Johns Hopkins University Press, 1995.

Cuthbertson, Debbie. 'Artist Phuong Ngo Revisits His Family's Life as Boat People'. *Sydney Morning Herald*, 3 May 2014. https://www.smh.com.au/entertainment/art-and-design/artist-phuong-ngo-revisits-his-familys-life-as-boat-people-20140502-37n4t.html.

DeBonis, Steven. *Children of the Enemy: Oral Histories of Vietnamese Amerasians and Their Mothers*. Jefferson, NC: McFarland, 1995.

Desbarats, Jacqueline. 'Human Rights: Two Steps Forward, One Step Back?' in *Vietnam Today: Assessing the New Trends*, edited by Thai Quang Trung, 47–64. New York: Crane Russak, 1990.

Eastmond, Marita. 'Stories as Lived Experience: Narratives in Forced Migration Research'. *Journal of Refugee Studies* 20, no. 2 (2007): 248–64.

Edkins, Jenny. *Missing: Persons and Politics*. Ithaca, NY: Cornell University Press, 2011.

Fadli. 'Vietnam Boat People's Plaque Torn Down'. *The Jakarta Post*, 20 June 2005. https://www.vnbp.org/vietnamese/memorial/baochi/newspaper01.htm.

Freeman, James M. and Nguyen Dinh Huu. *Voices from the Camps: Vietnamese Children Seeking Asylum*. Seattle: University of Washington Press, 2003.

Gemignani, Marco. 'The Past is Past: The Use of Memories and Self-Healing Narratives in Refugees from the Former Yugoslavia'. *Journal of Refugee Studies* 24, no. 1 (2011): 132–56.

Henke, Suzette A. *Shattered Subjects: Trauma and Testimony in Women's Life-Writing*. New York: St Martin's Press, 1998.

Hitchcox, Linda. *Vietnamese Refugees in Southeast Asian Camps*. Basingstoke: Macmillan in association with St. Antony's College, Oxford, 1990.

Jayawardena, Kumari. *Feminism and Nationalism in the Third World*. London: Zed Books, 1986.

Leydesdorff, Selma, Graham Dawson, Natasha Burchardt and T. G. Ashplant. 'Introduction', in *Trauma and Life Stories: International Perspectives*, edited by Kim Lacy Rogers, Selma Leydesdorff and Graham Dawson, 1–26. London: Routledge, 1999.

McKelvey, Robert S. *The Dust of Life: America's Children Abandoned in Vietnam*. Seattle: University of Washington Press, 1999.

Nguyen, Cam. 'East, West, and Vietnamese Women'. *The Journal of Vietnamese Studies* 5 (1992): 44–50.

Nguyen, Nathalie Huynh Chau. *Memory Is Another Country: Women of the Vietnamese Diaspora*. Santa Barbara, CA: Praeger, 2009.

Nguyen, Nathalie Huynh Chau. *Voyage of Hope: Vietnamese Australian Women's Narratives*. Altona, CA: Common Ground Publishing, 2005.

Robinson, W. Courtland. *Terms of Refuge: The Indochinese Exodus and the International Response*. London: Zed Books, 1998.

St. Cartmail, Keith. *Exodus Indochina*. Auckland: Heinemann, 1983.

Tai, Hue-Tam Ho. 'Faces of Remembrance and Forgetting', in *The Country of Memory: Remaking the Past in Late Socialist Vietnam*, edited by Hue-Tam Ho Tai, 167–95. Berkeley: University of California Press, 2001.

Tran, Quan Tue. 'Remembering the Boat People Exodus: A Tale of Two Memorials'. *The Journal of Vietnamese Studies* 7, no. 3 (2012): 80–121.

Valverde, Kieu-Linh Caroline. 'From Dust to Gold: The Vietnamese Amerasian Experience', in *Racially Mixed People in America*, edited by P. P. Maria Root, 144–61. Newbury Park, CA: Sage Publications, 1992.

Wajnryb, Ruth. *The Silence: How Tragedy Shapes Talk*. Crows Nest: Allen & Unwin, 2001.

Wayland, Sarah, Myfanwy Maple, Kathy McKay and Geoffrey Glassock. 'Holding on to Hope: A Review of the Literature Exploring Missing Persons, Hope and Ambiguous Loss'. *Death Studies* 40, no. 1 (2015): 54–60.

Wilmoth, Peter. 'Boat People Condemn Loss of Monument'. *The Age*, 26 June 2006. https://www.vnbp.org/vietnamese/memorial/baochi/1119321940275.pdf.

11

Refiguring trauma

Women's narratives of suffering in post-conflict Timor-Leste

Hannah Loney

The language of trauma occupies a prominent place in considerations of the legacies of violent conflict in contemporary Timor-Leste. It shapes and provokes a particular – and somewhat restricted – set of responses to continuing concerns in the newly independent, post-conflict state. This chapter examines how East Timorese women have engaged the term 'trauma' when recounting their experiences and memories of the Indonesian occupation of East Timor, which took place from 1975 to 1999.[1] Within this discussion, I seek to move beyond the dominant paradigms of trauma, the focus of which is primarily on an individual and pathologized subject. I suggest, instead, that trauma has been understood in Timor-Leste as a fundamentally corporeal emotion, that is both somatically transmittable and, simultaneously, able to suffuse the collective body of a social group. I argue that to understand East Timorese women's invocations of the trope of trauma as not purely an individual or psychological phenomenon, but rather, as embodied and social, can nuance our understanding of how trauma is experienced and understood in contemporary Timor-Leste.[2]

This chapter commences with a brief outline of the history of the Indonesian invasion and occupation of East Timor. It then moves to provide an overview of popular conceptualizations and theories of trauma, in order to contextualize my discussion of the particular ways in which the concept is invoked and understood within Timor-Leste today. Subsequently, I draw upon a series of oral history interviews with East Timorese women to explore some of the ways in which my interviewees used the term 'trauma', in relation to what particular circumstances or experiences, and how they described the feeling or effect of trauma upon their lives.[3] Finally, I reflect upon the dynamics of gender, trauma and social suffering in contemporary Timor-Leste.

Historical background and theoretical framework

When Indonesia invaded the former Portuguese colony of East Timor on 7 December 1975, a bloody and protracted campaign ensued. Indonesian security forces projected this campaign to be relatively quick and contained; however, it took several years, an increase in US-supplied aircraft and other military equipment, and the loss of thousands of civilian lives before the Indonesian National Armed Forces (*Angkatan Bersenjata Republik Indonesia*, ABRI) gained control over the territory and its people.[4] On 26 March 1979, the Indonesian government declared East Timor to be 'pacified' and established the militarized state structure that would administer the territory until 1999.

From the initial days of the invasion, Indonesian security forces terrorized the East Timorese civilian population into submission. Indeed, violence remained a feature of daily life throughout the subsequent military occupation of the territory. Up to 200,000 East Timorese people – nearly one-third of the territory's population – died over the twenty-four-year period.[5] Ongoing and systematic human rights violations were prevalent in all aspects of East Timorese daily life, including unlawful killings and disappearances; forced displacement and famine; arbitrary detention, torture and ill-treatment; and sexual violence.[6] These violations occurred throughout the occupation, reaching especially high levels in the lead-up to and in the aftermath of the United Nations' supervised independence referendum in 1999.

The violent repression that accompanied the Indonesian invasion and subsequent occupation of East Timor meant that my interviewees' memories, when recounting their lives during this time, were suffused with a deep sense of personal and collective suffering. They recalled many extreme and shocking events, including witnessing acts of tremendous violence; experiences of forced displacement; the destruction of their homes; enduring long periods of hunger; and separation from, and the loss of, multiple family members. Many of the women whom I interviewed had been directly affected by a traumatic event, were witnesses to one or more, or had heard about traumatic events that took place in the past and involved members of their family or community. As I have argued elsewhere, all of the women whom I interviewed experienced the Indonesian occupation as a traumatic *process*.[7]

As the introduction to this volume explores at length, the term 'trauma' is often interpreted within the scholarly literature in the sense that Cathy Caruth describes, as 'an overwhelming experience of sudden or catastrophic events, in which the response to the event occurs in the often delayed and uncontrollable repetitive occurrence of hallucinations and other intrusive phenomena'.[8] Traumatic episodes, Judith Herman similarly suggests, are those which 'overwhelm the ordinary systems of care that give people a sense of control, connection, and meaning. They confront human beings with the extremities of helplessness and terror, and evoke the responses of catastrophe'.[9] Indeed, much Western literature theorizes trauma in a similar manner; it generally involves the diagnosis of a traumatized individual, which necessitates a particular response by the state to manage such occurrences through medicalized treatment.

I argue that this framework, which places primary emphasis upon individual experiences of an event, is not automatically transferrable – nor directly translatable – to different cultural contexts. Indeed, much of the critical literature on trauma expresses concern that the concept of trauma, as it is understood in many official discourses, does not allow for a subtle understanding of the diverse forms that suffering takes in different individuals, let alone across a range of social and cultural contexts. Arthur and Joan Kleinman, for example, remind us that 'individuals do not suffer in the same way, any more than they live, talk about what is at stake, or respond to serious problems in the same way'.[10] Nevertheless, in many post-conflict societies across the world, conflict survivors have turned to the concept of trauma to describe their experiences of suffering. The concept of trauma has proven, therefore, to be somewhat contentious, yet also deeply compelling and malleable. In her examination of post-conflict Aceh, for example, Catherine Smith describes the way in which conflict survivors have taken up the concept of trauma and 'incorporated it into local languages, healing practices and political imaginaries'.[11] Trauma, Smith suggests, has become 'a powerful cultural idiom' in Aceh.[12] It shapes the ways in which many people reflect upon their own and others' experiences of suffering and, subsequently, embark upon the complex process of personal and social recovery.

In post-conflict Timor-Leste, the trope of trauma similarly occupies a prominent place in considerations of the legacies of violent conflict. The term has been adopted into Tetun, Timor-Leste's lingua franca, and has entered into everyday discourse. English-language emotional and character terms, Catharine Williams-van Klinken explains, cannot be simply mapped onto the Tetun language.[13] Yet, the term 'trauma' is frequently used with reference to individual and collective experiences of violence during the Indonesian occupation, as well as to its personal and social after-effects. This tendency is evident, for example, in the final report of the Timor-Leste Commission for Reception, Truth and Reconciliation (*Comissão de Acolhimento, Verdade e Reconciliação de Timor Leste*, CAVR). Established under the United

Nations Transitional Administration in East Timor (UNTAET) in 2002, the CAVR was an independent, statutory authority mandated to 'establish the truth' regarding human rights abuses committed in the territory between April 1974 and October 1999, to promote community reconciliation, and to prepare a report containing its findings and recommendations.[14]

Explicitly situated within a human rights framework, the Commission's final report refers frequently to Timor-Leste's traumatic struggle for national self-determination. The report describes, for example, the 'traumatic consequences' of the Indonesian occupation and the 'on-going trauma' experienced by survivors of the conflict, as well as the 'trauma' potentially associated with the act of giving testimony to the Commission itself.[15] Notably, the Commission found that East Timorese women who had experienced sexual violence during the Indonesian occupation were 'more likely to suffer symptoms of trauma than other victims', surpassed only by women who bore children as a result of rape or who had been involved in a coercive sexual relationship.[16] This observation speaks to the gendered dynamics of trauma and suffering in post-conflict Timor-Leste, as I elaborate later.

The Indonesian occupation of East Timor finally came to an end when, on 30 August 1999, an overwhelming 78.5 per cent of East Timorese voters rejected the proposal of special autonomy within the Republic of Indonesia. This event paved the way for full independence, which was finally realized on 20 May 2002.[17] In the aftermath of the independence referendum, Indonesian forces and East Timorese pro-integration supporters withdrew from East Timor, facilitating the forcible displacement of at least 200,000 people across the border to Indonesian West Timor. In the process, towns were burned to the ground and nearly 70 per cent of the territory's infrastructure was destroyed.[18] The United Nations subsequently established an interim civil administration and peacekeeping mission (UNTAET) to administer the territory until full independence.[19] In the aftermath of this violence, the various structures of UNTAET – as well as an impressive number of international aid and development agencies, health professionals, NGOs and other groups that flocked to the territory to witness these historic events – determined that the repeated human rights violations that had characterized the Indonesian occupation of East Timor necessitated multiple and ongoing assessments of the prevalence of trauma in the post-conflict state.

These international administrative bodies, accordingly, directed significant attention to the rehabilitation needs of conflict survivors in Timor-Leste. In 2000, for example, the International Rehabilitation Council for Torture Victims (IRCT) – an independent, international health professional organization – conducted a national psychological needs assessment in the territory.[20] The IRCT interviewed 1,033 households across all thirteen districts of Timor-Leste with the aim of assessing the extent of torture and trauma, as well as the health impact that it had upon the population. The IRCT determined that 97 per cent of those surveyed had experienced 'at least one traumatic event' during the conflict, including direct exposure to a combat situation, lack of shelter or ill health with no access to medical care.[21] The organization also classified 34 per cent of respondents as having 'post-traumatic stress disorder'.[22]

Some of the precipitating events had taken place within the context of the widespread conflict that broke out within the territory between local East Timorese resistance forces (*Forças Armadas da Libertação Nacional de Timor-Leste*, FALINTIL) and the Indonesian military following the invasion in December 1975. The ICRT also determined that other events – and the resultant trauma – had followed from explicit policies employed by the Indonesian security forces to inflict psychological harm on those East Timorese who were suspected of resisting Indonesia's annexation of the territory. Throughout the twenty-four-year military occupation, many East Timorese remained committed to the idea of national self-determination.[23] In response to these expressions of resistance and discontent, the military arm of the Indonesian occupying regime launched successive campaigns to eradicate the resistance movement. These campaigns included, for example, the establishment of highly trained local paramilitary units to conduct intelligence, reconnaissance and combat operations.[24] These deliberate attempts to divide and conquer the East Timorese had particularly devastating and lasting effects upon the local population.

This long history of violence both structured and informed my interviewees' narratives of the Indonesian occupation. The prevalence of the Western-derived language of trauma that my interviewees used to describe the violence and its effects, and the particular implications of this use of the term within the wider social context of Timor-Leste, also shaped their articulation of these experiences. To better understand the way that trauma has been understood and invoked in post-conflict Timor-Leste, I draw here upon the anthropological concept of 'social suffering'. This concept has been developed by Arthur Kleinman, Veena Das and Margaret Lock to explain how social and institutional structures, as well as various forms of political and economic power, shape and produce individual and collective experiences of suffering and trauma.[25] My analysis is also informed by recent feminist scholarship that aims to conceptualize trauma, suffering and witnessing beyond the dominant paradigm of trauma theory. Sara Ahmed and Lauren Berland, for example, approach emotions such as trauma in social and cultural terms, rather than exclusively through the lens of individual pathological affect.[26] These understandings provide a framework that is more attentive and responsive to the sociocultural dimensions of suffering in post-conflict Timor-Leste.

Gendered narratives of suffering

Many of my interviewees actively engaged the term 'trauma' to reflect upon their own and others' experiences of suffering that occurred during the Indonesian occupation of East Timor. They often explained that after experiencing particularly violent or shocking events, they 'began to feel trauma'. While violence was a constant feature of daily life throughout the Indonesian occupation, as I have outlined above, some of the most brutal instances of violence occurred during the lead-up to and following the independence referendum in 1999. The referendum took place within the context of momentous changes in the Indonesian political landscape. Amid growing public and political demands for reform, President Suharto resigned on 21 May 1998 after thirty-one years in office. Subsequently, Suharto's vice-president and nominated successor, B. J. Habibie, was sworn in as the new president of the Republic of Indonesia.[27] The new government faced a number of urgent challenges, including the devastating effects of the Asian Financial Crisis and the pro-democracy movement's demands for reform (*Reformasi*), as well as growing demands for greater autonomy from the provinces of Aceh, West Papua and East Timor.[28]

In occupied East Timor, in particular, the Indonesian military administration was unsettled by the increasing domestic and international momentum towards ending the violence and finding a peaceful solution to the territory's political future. The occupying regime thus established a number of pro-integration East Timorese militia groups in towns and villages across East Timor. Geoffrey Robinson, in a report commissioned by the United Nations Human Rights Office of the High Commissioner for Human Rights, draws upon substantial documentation and testimonial records to demonstrate that these local militia groups were 'conceived, created, and authorized by Indonesian authorities' as a conspicuous part of the government's strategy to discourage the population from voting for independence.[29] As the referendum drew closer, these groups embarked upon a widespread and systematic campaign of terrorizing and intimidating pro-independence supporters and the civilian population at large. These campaigns manifested in a number of brutal and premeditated attacks against unarmed civilians. One such event that featured prominently within my interviewees' narratives took place in the small town of Liquiçá.

Located some 15 kilometres to the west of the capital, Dili, Liquiçá witnessed a shocking massacre in 1999. At the Liquiçá Church on 6 April, between sixty and a hundred people were killed or disappeared in an attack by the notorious pro-integration East Timorese militia group, *Besi Merah Putih* (Red and White Iron). Around 2,000 people, including women and children, had sought refuge at the Church compound in response to escalating militia violence in the days prior.[30] Some people found sanctuary in the Church itself, while others sheltered in the adjacent residence of the local priest, Father Rafael dos Santos. Early on the morning of 6 April, local militiamen entered the Church compound and brutally attacked the terrified civilians with machetes, knives and guns. Members of the Indonesian military and the Police Mobile Brigades (*Brigade Mobile,* Brimob) reportedly backed up the militias and fired their weapons during the attack.[31]

Several of my interviewees recounted, in careful and extensive detail, the brutal nature of these killings and the effects that experiencing and witnessing such violence had upon their lives subsequently. One interviewee, Yolanda, for example, was born in 1971 in the nearby town of Maubara, but had lived in Liquiçá during the occupation. In the face of escalating militia violence in early April 1999, she had sought refuge at the Liquiçá Church compound. She had vivid memories of the massacre that ensued, as militiamen fired shots into the air, entered the Church compound and attacked the terrified civilians. Yolanda recalled, in particular, how the attackers stabbed and then trampled on her father. She remembered seeing militiamen stab and dismember villagers, putting various body parts into their mouths. 'There was so much blood', she recalled, 'the way they cut people was like they cut meat'.[32] Yolanda reflected upon this experience in light of the long history of violent conflict in the territory. She maintained, however, that there was something markedly different about the violence that took place in 1999, compared to earlier experiences:

> What I felt at that time was the war that happened in 1975, you saw people fighting each other with guns. But in this case, the *Besi Merah* was worse. I felt more afraid than before and really traumatized because they didn't shoot you but stabbed you, cut people into pieces. They didn't care if you were a child or an adult, they just kept going. . . . The way they killed people, it's like they had no heart. So, for me, if you talk about the war, crossfire is quite normal. But this case was really different, and I saw it with my own eyes.[33]

Yolanda experienced the 1999 violence as significantly more brutal than that of previous encounters. She felt it to be more visceral, immediate and indiscriminate. Indeed, it was the seemingly unpredictable nature of the killings that made this event particularly terrorizing for Yolanda, and which produced a deep sense of helplessness.

Yolanda was lucky enough to escape the Church compound physically unharmed, but she experienced profound emotional distress at having witnessed this shocking brutality. 'I couldn't eat and couldn't sleep for two months', she recalled.[34] Yolanda's affective state linked directly to witnessing a specific event, but this event had not been experienced in isolation. Yolanda understood her response to the massacre through the lens of prior experiences of violence. This event was distinguished not only by its brutality but also by its immediacy: it was 'really different', she explained, because 'I saw it with my own eyes'.[35] Only a small child when Indonesian forces had invaded East Timor in 1975, Yolanda had experienced the violence of this earlier period primarily through stories of the suffering of family and community members, as well as the broader social experiences of loss and displacement.[36] This earlier period of conflict Yolanda knew only abstractly;

in contrast, she had directly witnessed the violence and destruction of 1999 first-hand.

Other interviewees, too, placed great emphasis upon the fact that they had personally witnessed the violence in 1999, thus distinguishing it from a history of violence that they knew, albeit indirectly. With reference to the Liquiçá Church massacre, Bebe, for example, similarly emphasized: 'I saw these things'.[37] And, as she told me, many people had experienced 'very serious trauma' following this event.[38] Bebe was born in Liquiçá into a family of fifteen children in 1979, after the large-scale conflict between the Indonesian military and East Timorese resistance fighters had largely subsided. In our interview, she described a rather happy childhood, during which she worked hard at school. After high school, Bebe went to Surabaya, Indonesia, where she earned a university degree in electrical engineering. She returned to East Timor in early 1999. Bebe recalled that soon after her return, the situation in the territory began to change, and she had not wanted to return to Indonesia to continue her studies. Bebe's discussion of her first-hand experience of these unfolding events was demonstrative of a broader trend within East Timorese women's narratives to assert a space within Timor-Leste's history of occupation and resistance. During the Indonesian occupation, this agency sometimes took the form of returning home to East Timor after studying abroad, to witness and participate in the independence referendum in 1999. Retrospectively, this tendency can also be seen through the way in which many East Timorese women sought to integrate their memories, experiences – and indeed, their trauma – into the wider meaning of the independence struggle.[39]

Events that took place at the Liquiçá Church in April 1999 occupied a prominent place within many women's narratives of the Indonesian occupation. When violence broke out in early April, Bebe and her family had remained in their home, rather than seeking refuge in the Church compound. They had so many small children in their extended family, Bebe explained, that it was difficult to keep them all under control. Even though Bebe was at home when the massacre took place, she recalled hearing the sound of gunshots, and of militiamen shouting threats and insults at the population. Bebe described the violence as extending beyond the Church compound and into the nearby streets. She remembered, for example, that militiamen had thrown stones at houses and broken the windows; looting some houses, burning many others; and attacking civilians along the way. 'They destroyed many houses', she recounted. 'There was blood everywhere. . . . Many people were killed and bleeding'.[40] Bebe attested that in the days following the massacre, local militiamen and members of the Indonesian security forces had loaded the bodies of the victims into military trucks and discarded them in unknown locations. 'Until today', she explained, 'we still don't know where the bodies are [located]'.[41] Similar to other massacres that occurred in 1999, as I elaborate later, the systematic disposal of corpses following the

Liquiçá Church massacre disrupted mortuary rituals and compounded the distress caused by the violent and unexpected nature of these killings.[42]

The violence continued in the days and weeks following the massacre. Bebe explained that militiamen continued to rampage and terrorize villagers, to burn down houses, as well as to hunt down and kill suspected pro-independence supporters. 'Although we stayed in our houses', Bebe remembered, 'we felt unsafe. They kept burning houses . . . destroying houses, and if they found people who were their targets, they tried to kill them'.[43] Many people who were injured were afraid to go to hospital, she said, instead treating themselves at home despite the severity of their injuries. The violence and brutality of the massacre had a lingering effect on Bebe's life. 'I did not feel free at the time. For several months', she recounted, 'we didn't feel safe, even to go shopping. We couldn't do anything freely. We . . . were really afraid'.[44] Following the massacre, Bebe explained, 'our lives were full of trauma'.[45] Here, Bebe evoked the concept of trauma not solely to describe its effect upon herself as an individual, but also to describe a social response to a violent event both within and upon the community. Like much of the violence that occurred in 1999, the perpetrators in the Liquiçá Church massacre were predominantly local men who had been recruited, trained and equipped by the Indonesian security forces.[46] There were, therefore, often close familial and social ties between the perpetrators and victims of this violence. The violence, as Antonius Robben writes of another context, thus inflicted 'a wound to the social body and its cultural frame'.[47] And as Bebe suggested, the trauma that resulted from the massacre was not solely confined to the individual, but was one that manifested and circulated within a social group.

Considering these social dimensions, it is notable that the perpetrators of the violence wore masks to physically disguise themselves – and that when recounting these events, narrators discursively distanced themselves from the perpetrators by speaking in generalities. As Yolanda described, for example, the militiamen 'covered their faces so you couldn't see them'.[48] In addition, my interviewees largely referred to the perpetrators of this violence as a collective 'militia', rather than speaking more explicitly about the individuals enacting the violence. One can perhaps understand this distancing as a response to the deep anger, suspicion and distrust that permeated the community, fractured as it was by the occupying regime's deliberate and consistent attempts to divide it.[49] Indeed, this issue of East Timorese who sided with the Indonesians and perpetrated such violence remains a source of enduring tension in post-conflict Timor-Leste. Andrey Damaledo estimates that of the approximately 200,000 East Timorese – militiamen, military and civilian collaborators, as well as forcibly displaced people – who fled to Indonesian West Timor before and immediately following the independence referendum in 1999, approximately 88,000 remain in West Timor. This figure suggests, however, that a significant portion have since returned to Timor-Leste.[50] That conflict survivors such as Yolanda depersonalize this violence could, therefore, be seen as a means of transforming the experience into a memory with which they can live. To this day, most of the perpetrators of this violence also remain unpunished, an injustice that only intensifies individual and collective feelings of sadness and suffering.

Alongside this social context, gender also informed my interviewees' narratives of trauma and its after-effects. This theme was raised by Elisa, for example, whom I interviewed in June 2012 in Dili at the office of FOKUPERS (*Forum Komunikasi Perempuan*, Women's Communication Forum), an organization that was established in 1997 to address gender-based violence and human rights violations against women and children.[51] Elisa was involved in the organization's branch in Liquiçá, where she was born and had attended school. Her fiancé had been actively involved in the local resistance movement; when they married, Elisa became involved as well, helping to prepare supplies to send to the guerrilla fighters in the mountains.

Because of their involvement in the resistance, Elisa recalled feeling that everyday life was not peaceful and that she was constantly under surveillance by the various apparatuses of the occupying regime. Many East Timorese women who had connections to the resistance or were suspected by the Indonesian security forces to have links to them due to either their personal or family background, similarly described this sense of constantly being watched.[52] Elisa explained that this unease was something that she, as a woman, felt in particular. 'As a woman, I really felt that I had to overcome this situation', she explained. 'That was really difficult for me'.[53] Here, Elisa referred to the particular vulnerability that she felt because of her gender. During this time, many East Timorese women were vulnerable to sexual violence, but they also endured proxy violence as the military's means of targeting male relatives and the resistance at large.[54] In the 1980s, Elisa's husband was arrested for his involvement in the resistance. His arrest was not unusual; the Indonesian security forces employed arbitrary interrogation and detention throughout the occupation, often arresting and detaining – without trial, and for varying periods of time – individuals suspected of having links to the resistance.[55] At the time of her husband's arrest, Elisa was a new mother. Elisa described the fear and vulnerability that she felt at the time; she explained that she was 'really traumatized' by her husband's arrest.[56] What had concerned Elisa the most about her distress, however, was the effect that it would have upon her child.

For Elisa, experiencing emotional distress as a new mother transformed her trauma into something transmittable. Indeed, Elisa felt that she passed her trauma on to her baby while nursing; her fears and distress, held in her body, were imparted to her young daughter through her breast milk. There were thus gendered specificities to Elisa's experience of trauma.

As with her husband's arrest and imprisonment, gender also played a strong role in Elisa's description of the devastating impact that the Liquiçá

Church massacre had upon her family. By April 1999, Elisa's husband had been released from prison, and the family had sought refuge in the Church as violence had broken out: 'At that time, we were all there inside the Church because we thought that the Church was a safe place for us to hide',[57] Elisa recounted. At around noon, Elisa remembered, 'the militia came and attacked us all [. . .] they killed so many people, lots of people also got injured – including women and children'.[58] Among those killed was Elisa's husband. Elisa recounted these events plainly: 'My husband got killed in the Liquiçá Church. [. . .] They killed lots of people on 6 April 1999 and the dead bodies just disappeared'.[59] To this day, Elisa does not know where her husband's body is located.

Her inability to recover her husband's body means that Elisa remains unable to conduct the burial rituals that usually follow the death of a loved one. As Lia Kent explains, these rituals are important in Timor-Leste, 'both for the sake of the dead themselves as well as for the restoration of the order of the living and the re-establishment of social life'.[60] They are even more important when, like Elisa's husband, someone has died an unnatural or sudden death. Such disruptions of mortuary rituals by 'bad deaths' compound the distress of families and communities.[61] The perpetrators of this instance of violence were also local men. As Antonius Robben and Marcelo Suárez-Orozco write, such violence thus 'targets social bonds and cultural practices as much as it targets the body and psyche'.[62] The capacity to conduct such rituals, therefore, is a vital – but, for Elisa, as yet inaccessible – means of reconstructing everyday life in the aftermath of mass violence.[63]

As many of my interviewees suggested, the events that took place at the Liquiçá Church marked a moment of rupture in many women's lives. Afterwards, Elisa recalled, 'I had no idea what to do to continue to survive. It was a burden for me. [. . .] I had no idea how to continue my life. [. . .] I felt really stressed because I lost my husband. A family should be complete, so after I lost my husband it was really a burden'.[64] Elisa's desolation and desperation only increased when she learned that while she had been seeking refuge in the Church compound, members of the militia had burned down her house. 'I was thinking that I had to start from zero', Elisa remembered, 'I lost everything, and I lost my husband'.[65] Widowed, homeless and a young mother, Elisa had to rebuild her life and provide for her family alone. In response to the lingering violence in the streets of Liquiçá in the days following the massacre, and fearful that she may be a target for the militiamen, Elisa fled with her children to Dili. There, she 'had to play the role of mother and father', as childrearer and breadwinner.[66] Elisa's description of the after-effects of the massacre – her personal, social and economic vulnerability – were thus deeply gendered, embedded as they were in her identity as a wife and mother, her ideas about the role of men within families and the apparent separation of public and private spheres of life.

While many women's trauma was partly linked to a specific event, their feelings of distress and vulnerability had accumulated over time. In her discussion of the enduring implications of social trauma in post-conflict Timor-Leste, Victoria Sakti describes emotional distress as both arising from, and accumulated by, 'events succeeding and underlying the supposedly traumatizing incident'.[67] For Elisa, feelings of fear and emotional distress initially arose from her involvement in the resistance and the associated feeling of being watched. These fears – for Elisa herself, for her children and for their future – accumulated over time, as her husband was arrested and, eventually, brutally killed. This series of distressing events also provoked a lingering sense of vulnerability, stemming from the ongoing structural violence that she experienced. For women like Elisa, the emotional devastation of loss is compounded by its material consequences.

Many East Timorese women widowed in the violence of 1999 found support and solace in new forms of social organization that were established in local communities.[68] It is within this context that some of the ways in which attempts to heal trauma, to recover from decades of violent conflict, are made. Elisa described, for example, the critical role played by FOKUPERS in this regard. The organization provided support for women whose husbands were imprisoned or had been killed, particularly in the events of 1999, as well as assisted women who had experienced sexual violence at the hands of the Indonesian security forces. Representatives from the organization stayed with these women and provided them with counselling and support, Elisa explained, 'so that they wouldn't feel alone'.[69] Often with few resources to support themselves and their families, for many women, this organization presented a new support structure and form of solidarity beyond the immediate family network.

With the support of FOKUPERS, and at the initiative of women in local communities, a number of widows' groups were also established across the territory following the independence referendum in 1999. Elisa was involved in establishing one such group, *Rate Laek* (Without Graves), for women whose husbands had been killed in the Liquiçá Church massacre. Local women also established similar groups in Maliana, *Novi Novi* (Ninety-Nine), and in Covalima, *Mate Restu* (Remains of the Dead).[70] Representatives from these groups listened to women's stories, provided them with counselling and sought to address issues related to economic survival, for example, by helping women to establish a *kios* (small shop) to support themselves and their families. As their names indicate, these groups also played an active role in demanding justice and disclosure regarding the whereabouts of the disappeared. When the United Nations Commissioner for Human Rights, Mary Robinson, visited Liquiçá in August 2002, for example, the women from *Rate Laek* presented her with a petition that articulated their suffering and appealed for Robinson's support in their struggle for 'justice and healing'.[71] The prevalence of these groups suggests that many East Timorese women sought solace from other women, partly because of the gendered nature of conflict-related violence – many women had lost their husbands or other male relatives during the conflict – but also because of the gendered norms in East Timorese society, which stipulate that women often provide a source of emotional support for one another. That these groups were comprised mainly of women and were based in local communities sheds light upon the social and gendered dimensions of trauma, as it is understood within the context of post-conflict Timor-Leste.

In addition to these groups, faith also played a significant role for many East Timorese women in the healing process. Another of my interviewees, Jina, for example, attested to the violence that she witnessed at the Liquiçá Church massacre and the ways that she tries to manage her emotional distress. Jina explained that she reminds herself to have faith that God will not allow such events to happen again. It is this assurance, she told me, that allows her to live calmly with the past.[72] For Jina, therefore, it was important not to speak of the past in an effort to recuperate her subjectivity in the aftermath of trauma, but rather, to consign it to God. Indeed, the Catholic Church played a crucial role in providing support and comfort for many East Timorese over the course of the Indonesian occupation.

During the Indonesian occupation, the Church transformed from an institution entwined in Portuguese colonial rule to a critical source of sanctity and hope for many East Timorese people. For women, in particular, the Church provided comfort amid a violent and repressive regime. Catholicism saw explosive growth amid the occupation: approximately 30 per cent of East Timorese identified as Catholic in 1974; by 1999, this figure had increased to about 90 per cent.[73] This enormous rate of conversions can, in part, be explained with reference to the Indonesian state ideology of Pancasila. Under this system, which was introduced to East Timor following Indonesia's annexation of the territory, citizens were required to subscribe to one of five official religions: Islam, Hinduism, Buddhism, Catholicism or Protestantism.[74] Additionally, in response to the predominantly Muslim Indonesian population that comprised the occupying regime, becoming Catholic was a way for many East Timorese to express a subtle form of resistance. Due to this association between East Timorese identity and Catholicism, as well as the perceived sanctity of the Church as a place of worship, the Liquiçá Church was a particularly potent location for the massacre in April 1999.

Conclusion

The frequent evocation of the concept of trauma to describe responses to mass violence in the modern history of Timor-Leste is embedded in the context of humanitarian intervention in 1999 and the subsequent influx of international organizations advocating particular therapeutic models of healing. It is important, however, to understand the use of the term 'trauma' in post-conflict Timor-Leste beyond the discourse of psychic responses to shocking events or experiences. My interviewees described experiencing trauma and its ongoing effects, but they often did not mean this in strict accordance with the Western psychotherapeutic literature. Rather, they engaged the term trauma to convey the emotional distress caused by an event or experience and its long-term consequences, but not necessarily felt as an individualized, pathological, psychosomatic phenomenon.[75] My interviewees explained their distress and its aftermath not just as it related to themselves, but they embedded that affective experience in family networks and local communities. These accounts suggest that the experience of suffering is viewed in Timor-Leste as a deeply collective phenomenon that continues to shape the social and cultural worlds of conflict survivors.

There are also gendered dimensions to the nature of suffering in post-conflict Timor-Leste, as well as the way in which trauma is understood by East Timorese women. Women experienced the Indonesian occupation differently from men. The nature of violence – including women's experiences of suffering, as well as its broader implications – also differ. While the realm of the social was central to the experience of trauma, it is also notable that many women have found the strength, courage and resources to move forward with their lives within new social groups and networks that are comprised of other women. While the language of trauma may have been adopted by conflict survivors in Timor-Leste, this does not mean that associated therapeutic models and the medicalized discourse of trauma have been seamlessly incorporated. The ways that the language of trauma has been adapted, but has come to mean something different in Timor-Leste, therefore, call into question universalizing theories that see trauma as transcending time and space.

Notes

1 The official name of the territory today is the Democratic Republic of Timor-Leste (*República Democrática de Timor-Leste*, RDTL). In this chapter, I use the term 'East Timor' when referring to the period of Indonesian occupation (1975–99) and 'Timor-Leste' when referring to the period from 1999 to the present.

2 I extend my thanks to Paula Michaels and Christina Twomey for inviting me to participate in the workshop on Gender and Trauma at Monash University. Some material from this chapter was first published in my book, *In Women's Words: Violence and Everyday Life during the Indonesian Occupation of East Timor, 1975–1999* (Portland: Sussex Academic Press, 2018).

3 Ethics clearance was obtained for this project through the University of Melbourne Human Research Ethics Committee (HREC 1136578). With permission, I have referred to my interviewees using their first names. This research was made possible through the generous support of several travel

grants through the University of Melbourne: the School of Historical and Philosophical Studies Research and Graduate Studies Funding Scheme, the Faculty of Arts PhD Fieldwork Grant, the Graduate Research in Arts Travel Scheme, the MA Bartlett Special Travel Grant-in-aid, the Riady Scholarship, the Prue Torney Memorial Prize, and the Alma Hansen Scholarship.

4   The Indonesian military – which included the army, navy, air force and police – was referred to as ABRI under the New Order regime. In 1998, the name was changed to the Indonesian National Armed Forces (*Tentara Nasional Indonesia*, TNI) to reflect the separation of the police from the military.

5   Commission for Reception, Truth and Reconciliation in Timor-Leste (*Comissão de Acolhimento, Verdade e Reconciliação de Timor Leste*, CAVR), *Chega! The Final Report of the Timor-Leste Commission for Reception, Truth and Reconciliation*, Vol. 1 (Jakarta: KPG in cooperation with STP-CAVR, 2013), 491.

6   CAVR, Part 6. The Profile of Human Rights Violations in Timor-Leste, 1974–99.

7   Loney, *In Women's Words*, 31.

8   Cathy Caruth, *Unclaimed Experience: Trauma, Narrative, and History* (Baltimore, MD: Johns Hopkins University Press, 1996), 11.

9   Judith Herman, *Trauma and Recovery* (New York: Basic Books, 1992), 33.

10 Arthur Kleinman and Joan Kleinman, 'The Appeal of Experience; The Dismay of Images: Cultural Appropriations of Suffering in Our Times', in *Social Suffering*, ed. Arthur Kleinman, Veena Das and Margaret Lock (Berkeley: University of California Press, 1997), 2.

11 Catherine Smith, *Resilience and the Localisation of Trauma in Aceh, Indonesia* (Singapore: NUS Press, 2018), 2.

12 Smith, *Resilience and the Localisation of Trauma*, 1.

13 Catharina Williams-van Klinken, 'Is He Hot-Blooded or Hot Inside? Expression of Emotion and Character in Tetun Dili', *The 5th ENUS Conference on Language and Culture*, University of Nusa Cendana, Indonesia, 1–3 August 2007.

14 CAVR, *Chega*, 73–88.

15 CAVR, *Chega*, 706, 2228, 1256, 1916, 2034.

16 CAVR, *Chega*, 2562–3.

17 United Nations Security Council, 'Secretary General Informs Security Council People of East Timor Rejected Special Autonomy Proposed by Indonesia', Press Release SC/6721, 3 September 1999, in 'Meetings Coverage and Press Releases', *United Nations*. https://www.un.org/press/en/1999/19990903.sc6 721.html.

18 Susan Harris Rimmer and Juli Effi Tomaras, 'Aftermath Timor Leste: Reconciling Competing Notions of Justice', 22 May 2006, *Parliament of Australia*. https://www.aph.gov.au/About_Parliament/Parliamentary_Depart ments/Parliamentary_Library/Publications_Archive/archive/TimorLeste.

19 Sarah Smith, *Gendering Peace: UN Peacebuilding in Timor-Leste* (London; New York: Routledge, 2019).

20 J. Modvig, J. Pagaduan-Lopez, J. Rodenburg, C. M. D. Salud, R. V. Cabigon and C. I. A. Panelo, 'Torture and Trauma in Post-Conflict East Timor', *Lancet* 356, no. 9243 (2000): 1763.

21 Modvig et al., 'Torture and Trauma', 1763.

22 Modvig et al., 'Torture and Trauma', 1763.

23 CAVR, *Chega*, Part 3: History of the Conflict.

24 CAVR, *Chega*, 367.

25 Arthur Kleinman, Veena Das and Margaret Lock, 'Introduction', in *Social Suffering*, ix.

26 Sara Ahmed, *The Cultural Politics of Emotion* (Edinburgh: Edinburgh University Press, 2014); and Lauren Berlant, ed., *Compassion: The Cultural and Politics of an Emotion* (New York; London: Routledge, 2004).

27 Edward Aspinall and Greg Fealy, ed., *Soeharto's New Order and Its Legacy: Essays in Honour of Harold Crouch* (Acton: ANU E Press, 2010).

28 Clinton Fernandes, *The Independence of East Timor: Multidimensional Perspectives – Occupation, Resistance, and International Political Activism* (Portland: Sussex Academic Press, 2011).

29 Geoffrey Robinson, *East Timor 1999: Crimes against Humanity. A Report Commissioned by the United Nations Office of the High Commissioner for Human Rights (OHCHR)* (Jakarta: Elsam and Hak, 2006), 6.

30 CAVR, *Chega*, 2806–10.

31 Robinson, *East Timor 1999*, 192.

32 Yolanda, interview with the author, Liquiçá, 15 July 2012.

33 Yolanda, interview.

34 Yolanda, interview.

35 Yolanda, interview.

36 Hannah Loney, '"And I Started to Understand": Moments of Illumination within Women's Oral Narratives from Indonesian-Occupied East Timor', *Oral History Australia Journal*, 36 (2014): 61–71.

37 Loney, '"And I Started to Understand"', 61–71.

38 Bebe, interview with the author, Liquiçá, 3 June 2012.

39 Amanda Wise, 'Embodying Exile: Collective Identities among East Timorese Refugees in Australia', *Social Analysis* 48, no. 3 (2004): 24–39.

40 Bebe, interview.

41 Bebe, interview.

42 Robinson, *East Timor 1999*, 195; and Victoria Kumala Sakti, '"Thinking Too Much": Tracing Local Patterns of Emotional Distress after Mass Violence in Timor-Leste', *The Asia Pacific Journal of Anthropology* 14, no. 5 (2013): 438–54.

43 Bebe, interview.

44 Bebe, interview.

45 Bebe, interview.

46 See Robinson, *East Timor 1999*.
47 Antonius C. G. M. Robben, 'How Traumatized Societies Remember: The Aftermath of Argentina's Dirty War', *Cultural Critique* 59 (Winter 2005): 125.
48 Yolanda, interview.
49 Wise, 'Embodying Exile', 32.
50 Andrey Damaledo, *Divided Loyalties: Displacement, Belonging and Citizenship among East Timorese in West Timor* (Acton: ANU Press, 2018), 16.
51 Janet Hunt, 'FOKUPERS – The East Timorese Women's Communication Forum: The Development of Timor-Leste's First Women's NGO', in *Women and the Politics of Gender in Post-Conflict Timor-Leste*, ed. Sara Niner (Florence: Taylor and Francis, 2016), 65–82.
52 Loney, *In Women's Words*, 85.
53 Elisa, interview with the author, Dili, 27 June 2012.
54 Loney, *In Women's Words*, Chapter Three.
55 Loney, *In Women's Words*, 65–70.
56 Elisa, interview.
57 Elisa, interview.
58 Elisa, interview.
59 Elisa, interview.
60 Lia Kent, 'Interrogating the "Gap" Between Law and Justice: East Timor's Serious Crimes Process', *Human Rights Quarterly* 34, no. 4 (2012): 1037.
61 James Fox, 'On Bad Death and the Left Hand: A Study of Rotinese Symbolic Inversions', in *Right and Left: Essays on Dual Symbolic Classification*, ed. Rodney Needham, 342–68 (Chicago: The University of Chicago Press, 1973).
62 Antonius C. G. M. Robben and Marcelo M. Suárez-Orozco, 'Introduction: Interdisciplinary Perspectives on Violence and Trauma', in *Cultures under Siege: Collective Violence and Trauma,* ed. Antonius C. G. M. Robben and Marcelo M. Suárez-Orozco (Cambridge: Cambridge University Press, 2000), 10.
63 Lia Kent, 'Local Memory Practices in East Timor: Disrupting Transitional Justice Narratives', *The International Journal of Transitional Justice* 5 (2011): 434–55.
64 Elisa, interview.
65 Elisa, interview.
66 Elisa, interview.
67 Sakti, 'Thinking Too Much', 450.
68 Galuh Wandita, Karen Campbell-Nelson and Manuela Leong Pereira, 'Learning to Engender Reparations in Timor-Leste: Reaching Out to Female Victims', in *What Happened to the Women? Gender and Reparations for Human Rights Violations*, ed. Ruth Rubio-Marín (Brooklyn, NY: Social Science Research Council, 2006), 292.

69 Elisa, interview.
70 Kent, 'Local Memory Practices in East Timor', 445–6; and Wandita et al., 'Learning to Engender Reparations in Timor-Leste', 297.
71 'Widows' Group Demands International Tribunal', 24 August 2002, *ETAN*. http://etan.org/et2002c/august/25-31/24widows.htm.
72 Jina, interview with the author, Liquiçá, 3 June 2012.
73 Peter Carey, 'The Catholic Church, Religious Revival, and the Nationalist Movement in East Timor, 1975–98', *Indonesia and the Malay World* 27, no. 78 (1999): 86.
74 During the New Order, Confucianism was de-recognized, but was reinstated with the fall of Suharto in 1998. Helen Pausacker, 'The Sixth Religion', *Inside Indonesia* 89 (2007). https://www.insideindonesia.org/the-sixth-religion.
75 I am grateful to Mica Barreto Soares for her insights here.

Works cited

Ahmed, Sara. *The Cultural Politics of Emotion*. Edinburgh: Edinburgh University Press, 2014.
Aspinall, Edward and Greg Fealy, eds. *Soeharto's New Order and Its Legacy: Essays in Honour of Harold Crouch*. Acton: ANU E Press, 2010.
Berlant, Lauren, ed. *Compassion: The Cultural and Politics of an Emotion*. New York; London: Routledge, 2004.
Carey, Peter. 'The Catholic Church, Religious Revival, and the Nationalist Movement in East Timor, 1975–98'. *Indonesia and the Malay World* 27, no. 78 (1999): 77–95.
Caruth, Cathy. *Unclaimed Experience: Trauma, Narrative, and History*. Baltimore, MD: Johns Hopkins University Press, 1996.
Commission for Reception, Truth and Reconciliation in Timor-Leste (*Comissão de Acolhimento, Verdade e Reconciliação de Timor Leste*, CAVR). *Chega! The Final Report of the Timor-Leste Commission for Reception, Truth and Reconciliation*, Vol. 1. Jakarta: KPG in cooperation with STP-CAVR, 2013.
Damaledo, Andrey. *Divided Loyalties: Displacement, Belonging and Citizenship among East Timorese in West Timor*. Acton: ANU Press, 2018.
Fernandes, Clinton. *The Independence of East Timor: Multidimensional Perspectives – Occupation, Resistance, and International Political Activism*. Portland: Sussex Academic Press, 2011.
Fox, James. 'On Bad Death and the Left Hand: A Study of Rotinese Symbolic Inversions', in *Right and Left: Essays on Dual Symbolic Classification*, edited by Rodney Needham, 342–68. Chicago: The University of Chicago Press, 1973.
Harris Rimmer, Susan and Juli Effi Tomaras. 'Aftermath Timor Leste: Reconciling Competing Notions of Justice'. 22 May 2006. *Parliament of Australia*. https://www.aph.gov.au/About_Parliament/Parliamentary_Departments/Parliamentary_Library/Publications_Archive/archive/TimorLeste.
Herman, Judith. *Trauma and Recovery*. New York: Basic Books, 1992.
Hunt, Janet. 'FOKUPERS – The East Timorese Women's Communication Forum: The Development of Timor-Leste's First Women's NGO', in *Women and the*

Politics of Gender in Post-Conflict Timor-Leste, edited by Sara Niner, 65–82. Florence: Taylor and Francis, 2016.

Kent, Lia. 'Interrogating the "Gap" Between Law and Justice: East Timor's Serious Crimes Process'. *Human Rights Quarterly* 34, no. 4 (2012): 1021–44.

Kent, Lia. 'Local Memory Practices in East Timor: Disrupting Transitional Justice Narratives'. *The International Journal of Transitional Justice* 5 (2011): 434–55.

Kleinman, Arthur and Joan Kleinman. 'The Appeal of Experience; The Dismay of Images: Cultural Appropriations of Suffering in Our Times', in *Social Suffering*, edited by Arthur Kleinman, Veena Das and Margaret Lock, 1–24. Berkeley: University of California Press, 1997.

Kleinman, Arthur, Veena Das and Margaret Lock. 'Introduction', in *Social Suffering*, edited by Arthur Kleinman, Veena Das and Margaret Lock, ix–xxvii. Berkeley: University of California Press, 1997.

Loney, Hannah. '"And I Started to Understand": Moments of Illumination within Women's Oral Narratives from Indonesian-Occupied East Timor'. *Oral History Australia Journal* 36 (2014): 61–71.

Loney, Hannah. *In Women's Words: Violence and Everyday Life during the Indonesian Occupation of East Timor, 1975–1999*. Portland: Sussex Academic Press, 2018.

Modvig, J., J. Pagaduan-Lopez, J. Rodenburg, C. M. D. Salud, R. V. Cabigon and C. I. A. Panelo. 'Torture and Trauma in Post-Conflict East Timor'. *Lancet* 356, no. 9243 (2000): 1763.

Pausacker, Helen. 'The Sixth Religion'. *Inside Indonesia* 89 (2007). https://www.insideindonesia.org/the-sixth-religion.

Robben, Antonius C. G. M. 'How Traumatized Societies Remember: The Aftermath of Argentina's Dirty War'. *Cultural Critique* 59 (Winter 2005): 120–64.

Robben, Antonius C. G. M. and Marcelo M. Suárez-Orozco. 'Introduction: Interdisciplinary Perspectives on Violence and Trauma', in *Cultures under Siege: Collective Violence and Trauma*, edited by Antonius C. G. M. Robben and Marcelo M. Suárez-Orozco, 1–41. Cambridge: Cambridge University Press, 2000.

Robinson, Geoffrey. *East Timor 1999: Crimes against Humanity. A Report Commissioned by the United Nations Office of the High Commissioner for Human Rights (OHCHR)*. Jakarta: Elsam and Hak, 2006.

Sakti, Victoria Kumala. '"Thinking Too Much": Tracing Local Patterns of Emotional Distress After Mass Violence in Timor-Leste'. *The Asia Pacific Journal of Anthropology* 14, no. 5 (2013): 438–54.

Smith, Catherine. *Resilience and the Localisation of Trauma in Aceh, Indonesia*. Singapore: NUS Press, 2018.

Smith, Sarah. *Gendering Peace: UN Peacebuilding in Timor-Leste*. London; New York: Routledge, 2019.

United Nations Security Council. 'Secretary General Informs Security Council People of East Timor Rejected Special Autonomy Proposed by Indonesia'. Press Release SC/6721, 3 September, 1999. In 'Meetings Coverage and Press Releases'. *United Nations*. https://www.un.org/press/en/1999/19990903.sc6721.html.

Wandita, Galuh, Karen Campbell-Nelson and Manuela Leong Pereira. 'Learning to Engender Reparations in Timor-Leste: Reaching Out to Female Victims', in *What Happened to the Women? Gender and Reparations for Human Rights Violations*, edited by Ruth Rubio-Marín, 284–334. Brooklyn, NY: Social Science Research Council, 2006.

'Widows' Group Demands International Tribunal'. 24 August 2002. *ETAN*. http://etan.org/et2002c/august/25-31/24widows.htm.

Williams-van Klinken, Catharina. 'Is He Hot-Blooded or Hot Inside? Expression of Emotion and Character in Tetun Dili'. *The 5th ENUS Conference on Language and Culture*, University of Nusa Cendana, Indonesia, 1–3 August 2007.

Wise, Amanda. 'Embodying Exile: Collective Identities among East Timorese Refugees in Australia'. *Social Analysis* 48, no. 3 (2004): 24–39.

12

Changing the story

Women and trauma in Australian narratives of mental illness

Katie Holmes

Suzie Quartermaine's Expression of Interest (EOI) for the Australian Generations Oral History project was upbeat. As requested, she had succinctly summarized the 'main experiences, issues and events' in her life history. These included being adopted and meeting her biological family; studying; travelling; meeting her partner; her brother's struggle with schizophrenia and subsequent suicide, an event which coincided with her pregnancy; and then abandonment by her partner: 'Suddenly I was a single parent to a newborn, living on the pension and in grief and shock over my brother's death and my partner leaving me. Over the next eight years, my strength and my education brought me back from the brink of my own suicide and depression'. In the time between Suzie submitting her EOI and her interview, however, her life had once again changed dramatically. The sudden death of her mother in a bicycle accident left Suzie bereft, barely able to summon the strength to leave her home for at least a year. Rather than a forward-looking story of recovery and hope, her narrative was one haunted by grief and despair. Suzie was thoughtful and articulate about her life and the recurring experiences of depression which shaped it. Her intensely moving story of private pain finds echoes in more public narratives about women and depression.

In this chapter I explore the life histories of three women and consider the frameworks within which they made sense of their experience of mental illness and the gendered nature of these narratives. Mental illness comes in many varieties and degrees of severity. The three women discussed here all experienced what they labelled as 'depression' or, sometimes, 'post-natal depression'. Although many interviewees spoke about depression, I focus on these particular women because of the richness of their discussions.[1] My interest is not in the clinical accuracy of their self-diagnosis. Rather, I accept their terminology, while recognizing that what is today labelled 'depression' derives meaning from a particular historical and cultural context; it is not 'a unitary, global, trans-historical pathology'.[2] My focus is on how changing historical conditions have provided different narrative frames within which women talked about the trauma of mental illness. I also suggest that gender shapes both their experience of mental illness and their ways of telling; as important as what they say, is the way they say it.[3]

When we embarked on the Australian Generations project, which gathered life histories from 300 individuals, we did not set out to find people with experiences of mental illness but, like Suzie (b.1975), many volunteered this information.[4] Thanks to the rise of a 'therapeutic culture' that encourages talking about self, there was a greater willingness to talk about mental illness than participants had displayed in a similar project conducted in the 1980s.[5] In economically developed countries, therapeutic culture is fascinated with emotional and psychological life and this pervasive interest now manifests in a range of discourses, social practices and cultural artefacts, including the life history interview.[6] The narratives of self which emerged from the Australian Generations project are themselves historically shaped and located, and this is evident in the discussions of mental illness and the readiness of many interviewees to talk about emotional trauma.

It is implicit in the interviews that the experience of depression was itself traumatic and linked to other traumatizing experiences, although the women discussed here did not invoke the word 'trauma'. Sexual and domestic abuse have been widely recognized as traumatic; as sociologist Katie Wright notes, 'the concept of trauma has become the dominant way of understanding the psychological effects of abuse'.[7] Such recognition has been the result of feminism's exposure of the realities of many women's lives. As the opening chapter in this collection notes, women's trauma, so often the result of domestic and sexual violence experienced as part of their everyday lives, is ubiquitous. Feminism located the source of much of women's trauma in the family and the unequal power relations between men and women, which can remain hidden behind closed doors to the detriment of women's mental health.[8] The language used to talk about this kind of trauma is noticeably different from that of post-traumatic stress disorder (PTSD). It is private, feminized and inherently political. The articulation of such trauma as 'depression' provides a label that is both socially acceptable and that privileges a psychological, rather than a political or structural, understanding of the underlying causes.[9]

In Australia, successful men, especially politicians, judges and sportsmen, have been among the most outspoken advocates for mental health awareness and their stories have helped to normalize public discussion of this once-taboo topic.[10] Their narratives have generally told of the stress of their public lives, the pressure upon them to perform, the challenges they experienced as men in accepting their mental illness and the relief they have received through medication and counselling. It took courage for these men to come forward, and their trauma is evident. It in no way diminishes their suffering or the value of the public efforts to observe that the number of men who have spoken publicly about their struggles with mental illness far outweighs that of high-profile women who have felt able to endure public scrutiny of their private pain. One exception was media personality and model Charlotte Dawson, who had been very public about her anxiety and depression and was vilified on social media for her openness. She took her own life in 2014.[11]

Despite the high visibility of men in recent efforts to destigmatize mental illness, women historically have far outnumbered men in the treatment and incarceration for it.[12] Contemporary studies suggest that women are one and a half to two times more likely than men to report or be diagnosed with depression and twice as likely to be prescribed psychotropic drugs.[13] Nonetheless, their stories do not feature prominently in public narratives. For women, long-held gendered archetypes of the hysterical or overly emotional woman make public disclosure a far more treacherous path to navigate than it has become for men.[14]

The dominance of such notions has significant implications for the ways in which women can talk about mental illness. As Kimberly Emmons observes, 'while depression in men tends to be presented as a stark departure from "normal" feelings or emotions, depression in women is more likely to be understood as an outgrowth of women's complex emotional lives'.[15] For women whose lives have historically been lived within the 'private', domestic sphere, depression can be seen as an exaggeration of this state, when sufferers experience being overwhelmed by the quotidian demands of life.[16] These cultural and structural contexts of women's lives are entwined in their 'lifeworlds' – the 'routinely patterned everyday world in which [individuals] exist'.[17]

The intimate environment of an oral history interview creates a space in which women can attest to experiences of mental illness that diverge from the more visible accounts of prominent men in important ways. Talking about a world of relationships, family and emotions is something for which women have an available language. Having spent time in therapy, the three women discussed in this chapter demonstrate an ease in telling their narratives of depression. In doing so they reflected different interpretive frames for their experiences and in particular the therapy they received: depression as circumstantial, as a result of trauma, as a chemical imbalance; therapy as treatment, as empowerment, as medication. They also revealed the ways in which public discourses have shaped individual subjectivities and offered individuals the language through which to contest gender ideologies and make sense of individual trauma.

These women are products of their times, which shape how lives unfold and how they make meaning of those experiences. Two of the women I discuss here – Sandy and Alison – come from the post-war, baby boomer generation. Suzie is of the next cohort, the so-called Gen X. The major social changes which their lives traverse provide the context for their life experiences. One of the most dramatic changes was in the position of women and the new opportunities for them to pursue an education and career.[18] Second-wave feminism drove these broadening horizons and, in the notion that 'the personal is political', provided a new form of critique. Thus, at the same time as it was becoming more acceptable to talk about private life and private pain, feminism provided a language with which to analyse the political structures which formed the source of much of women's suffering.[19] The three stories examined here reflect the legacies of these two interlinked developments. Although the women did not necessarily identify as feminists, their lives and their stories reveal the impact of feminism on the opportunities available to them, and the ways they understood their experience of depression and the trauma.

Sandy

Sandy Carter (b. 1947) came from a working-class background and was the first in her family to finish high school. At the age of thirteen she was assessed as overstressed with the worry of exams and prescribed Valium for depression. 'When I was in school it was definitely seen to be something really wrong with me. . . . Now I see that there was something wrong with the circumstances . . . it was a normal reaction to a bad situation'.[20] Sandy's 'circumstances' included a mother who suffered depression and took 'under-the-counter' weight-loss pills, which made her moody, volatile and liable to 'take to her bed' for days. Sandy now interprets her mother's mental health issues, and those of her grandmother, as appropriate responses to their circumstances: poverty, difficult marriages and home environments, and social expectations that could not be met. With the exception of poverty, those conditions were repeated for Sandy.

In Sandy's narrative the mental health problems of her grandmother and mother were seen at the time to lie with the individual: they were the problem, not the circumstances, and there was no 'treatment'. In the mid-1970s, a time when 'the normal thing was to take medication', she was diagnosed with depression. 'It was seen as something wrong with me . . . and in retrospect, the same as my mother, it was the circumstances that were pretty difficult'. Only eighteen months after the birth of her second child, Sandy 'wasn't doing that well. . . . For the next 20 years I was intermittently treated for depression because it became quite the thing to do ... if somebody wasn't coping'.

Reflecting a shift in psychiatric thinking about the aetiology of depression, Sandy now locates the sources of her depression externally. In the 1970s, counselling 'started out being how to convince you that the situation you were in was ok' and working out how to put up with it. She believes the counselling and medical professions simply prescribed medication, rather than helping her – or other women – to address problems in their circumstances. By the early 1990s, Sandy came to see that her commitment to looking after her six children, keeping house, moving countries and cities regularly as she followed her husband for work came 'at my expense'. Sandy's husband had numerous extramarital affairs and the marriage finally ended when she learnt that he had passed a sexually transmitted disease to her, and that a number of the illnesses and an ectopic pregnancy she had suffered could be traced to it. Sandy's realization that the marriage was making her physically and psychologically ill – that the situation, and not she, was the problem – enabled her to leave the relationship. By this time, the attitude she encountered in therapy was, '"maybe you're right, maybe your circumstances are not ok and what do you want to do about it?", which gave you a bit more independence – treated you like a normal person'.

Sandy's understanding of her life history is refracted through the lens of the women's liberation movement and its impact on popular and medical understandings of the family, gender roles and the oppressive nature of patriarchal power, an issue she drew attention to in her EOI. The narrative arc of her interview moved from a life of significant restrictions to one of greater independence and empowerment. As indicated through her mother's and grandmother's experiences, women's disempowerment had implications for their mental health, what Betty Friedan called 'the problem that has no name'.[21] Sandy linked her personal struggle with mental illness to the changing historical position of women, and her story of healing became a narrative where the cause of mental illness shifted from the individual to the environment. Evident throughout the interview is a feminist critique of patriarchy, which enacted a gender hierarchy to the detriment of women's mental health.[22]

The growing awareness of the oppressive nature of the family among the counselling services Sandy accessed, and the increasing legitimacy of those services, is also evident in her interview.[23] The initial blindness of counsellors or doctors to the role of Sandy's circumstances in her distress suggests an unwillingness or inability to question a model of marriage that saw it as the woman's responsibility to subsume her own needs in those of her husband. The shift between her earlier and later encounters with mental health care also reflects a growing awareness among health professionals and the general public of trauma as more commonplace (not just restricted to Holocaust survivors and war veterans) and as rooted in an external event, not a personal failing.

The challenge to traditional family structures that empowered Sandy to free herself from an abusive and exploitative marriage could also serve to fuel a backlash against women who dared to resist oppression. With greater financial resources and professional connections, Sandy's husband fought for and won custody of their three sons, claiming that she was 'abandoning her children'. The court's judgement hints at an insidious and pervasive mindset: What 'sane' mother would abandon her children? In choosing to leave her abusive husband, Sandy implicitly challenged the family structure – the core unit of patriarchal power. In doing so she jeopardized her capacity to be seen and treated as a responsible, capable mother. Sandy's experience points to the limits of the seemingly unlikely alliance that developed between the mental health professionals and feminism, with the former lacking a critique of the revolutionary structural change needed to fundamentally alter power relations.[24]

Alison

Sandy's experience pinpoints the decades of the 1970s and 1980s as a hinge for changing narratives of women and mental illness. Just five years younger than Sandy, Alison Fettell (b.1952) had a more positive experience navigating mental illness and accessing empowering support to escape a destructive marriage.[25] Alison also grew up in a working-class household in western Sydney with a mother who, like Sandy's, had struggled with depression. Alison described her mother as 'often sad', perhaps grieving the death of her second child, who died two days after birth. Alison and her siblings made their own way to school in the mornings, while her mother stayed in bed, 'in her own funk'. At the age of four, Alison was sexually abused by a neighbour, a 'white-haired old man'. She recalled this abuse only decades later, during a gynaecological examination by a doctor who 'was the spitting image' of her abuser. She 'freaked out' and had an 'instant memory' of the abuse. Alison identified this as a 'repressed memory' – a term which became used, somewhat controversially, in the 1980s and 1990s for the recollection of (usually sexual) abuse, sometimes decades after it had occurred.[26] Less repressed for Alison was the memory of sexual abuse endured over a number of years at the hands of the neighbour's son. He was a teenager – already 'a young man' – and she was 'probably six, seven, and eight'.

It was many years before Alison was able to deal with the legacy of this trauma. Her older abuser owned the foundry where her father worked. She described her father as her 'protector', but she felt unable to tell him, fearing that 'he'd have killed them . . . or something would have happened and he would have lost his job'. She thinks she tried to tell her mother, but couldn't 'verbalise it properly'. When Alison subsequently remembered the abuse and discussed it with her mother, her mother remembered that Alison used to hide behind her legs whenever the neighbour was around. Alison observed: 'but she didn't put it together, or chose not to – I don't, I don't know what'. The ambivalence in this comment suggests a wish perhaps that her mother had been more attentive to Alison's childhood distress and able to see her child's pain. Her mother had a breakdown about the time of the first abuse Alison suffered, compounding her sense of abandonment.

Alison is clear about the impact of the abuse. She blames the repeated abuse by her teenage neighbour for her 'incredible shyness', her inability to concentrate at school and her consequent poor academic performance. Her suffering is evident in suicidal ideation at age fifteen: 'something in me jumped in front of that train but I was still on the platform'. Suicidal thoughts were the catalyst for Alison to leave school and find work. She married at seventeen and had two children by the age of twenty. In her mid-twenties she had her 'first hit with anxiety'. After the birth of her third child in 1982, at the age of thirty, she suffered post-natal depression. Alison was careful to note that she did not think of hurting her child, but the three children 'were at risk of not having a mother'. Alison's clarification of this point suggests her awareness of the broader 1970s discussion about the prevalence of child abuse (physical and emotional, rather than sexual) and post-natal depression.[27] She sought help from a therapist, 'thinking they'd lock me up'. Instead, her 'sojourn into therapy' began. One of the therapists she saw taught her self-hypnosis and meditation: 'I think it saved my life'. The contrast with Sandy's experience is striking. Alison made no mention of being prescribed medication; indeed, she made no mention of seeing a doctor – it was a therapist who offered her life-saving strategies that she still practises for dealing with her depression.

Post-natal depression brought Alison to therapy, but that encounter led her to far-reaching insights about her past and present. Therapy helped her to recognize her husband's 'manipulative' behaviour and to acknowledge that by the time her daughter 'was about two, the marriage was over and I was sleeping in the lounge room. . . . And I, I decided that, you know, I probably wasn't going to survive really if I stayed. . . . I thought that I would not exist. That I would almost be annihilated if I stayed'. Therapy gave Alison the tools for recognizing the existential threat posed to her by her marriage, and the fortitude to extricate herself.

Alison's narratives about her childhood abuse and dysfunctional marriage harness the feminist critique of the 1970s, which, in turn, informed the increasing attention on child sexual abuse that marked the 1980s. As Shurlee Swain notes, the '(re)discovery of child abuse in the 1960s was, by the 1980s, overwhelmed by a focus on child sexual abuse, characterised as the most extreme transgression of the supposed innocence of childhood'. Children were seen to be innocent victims, most vulnerable in the family home, a place 'made dangerous by the patriarchal power that it embodied'.[28] By the 1980s, child sexual abuse was a concern of legal, political and media attention, with a focus on the mental health implications.[29] Although Alison did not use the language of 'trauma', her account draws directly from the feminist recognition of child sexual abuse as traumatic, with enduring legacies.

Feminism's critique of the traditional family called into question conventional notions of marriage and sexuality, opening up the possibility of a lesbian alternative. One of the other crucial factors in Alison's narrative about this time is her involvement in a women's soccer team. Here she found friendship, camaraderie and a glimpse of an alternative life. A lesbian couple on the team was Alison's first encounter with homosexuality. Alison decided that she 'would possibly try what it was like to be with another woman'. Her first sexual experience with a woman was a 'defining moment', when she 'decided that [she'd] be staying on that side of the fence'. The axis of her lifeworld shifted, even if, as Alison notes, she was 'the only gay in the village' for many years.[30]

Therapy continued to feature centrally in Alison's narrative. In the 1990s, in a stable relationship with her partner, Alison found 'an excellent therapist in the city'. The work of addressing the legacy of her childhood sexual abuse commenced in earnest. One day, 'on the spur of the moment', she decided to confront the younger of her two abusers. She found him at his work. Legs shaking, she

> sat opposite him with his big desk and just told him what I thought of him and got an apology. He said 'What do you want from me?' And I said, 'Just an apology. You need to know how important that was and how wrong it was and that I want to make sure you're not doing any of that again. And that you are sorry that you did it'.

Buttressed by the support of her therapist (and her partner), Alison had grown from an 'incredibly shy' teenager to a courageous woman with an unflinching desire to face the traumatic legacies of her past.

Suzie

Despite different experiences of therapy, Alison and Sandy shared an understanding of emotional pain as intensely private, even if they appreciated its broader political context. Suzie Quartermaine, whose story opened this chapter, is of a younger generation than Sandy and Alison, and her experience of mental illness and the way she spoke about it reflects this generational difference.

In the mid-1970s, her maternal grandparents forced their unwed seventeen-year-old daughter to give Suzie up for adoption, despite the willingness of her paternal grandparents to raise her. Her adoptive parents had adopted a son, and three years after Suzie's adoption, had a biological son. Aware that she was adopted, she had what she describes as a happy childhood in central Victoria.[31] Suzie's first encounter with mental illness was through her brother's schizophrenia. She described him as 'beautiful, kind hearted – all of that – but socially he just, his whole life he never fitted in'. One night, at age thirty, he 'made himself a cup of coffee, put the coffee cup on the washing machine as he went out the laundry door for a smoke, and he never came back inside. He hung himself. Just spur of the moment'. Suzie was pregnant at the time and building a new house in Melbourne with her partner. Suzie 'couldn't really plunge into too deep a depression. I was really aware of looking after my baby. But then I had Ava and her dad left me. So that all happened within five months'. Suzie's suggestion that her responsibility to her unborn child initially staved off depression supports her belief that her first experience of depression resulted from an accumulation of traumatic events, which shattered her resilience.

Suzie's partner had begun an affair while she was pregnant. With a three-week-old baby and in the car on their way to choose a carpet for their new house, he told her, 'I don't want to be with you anymore'. Suzie recalls: 'My God, I had this brand-new baby. Oh, brand new house that we hadn't even moved into and he just bailed on me'. The narrative of the deceitful male partner was a powerful one in Suzie's story, as it had been in Sandy's, with a marked impact on their mental health. Suzie moved back to Wangaratta to be close to her parents but, needing to distance herself from their grief over their son's recent suicide, she moved into her own place. That was 'when things got pretty dark for me. Um 'cause I was home alone with the baby all the time and she was so easy I had a lot of thinking time'.

In this period, Suzie regularly fantasized about suicide, planning how to kill herself and have someone find Ava. One night as she imagined this scenario, she looked down the hallway and saw her dead brother

> standing at the very end of the hallway and his eyes were burning bright like light. Like he was just staring at me. Not evil but like, 'You've gotta get past me first if you wanna go and do that'. That's the message I got from the way he was staring at me. And, yeah, never thought about it again after that.

In discussing her readiness to contemplate suicide, Suzie recalls that 'it took me a long time to fall in love with Ava'. She believes this to be the result of a very difficult labour, which Ava almost did not survive and a traumatic post-delivery experience. Desperate to save the baby, the doctors and nurses took her away and Suzie was left in the birthing room 'all by myself in these stirrups'. Ava was in a humidicrib, which stymied Suzie's ability to bond with her newborn in the first few days of Ava's life. When discussing her readiness to contemplate suicide, Suzie observed that without a powerful connection to her baby, 'taking my own life didn't seem as bad'. Suzie sought help for her depression, saying that she 'did have counselling and stuff but at the end of the day it didn't change anything'. In light of her brother's death and her partner's betrayal, her depression was an appropriate response to her circumstances. Significantly, Suzie did not name this period of depression as 'post-natal depression', preferring to see it as a response to her life situation.[32]

Suzie got a job in Melbourne when Ava was eighteen months old and began to reconstruct her life, but not for long. Suzie soon

> fell into a massive depression. . . . The first bout was circumstantial – I was just shattered. That second bout when [Ava] was about two was depression as diagnosed, chemical. Yeah, that was really bad. But I managed to hide it. Like I managed to keep working and all of that.

Prompted by a friend who had suffered depression, Suzie went to a doctor who prescribed medication and told her it would take about two weeks to work. 'And one day I'm lying on the couch – 'cause that's all I'd ever do when I was at home – and I remember the moment those tablets kicked in. And this black fog just lifted and it was gone just like that. And I'm still on tablets today'.

Suzie's understanding of her different experiences of mental illness is striking and reflects two different ways of understanding and treating depression. The most significant factor in her first depression seems to be her partner's abandonment and financial abuse. Years later she came to believe that he had a 'fear of commitment' – a common cultural narrative about men in relationships – but at the time she experienced his desertion as deeply personal: 'I felt like I was nothing'. Suzie describes this first depression as 'so slow . . . it had been kind of circumstantial. So I just, how can you change your circumstances? You can't really'. In contrast, during her subsequent 'massive depression', the circumstances did not seem to warrant the intensity of her experience and a clinical diagnosis and medication, and her strikingly positive reaction to the medication, seemed to confirm a chemical cause. All it took was a visit to a doctor: 'it was as easy as that really'.

The two types of depression Suzie talked about are known in the medical literature as 'reactive' depression, a response to life experience and circumstances, and 'endogenous' depression, a chemical imbalance in the brain. The idea that depression could be caused by a chemical imbalance – primarily low levels of serotonin – was first hypothesized in the 1960s and tested in the 1970s. In the 1990s a range of drugs to treat this 'imbalance' became widely prescribed. There is now considerable debate about the validity of the hypothesis that a chemical imbalance causes depression.[33] But for Suzie and millions like her, the belief that her depression had a chemical basis made sense and the drugs seemed to work.

When Sandy and Alison sought treatment for depression, the idea of it being caused by a chemical imbalance was not the dominant understanding. Sandy had been prescribed Valium not as a fix for a chemical imbalance, but as a treatment for something wrong with her emotional self-regulation, notably anxiety and depression. Both women posited the structural conditions of their lives and, in Alison's case, the childhood trauma of sexual abuse, as the underlying causes of their mental illness. In Suzie's narrative, the cause was her circumstances or, alternatively, faulty brain chemistry; the first she felt she had no control over, and the second seemed easily fixed.

Conclusion

The idea of 'life's circumstances' hides a multitude of meanings and factors. The lives of all three women, and the nature of their trauma, were profoundly shaped by gender, as was the telling of their experiences. Through their own experience of depression, both Sandy and Alison came to understand that their mothers had also suffered depression and were not emotionally available, or, in Alison's case, able to protect her from the abusive, predatory neighbours. All three women were in relationships with men who were emotionally, physically or financially abusive, or all three. They all suffered depression following the birth of a child; their reproductive lives were thus a powerful embodied context for the contours of their depression. As Jane Ussher observes in her discussion of the medicalization of 'women's misery', the 'very use of the medicalized term "depression"' among women in oppressive heterosexual relationships 'acts to depoliticize women's distress'.[34] The lifeworlds of all the women indict structural inequalities in the family and the broader culture and society.

In talking about their life circumstances, Sandy, Alison and Suzie crafted the narrative arc of their stories in ways that reflected both their gender and their generation. Sandy's and Alison's narratives ride a wave of changing historical conditions, which offered them personal opportunities unavailable to their mothers. Propelling both their lives and their narratives, broader social changes, spurred largely by feminist liberationist ideas and agitation for women's opportunities, helped them to understand and escape oppressive relationships. Each woman seemed also to acknowledge, implicitly in Alison's case, and more explicitly in Sandy's, that the story she was telling had a political edge: their intimate lives, including the experience and nature of their depression, exposed the truth of the 1970s feminist message that 'the personal is political'. Also telling is the fact that neither mentioned her experiences of depression in her EOI. This part of their story was revealed only in the context of the oral history interview. While the therapeutic culture has made talk of personal suffering acceptable, mental health was not revealed as a motivating reason for contacting the Australian Generations project.

Suzie's EOI showed no such reticence. Suzie came of age in a therapeutic culture, unlike the baby-boomers Sandy and Alison. Recent changes in media and entertainment have also affected a shift to a public confessional mode and have created an online culture of constant self-narrativization, whereby Facebook and Twitter naturalize the generation of public narrative out of private experience. For Suzie, technology had played an important part in her recent period of deep mourning and depression following the loss of her mother. The iPhone, an invention she described as 'awesome', enabled her to maintain contact with the outside world when she felt unable to be physically social.

Aged thirty-eight when I interviewed her, Suzie's life story was not as distilled as Sandy's or Alison's, whose narrative arcs are clearer to them in the fullness of time. Her EOI suggested that it was her 'strength and education' which 'brought [her] back from the brink of [her] own suicide and depression', reflecting, perhaps, the currently vogue idea of resilience as the antidote to trauma and mental illness. Subsequent events challenged that trajectory. Whereas feminism had been central to the two older women, it was taken for granted in Suzie's narrative. 'I never let being a girl stop me doing anything,' she observed confidently, and was determined that she would not repeat the gendered division of labour which had characterized her parents' marriage. But gender shaped her life in other ways: in her choice to be a preschool teacher (and the lack of other options put forward by the school's career counsellor); in the trauma of her daughter's birth; in her financial and emotional vulnerability when her partner deserted her; in raising a daughter as a single mother; in the depression she suffered as she grieved the dramatic, rapid changes in her circumstances. Despite these reproductive and economic constraints, Suzie implicitly rejected the idea that her gender might have limited her options, or that she might want to pursue a career: 'It hasn't been about my career at all. 'Cause, you know, being a single parent, you just have to do what you can'. For Suzie, being a mother was her 'number one job'. In claiming the importance of her work as a mother, Suzie was also creating a narrative she could live with.[35] She asserted choice in the context of shattering events beyond her control.

A further way in which the narratives of all three women are shaped by gender is their focus on the intimate, domestic nature of their circumstances and their pain. Their narratives not only reveal the embodied nature of mental illness and its relationship to women's reproductive lives; they also take us into the heart of their relationships and expose the ways in which, as the opening chapter of this book argues, much of women's trauma is a function of everyday life experiences. This is in stark contrast to the public narratives of elite men's struggles with depression where the context and pressure of their professional lives appears to trigger an emotional unravelling. In men's public 'truth-telling' about mental illness, their narratives of depression invariably describe 'falling into' an intensely emotional space – one usually reserved for women – and an emergence from it with the aid of medication. Depression is thus an aberration, although the idea that it is acceptable for some men – particularly privileged white men – to talk about their emotional state and thus challenge dominant understandings of masculinity has been welcomed by many.[36] For Sandy, Alison and Suzie, who as women are culturally identified as more emotional than men, their narratives of depression suggest an extension and intensification of that emotional, domestic realm. In the arc of their life stories, coming out of depression is expressed as an entry, and for Suzie a re-entry, into the possibilities of education and employment.

Women's entry into public life carries many perils, including the risk of being seen as too emotional and, relatedly, too bound by the hazards and demands of their reproductive capacities. It has thus been important for women to cordon off their private selves from their public, professional lives. To speak openly about mental illness risks being seen as an unstable woman and a possible risk to one's children. Sandy's experience is a reminder of this harsh reality and the potential for charges of madness or mental instability to be mobilized against women. Alison's explicit assurance that, despite her own profound depression, she was not a risk to her children echoes this fear. In this context, the private narrative of sexual or domestic trauma bequeathed by feminism is far more empowering: if a woman's mental illness is rooted in patriarchy's treatment of her, as opposed, for example, to a biologically determined emotional instability, then a safer space is opened in which women can articulate their narratives of trauma with less risk to their position in the family. Freed from her oppressive husband, for example, a mother's mental health can stabilize and her capacity to care for her children be enhanced.

The stories of the women discussed here remind us that mental health constructs, such as trauma, depression and their treatments, have a history. The readiness of Sandy, Alison and Suzie to talk about their periods of depression reflects the therapeutic culture in which they live, just as their experiences reflect changes in that culture over time. Suzie's second and most recent experience of depression (*c*. 2007) suggests the increasing use of medication as a treatment; her understanding of it as a chemical imbalance reveals both the pathologization of depression as an illness at the same time as suggesting the return to an understanding of the individual as the problem, even if its basis is 'chemical'. Given the preponderance of women among the sufferers of depression, this has significant implications for how women are treated and how they understand their condition. Sandy and Alison's stories suggest the importance of feminism, as critique and as a social movement, in enabling them to make sense of their lives and their psyches. The more depression is viewed and treated as a chemical imbalance, the easier it will be to dissociate it from the circumstances of women's lives and the cultural context in which they live. And the more readily the political and structural nature of women's private trauma will be rendered, once again, invisible.

Acknowledgements

My thanks to Lindsey Earner-Byrne for the conversations which helped shape this chapter, the Melbourne Life Writers and Christine Brett-Vickers for their helpful suggestions on earlier iterations of it and the editors for their excellent work. The Australian Generations project was funded by an Australian Research Council Linkage Grant, supplemented with financial and in-kind contributions from the National Library of Australia, ABC Radio National, Monash University and La Trobe University.

Notes

1. For further discussion about the extent of mental illness among participants in the Australian Generations project, see Katie Holmes, 'Talking about Mental Illness: Life Histories and Mental Health in Modern Australia', *Australian Historical Studies* 47, no. 1 (2016): 25–40. Although the three women discussed here were from different generations, they shared the privilege of being white women in a country where the rates of mental illness among Aboriginal women far exceed those within the majority white population.

2. For an extensive discussion of the medical history of the term 'depression', and the association of women with it, see Jane M. Ussher, 'Are We Medicalizing Women's Misery? A Critical Review of Women's Higher Rates of Reported Depression', *Feminism & Psychology* 20, no. 1 (2010): 10–11, 24.

3. I have discussed elsewhere the ways that key structural patterns of class and gender inequality shape the stories about mental illness. See Holmes, 'Talking about Mental Illness'.

4. The Australian Research Council funded the Australian Generations Project (2011–14), which was a collaboration between Monash University, LaTrobe University, the National Library of Australia and the Australian Broadcasting Commission. Each of the interviews ran for approximately four hours and traversed the life course of the interviewee.

5. Katie Wright, *The Rise of the Therapeutic Society: Psychological Knowledge & the Contradictions of Cultural Change* (Washington, DC: New Academia, 2011), 8.

6. On social practices and cultural artefacts of the therapeutic culture, see Wright, *The Rise of the Therapeutic Society*, 1–2. For a discussion of the rise of the therapeutic culture in Britain, see Hera Cook, 'From Controlling Emotion to Expressing Feelings in Mid-Twentieth-Century England', *Journal of Social History* 47, no. 3 (2014): 627–46. For a discussion of the life history interview, see Alexander Freund, '"Confessing Animals": Toward a Longue Durée History of the Oral History Interview', *Oral History Review* 41, no. 1 (2014): 1–26.

7. Katie Wright, 'Speaking Out: Representations of Childhood and Sexual Abuse in the Media, Memoir and Public Inquiries', *Red Feather Journal* 7, no. 2 (2016): 25.

8. Wright, *The Rise of the Therapeutic Society*, 21. Joseph E. Davis locates the first public articulation of child sexual abuse as a narrative with the victim at its centre, as occurring in New York in 1971 at the New York Radical Feminists' first conference on rape. Davis suggests that the power of this new

narrative was its bringing together the discourses from 'child protection and anti-rape movements' and their attention to 'the victim of abuse and emphasis on victim innocence and injury'. Joseph E. Davis, *Accounts of Innocence: Sexual Abuse, Trauma and the Self* (Chicago: University of Chicago Press, 2005), 29.

9   See Davis, *Accounts of Innocence*, ch. 9, for an extended discussion of this issue, and the implications of an approach where sexual abuse becomes a 'signifier of psychological problems' (9) in adults, irrespective of other circumstances.

10 The list is long, including West Australian Premier Geoff Gallop; former federal Minister for Trade, Andrew Robb; Federal Court judge Justice Shane Marshall; actor Garry McDonald; footballers Nathan Thomson, Wayne Schwass and Alex Fasolo; Olympic swimmers Kieran Perkins and Ian Thorpe; and businessman James Packer. See Wright, *The Rise of the Therapeutic Society*, 171–2.

11 https://www.news.com.au/charlotte-dawson-found-dead-after-long-and-public-battle-with-depression/news-story/4d3f4302f5fad49af82ffab4b90e6e8e (Accessed 26 April 2019). Other examples of prominent women who have spoken publicly about their mental illness include Queensland parliamentarian Linda Levage and sportswomen Lauren Jackson and Jana Pittman. The greater readiness of younger women to speak and write about their experiences of mental illness is reflected in two 2019 publications: Clare Bowditch, *Your Own Kind of Girl* (Crows Nest: Allen & Unwin, 2019); and Georgie Dent, *Breaking Badly: How I Worried Myself Sick* (South Melbourne: Affirm Press, 2019).

12 Barbara Taylor, *The Last Asylum: A Memoir of Madness in Our Times* (London: Hamish Hamilton, 2013), ch. 19. See also Jill Julius Matthews, *Good and Mad Women: The Historical Construction of Femininity in Twentieth-Century Australia* (Sydney: George Allen & Unwin, 1984). For a more detailed discussion of the over-representation of women among those being treated for mental illness, see Bernadette C. Hayes and Pauline M. Prior, 'Women as the "Madder" Sex', in *Gender and Health Care in the United Kingdom: Exploring the Stereotypes*, ed. Bernadette C. Hayes, Pauline M. Prior and Jo Campling (London: Macmillan Education UK, 2003), 123–39.

13 M. Piccinelle and F. G. Homen, *Gender Differences in the Epidemiology of Affective Disorders and Schizophrenia* (Geneva: World Health Organization, 2007). See also Ussher, 'Are We Medicalizing Women's Misery?'.

14 Elaine Showalter, *The Female Malady: Women, Madness, and English Culture, 1830-1980* (New York: Pantheon Books, 1985); and Phyllis Chesler, *Women and Madness* (New York: Doubleday, 1972).

15 Kimberly Emmons, 'Narrating the Emotional Woman: Uptake and Gender in Discourses on Depression', in *Depression and Narrative: Telling the Dark*, ed. Hilary Anne Clark (Albany: State University of New York Press, 2008), 112.

16 Suzanne England, Carol Ganzer and Tracy Tosone, 'Storying Sadness: Representations of Depression in the Writings of Sylvia Plath, Louise Gliick and Tracey Thompson', in *Depression and Narrative: Telling the Dark*, 83–4.

17 The term comes from phenomenologist Edmuns Husserl. See Cook, 'From Controlling Emotion to Expressing Feelings in Mid-Twentieth-Century England', 630.

18 Michelle Arrow, *The Seventies: The Personal, the Political and the Making of Modern Australia* (Sydney: NewSouth, 2019), 11.

19 Jenny Kitzinger, 'Transformations of Public and Private Knowledge: Audience Reception, Feminism and the Experience of Childhood Sexual Abuse', in *Memory Matters: Contexts of Understanding Sexual Abuse Recollections*, ed. Janice Haaken and Paula Reavey (London; New York: Routledge, 2009), 86–104.

20 Closed interview, pseudonym.

21 Betty Friedan famously suggested that post-war American women's widespread unhappiness and fatigue was related to their lack of fulfilment in their roles as wife/mother/housewife. She described this as 'the problem that has no name'. Betty Friedan, *The Feminine Mystique* (Melbourne: Penguin, 1963), 16.

22 Feminism has also been highly critical of the therapeutic culture and the tendency of the therapeutic to be oppressive of women. See Wright, *The Rise of the Therapeutic Society*, 36–7; Matthews, *Good and Mad Women*.

23 For a discussion of the rise of the counselling profession in Australia, see Wright, *The Rise of the Therapeutic Society*, ch. 4.

24 On the alliance between the mental health professions and feminism, see Eva Illouz, *Saving the Modern Soul: Therapy, Emotions, and the Culture of Self-Help* (Berkeley: University of California Press, 2008), 115, 122. For a feminist critique of this argument, see Ussher, 'Are We Medicalizing Women's Misery?'.

25 Alison Fettell, interview with Roslyn Burge, 25 and 26 August 2014, Australian Generations Project, transcript and audio recording, National Library of Australia, Canberra. https://catalogue.nla.gov.au/Search/Home?lookfor=Fettell%2C+Alison&type=all&limit%5B%5D=&submit=Find&limit%5B%5D=format%3AAudio.

26 For an extended discussion of the 'Memory Wars', see Davis, *Accounts of Innocence*, ch. 8. See also Janice Haaken, 'Transformative Remembering: Feminism, Psychoanalysis, and Recollections of Abuse', in *Memory Matters*.

27 Arrow, *The Seventies*, 167.

28 Shurlee Swain, 'Giving Voice to Narratives of Institutional Sex Abuse', *Australian Feminist Law Journal* 41, no. 2 (2015): 289, 293.

29 Kate Gleeson and Timothy Willem Jones, 'Feminist Contributions to Justice for Survivors of Clerical Child Sexual Abuse', *Australian Feminist Law Journal* 41, no. 2 (2015): 202. See also Dorothy Scott and Shurlee Swain, *Confronting Cruelty: Historical Perspectives on Child Protection in Australia* (Carlton: Melbourne University Press, 2002), ch. 9; and Wright, 'Speaking Out', 21.

30 For a broader discussion of the relationship between women's liberation and lesbianism, see Arrow, *The Seventies*, 63–70.

31 Suzie Quartermaine, interview with Katie Holmes, 16 April 2013, Australian Generations Project, transcript and audio recording, National Library of

Australia, Canberra. https://catalogue.nla.gov.au/Record/6290934?lookfor =quartermaine%20%23[format:Audio]&offset=3&max=3. For further details about Suzie's life and excerpts from her transcript, see *Australian Lives: An Intimate History,* ed. Anisa Puri and Alistair Thomson (Clayton: Monash University Publishing, 2017). Suzie's story of discovering the details of her biological parents can be found on pp. 141–2. For Alison Fettell's story, see *Australian Lives*, especially pp. 60–2, 170, 258–60, 365–6.

32 Suzie's symptoms and circumstances are well recognized as risk factors for post-natal depression. See: https://www.panda.org.au/images/resources/Resources-Factsheets/Anxiety-And-Depression-In-Early-Parenthood-And-Pregnancy.pdf.

33 See Johann Hari, *Lost Connections: Uncovering the Real Causes of Depression - and the Unexpected Solutions* (London: Bloomsbury, 2018), 33. See also Ussher, 'Are We Medicalizing Women's Misery?', 14–15.

34 Ussher, 'Are We Medicalizing Women's Misery?', 21.

35 The phrase comes from Alistair Thomson. See Alistair Thomson, 'Anzac Memories: Putting Popular Memory Theory into Practice in Australia', *Oral History* 18, no. 1 (1990): 25–31.

36 Wright, *The Rise of the Therapeutic Society,* xx. Class remains a determining factor in both ideas and expressions of masculinity. Elite men have benefited from a feminist movement that allows them a broader range of masculine behaviour, including the ability to break with gender conventions in relation to the expression of emotion and discussion of mental illness, without compromising masculinity.

Works cited

Arrow, Michelle. *The Seventies: The Personal, the Political and the Making of Modern Australia.* Sydney: NewSouth, 2019.

Bowditch, Clare. *Your Own Kind of Girl.* Crows Nest: Allen & Unwin, 2019.

Cook, Hera. 'From Controlling Emotion to Expressing Feelings in Mid-Twentieth-Century England'. *Journal of Social History* 47, no. 3 (2014): 627–46.

Davis, Joseph E. *Accounts of Innocence: Sexual Abuse, Trauma, and the Self.* Chicago: University of Chicago Press, 2005.

Dent, Georgie. *Breaking Badly: How I Worried Myself Sick.* South Melbourne: Affirm Press, 2019.

Dubus, Alexis, Geradine Hickey, Simon Keck, Rhys Nicolson and Felicity Ward. *Felicity's Mental Mission.* Informit, Melbourne, 2014. https://edutv.informit.com.au/watch-screen.php?videoID=817720.

Emmons, Kimberly. 'Narrating the Emotional Woman: Uptake and Gender in Discourses on Depression', in *Depression and Narrative: Telling the Dark*, edited by Hilary Anne Clark, 111–25. Albany: State University of New York Press, 2008.

England, Suzanne, Carol Ganzer and Tracy Tosone. 'Storying Sadness: Representations of Depression in the Writings of Sylvia Plath, Louise Gliick, and

Tracey Thompson', in *Depression and Narrative: Telling the Dark*, edited by Hilary Anne Clark, 83–95. Albany: State University of New York Press, 2008.

Fettell, Alison. Interview by Roslyn Burge, 25 and 26 August 2014, Australian Generations Project, transcript and audio recording, National Library of Australia, Canberra. https://catalogue.nla.gov.au/Search/Home?lookfor=Fettel l%2C+Alison&type=all&limit%5B%5D=&submit=Find&limit%5B%5D=fo rmat%3AAudio.

Freund, Alexander. '"Confessing Animals": Toward a Longue Durée History of the Oral History Interview'. *Oral History Review* 41, no. 1 (2014): 1–26.

Friedan, Betty. *The Feminine Mystique*. Melbourne: Penguin, 1963.

Gleeson, Kate and Timothy Willem Jones. 'Feminist Contributions to Justice for Survivors of Clerical Child Sexual Abuse'. *Australian Feminist Law Journal* 41, no. 2 (2015): 201–5.

Hari, Johann. *Lost Connections: Uncovering the Real Causes of Depression – and the Unexpected Solutions*. London: Bloomsbury, 2018.

Hayes, Bernadette C. and Pauline M. Prior. 'Women as the "Madder" Sex', in *Gender and Health Care in the United Kingdom: Exploring the Stereotypes*, edited by Bernadette C. Hayes, Pauline M. Prior and Jo Campling, 123–39. London: Macmillan Education UK, 2003.

Holmes, Katie. 'Talking about Mental Illness: Life Histories and Mental Health in Modern Australia'. *Australian Historical Studies* 47, no. 1 (2016): 25–40.

Illouz, Eva. *Saving the Modern Soul: Therapy, Emotions, and the Culture of Self-Help*. Berkeley: University of California Press, 2008.

Kitzinger, Jenny. 'Transformations of Public and Private Knowledge: Audience Reception, Feminism and the Experience of Childhood Sexual Abuse', in *Memory Matters: Contexts of Understanding Sexual Abuse Recollections*, edited by Janice Haaken and Paula Reavey, 86–104. London; New York: Routledge, 2009.

Matthews, Jill Julius. *Good and Mad Women: The Historical Construction of Femininity in Twentieth-Century Australia*. Sydney: George Allen & Unwin, 1984.

Puri, Anisa and Alistair Thomson, eds. *Australian Lives: An Intimate History*. Clayton: Monash University Publishing, 2017.

Quartermaine, Suzie. Interview with Katie Holmes, 16 April 2013, Australian Generations Project, transcript and audio recording, National Library of Australia, Canberra. https://catalogue.nla.gov.au/Record/6290934?lookfor=qua rtermaine%20%23[format:Audio]&offset=3&max=3.

Showalter, Elaine. *The Female Malady: Women, Madness, and English Culture, 1830–1980*. New York: Pantheon Books, 1985.

Swain, Shurlee. 'Giving Voice to Narratives of Institutional Sex Abuse'. *Australian Feminist Law Journal* 41, no. 2 (2015): 289–304.

Taylor, Barbara. *The Last Asylum: A Memoir of Madness in Our Times*. London: Hamish Hamilton, 2013.

Thomson, Alistair. 'Anzac Memories: Putting Popular Memory Theory into Practice in Australia'. *Oral History* 18, no. 1 (1990): 25–31.

Ussher, Jane M. 'Are We Medicalizing Women's Misery? A Critical Review of Women's Higher Rates of Reported Depression'. *Feminism & Psychology* 20, no. 1 (2010): 9–35.

Wright, Katie. 'Speaking Out: Representations of Childhood and Sexual Abuse in the Media, Memoir and Public Inquiries'. *Red Feather Journal* 7, no. 2 (2016): 17–30.

Wright, Katie. *The Rise of the Therapeutic Society: Psychological Knowledge & the Contradictions of Cultural Change*. Washington, DC: New Academia, 2011.

CONSOLIDATED BIBLIOGRAPHY

Aarons, Mark. *The Family File*. Melbourne: Black Inc., 2015.
Adler, Robert. 'Doctors and the Sexually Abused Child'. *Medical Journal of Australia* 145, no. 7 (1986): 305.
Ahmed, Sara. *The Cultural Politics of Emotion*. Edinburgh: Edinburgh University Press, 2014.
Allport, Alan. *Demobbed: Coming Home After World War Two*. New Haven, CT: Yale University Press, 2010.
Alvarado, Carlos S. 'Nineteenth-Century Hysteria and Hypnosis: A Historical Note on Blanche Wittmann'. *Australian Journal of Clinical and Experimental Hypnosis* 37, no. 1 (2009): 21–36.
American Psychiatric Association. *Diagnostic and Statistical Manual of Mental Disorders, Third Volume*. Washington, DC: American Psychiatric Association, third printing 1987.
Arrow, Michelle. *The Seventies: The Personal, the Political and the Making of Modern Australia*. Sydney: NewSouth, 2019.
Asiimwe, Godfrey B. 'Household Gender and Resource Relations: Women in the Marketing of Income Generating Crops in Uganda'. *Eastern Africa Social Science Research Review* 26, no. 2 (2010): 1–30.
Aspinall, Edward and Greg Fealy, eds. *Soeharto's New Order and Its Legacy: Essays in Honour of Harold Crouch*. Acton: ANU E Press, 2010.
Atti della III Conferenza interalleata per l'assistenza agli invalidi di guerra (Roma, 12–17 ottobre 1919). Roma: Stab. tip. La Rapida, 1919.
Auerbach, Sgt. A. J. 'It's All in Your Mind'. *Yank*, 14 December 1945, 31.
Ayers, Susan. 'Fear of Childbirth, Postnatal Post-Traumatic Stress Disorder and Midwifery Care'. *Midwifery* 30, no. 2 (2014): 145–8.
Babini, Valeria Paola. 'Looking Back: Italian Psychiatry From Its Origins to Law 180 of 1978'. *The Journal of Nervous and Mental Disease* 202, no. 6 (June 2014): 428–31.
bad_muthafucka. Comment on Germanych, 'Vopros k zhenskoi auditoria'. LiveJournal. *1965* (blog), 20 May 2009. https://germanych.livejournal.com/138984.html.
Baer, Elizabeth Roberts and Myrna Goldenberg, eds. *Experience and Expression: Women, the Nazis, and the Holocaust*. Detroit, MI: Wayne State University Press, 2003.
Bantebya-Kyomuhendo, Grace and Marjorie Keniston McIntosh. *Women, Work and Domestic Virtue in Uganda, 1900–2003*. Athens: Ohio University Press, 2006.

Bar-Haim, Shaul. '"The Drug Doctor": Michael Balint and the Revival of General Practice in Postwar Britain'. *History Workshop Journal* 86 (2018): 114–32.

Barker, Pat. *Regeneration*. London: Viking, 1991.

Baskakov, V. 'Vopros-otvet'. *Argumenty i fakty*, 19 September 1991, 7.

Baumel, Judith Tydor. *Double Jeopardy: Gender and the Holocaust*. London: Vallentine, Mitchell, 1998.

Bay Area Holocaust Oral History Project, United States Holocaust Memorial Museum, Washington, DC.

Bean, Jessica S. '"To help keep the home going": Female Labour Supply in Interwar London'. *Economic History Review* 68, no. 2 (2015): 441–70.

Beck, Cheryl Tatano. 'Birth Trauma: In the Eye of the Beholder'. *Nursing Research* 53, no. 1 (2004): 28–35.

Becker, Thomas, Heiner Fangerau, Peter Fassl and Hans-Georg Hofer, eds. *Psychiatrie im Erstern Weltkrieg*. Konstanz: UVK Verlagsgesellschaft, 2018.

Berg, Charles. 'Clinical Notes on the Analysis of a War Neurosis'. *The British Journal of Medical Psychology* XIX (1941–3): 155–85.

Bergen, Leo van. 'Medicine and Medical Service', in *1914–1918 Online: International Encyclopedia of the First World War*, edited by Ute Daniel, Peter Gatrell, Oliver Janz, Heather Jones, Jennifer Keene, Alan Kramer and Bill Nasson. Berlin: Freie Universität Berlin, 2014. DOI: 10.15463/ie1418.10221.

Berghahn, Marion. *German-Jewish Refugees in England: The Ambiguities of Assimilation*. London: St Martin's, 1984.

Berk, J. H. 'Trauma and Resilience during War: A Look at the Children and Humanitarian Aid Workers of Bosnia'. *Psychoanalytic Review* 85, no. 4 (1998): 640–58.

Berlant, Lauren, ed. *Compassion: The Culture and Politics of an Emotion*. New York; London: Routledge, 2004.

Berman, Harold J. 'Soviet Family Law in the Light of Russian History and Marxist Theory'. *Yale Law Journal* 56, no. 1 (1946): 26–57.

Bérubé, Alan. *Coming Out Under Fire: The History of Gay Men and Women in World War II*. New York: The Free Press, 1990.

Bettiol, Nicola. 'Destini della follia in guerra: vivere, sopravvivere e scrivere al S. Artemio di Treviso', in *Dalle trincee al manicomio: Esperienza bellica e destino di matti e psichiatri nella Grande guerra*, edited by Andrea Scartabellati, 221–329. Torino: Marco Valerio, 2008.

Bettiol, Nicola. *Feriti nell'anima: storie di soldati dai manicomi del Veneto: 1915–1918*. Treviso: Istresco, 2008.

Bezzoli, Belinda. 'Memory, Forgetting, and the Alexandra Rebellion of 1986', in *States of Violence: Politics, Youth, and Memory in Contemporary Africa*, edited by Edna G. Bay and Donald L. Donham, 179–214. Charlottesville: University of Virginia Press, 2007.

Bianchi, Bruna. 'Psychiatrists, Soldiers, and Officers in Italy during the Great War', in *Traumatic Pasts: History, Psychiatry, and Trauma in the Modern Age, 1870–1930*, edited by Mark S. Micale and Paul Frederick Lerner, 222–52. Cambridge; New York: Cambridge University Press, 2001.

Black, Michele C., Kathleen C. Basile, Matthew J. Breiding, Sharon G. Smith, Mikel L. Walters, Melissa T. Merrick, Jieru Chen and Mark R. Stevens. 'National Intimate Partner and Sexual Violence Survey: 2010 Summary Report'. Atlanta: National Center for Injury Prevention and Control of the Centers for Disease

Control and Prevention, November 2011. https://www.cdc.gov/ViolencePrevention/pdf/NISVS_Report2010-a.pdf.
Blas, Veronica Sierra. 'Educating the Communists of the Future: Notes on the Educational Life of the Spanish Children Evacuated to the USSR during the Spanish Civil War'. *Paedagogica Historica: International Journal of the History of Education* 51, no. 4 (2015): 496–519.
Block, Sharon. *Rape and Sexual Power in Early America*. Chapel Hill: University of North Carolina Press, 2017.
bormental r. Comment on Germanych, 'Vopros k zhenskoi auditoria'. LiveJournal. *1965* (blog), 20 May 2009. https://germanych.livejournal.com/138984.html.
Boss, Pauline and Janet R. Yeats. 'Ambiguous Loss: A Complicated Type of Grief When Loved Ones Disappear'. *Bereavement Care* 33, no. 2 (2014): 63–9.
Bouju, Jacky and Mirjam de Bruijn. 'Introduction: Ordinary Violence in Africa', in *Ordinary Violence and Social Change in Africa*, edited by Jacky Bouju and Mirjam de Bruijn, 1–11. Leiden: Brill, 2014.
Bourke, Joanna. *Dismembering the Male: Men's Bodies, Britain, and the Great War*. Chicago: University of Chicago Press, 1996.
Bourke, Joanna. *Rape: A History from 1860 to the Present Day*. London: Virago, 2007.
Bourke, Joanna. 'Shell Shock and Australian Soldiers in the Great War'. *Sabretache* 36, no. 3 (1995): 3–10.
Bowditch, Clare. *Your Own Kind of Girl*. Crows Nest: Allen & Unwin, 2019.
Bowman, Karl M. 'Psychiatry at War: An Answer to "The Errors of Psychiatry"'. *American Mercury*, September 1944, 336–43.
Brégain, Gildas. 'Un problème national, interallié ou international ? La difficile gestion transnationale des mutilés de guerre (1917–1923); A National, an Inter-Allied or an International Problem? The Difficult Transnational Management of Disabled War Veterans (1917–1923)'. *Revue d'histoire de la protection sociale* 9, no. 1 (2016): 110–32.
Bresnahan, Josephine Callisen. 'Danger in Paradise: The Battle against Combat Fatigue in the Pacific War'. PhD diss., Harvard University, 1999.
Broadberry, Stephen and Peter Howlett. 'Blood, Sweat and Tears: British Mobilization for World War II', in *A World at Total War: Global Conflict and the Politics of Destruction, 1937–1945*, edited by Roger Chickering, Stig Förster and Bernd Greiner, 157–76. Cambridge: Cambridge University Press, 2005.
Brown, Laura S. 'Treating the Effects of Psychological Trauma', in *Psychologists' Desk Reference*, edited by Gerald P. Koocher, John C. Norcross and Beverly A. Greens, 3rd edn, 289–93. New York: Oxford University Press, 2013.
Brownmiller, Susan. *Against Our Will: Men, Women and Rape*. New York: Simon and Schuster, 1975.
Burges Watson, Ian P. 'Post-Traumatic Stress Disorder in Australian Prisoners of the Japanese: A Clinical Study'. *Australian and New Zealand Journal of Psychiatry* 27, no. 1 (1993): 20–9.
Burgess, Ann Wolbert and Lynda Lytle Holmstrom. 'Rape Trauma Syndrome'. *American Journal of Psychiatry* 131, no. 9 (1974): 981–6.
Cardozo, Barbara, Carol Gotway Crawford, Cynthia Eriksson, Julia Zhu, Miriam Sabin, Alastair Ager, David Foy, Leslie Snider, Willem Scholte, Reinhard Kaiser, Miranda Olff, Bas Rijnen and Winnifred Simon. 'Psychological Distress,

Depression, Anxiety, and Burnout among International Humanitarian Aid Workers: A Longitudinal Study'. *PLOS One* 7, no. 9 (2012): e44948.

Carey, Peter. 'The Catholic Church, Religious Revival, and the Nationalist Movement in East Timor, 1975–98'. *Indonesia and the Malay World* 27, no. 78 (1999): 77–95.

Cargill, Mary Terrell and Jade Quang Huynh. *Voices of Vietnamese Boat People: Nineteen Narratives of Escape and Survival*. Jefferson, NC: McFarland, 2000.

Carruthers, Ashley and Boitran Huynh-Beattie. 'Dark Tourism, Diasporic Memory and Disappeared History', in *The Chinese/Vietnamese Diaspora*, edited by Chan Yuk Wah, 147–60. London: Taylor and Francis, 2012.

Caruth, Cathy. 'Introduction', in *Trauma: Explorations in Memory*, edited by Cathy Caruth, 3–12. Baltimore, MD: The Johns Hopkins University Press, 1995.

Caruth, Cathy. *Unclaimed Experience: Trauma, Narrative, and History*. Baltimore, MD: Johns Hopkins University Press, 1996.

Cassell, Eric J. *The Nature of Suffering and the Goals of Medicine*. New York: Oxford University Press, 1994.

Central Committee on Women's Training and Employment. *Second Interim Report*. London: HMSO, 1923.

Chappell, Duncan. 'Compensating Australian Victims of Crime'. *Australian Law Journal* 41 (1967): 3–11.

Charon, Rita. *Narrative Medicine: Honoring the Stories of Illness*. New York: Oxford University Press, 2008.

Charon, Rita. *The Principles and Practice of Narrative Medicine*. New York: Oxford University Press, 2017.

Chauncey, George. 'The Postwar Sex Crime Panic', in *True Stories from the American Past*, edited by William Graebner, 160–78. New York: McGraw-Hill, 1993.

Chettiar, Terri. 'Democratizing Mental Health: Motherhood, Therapeutic Community and the Emergence of the Psychiatric Family at the Cassel Hospital in Post-Second World War Britain'. *History of the Human Sciences* 25, no. 5 (2012): 107–22.

Chettiar, Terri. '"More than a Contract"?: The Emergence of a State-Supported Marriage Welfare Service and the Politics of Emotional Life in Post-1945 Britain'. *Journal of British Studies* 55, no. 3 (2016): 566–91.

'Children's Republic'. *Townsville Daily Bulletin*, 26 February 1941, 10.

Chirot, Daniel, Shin Gi-Wook and Sneider Daniel, eds. *Confronting Memories of World War II: European and Asian Legacies*. Seattle: University of Washington Press, 2014.

Cipriani, Gabriele, Lucia Picchi, Marcella Vedovello, Angelo Nuti and Mario Di Fiorino. 'The Phantom and the Supernumerary Phantom Limb: Historical Review and New Case'. *Neuroscience Bulletin* 27, no. 6 (December 2011): 359–65.

Commission for Reception, Truth and Reconciliation in Timor-Leste (*Comissão de Acolhimento, Verdade e Reconciliação de Timor Leste*, CAVR). *Chega! The Final Report of the Timor-Leste Commission for Reception, Truth and Reconciliation*, vol. 1. Jakarta: KPG in cooperation with STP-CAVR, 2013.

Connell, H. M. 'Incest: A Family Problem'. *Medical Journal of Australia* 2, no. 8 (1978): 362.

Connell, H. M. 'The Wider Spectrum of Child Abuse'. *Medical Journal of Australia* 2, no. 8 (1978): 391–2.
Connorton, Ellen, Melissa J. Perry, David Hemenway and Matthew Miller. 'Humanitarian Relief Workers and Trauma-related Mental Illness'. *Epidemiologic Reviews* 34, no. 1 (2012): 145–55.
Consiglio, Placido. 'Il centro psichiatrico militare di 1a raccolta di Reggio Emilia'. *Gionale di medicina militare* 67, no. 3 (1919): 340–55.
Consiglio, Placido. 'Il servizio neuropsichiatrico di guerra in Italia', in *Atti della III Conferenza interalleata per l'assistenza agli invalidi di Guerra*, 499–510. Roma: Tip. La Rapida, 1919.
Consiglio, Placido. 'Le psicosi, le nevrosi e la delinquenza militare in guerra'. *Rivista sperimentale di freniatria e medicina legale delle alienazioni mentali* 47, nos. 3–4 (1923): 617–29.
Consiglio, Placido. 'Un villagio neuro-psichiatrico in zona di guerra'. *Rivista sperimentale di psichiatria* 42, no. 2 (1918): 175–82.
Cook, Hera. 'From Controlling Emotion to Expressing Feelings in Mid-Twentieth-Century England'. *Journal of Social History* 47, no. 3 (2014): 627–46.
Cook, Joan M., David S. Riggs, Richard Thompson, James C. Coyne and Javaid I. Sheikh. 'Posttraumatic Stress Disorder and Current Relationship Functioning among World War II Ex-Prisoners of War'. *Journal of Family Psychology* 18, no. 1 (2004): 36–45.
Coser, Lewis. *Refugee Scholars in America: Their Impact and Their Experiences*. New Haven, CT: Yale University Press, 1984.
Craig-Norton, Jennifer. *The Kindertransport: Contesting Memory*. Bloomington: Indiana University Press, 2019.
Craig-Norton, Jennifer. 'Refugees at the Margins: Jewish Domestics in Britain 1939–1945'. *Shofar* 37, no. 3 (2019): 296–330.
Creedy, Debra K., Ian M. Shochet and Jan Horsfall. 'Childbirth and the Development of Acute Trauma Symptoms: Incidence and Contributing Factors'. *Birth* 27, no. 2 (2000): 104–11.
Crouthamel, Jason. *The Great War and German Memory: Society, Politics and Psychological Trauma, 1914–1945*. Exeter: University of Exeter Press, 2009.
Crouthamel, Jason and Peter Leese, eds. *Psychological Trauma and the Legacies of the First World War*. Basingstoke: Palgrave Macmillan, 2017.
Crouthamel, Jason and Peter Leese, eds. *Traumatic Memories of the Second World War and After*. Basingstoke: Palgrave Macmillan, 2016.
Curle, Adam and E. L. Trist. 'Transitional Communities and Social Re-connection: A Follow-Up Study of the Civil Resettlement of British Prisoners of War. Part II'. *Human Relations* 1, no. 2 (1947): 240–88.
Cuthbertson, Debbie. 'Artist Phuong Ngo Revisits His Family's Life as Boat People'. *Sydney Morning Herald*, 3 May 2014. https://www.smh.com.au/entertainment/art-and-design/artist-phuong-ngo-revisits-his-familys-life-as-boat-people-20140502-37n4t.html.
Dal Lago, Enrico and Kevin O'Sullivan. 'Prosopographies, Transnational Lives, and Multiple Identities and Global Humanitarianism'. *Moving the Social: Journal of Social History and the History of Social Movements* 57, no. 160 (2017): 159–74.
Damaledo, Andrey. *Divided Loyalties: Displacement, Belonging and Citizenship among East Timorese in West Timor*. Acton: ANU Press, 2018.

Damousi, Joy. *Freud in the Antipodes: A Cultural History of Psychoanalysis in Australia*. Sydney: UNSW Press, 2005.

Das, Veena. *Life and Words: Violence and the Descent into the Ordinary*. Berkeley: University of California Press, 2007.

Davis, Joseph E. *Accounts of Innocence: Sexual Abuse, Trauma, and the Self*. Chicago: University of Chicago Press, 2005.

Daws, Gavan. *Prisoners of the Japanese: POWs in World War II in the Pacific*. New York: Harper Perennial, 1994.

De Santis, Dario, ed. *Guerra e scienze della mente in Italia nella prima metà del novecento*. Canterano: Aracne editrice, 2020.

De Santis, Dario, ed. 'Introduzione. Una fucina di traumatizzati', in *Guerra e scienze della mente in Italia nella prima metà del novecento*, edited by Dario De Santis, 17–36. Canterano: Aracne editrice, 2020.

DeBonis, Steven. *Children of the Enemy: Oral Histories of Vietnamese Amerasians and Their Mothers*. Jefferson, NC: McFarland, 1995.

Decker, Alicia C. *In Idi Amin's Shadow: Women, Gender, and Militarism in Uganda*. Athens: Ohio University Press, 2014.

Delap, Lucy. *Knowing Their Place: Domestic Service in Twentieth-Century Britain*. New York: Oxford University Press, 2011.

Delaporte, Sophie. 'Making Trauma Visible', in *Traumatic Memories of the Second World War and After*, edited by Peter Leese and Jason Crouthamel, 23–46. Cham: Palgrave Macmillan, 2016.

Dent, Georgie. *Breaking Badly: How I Worried Myself Sick*. South Melbourne: Affirm Press, 2019.

Derickson, Alan. '"No Such thing as a Night's Sleep": The Embattled Sleep of American Fighting Men from World War II to the Present'. *Journal of Social History* 47, no. 1 (2013): 1–26.

Desbarats, Jacqueline. 'Human Rights: Two Steps Forward, One Step Back?', in *Vietnam Today: Assessing the New Trends*, edited by Thai Quang Trung, 47–64. New York: Crane Russak, 1990.

Deutsch, Helene. *The Psychology of Women: A Psychoanalytic Interpretation*, 2 vols. New York: Grune & Stratton, 1944.

Didi-Huberman, Georges. *The Invention of Hysteria: Charcot and the Photographic Iconography of the Salpêtrière*. Translated by Alisa Hartz. Cambridge, MA: MIT Press, 2003.

Ditlevsen, Daniel N. and Ask Elklit. 'Gender, Trauma Type, and PTSD Prevalence: A Re-Analysis of 18 Nordic Convenience Samples'. *Annals of General Psychiatry* 11, no. 1 (2012): 26.

Dower, John W. *War Without Mercy: Race and Power in the Pacific War*. New York: Pantheon Books, 1993.

Downs, Laura Lee. 'Au Revoir les Enfants: Wartime Evacuation and the Politics of Childhood in Britain and France, 1939–1940'. *History Workshop Journal* 82, no. 1 (Autumn 2016): 121–50.

Dubus, Alexis, Geradine Hickey, Simon Keck, Rhys Nicolson and Felicity Ward. *Felicity's Mental Mission*. Informit, Melbourne, 2014. https://edutv.informit.com.au/watch-screen.php?videoID=817720.

Dwork, Deborah and Robert Jan van Pelt. *Flight from the Reich: Refugee Jews 1933–1946*. New York: Norton, 2009.

Dwyer, Ellen. 'Psychiatry and Race During World War II'. *Journal of the History of Medicine and Allied Sciences* 61, no. 2 (2005): 117–43.

Eastmond, Marita. 'Stories as Lived Experience: Narratives in Forced Migration Research'. *Journal of Refugee Studies* 20, no. 2 (2007): 248–64.

Edkins, Jenny. *Missing: Persons and Politics*. Ithaca, NY: Cornell University Press, 2011.

Ehrenreich, Barbara and Deirdre English. *Complaints and Disorders: The Sexual Politics of Sickness*. Old Westbury, NY: The Feminist Press, 1975.

Ehrenreich, John H. and Teri L. Elliot, 'Managing Stress in Humanitarian Aid: A Survey of Humanitarian Aid Agencies' Psychosocial Training and Support of Staff'. *Peace and Conflict: Journal of Peace Psychology* 10, no. 1 (2004): 53–66.

Ellenberger, Henri F. *The Discovery of the Unconscious: The History and Evolution of Dynamic Psychiatry*. London: Fontana Press, 1994.

Ells, Mark Van. Transcript of oral history interview with Francis R. Johnston. Wisconsin Veteran Center, 1997.

Emmons, Kimberly. 'Narrating the Emotional Woman: Uptake and Gender in Discourses on Depression', in *Depression and Narrative: Telling the Dark*, edited by Hilary Anne Clark, 111–25. Albany: State University of New York Press, 2008.

Emmot, Gertrud. *Report of the Women's Advisory Committee of the Ministry of Reconstruction on the Domestic Servant Problem*. London: HMSO, 1919.

England, Suzanne, Carol Ganzer and Tracy Tosone. 'Storying Sadness: Representations of Depression in the Writings of Sylvia Plath, Louise Gliick, and Tracey Thompson', in *Depression and Narrative: Telling the Dark*, edited by Hilary Anne Clark, 83–95. Albany: State University of New York Press, 2008.

Enloe, Cynthia. *Maneuvers: The International Politics of Militarizing Women's Lives*. Los Angeles: University of California Press, 2000.

Enquist, Per Olov. *The Story of Blanche and Marie*. London: Vintage Books, 2007.

Ernst, Waltraud, ed. *Work, Psychiatry and Society, c.1750–2015*. Manchester: Manchester University Press, 2016.

Estrich, Susan. *Real Rape: How the Legal System Victimizes Women Who Say No*. Cambridge, MA: Harvard University Press, 1987.

Evatt, Elizabeth. *Royal Commission on Human Relationships: Official Transcript of Proceedings*, vol. 1. Sydney: Sydney Commonwealth Reporting Service, 1974–6.

Evatt, Felix Arnott and Anne Deveson. *Royal Commission on Human Relationships: Final Report*, vol 5. Canberra: Australian Government Publishing Service, 1977.

Fadli. 'Vietnam Boat People's Plaque Torn Down'. *The Jakarta Post*, 20 June 2005. https://www.vnbp.org/vietnamese/memorial/baochi/newspaper01.htm.

Family Law Council. *Child Sexual Abuse Report September 1988*. Canberra: Commonwealth Government, 1988.

Farrell, Malcolm J. and Marie Beynon Ray. 'Will the Battle-Shocked Come Home Cured?' *Woman's Home Companion*, April 1944, 48–50.

Fassin, Didier and Richard Rechtman. *The Empire of Trauma: An Inquiry into the Condition of Victimhood*. Translated by Rachel Gomme. Princeton, NJ: Princeton University Press, 2009.

Featherstone, Lisa. '"Children in a terrible state": Understandings of Trauma and Child Sexual Assault in 1970s and 1980s Australia'. *Journal of Australian Studies* 42, no. 2 (2018): 164–76.

Featherstone, Lisa. '"That's what being a woman is for": Opposition to Marital Rape Law Reform in Late Twentieth Century Australia'. *Gender and History* 29, no. 1 (2017): 87–103.

Featherstone, Lisa and Andy Kaladelfos. *Sex Crimes in the Fifties*. Melbourne: Melbourne University Publishing, 2015.

Feklistov, Iurii. 'Rozhaem vmeste'. *Ogonek*, May 1989, 32–3.

Fermi, Laura. *Illustrious Immigrants: The Intellectual Migration from Europe, 1930–1941*. Chicago: University of Chicago Press, 1968.

Fernandes, Clinton. *The Independence of East Timor: Multidimensional Perspectives – Occupation, Resistance, and International Political Activism*. Portland: Sussex Academic Press, 2011.

Fettell, Alison. Interview with Roslyn Burge, 25 and 26 August 2014, Australian Generations Project, transcript and audio recording, National Library of Australia, Canberra. https://catalogue.nla.gov.au/Search/Home?lookfor=Fettell%2C+Alison&type=all&limit%5B%5D=&submit=Find&limit%5B%5D=format%3AAudio.

Fiorino, Vinzia. 'First World War Neuroses in Italy: Emergency Management, Therapies and Some Reflections on Male Hysteria', in *Psychiatrie im Ersten Weltkrieg*, edited by Thomas Becker, Heiner Fangerau, Peter Fassl and Hans-Georg Hofer, 211–26. Konstanz: UVK Verlagsgesellschaft, 2018.

Firth, Violet. *The Psychology of the Servant Problem: A Study in Social Relationships*. London: C. W. Daniel, 1925.

Forcella, Enzo and Alberto Monticone. *Plotone d'esecuzione. I processi della prima guerra mondiale*. Bari: Laterza, 1968.

Foucault, Michel. *The History of Sexuality*. Translated by Robert Hurley. New York: Pantheon, 1978.

Fox, James. 'On Bad Death and the Left Hand: A Study of Rotinese Symbolic Inversions', in *Right and Left: Essays on Dual Symbolic Classification*, edited by Rodney Needham, 342–68. Chicago: The University of Chicago Press, 1973.

Freedman, Estelle. '"Uncontrolled desires": The Response to the Sexual Psychopath, 1920–1960', in *Passion and Power: Sexuality in History*, edited by K. Peiss and C. Simmons, 199–225. Philadelphia, PA: Temple University Press, 1989.

Freeman, James M. and Nguyen Dinh Huu. *Voices from the Camps: Vietnamese Children Seeking Asylum*. Seattle: University of Washington Press, 2003.

Fremlin, Celia. *The Seven Chars of Chelsea*. London: n.p. 1940.

Freund, Alexander. '"Confessing Animals": Toward a Longue Durée History of the Oral History Interview'. *Oral History Review* 41, no. 1 (2014): 1–26.

Friedan, Betty. *The Feminine Mystique*. Melbourne: Penguin, 1963.

Friedman, Matthew J. 'PTSD History and Overview'. https://www.ptsd.va.gov/professional/treat/essentials/history_ptsd.asp.

Fyrth, Jim and Alexander Sally, eds. *Women's Voices from the Spanish Civil War*. London: Lawrence and Wishart 1991.

Gamble, Jenny and Debra Creedy. 'Psychological Trauma Symptoms of Operative Birth'. *British Journal of Midwifery* 13, no. 4 (2005): 218–24.

Garton, Stephen. *The Cost of War: Australians Return*. Melbourne: Oxford University Press, 1996.

Garton, Stephen. 'Freud and the Psychiatrists: The Australian Debate 1900 to 1940', in *Intellectual Movements and Australian Society*, edited by Brian Head and James Walter, 170–87. Melbourne: Oxford University Press, 1988.
Garton, Stephen. 'Freud versus the Rat: Understanding Shell Shock in World War I'. *Australian Cultural History* 16–17 (1997–8): 45–59.
Garton, Stephen. 'The Melancholy Years: Psychiatry in New South Wales, 1900–1940', in *Australian Welfare History: Critical Essays*, edited by Richard Kennedy, 138–66. Melbourne: Macmillan, 1982.
Garton, Stephen. 'The Rise of the Therapeutic State: Psychiatry and the System of Criminal Jurisdiction in New South Wales, 1890–1940'. *Australian Journal of Politics and History* 32, no. 3 (1986): 378–88.
Gatrell, Peter. *The Making of the Modern Refugee*. Oxford: Oxford University Press, 2013.
Gebhardt, Miriam. *Crimes Unspoken: The Rape of German Women at the End of the Second World War*. Cambridge: Polity, 2017.
Gemelli, Agostino. *Il nostro soldato. Saggi di psicologia militare*. Milano: Treves, 1917.
Gemelli, Agostino. *La filosofia del cannone e altri scritti di psicologia del soldato*. Edited by Dario De Santis. Pisa: ETS, 2018.
Gemignani, Marco. 'The Past Is Past: The Use of Memories and Self-Healing Narratives in Refugees from the Former Yugoslavia'. *Journal of Refugee Studies* 24, no. 1 (2011): 132–56.
General Board (Medical), United States Forces, European Theater. 'Combat Fatigue', Study No. 91, 1945.
German and Austrian Exile Studies Centre, University of London.
Germanych. 'Vopros k zhenskoi auditorii'. LiveJournal. *1965* (blog), 20 May 2009. https://germanych.livejournal.com/138984.html.
Gerrard, Hilde. 'We Were Lucky'. Wiener Holocaust Library 4011, 1984.
Gibson, Mary. *Born to Crime: Cesare Lombroso and the Origins of Biological Criminology*. Westport, CT: Praeger, 2002.
Gijn, J. van. 'In Defence of Charcot, Curie, and Wittmann'. *The Lancet* 369, no. 9560 (2007): 462.
Gijswijt-Hofstra, Marijke and Roy Porter, eds. *Cultures of Neurasthenia from Beard to the First World War*. Amsterdam: Editions Rodopi B.V., 2001.
Giles, Judy. *The Parlour and the Suburb: Domestic Identities, Class, Femininity and Modernity*. Oxford: Berg, 2004.
Gilmore, Jane. *Fixed It: Violence and the Representation of Women in the Media*. Sydney: Viking, 2019.
Giourou, Evangelia, Maria Skokou, Stuart P. Andrew, Konstantina Alexopoulou, Philippos Gourzis and Eleni Jelastopulu. 'Complex Posttraumatic Stress Disorder: The Need to Consolidate a Distinct Clinical Syndrome or to Reevaluate Features of Psychiatric Disorders Following Interpersonal Trauma?' *World Journal of Psychiatry* 8, no. 1 (2018): 12–19.
'Give Us a Break!' *Woman's Home Companion*, October 1944, 80–1.
Gleeson, Kate and Timothy Willem Jones. 'Feminist Contributions to Justice for Survivors of Clerical Child Sexual Abuse'. *Australian Feminist Law Journal* 41, no. 2 (2015): 201–5.
Goldenberg, Myrna and Amy H. Shapiro, eds. *Different Horrors/Same Hell: Gender and the Holocaust*. Seattle; London: University of Washington Press, 2013.

Gorlanova, Nina. 'How Lake Jolly Came About', in *Nine of Russia's Foremost Women Writers*, translated by Jane Chamberlain, 30:67–90. Glas: New Russian Writing. Moscow: Glas, 2003.

Goscilo, Helena. *Dehexing Sex: Russian Womanhood During and After Glasnost*. Ann Arbor: University of Michigan Press, 1996.

greenbat. Comment on Germanych, 'Vopros k zhenskoi auditorii'. LiveJournal. 1965 (blog), 20 May 2009. https://germanych.livejournal.com/138984.html.

Greene, Rebecca Schwartz. 'The Role of the Psychiatrist in World War II'. PhD diss., Columbia University, 1977.

Griffin, Ben. 'Hegemonic Masculinity as a Historical Problem'. *Gender & History* 30, no. 2 (2018): 377–400.

Grillini, Anna. 'Fast Therapy and Fast Recovery: The Role of Time for the Italian Neuropsychiatric Service in the War Zones', in *War Time: First World War Perspectives on Temporality*, edited by Louis Halewood, Adam Luptak and Hanna Smyth, 36–50. London; New York: Routledge, 2018.

Grinker, Roy R. and John P. Spiegel. *War Neuroses in North Africa: The Tunisian Campaign, January–May 1943*. New York: Josiah Macy, Jr., Foundation, 1943.

Grob, Gerald. *From Asylum to Community: Mental Health Policy in Modern America*. Princeton, NJ: Princeton University Press, 1991.

Grob, Gerald. *Mental Illness and American Society, 1875–1940*. Princeton, NJ: Princeton University Press, 1983.

Grove, Herta. Interview V.T/3152-0.3/4025911,2001, Yad Vshaem, Jerusalem, Israel.

Grunseit, Ferry. 'Child Abuse'. *Medical Journal of Australia* 2, no. 11 (1983): 527–8.

Guerrini, Irene and Marco Pluviano. 'Discipline and Military Justice in the Italian Army', in *Italy in the Era of the Great War*, edited by Vanda Wilcox, 80–98. Leiden; Boston, MA: Brill, 2018.

Guerrini, Irene and Marco Pluviano. *Fucilati senza un processo: il 'Memoriale Tommasi' sulle esecuzioni sommarie nella Grande Guerra*. Udine: Gaspari, 2019.

Hale, Jr, Nathan G. *The Rise and Crisis of Psychoanalysis in the United States: Freud and the Americans, 1917–1985*. Oxford: Oxford University Press, 1995.

Hallett, Christine E. *Containing Trauma: Nursing Work in the First World War*. Manchester: Manchester University Press, 2009.

Hari, Johann. *Lost Connections: Uncovering the Real Causes of Depression – and the Unexpected Solutions*. London: Bloomsbury, 2018.

Harrington, Anne. *The Cure Within: A History of Mind-Body Medicine*. New York; London: W. W. Norton, 2009.

Harris Rimmer, Susan and Juli Effi Tomaras. 'Aftermath Timor Leste: Reconciling Competing Notions of Justice'. *Parliament of Australia*, 22 May 2006. https://www.aph.gov.au/About_Parliament/Parliamentary_Departments/Parliamentary_Library/Publications_Archive/archive/TimorLeste.

Harrison, Tom. *Bion, Rickman, Foulkes and the Northfield Experiments: Advancing on a Different Front*. London: Jessica Kingsley Publishers, 2000.

Hastings, Maj. Donald W., Capt. David G. Wright and Capt. Bernard C. Glueck. *Psychiatric Experiences of the Eighth Air Force: First Year of Combat, July 4, 1942–July 4, 1943*. New York: Josiah Macy, Jr., Foundation, 1944.

Hayes, Bernadette C. and Pauline M. Prior. 'Women as the "Madder" Sex', in *Gender and Health Care in the United Kingdom: Exploring the Stereotypes*,

edited by Bernadette C. Hayes, Pauline M. Prior and Jo Campling, 123–39. London: Macmillan Education UK, 2003.
Heineman, Elizabeth D, ed. *Sexual Violence in Conflict Zones: From the Ancient World to the Era of Human Rights*. Philadelphia: University of Pennsylvania Press, 2013.
Heinemann, Marlene. *Gender and Destiny: Women Writers and the Holocaust*. New York: Greenwood Press, 1986.
Henke, Suzette A. *Shattered Subjects: Trauma and Testimony in Women's Life-Writing*. New York: St Martin's Press, 1998.
Henriques, Tatiana, Claudia Leite de Moraes, Michael E. Reichenheim, Gustavo Lobato de Azevedo, Evandro Silva Freire Coutinho and Ivan Luiz de Vasconcellos Figueira. 'Postpartum Posttraumatic Stress Disorder in a Fetal High-Risk Maternity Hospital in the City of Rio de Janeiro, Brazil'. *Cadernos De Saúde Pública* 31, no. 12 (2015): 2523–34.
Herman, Ellen. *The Romance of American Psychology: Political Culture in the Age of the Experts*. Berkeley: University of California Press, 1995.
Herman, Judith Lewis. 'Complex PTSD: A Syndrome in Survivors of Prolonged and Repeated Trauma'. *Journal of Traumatic Stress* 5, no. 3 (1992): 377–91.
Herman, Judith Lewis. *Trauma and Recovery*. New York: BasicBooks, 1992.
Hinch, Derryn. 'Saving 2,000 Youngsters'. *The Sun-Herald*, 21 July 1985.
Hinton, Devon E. and Athanase Hagengimana. '"Ihahamuka": A Rwandan Syndrome of Response to the Genocide: Blocked Flow, Spirit Assualt, and Shortness of Breath', in *Culture and Panic Disorder*, edited by Byron Good and Devon Byron, 205–29. Palo Alto, CA: Stanford University Press, 2009.
Hitchcox, Linda. *Vietnamese Refugees in Southeast Asian Camps*. Basingstoke: Macmillan in association with St. Antony's College, Oxford, 1990.
Holmes, Katie. 'Talking about Mental Illness: Life Histories and Mental Health in Modern Australia'. *Australian Historical Studies* 47, no. 1 (2016): 25–40.
Holocaust Video Testimonies, Yale Fortunoff Library, New Haven, CT.
Horowitz, Mardi J. 'Introduction', in *Essential Papers on Post Traumatic Stress Disorder*, edited by Mardi J. Horowitz, 1–17. New York: New York University Press, 1999.
Horwitz, Allan V. *PTSD: A Short History*. Baltimore, MD: Johns Hopkins University Press, 2018.
Hughes, H. Stuart. *The Sea Change: The Migration of Social Thought, 1930–1965*. New York: Harper and Row, 1975.
Hunt, Janet. 'FOKUPERS – The East Timorese Women's Communication Forum: The Development of Timor-Leste's First Women's NGO', in *Women and the Politics of Gender in Post-Conflict Timor-Leste*, edited by Sara Niner, 65–82. Florence: Taylor and Francis, 2016.
Hustvedt, Asti. *Medical Muses: Hysteria in Nineteenth-Century Paris*. London: Bloomsbury, 2012.
Iliffe, John. *Honour in African History*. Cambridge: Cambridge University Press, 2005.
Illouz, Eva. *Saving the Modern Soul: Therapy, Emotions, and the Culture of Self-Help*. Berkeley: University of California Press, 2008.
'Incest – the hidden crime you want brought into the open'. *Australian Women's Weekly*, 30 April 1980.

Inglis, Amirah. *Australians in the Spanish Civil War*. Sydney: Allen and Unwin, 1987.
Ispa, Jean. 'Soviet and American Childbearing Experiences and Attitudes: A Comparison'. *Slavic Review* 42, no. 1 (1983): 1–13.
'It's Evil'. *The Sun*, 5 July 1985.
Jacoby, Russell. *The Repression of Psychoanalysis: Otto Fenichel and the Political Freudians*. Chicago: University of Chicago Press, 1983.
Jahoda, Marie. 'The Migration of Psychoanalysis: Its Impact on American Psychology', in *The Intellectual Migration: Europe and America, 1930–1960*, edited by Donald Fleming and Bernard Bailyn, 420–62. Cambridge, MA: Harvard University Press, 1969.
Jarvis, Christina S. '"If He Comes Home Nervous": U.S. World War II Neuropsychiatric Casualties and Postwar Masculinities'. *Journal of Men's Studies* 17, no. 2 (2010): 97–115.
Jay, Martin. *The Dialectical Imagination: A History of the Frankfurt School and the Institute for Social Research, 1923–1950*. Berkeley: University of California Press, 1973.
Jayawardena, Kumari. *Feminism and Nationalism in the Third World*. London: Zed Books, 1986.
Jones, Edgar and Simon Wessely. 'British Prisoners-of-War: From Resilience to Psychological Vulnerability: Reality or Perception'. *Twentieth Century British History* 21, no. 2 (2010): 163–83.
Jones, Edgar and Simon Wessely. *Shell Shock to PTSD: Military Psychiatry from 1900 to the Gulf War*. Hove; New York: Psychology Press, 2005.
Jones, Edgar, Robert Hodgins Vermaas, Helen McCartney, Charlotte Beech, Ian Palmer, Kenneth Hyams and Simon Wessely. 'Flashbacks and Post-Traumatic Stress Disorder: The Genesis of a 20th-Century Diagnosis'. *The British Journal of Psychiatry* 182, no. 2 (2003): 158–63.
Jones, Maxwell. 'Rehabilitation of Forces Neurosis Patients to Civilian Life'. *British Medical Journal* 1, no. 4448 (6 April 1946): 533–5.
Jones, Maxwell. 'Why Two Therapeutic Communities?' *Journal of Psychoactive Drugs* 16, no. 1 (1984): 23–6.
Jones, Maxwell and J. M. Tanner. 'The Clinical Characteristics, Treatment, and Rehabilitation of Repatriated Prisoners of War with Neurosis'. *Journal of Neurology, Neurosurgery and Psychiatry* 11, no. 1 (1948): 53–60.
'Judge: Parents must be Alert'. *West Australian*, 18 October 1980.
'A justifiable risk?' *WEL-Informed*, September 1979.
Kaminer, Jenny. *Women with a Thirst for Destruction: The Bad Mother in Russian Culture*. Evanston, IL: Northwestern University Press, 2015.
Karageorgos, Effie. 'Mental Illness, Masculinity, and the Australian Soldier: Military Psychiatry from South Africa to the First World War'. *Health and History* 20, no. 2 (2018): 10–29.
Karp, Ivan. 'Deconstructing Culture-Bound Syndromes'. *Social Science & Medicine* 21, no. 2 (1985): 221–8.
Kefford, Alistair. 'Housing the Citizen-Consumer in Post-war Britain: The Parker Morris Report, Affluence and the Even Briefer Life of Social Democracy'. *Twentieth Century British History* 29, no. 2 (2018): 225–58.
Kent, Lia. 'Interrogating the "Gap" Between Law and Justice: East Timor's Serious Crimes Process'. *Human Rights Quarterly* 34, no. 4 (2012): 1021–44.

Kent, Lia. 'Local Memory Practices in East Timor: Disrupting Transitional Justice Narratives'. *The International Journal of Transitional Justice* 5 (2011): 434–55.

Killingray, David. *Fighting for Britain: African Soldiers in the Second World War*. Rochester, NY: James Currey, 2010.

Kingsley Kent, Susan. *Gender and Power in Britain, 1640–1990*. London: Routledge, 2002.

Kitzinger, Jenny. 'Transformations of Public and Private Knowledge: Audience Reception, Feminism and the Experience of Childhood Sexual Abuse', in *Memory Matters: Contexts of Understanding Sexual Abuse Recollections*, edited by Janice Haaken and Paula Reavey, 86–104. London; New York: Routledge, 2009.

Kleinman, Arthur and Joan Kleinman. 'The Appeal of Experience; The Dismay of Images: Cultural Appropriations of Suffering in Our Times', in *Social Suffering*, edited by Arthur Kleinman, Veena Das and Margaret Lock, 1–24. Berkeley: University of California Press, 1997.

Kleinman, Arthur, Veena Das and Margaret Lock. 'Introduction', in *Social Suffering*, edited by Arthur Kleinman, Veena Das and Margaret Lock, ix–xxvii. Berkeley: University of California Press, 1997.

Kolk, Bessel A. van der. *The Body Keeps the Score: Brain, Mind, and Body in the Healing of Trauma*. New York: Penguin Books, 2015.

Koreman, Megan. 'The Collaborator's Penance: The Local Purge, 1944–5'. *Contemporary European History* 6, no. 2 (1997): 177–92.

Kubie, Lawrence. Papers. Library of Congress, Washington, DC.

Kushner, Tony. 'An Alien Occupation – Jewish Refugees and Domestic Service in Britain, 1933–1948', in *Second Chance: Two Centuries of German-Speaking Jews in the United Kingdom*, edited by Werner Mosse, Julius Carlebach, Gerhard Hirschfeld, Aubrey Newman, Arnold Pauker and Peter Pulzer, 553–78. Tübingen: Mohr Siebeck, 1991.

Kushner, Tony. *Journeys from the Abyss: The Holocaust and Forced Migration from the 1880s to the Present*. Liverpool: Liverpool University Press, 2016.

Kushner, Tony. *Remembering Refugees: Then and Now*. Manchester: Manchester University Press, 2006.

Kyemba, Henry. *A State of Blood: The Inside Story of Idi Amin*. New York: Grosset & Dunlap, 1977.

LaCapra, Dominick. 'Trauma, History, Memory, Identity: What Remains?' *History and Theory* 55, no. 3 (2016): 375–400.

LaCapra, Dominick. *Writing History, Writing Trauma*. Parallax. Baltimore, MD: Johns Hopkins University Press, 2001.

Lamb, S. D. *Pathologist of the Mind: Adolf Meyer and the Origins of American Psychiatry*. Baltimore, MD: Johns Hopkins University Press, 2014.

Langer, Lawrence. *Holocaust Testimonies: The Ruins of Memory*. New Haven, CT; London: Yale University Press, 1991.

Leinweber, Julia, Debra K. Creedy, Heather Rowe and Jenny Gamble. 'A Socioecological Model of Posttraumatic Stress among Australian Midwives'. *Midwifery* 45 (2017): 7–13.

Lerner, Paul. *Hysterical Men: War, Psychiatry, and the Politics of Trauma in Germany, 1890-1930*. Ithaca, NY: Cornell University Press, 2003.

Levine, Peter A. *Waking the Tiger: Healing Trauma*. Berkeley, CA: North Atlantic Books, 1997.

Levy, David. Papers. Oskar Diethelm Library, Weill Medical College of Cornell University, New York, NY.

Leydesdorff, Selma, Graham Dawson, Natasha Burchardt and T. G. Ashplant. 'Introduction', in *Trauma and Life Stories: International Perspectives*, edited by Kim Lacy Rogers, Selma Leydesdorff and Graham Dawson, 1–26. London: Routledge, 1999.

Leys, Ruth. *Trauma: A Genealogy*. Chicago: University of Chicago Press, 2000.

Lifton, Robert Jay. *Death in Life: Survivors of Hiroshima*. Chapel Hill: University of North Carolina Press, 1987.

Lifton, Robert Jay. *Home from the War: Vietnam Veterans, Neither Victims nor Executioners*. New York: Simon and Schuster, 1973.

Lilly, J. Robert. *Taken by Force: Rape and American GIs in Europe during World War II*. New York: Palgrave Macmillan, 2011.

Link, Henry C. 'The Errors of Psychiatry'. *American Mercury*, July 1944, 72–8.

Littleton, Heather L., Deborah L. Rhatigan and Danny Axsom. 'Unacknowledged Rape: How Much Do We Know About the Hidden Rape Victim?' *Journal of Aggression, Maltreatment & Trauma* 14, no. 4 (2007): 57–74.

Living Memory of the Jewish Community, British Library, London.

Lockhart, Alastair. 'The "Parson's Clinic": Religion and Psychology at the Interwar Tavistock Clinic'. *History & Philosophy of Psychology* 12, no. 2 (2010): 11–23.

Lomax, Eric. *The Railway Man*. London: Vintage, 1996.

Loney, Hannah. '"And I Started to Understand": Moments of Illumination Within Women's Oral Narratives from Indonesian-Occupied East Timor'. *Oral History Australia Journal* 36 (2014): 61–71.

Loney, Hannah. *In Women's Words: Violence and Everyday Life during the Indonesian Occupation of East Timor, 1975–1999*. Portland: Sussex Academic Press, 2018.

Loughran, Tracey. 'Shell Shock'. *The British Library*, 7 November 2018. https://www.bl.uk/world-war-one/articles/shell-shock.

Loughran, Tracey. *Shell-Shock and Medical Culture in First World War Britain*. Cambridge: Cambridge University Press, 2017.

Lupton, John A. Transcript of Oral History interview with John J. Stamos, Illinois Supreme Historic Preservation Commission, 2010.

Mackenzie, S. P. *The Colditz Myth: British and Commonwealth Prisoners of War in Nazi Germany*. Oxford: Oxford University Press, 2006.

MacKinnon, Gilles, dir. *Regeneration*. London: BBC Films, 1997.

MacLeish, Kenneth. 'On "moral injury": Psychic Fringes and War Violence'. *History of the Human Sciences* 31, no. 2 (2018): 128–46.

madlesha. Comment on Germanych, 'Vopros k zhenskoi auditorii'. LiveJournal. *1965* (blog), 20 May 2009. https://germanych.livejournal.com/138984.html.

Makarova, Elena. 'Na sokhranenii', in *Otkrytyi final: povesti*, 58–126. Moscow: Sovetskii pisatel', 1989.

Makepeace, Clare. *Captives of War: British Prisoners of War in Europe in the Second World War*. Cambridge: Cambridge University Press, 2017.

Malone, Hannah. 'Legacies of Fascism: Architecture, Heritage and Memory in Contemporary Italy'. *Modern Italy* 22, no. 4 (November 2017): 445–70.

Mama, Amina and Margo Okazawa-Rey. 'Editorial: Militarism, Conflict and Women's Activism'. *Feminist Africa* 10, no. 1 (2008): 1–8.

Mandel family letters, 1938–46: Letters and other documents concerning the experiences of Hermann and Tony Mandel, of Vienna, during the time of the Nazis, LBIJMB MSF 62/MS650 Leo Baeck Institute Archives, New York.

Mandler, Peter. *Return from the Natives: How Margaret Mead Won the Second World War and Lost the Cold War*. New Haven, CT: Yale University Press, 2013.

Marco, Mondini. *Il capo: la grande guerra del generale Luigi Cadorna*. Bologna: Il Mulino, 2017.

Marshall, Dominique. 'International Child Saving', in *The Routledge History of Childhood in the Western World*, edited by Paula S. Fass, 469–90. London: Routledge, 2013/2015.

Mason, Gail. 'Reforming the Law of Rape: Incursions into the Masculinist Sanctum', in *Sex, Power and Justice: Historical Perspectives on Law in Australia*, edited by Diane Kirkby, 50–69. Melbourne: Oxford University Press, 1990.

Materiam i detiam. Kievskaia kinostudiia nauchno-populiarnykh fil'mov, 1970.

Matthews, Jill Julius. *Good and Mad Women: The Historical Construction of Femininity in Twentieth-Century Australia*. Sydney: George Allen & Unwin, 1984.

McKay, Lisa. *Understanding and Coping with Traumatic Stress*. Pasadena, CA: Headington Institute, 2007.

McKelvey, Robert S. *The Dust of Life: America's Children Abandoned in Vietnam*. Seattle: University of Washington Press, 1999.

McLaren, Angus. *Impotence: A Cultural History*. Chicago: University of Chicago Press, 2008.

McNally, Richard J. 'Is PTSD a Transhistorical Phenomenon?', in *Culture and PTSD: Trauma in Global and Historical Perspective*, edited by Devon E. Hinton and Byron J. Good, 117–34. Philadelphia: University of Pennsylvania Press, 2016.

Medlicott, R. W. 'Parent-Child Incest'. *Australian and New Zealand Journal of Psychiatry* 1, no. 4 (1967): 180–7.

Menninger, William C. *Psychiatry in a Troubled World: Yesterday's War and Today's Challenge*. New York: MacMillan, 1948.

Menninger, William C. 'Psychoneurosis—A Summary for the Nurse'. *American Journal of Nursing* 45, no. 5 (1945): 348–50.

Menninger Foundation Archives. Kansas Historical Society, Topeka.

Mészáros, Judit. *Ferenczi and Beyond: Exile of the Budapest School and Solidarity in the Psychoanalytic Movement during the Nazi Years*. London: Karnac Books, 2014.

Meyer, Jessica. *Men of War: Masculinity and the First World War in Britain*. London: Palgrave Macmillan, 2009.

Micale, Mark S. *Hysterical Men: The Hidden History of Male Nervous Illness*. Cambridge, MA: Harvard University Press, 2009.

Micale, Mark S. 'Toward A Global History of Trauma', in *Psychological Trauma and the Legacies of the First World War*, edited by Jason Crouthamel and Peter Leese, 289–310. Basingstoke: Palgrave Macmillan, 2017.

Micale, Mark S. and Paul Lerner. 'Trauma, Psychiatry, and History: A Conceptual and Historiographical Introduction', in *Traumatic Pasts: History, Psychiatry, and Trauma in the Modern Age, 1870–1930*, edited by Paul Lerner and Mark S. Micale, 1–27. Cambridge; New York: Cambridge University Press, 2001.

Micale, Mark S. and Paul Lerner, eds. *Traumatic Pasts: History, Psychiatry, and Trauma in the Modern Age, 1870–1920*. Cambridge: Cambridge University Press, 2001.

Michaels, Paula A. 'Childbirth and Trauma, 1940s–1980s'. *Journal of the History of Medicine and Allied Sciences* 73, no. 1 (2018): 52–72.

Michaels, Paula A. *Lamaze: An International History*. New York: Oxford University Press, 2014.

Miller, Martin Alan. *Freud and the Bolsheviks: Psychoanalysis in Imperial Russia and the Soviet Union*. New Haven, CT: Yale University Press, 1998.

Ministry of Labour. *Report to the Ministry of Labour on the Committee Appointed to Enquire into the Present Conditions as to the Supply of Female Domestic Servants*. London: HMSO, 1923.

Modvig, J., J. Pagaduan-Lopez, J. Rodenburg, C. M. D. Salud, R. V. Cabigon and C. I. A. Panelo. 'Torture and Trauma in Post-Conflict East Timor'. *Lancet* 356, no. 9243 (2000): 1763.

Moffett, Helen. '"These Women, They Force Us to Rape Them": Rape as Narrative of Social Control in Post-Apartheid South Africa'. *Journal of Southern African Studies* 32, no. 1 (2015): 129–44.

Molumphy, Henry D. *For Common Decency: The History of Foster Parents Plan, 1937–1983*. Warwick, RI: Foster Parents International, 1984.

Moore, Alison M. 'Victorian Medicine Was Not Responsible for Repressing the Clitoris: Rethinking Homology in the Long History of Women's Genital Anatomy'. *Signs: Journal of Women in Culture and Society* 44, no. 1 (2018): 53–81.

Morgan, Robin. *Going Too Far*. New York: Vintage, 1978.

Morlock, Forbes. 'The Very Picture of a Primal Scene: Une Leçon Clinique à La Salpêtrière'. *Visual Resources* 23, nos. 1–2 (2007): 129–46.

Morris, David J. *The Evil Hours: A Biography of Post-Traumatic Stress Disorder*. Boston: Houghton Mifflin Harcourt, 2016.

Moskowitz, Eva S. *In Therapy We Trust: America's Obsession with Self-Fulfillment*. Baltimore, MD: Johns Hopkins University Press, 2001.

Mosse, George. 'Shell-Shock as a Social Disease'. *Journal of Contemporary History* 35, no. 1 (2000): 101–8.

Munday, Rosemary. 'Rape The Victims'. *Australian Women's Weekly*, 3 May 1978.

Musisi, Nakanyike B. 'Gender and the Cultural Construction of "Bad Women" in the Development of Kampala-Kibuga, 1900–1962', in *"Wicked" Women and the Reconfiguration of Gender in Africa*, edited by Dorothy Louise Hodgson and Sheryl McCurdy, 171–87. Portsmouth, NH: Heinemann, 2001.

Nakachi, Mie. 'N. S. Khrushchev and the 1944 Soviet Family Law: Politics, Reproduction, and Language'. *East European Politics & Societies* 20, no. 1 (2006): 40–68.

Nakachi, Mie. 'Replacing the Dead: The Politics of Reproduction in the Postwar Soviet Union, 1944–1955', PhD diss., University of Chicago, 2008.

Nannyonga-Tamusuza, Sylvia. *Baakisimba: Music, Dance and Gender of the Baganda People of Buganda*. Pittsburgh, PA: University of Pittsburgh Press, 1999.

Nayeri, Dina. *The Ungrateful Refugee: What Immigrants Never Tell You*. Edinburgh: Cannongate, 2019.

'New Post for Esme Odgers: Five Children's Colonies', *Workers' Weekly*, 20 June 1939, 3.

New South Wales. *Report of the NSW Child Sexual Assault Task Force*. Sydney: Government Printer, 1985.
Nguyen, Cam. 'East, West, and Vietnamese Women'. *The Journal of Vietnamese Studies* 5 (1992): 44–50.
Nguyen, Nathalie Huynh Chau. *Memory Is Another Country: Women of the Vietnamese Diaspora*. Santa Barbara, CA: Praeger, 2009.
Nguyen, Nathalie Huynh Chau. *Voyage of Hope: Vietnamese Australian Women's Narratives*. Altona, CA: Common Ground Publishing, 2005.
nnagina. Comment on Germanych, 'Vopros k zhenskoi auditorii'. LiveJournal. *1965* (blog), 20 May 2009. https://germanych.livejournal.com/138984.html.
O'Connor, Deidre. 'Rape Law Reform – The Australian Experience. Part 1'. *Criminal Law Journal* 1 (1977): 305–19.
Obbo, Christine. *African Women: Their Struggle for Economic Independence*. London: Zed Press, 1980.
Odgers, Esme. 'Children of Spain'. *Woman Today*, August 1937, 4.
Omara-Otunnu, Amii. *Politics and the Military in Uganda (1890–1985)*. New York: St. Martin's Press, 1987.
Opera nazionale per la protezione ed assistenza degli invalidi di guerra. *Per La Tutela Dei Dementi Di Guerra*. Roma: Coop. Tip. Castaldi, 1926.
Ordynskii, Vasilii, dir. *Chelovek rodilsia*. Moscow: Mosfilm Studios, 1956.
Palei, Marina. 'The Bloody Women's Ward', in *Women's View*, 3:74–93. Glas: New Russian Writing. Moscow: Glas, 1992.
Palei, Marina. 'The Losers' Division', in *Lives in Transit: A Collection of Recent Russian Women's Writings*, edited by Helena Goscilo, translated by Jehanne Gheith, 191–202. Dana Point, CA: Ardis, 1995.
Palmer, Ian. 'Psychological Aspects of Providing Medical Humanitarian Aid'. *British Medical Journal* 331, no. 7509 (2005): 152–4.
Paolella, Francesco. 'Un laboratorio di medicina politica. Placido Consiglio e il Centro psichitrico militare di prima raccolta', in *Piccola patria, Grande guerra. La prima guerra mondiale a Reggio Emilia*, edited by Marco Carrattieri and Alberto Ferraboschi, 187–204. Bologna: CLUEB, 2008.
Papers of the Polish Jewish Refugee Fund MS 190 AJ 390; The Papers of Rabbi Dr Solomon Schonfeld, MS183; The Papers of the West London Synagogue, MS140, University of Southampton Hartley Library, Southampton.
Papers related to Selma Weil and her children Marianne and Robby, 0.75/1576, Yad Vashem, Jerusalem.
Parker, Gordon. 'Incest'. *Medical Journal of Australia* 1, no. 13 (1974): 488–90.
Pattinson, Juliette. '"Shirkers", "Scrimjacks" and "Scrimshanks"?: British Civilian Masculinity and Reserved Occupations, 1914–45'. *Gender & History* 28, no. 3 (2016): 709–27.
Pausacker, Helen. 'The Sixth Religion'. *Inside Indonesia* 89 (2007). https://www.insideindonesia.org/the-sixth-religion.
Pellacani, Giuseppe. 'Le neuropatie emotive e le psiconevrosi nei combattenti'. *Rivista sperimentale di freniatria*, 44, nos. 1–2 (1920): 1–65.
Pengally, Beth. 'A Feminist Critique of the Idea of Incest as a Product of the Dysfunctional Family', in *Incest and the Community: Australian Perspectives*, edited by Penelope Hetherington, 184–97. Perth: University of Western Australia, 1991.

Perlow, J. H., T. Wigton, J. Hart, H. T. Strassner, M. P. Nageotte and B. M. Wolk. 'Birth Trauma: A Five-Year Review of Incidence and Associated Perinatal Factors'. *The Journal of Reproductive Medicine* 41, no. 10 (1996): 754–60.

Personal and subject files, 1920–1960, A6126, National Archives of Australia, Canberra.

Pether, G. C. 'The Returned Prisoner-of-War'. *The Lancet*, 5 May 1945, 571–2.

phd_paul_lector. Comment on Germanych, 'Vopros k zhenskoi auditorii'. LiveJournal. *1965* (blog), 20 May 2009. https://germanych.livejournal.com/138984.html.

Pick, Daniel. *The Pursuit of the Nazi Mind: Hitler, Hess, and the Analysts*. Oxford: Oxford University Press, 2012.

Pighini, Giacomo. 'Considerazioni patogeniche sulle psiconevrosi emotive osservate al fronte'. *Il Policlinico* 24, no. 6 (1917): 3–28.

Pisani, Daniele. 'From Italian Monuments to the Fallen of World War I to Fascist War Memorials'. *RIHA Journal*. Accessed 17 April 2020. https://www.riha-journal.org/articles/2017/0150-0176-special-issue-war-graves/0165-pisani.

Plant, Rebecca Jo. 'Preventing the Inevitable: John W. Appel and the Problem of Psychiatric Casualties in the U.S. Army during World War II', in *Science and Emotions after 1945: A Transatlantic Perspective*, edited by Frank Biess and David M. Gross, 209–38. Chicago: University of Chicago Press, 2014.

Plant, Rebecca Jo. 'The Veteran, His Wife and Their Mothers: Prescriptions for Psychological Rehabilitation After World War II', in *Tales of the Great American Victory: World War II in Politics and Poetics*, edited by Diederik Oostdijk and Markha G. Valenta, 95–106. Amsterdam: Vrije University Press, 2006.

Plant, Rebecca Jo. 'William Menninger and American Psychoanalysis, 1946–1984'. *History of Psychiatry* 16, no. 2 (June 2005): 181–202.

Pluviano, Marco and Irene Guerrini. *Le fucilazioni sommarie nella prima guerra mondiale*. Udine: Paolo Gaspari, 2004.

Pollock, Ethan. *Stalin and the Soviet Science Wars*. Princeton, NJ: Princeton University Press, 2009.

Pols, Hans. 'The Tunisian Campaign, War Neuroses, and the Reorientation of American Psychiatry during World War II'. *Harvard Review of Psychiatry* 19, no. 6 (2011): 313–20.

Procacci, Giovanna. 'The Disaster of Caporetto', in *Disastro! Disasters in Italy since 1860: Culture, Politics, Society*, edited by John Dickie, John Foot and Frank M. Snowden, 141–64. New York: Palgrave, 2002.

Pugliese, Joseph. 'The Gendered Figuring of the Dysfunctional Serviceman in the Discourses of Military Psychiatry', in *Gender and War: Australians at War in the Twentieth Century*, edited by Joy Damousi and Marilyn Lake, 162–77. Cambridge: Cambridge University Press, 1995.

Puri, Anisa and Alistair Thomson, eds. *Australian Lives: An Intimate History*. Clayton: Monash University Publishing, 2017.

Qualls, Karl D. *Stalin's Niños: Educating Spanish Civil War Refugees in the Soviet Union, 1937–1951*. Toronto: University of Toronto Press, 2020.

Quartermaine, Suzie, interview with Katie Holmes, 16 April 2013, Australian Generations Project, transcript and audio recording, National Library of Australia, Canberra. https://catalogue.nla.gov.au/Record/6290934?lookfor=quartermaine%20%23[format:Audio]&offset=3&max=3.

Randall, Amy E., ed. *Genocide and Gender in the Twentieth Century: A Comparative Survey*. London; New York: Bloomsbury Academic, 2015.
'Rape crisis'. *Vashti's Voice*, March 1974.
Records of Foster Parents Plan International. Special Collections and Archives, University of Rhode Island, Kingston.
Rees, Jaqueline. 'Researching the Hidden Crime of Family Violence'. *Australian Women's Weekly*, 13 December 1978.
Refugee Voices, Association of Jewish Refugees, London.
Reid, Fiona. *Broken Men: Shell Shock, Treatment and Recovery in Britain, 1914–1930*. London: Continuum, 2010.
Reid, Fiona. 'Losing Face: Trauma and Maxillofacial Injury in the First World War', in *Psychological Trauma and the Legacies of the First World War*, edited by Peter Leese and Jason Crouthamel, 25–47. Cham: Palgrave Macmillan/Springer International Publishing, 2017.
Reid, Fiona. 'War Psychiatry and Shell Shock', in *1914–1918 Online: International Encyclopedia of the First World War*, edited by Ute Daniel, Peter Gatrell, Oliver Janz, Heather Jones, Jennifer Keene, Alan Kramer and Bill Nasson. Berlin: Freie Universität Berlin, 2019. DOI: 10.15463/ie1418.10288/2.0.
Reid, Richard and Henri Medard. 'Merchants, Missions and the Remaking of the Urban Environment in Buganda, c. 1840–90', in *Africa's Urban Past*, edited by David M. Anderson and Richard Rathbone, 98–108. Portsmouth, NH: Heinemann, 2000.
Republic of Uganda. *Report of the Commission of Inquiry into Violations of Human Rights: Verbatim Record of Proceedings*. Kampala: The Government of Uganda, 1995.
Reynolds, J. L. 'Post-Traumatic Stress Disorder after Childbirth: The Phenomenon of Traumatic Birth'. *Canadian Medical Association Journal* 156, no. 6 (1997): 831–5.
Rivkin-Fish, Michele. *Women's Health in Post-Soviet Russia: The Politics of Intervention*. Bloomington: Indiana University Press, 2005.
Robben, Antonius C. G. M. 'How Traumatized Societies Remember: The Aftermath of Argentina's Dirty War'. *Cultural Critique* 59 (Winter 2005): 120–64.
Robben, Antonius C. G. M. and Marcelo M. Suárez-Orozco. 'Introduction: Interdisciplinary Perspectives on Violence and Trauma', in *Cultures Under Siege: Collective Violence and Trauma*, edited by Antonius C. G. M. Robben and Marcelo M. Suárez-Orozco, 1–41. Cambridge: Cambridge University Press, 2000.
Roberts, Mary Louise. 'Beyond "Crisis" in Understanding Gender Transformation'. *Gender & History* 28, no. 2 (2016): 358–66.
Roberts-Pedersen, Elizabeth. 'Introduction: Trauma and Its Histories in Australia'. *Health and History* 20, no. 2 (2018): 1–9.
Roberts-Pedersen, Elizabeth. 'A Weak Spot in the Personality? Conceptualising "War Neurosis" in British Medical Literature of the Second World War'. *Australian Journal of Politics and History* 58, no. 3 (2012): 408–20.
Robinson, Emily, Camilla Schofield, Florence Sutcliffe-Braithwaite and Natalie Thomson. 'Telling Stories about Post-war Britain: Popular Individualism and the "Crisis" of the 1970s'. *Twentieth Century British History* 28, no. 2 (2017): 268–304.

Robinson, Geoffrey. *East Timor 1999: Crimes against Humanity. A Report Commissioned by the United Nations Office of the High Commissioner for Human Rights (OHCHR)*. Jakarta: Elsam and Hak, 2006.

Robinson, W. Courtland. *Terms of Refuge: The Indochinese Exodus and the International Response*. London: Zed Books, 1998.

Rockefeller Foundation Records, Projects. Rockefeller Archive Center, Tarrytown, NY.

Roper, Michael. *The Secret Battle: Emotional Survival in the First World War*. Manchester: Manchester University Press, 2009.

Rosalyn Manowitz/Hebrew Tabernacle Congregation Collection, United States Holocaust Memorial Museum, Washington, DC.

Roth, Michael S. *Memory, Trauma and History: Essays on Living with the Past*. New York: Columbia University Press, 2012.

Rotskoff, Lori. *Love on the Rocks: Men, Women, and Alcohol in Post-World War II America*. Chapel Hill: The University of North Carolina Press, 2002.

Rumiz, Paolo. 'L'ultima ferita della Grande guerra "L'Italia riabiliti i militari fucilati"'. la Repubblica, 6 November 2014. https://www.repubblica.it/cronaca/2014/10/31/news/l_ultima_ferita_della_grande_guerra_l_italia_riabiliti_i_militari_fucilati-99937510/.

Ryan, M. G., A. A. Davis and R. K. Oates. 'One Hundred and Eighty-Seven Cases of Child Abuse and Neglect'. *Medical Journal Australia* 2, no. 19 (1977): 623–8.

Sadilova, Larisa, dir. *S dnem rozhdeniia!*. Moscow: Gosudarstvennyi komitet Rossiiskoi Federatsii po kinomatografii; Regional'nyi obshchestvenii fond podderzhki kino, 1998.

Saikia, Yasmin. *Women, War, and the Making of Bangladesh: Remembering 1971*. Durham, NC: Duke University Press, 2011.

Sakti, Victoria Kumala. '"Thinking Too Much": Tracing Local Patterns of Emotional Distress After Mass Violence in Timor-Leste'. *The Asia Pacific Journal of Anthropology* 14, no. 5 (2013): 438–54.

Salvante, Martina. '"Thanks to the Great War the Blind Gets the Recognition of His Ability to Act": The Rehabilitation of Blinded Servicemen in Florence'. *First World War Studies* 6, no. 1 (2015): 21–35.

Salvante, Martina. 'The Wounded Male Body: Masculinity and Disability in Wartime and Post-WWI Italy'. *Journal of Social History* 53, no. 3 (2020): 644–66.

Samuel, Lawrence R. *Shrink: A Cultural History of Psychoanalysis in America*. Lincoln: University of Nebraska Press, 2013.

Santin, Luciano and Andrea Zannini, eds. *Fucilati per l'esempio: la giustizia militare nella Grande Guerra e il caso di Cercivento*. Udine: Forum, 2017.

Saul, Leon J. 'Book review of Roy R. Grinker and John P. Spiegel's *Men Under Stress* (Philadelphia, PA: Blakison, 1945)'. *Psychosomatic Medicine* 8, no. 1 (1946): 69–71.

Scartabellati, Andrea. 'Un Wanderer dell'anormalità? Un invito allo studio di Placido Consiglio (1877–1959)'. *Rivista sperimentale di freniatria* 134, no. 3 (2010): 89–112.

Schneider, Bronka. *Exile: A Memoir of 1939*. Edited by Erika Bourginon and Barbara Hill Rigney. Columbus: Ohio State University Press, 1998.

Schuster, David G. *Neurasthenic Nation: America's Search for Health, Happiness, and Comfort, 1869–1920*. New Brunswick, NJ: Rutgers University Press, 2011.

Scolè, Pierluigi. 'I morti', in *Dizionario storico della prima guerra mondiale*, edited by Nicola Labanca. Roma-Bari: Laterza, 2014.
Scott, Wilbur. 'PTSD in DSM-III: A Case in the Politics of Diagnosis and Disease'. *Social Problems* 37, no. 3 (1990): 294–310.
Scull, Andrew. 'The Mental Health Sector and the Social Sciences in Post-World War II USA. Part 1: Total War and Its Aftermath'. *History of Psychiatry* 22, no. 1 (2011): 3–19.
Segal, Lore. *Other People's Houses*, 40th anniversary edn. New York: New Press, 2004.
'Sexual Abuse of Children "Prevalent"'. *Courier Mail*, 17 October 1980.
'Sexual Abuse of Children'. *WEL-Informed*, August 1978.
'Sexual Abuse: Could Your Child be a Victim?' *Woman's Day*, 2 December 1985.
Shapira, Michal. *The War Inside: Psychoanalysis, Total War, and the Making of the Democratic Self in Postwar Britain*. Cambridge: Cambridge University Press, 2013.
Shapiro, Johanna. 'Illness Narratives: Reliability, Authenticity and the Empathic Witness'. *Medical Humanities* 37, no. 2 (2011): 68–72.
Shatan, Chaim F. 'Post-Vietnam Syndrome'. *The New York Times*, 6 May 1972.
Shay, Jonathan. *Achilles in Vietnam Combat Trauma and the Undoing of Character*. New York: Scribner, 2005.
Shay, Jonathan. *Odysseus in America: Combat Trauma and the Trials of Homecoming*. New York: Scribner, 2002.
Sheen, Kayleigh, Helen Spiby and Pauline Slade. 'Exposure to Traumatic Perinatal Experiences and Posttraumatic Stress Symptoms in Midwives: Prevalence and Association with Burnout'. *International Journal of Nursing Studies* 52 (2015): 578–87.
Shenker, Noah. *Reframing Holocaust Testimony*. Bloomington: Indiana University Press, 2015.
Shephard, Ben. 'Risk Factors and PTSD: A Historian's Perspective', in *Posttraumatic Stress Disorder: Issues and Controversies*, edited by Gerald M. Rosen, 39–61. Chichester: Wiley, 2004.
Shephard, Ben. *A War of Nerves: Soldiers and Psychiatrists in the Twentieth Century*. Cambridge, MA: Harvard University Press, 2001.
Shiraev, Eric. *Personality Theories: A Global View*. Los Angeles: Sage Publications, 2016.
Showalter, Elaine. *The Female Malady: Women, Madness, and English Culture, 1830–1980*. New York: Pantheon Books, 1985.
'Silence on Child Abuse Alleged'. *Sydney Morning Herald*, 25 September 1980.
Simkin, Penny. 'Pain, Suffering, and Trauma in Labor and Prevention of Subsequent Posttraumatic Stress Disorder'. *The Journal of Perinatal Education* 20, no. 3 (2011): 166–76.
Simpson, Madeleine and Christine Catling. 'Understanding Psychological Traumatic Birth Experiences: A Literature Review'. *Women and Birth* 29, no. 3 (2016): 203–7.
Skomp, Elizabeth. 'Russian Women's Publishing at the Beginning of the 1990s: The Case of the New Amazons'. *The Soviet and Post-Soviet Review* 33, no. 1 (2006): 85–98.
Slight, David. 'Society Transactions: Illinois Psychiatric Society and the Chicago Neurological Society'. *Archives of Neurology and Psychiatry* 55, no. 2 (1946): 151–2.

Smith, Catherine. *Resilience and the Localisation of Trauma in Aceh, Indonesia*. Singapore: NUS Press, 2018.

Smith, Sarah. *Gendering Peace: UN Peacebuilding in Timor-Leste*. London; New York: Routledge, 2019.

Sobocinska, Agnieszka. '"The Language of Scars": Australian Prisoners of War and the Colonial Order'. *History Australia* 7, no. 3 (2010): 58.1–58.19.

Soet, Johanna E., Gregory A. Brack and Colleen DiIorio. 'Prevalence and Predictors of Women's Experience of Psychological Trauma During Childbirth'. *Birth* 30, no. 1 (2003): 36–46.

'Soldiers Named in Sex Scandal with Suspects'. *The Monitor*, 5 December 2001, n.p.

Southall, Aidan William and Peter C. W. Gutkind. *Townsmen in the Making: Kampala and Its Suburbs*. Kampala: East African Institute of Social Research, 1953.

St. Cartmail, Keith. *Exodus Indochina*. Auckland: Heinemann, 1983.

Stafford, Katherine O. *Narrating War in Peace: The Spanish Civil War in the Transition and Today*. London: Palgrave Macmillan 2015.

State Records New South Wales. Court Reporting Branch; NRS 2713, Criminal Transcripts.

Stevenson, Kim. 'Unequivocal Victims: The Historical Roots of the Mystification of the Female Complainant in Rape Cases'. *Feminist Legal Studies* 8, no. 3 (2000): 343–66.

Stiglmayer, Alexandra. *Mass Rape: The War against Women in Bosnia-Herzegovina*. Lincoln: University of Nebraska Press, 1994.

Stookey, Byron. 'Society Transactions: New York Neurological Society and New York Academy of Medicine, Section of Neurology and Psychiatry'. *Archives of Neurology and Psychiatry* 55, no. 2 (1946): 157–61.

Strecker, Edward. Papers. Institute of Pennsylvania Hospital, Philadelphia.

Sukhanova, Natalia. 'Delos', in *Zal ozhidaniia: rassakzy*, 3–28. Moscow: Sovremennik, 1990.

Summers, Anne. 'How Women Are Trained'. *National Times*, 29 November 1976.

Swain, Shurlee. 'Giving Voice to Narratives of Institutional Sex Abuse'. *Australian Feminist Law Journal* 41, no. 2 (2015): 289–304.

Swank, Roy L. and Walter E. Marchand. 'Combat Neuroses: Development of Combat Exhaustion'. *Archives of Neurology and Psychiatry* 55, no. 3 (1946): 236–47.

Tai, Hue-Tam Ho. 'Faces of Remembrance and Forgetting', in *The Country of Memory: Remaking the Past in Late Socialist Vietnam*, edited by Hue-Tam Ho Tai, 167–95. Berkeley: University of California Press, 2001.

Taithe, Bertrand and Borton John. 'History, Memory and "Lessons Learnt" for Humanitarianism'. *European Review of History* 23, nos. 1–2 (2016): 210–24.

'Tantrum or Neurosis'. *Time Magazine*, 7 August 1944, 30.

Tavistock Institute of Human Relations, Civil Resettlement Units, Wellcome Collection Archives and Manuscripts, London.

Taylor, Barbara. *The Last Asylum: A Memoir of Madness in Our Times*. London: Hamish Hamilton, 2013.

Taylor, Christopher C. 'Ihahamuka—PTSD in Post-Genocidal Rwanda: Culture, Continuity and Change in Rwandan Therapeutics', in *African Medical*

Pluralism, edited by William C. Olsen and Carolyn Sargent, 170–84. Bloomington: Indiana University Press, 2017.
'Teacher Admits to 2000 Sex Attacks'. *Daily Mirror*, 5 July 1985.
Thalassis, Nafiska. 'Soldiers in Psychiatric Therapy: The Case of Northfield Military Hospital 1942–1946'. *Social History of Medicine* 20, no. 2 (2007): 351–68.
Thomson, Alistair. 'Anzac Memories: Putting Popular Memory Theory into Practice in Australia'. *Oral History* 18, no. 1 (1990): 25–31.
Thomson, Mathew. *Psychological Subjects: Identity, Culture, and Health in Twentieth-Century Britain*. Oxford: Oxford University Press, 2006.
Todes, Daniel P. *Ivan Pavlov: A Russian Life in Science*. Oxford: Oxford University Press, 2015.
'Topics of *The Times*'. *New York Times*, 30 August 1944, 16.
Torrie, Alfred. 'The Return of Odysseus: The Problem of Marital Infidelity for the Repatriate'. *British Medical Journal*, 11 August 1945, 192–3.
Tran, Quan Tue. 'Remembering the Boat People Exodus: A Tale of Two Memorials'. *The Journal of Vietnamese Studies* 7, no. 3 (2012): 80–121.
'Trauma- and Stressor-Related Disorders', in *Diagnostic and Statistical Manual of Mental Disorders*, 5th edn. DSM Library. Washington, DC: American Psychiatric Association, 2013.
Twagira, Benjamin. '*Bajeemi* Urbanites: Roots of Social Resilience in Militarized Kampala, ca. 1966–1986'. PhD diss., Boston University, 2018.
Twagira, Benjamin. '"The Men Have Come": Gender and Militarisation in Kampala, 1966-86'. *Gender & History* 28, no. 3 (2016): 813–32.
Twomey, Christina. *The Battle Within: POWs in Postwar Australia*. Sydney: NewSouth Publishing, 2018.
Twomey, Christina. 'Trauma and the Reinvigoration of Anzac: An Argument'. *History Australia* 10, no. 3 (2013): 85–105.
United Nations Security Council. 'Secretary General Informs Security Council People of East Timor Rejected Special Autonomy Proposed by Indonesia'. Press Release SC/6721, 3 September, 1999. In 'Meetings Coverage and Press Releases'. *United Nations*. https://www.un.org/press/en/1999/19990903.sc6721.html.
U.S. Army Medical Department. *Neuropsychiatry in World War II, vol. 1: Zone of Interior*. Washington, DC: Office of the Surgeon General, Department of the Army, 1966.
Ussher, Jane M. 'Are We Medicalizing Women's Misery? A Critical Review of Women's Higher Rates of Reported Depression'. *Feminism & Psychology* 20, no. 1 (2010): 9–35.
Valverde, Kieu-Linh Caroline. 'From Dust to Gold: The Vietnamese Amerasian Experience', in *Racially Mixed People in America*, edited by P. P. Maria Root, 144–61. Newbury Park, CA: Sage Publications, 1992.
Vansina, Jan. *Oral Tradition as History*, 1965; repr. Madison: University of Wisconsin Press, 1985.
Vel'vovskii, I. Z. *Sistema psikhoprofilakticheskogo obezbolivaniia rodov*. Moscow: Medgiz, 1963.
Visual History Archive, USC Shoah Foundation.
vladimirgin. Comment on Germanych, 'Vopros k zhenskoi auditorii'. LiveJournal. *1965* (blog), 20 May 2009. https://germanych.livejournal.com/138984.html.

Wajnryb, Ruth. *The Silence: How Tragedy Shapes Talk*. Crows Nest: Allen & Unwin, 2001.
Wake, Naoke. *Private Practices: Harry Stack Sullivan, Homosexuality, and American Liberalism*. Rutgers, NJ: Rutgers University Press, 2011.
Waldby, Cathy. *Breaking the Silence: A Report Based Upon the Findings of the Women Against Incest Phone-in Survey*. Sydney: Women Against Incest, 1985.
Wandita, Galuh, Karen Campbell-Nelson and Manuela Leong Pereira. 'Learning to Engender Reparations in Timor-Leste: Reaching Out to Female Victims', in *What Happened to the Women? Gender and Reparations for Human Rights Violations*, edited by Ruth Rubio-Marín, 284–334. Brooklyn, NY: Social Science Research Council, 2006.
Watson, Laurel B., Cirleen DeBlaere, Kimberly J. Langrehr, David G. Zelaya and Mirella J. Flores. 'The Influence of Multiple Oppressions on Women of Color's Experiences with Insidious Trauma'. *Journal of Counseling Psychology* 63, no. 6 (2016): 656–67.
Watters, Ethan. 'The Americanization of Mental Illness'. *The New York Times*, 8 January 2010, sec. Magazine.
Watters, Ethan. *Crazy Like Us: The Globalization of the Western Mind*. London: Robinson, 2010.
Watters, Ethan. 'Suffering Differently'. *The New York Times*, 12 August 2007, sec. Magazine. https://www.nytimes.com/2007/08/12/magazine/12wwln-idealab-t.html.
Wayland, Sarah, Myfanwy Maple, Kathy McKay and Geoffrey Glassock. 'Holding on to Hope: A Review of the Literature Exploring Missing Persons, Hope and Ambiguous Loss'. *Death Studies* 40, no. 1 (2015): 54–60.
Welch, Steven R. 'Military Justice', in *1914–1918 Online: International Encyclopedia of the First World War*, edited by Ute Daniel, Peter Gatrell, Oliver Janz, Heather Jones, Jennifer Keene, Alan Kramer and Bill Nasson. Berlin: Freie Universität Berlin, 2014.
Wetherby, Aeiwen D. *Private Aid, Political Activism: American Medical Relief to Spain and China, 1936–1949*. Columbia: University of Missouri Press, 2017.
White, Luise. *Speaking with Vampires: Rumor and History in Colonial Africa*. Berkeley: University of California Press, 2000.
White, Luise S., Stephan Miescher and David William Cohen, eds. *African Words, African Voices: Critical Practices in Oral History*. Bloomington: Indiana University Press, 2001.
White, Tracey, Stephen Matthey, Kim Boyd and Bryanne Barnett. 'Postnatal Depression and Post-traumatic Stress after Childbirth: Prevalence, Course and Co-occurrence'. *Journal of Reproductive and Infant Psychology* 24, no. 2 (2006): 107–20.
'Widows' Group Demands International Tribunal'. *ETAN*, 24 August 2002. http://etan.org/et2002c/august/25-31/24widows.htm.
Wilcox, Vanda. 'The Catastrophe at Caporetto'. *History Today*. Accessed 2 August 2019. https://www.historytoday.com/miscellanies/catastrophe-caporetto.
Wilcox, Vanda. 'From Heroic Defeat To Mutilated Victory: The Myth of Caporetto in Fascist Italy', in *Defeat and Memory: Cultural Histories of Military Defeat in the Modern Era*, edited by Jenny Macleod, 46–60. Basingstoke; New York: Palgrave Macmillan, 2008.

Wilcox, Vanda. *Morale and the Italian Army during the First World War*. Cambridge Military Histories. Cambridge: Cambridge University Press, 2016.
Williams-van Klinken, Catharina. 'Is He Hot-Blooded or Hot Inside? Expression of Emotion and Character in Tetun Dili'. *The 5th ENUS Conference on Language and Culture*, University of Nusa Cendana, Indonesia, 1–3 August 2007.
Wilmoth, Peter. 'Boat People Condemn Loss of Monument'. *The Age*, 26 June 2006. https://www.vnbp.org/vietnamese/memorial/baochi/1119321940275.pdf.
Winefield, Helen R. and Sally N. Castell-McGregor. 'Experiences and Views of General Practitioners'. *Medical Journal of Australia* 145, no. 7 (1986): 311–13.
Winter, Jay. 'Shell Shock and the Cultural History of the Great War'. *Journal of Contemporary History* 35, no. 1 (2000): 7–11.
Winter, Jay M. 'Shell Shock', in *The Cambridge History of the First World War*, edited by Jay M. Winter, vol. 3: Civil Society, 310–33. Cambridge: Cambridge University Press, 2014.
Winter, Jay M. *War beyond Words: Languages of Remembrance from the Great War to the Present*. Cambridge: Cambridge University Press, 2018.
Wise, Amanda. 'Embodying Exile: Collective Identities among East Timorese Refugees in Australia'. *Social Analysis* 48, no. 3 (2004): 24–39.
'Women Against Rape'. *Sydney Women's Liberation Newsletter*, May 1976.
Wright, Katie. *The Rise of the Therapeutic Society: Psychological Knowledge & the Contradictions of Cultural Change*. Washington, DC: New Academia, 2011.
Wright, Katie. 'Speaking Out: Representations of Childhood and Sexual Abuse in the Media, Memoir and Public Inquiries'. *Red Feather Journal* 7, no. 2 (2016): 17–30.
Yap, Felicia. 'Prisoners of War and Civilian Internees of the Japanese in British Asia: The Similarities and Contrasts of Experience'. *Journal of Contemporary History* 47, no. 2 (2012): 317–46.
Yehuda, Rachel and Alexander C. McFarlane. 'Introduction', in *Psychobiology of Post-Traumatic Stress Disorder*, edited by Rachel Yehuda and Alexander C. McFarlane, xi–xv. New York: New York Academy of Sciences, 1997.
Young, Allan. *The Harmony of Illusions: Inventing Post Traumatic Stress Disorder*. Princeton, NJ: Princeton University Press, 1995.
Young, Allan and Naomi Breslau. 'What Is "PTSD"?: The Heterogeneity Thesis', in *Culture and PTSD: Trauma in Global and Historical Perspective*, edited by Devon E. Hinton and Byron J. Good, 135–54. Philadelphia: University of Pennsylvania Press, 2016.
Zaretsky, Eli. *Secrets of the Soul: A Social and Cultural History of Psychoanalysis*. New York: Knopf, 2004.
Zimmerman, Grace. 'Birth Trauma: Posttraumatic Stress Disorder After Childbirth'. *International Journal of Childbirth Education* 28, no. 3 (2013): 61–6.

INDEX

African post-colonial militarism
 163–4
 importance of oral histories 165
Ahmed, Sara 205
Alison (Australian Generations
 interviewee) 224
Alison, Rita 52
ambiguous loss 193, 194
American Medical Bureau to Aid
 Spanish Democracy 46
American Mercury 79, 80
American Psychiatric Association 80,
 90, 91
Amin, Hussein Lumumba 165
Amin, Idi 163–4, 176
Amin, Kay 164
Amin regime 163–4, 166, 174
amnesia, episodic 6
*Angkatan Bersenjata Republik
 Indonesia* (ABRI) 202
Anh (Vietnamese interviewee) 192–3
Appel, Kenneth 85
Archive of Vietnamese Boat
 People 188
Army Air Forces 89
Article 14.1 (Ngo) 195–6
Australian Generations Oral History
 project 222, 223
 Expression of Interest (EOI) 221
 interviews 224–31
Australian Royal Commission into
 Institutional Responses to Child
 Sexual Abuse (2013–17) 146
Australia–Vietnam Human Rights
 Committee 188
Auxiliary Territorial Service 109

barbed wire syndrome 101, 103
Beaton, Lindsay 81

Bebe (East Timorese interviewee)
 206, 209
Berland, Lauren 205
Besi Merah Putih (Red and White
 Iron) 206, 207
Bianchi, Bruna 22
Bianchi, Leonardo 21
Biarritz children colony 44, 46
biography as framework for recording
 trauma 43, 53
Bion, Wilfred 106
birth trauma
 camaraderie and bonding of new
 mothers 134–5
 language used around 126
 maternity wards as contributing
 factor 129–30, 131, 135
 medical narrative 128–9
Boss, Pauline 193
Bouju, Jacky 10
Bowman, Karl 80
Bradley, Omar 86
Breuer, Joseph 7
Brigade Mobile (Brimob) 206
Brouillet, Pierre Aristide André
 1, 2
Bruijn, Mirjam de 10
Buchler, Gertrude 64–5
Burgess, Ann 8

Cadorna, Luigi 27, 29, 30
Calder, Alice 72
Callman, Ann 65
Cap Anamur 190
Caporetto defeat 1917 20, 23, 28
 memorial for Italian casualties
 30–1
 as propaganda tool by
 Mussolini 29–30

Carter, Sandy (Australian Generations interviewee) 224–6
Caruth, Cathy 4, 192, 203
Cassell, Eric 125
Catholic Church 187, 191, 213
Charcot, Jean-Martin 1, 2, 6
Chettiar, Teri 108
Chicago Neurological Society 88
child sexual abuse
 Australian Generations interview 226–8
 growing awareness of trauma from 146, 227–8
 models based on family unit reintegration 152
 socio-medical interest in 147, 148
Christian Century 85–6
Chuong (Vietnamese refugee) 190
circumstantial depression 223, 229–30
Civil Resettlement Unit (CRU) scheme
 aims and operations 102–3, 106
 Impotence in Repatriates (1945) 110
 reharmonizing POWs' marriages and families 108–10
 reintegrating POWs into civilian employment 107–8
 Settling Down in Civvy Street (1945) 104, 105
civil wars as emerging area of trauma studies 43
class
 interactions between Jewish domestics and employers 61, 65–6
 military psychiatrists and soldiers 22–3
 Ugandan soldiers and urban men 174
Clifford, Esther 71
collective memory
 Italians' experience of fascism 19, 20, 27–31
 Vietnamese diaspora 194–5
collective trauma 194–5
combat exhaustion 81, 82, 87–9, 91, *see also* combat fatigue; gross stress reaction

combat fatigue 81, 88–9, 90
combat neurosis 2–3
combat-related trauma 5
Comissao de Acolhimento, Verdade e Reconcilição de Timor Leste (CAVR) 203–4
Communist Party of Australia 44
compensation for trauma 152–5
 victim impact statements 154–5
complex PTSD 9
Connell, H. M. 147
consent 150–1
Consiglio, Placido 23, 24
counselling models 1970s 225
court cases, *see* rape cases; sexual assault criminal trials
Craiglockhart War Hospital 2

Damaledo, Andrey 209
Dao, Quynh 188
Das, Veena 205
Dawson, Charlotte 223
Decker, Alicia 164, 169
De Lisi, Lionello 22
depression
 chemical imbalance 223, 230
 circumstantial 223, 229–30
 counselling models 1970s 225
 counselling models 1980s 227–8
 endogenous 230
 evolving treatments for 230–1
 post-natal 227, 230
 reactive 230
 as trauma 222
 treatment with medication 230–1, 233
Derickson, Alan 81
Deutsch, Helen 128, 129
Diagnostic Statistical Manual (DSM) 81, 91
Diagnostic Statistical Manual (DSM-II) 91
Diagnostic Statistical Manual (DSM-III) (1980), official diagnosis of PTSD 8, 90, 91, 112, 147–8
Diagnostic Statistical Manual (DSM-III) (1987) 5

INDEX

Diagnostic Statistical Manual (DSM-V) (2013) 5
diasporic history, Vietnamese collective 194–5
direct trauma 9
distress
  emotional 212, 214
  evolution of understanding 135
  through disruption of mortuary rituals 211
Domar, Carola 64
Downs, Laura Lee 49
Dzung (Vietnamese interviewee) 190–1, 193, 194

Eastmond, Marita 195
East Timor, *see also* Timor-Leste (post-conflict)
  distress of disrupted mortuary rituals 211
  growth of Catholicism during occupation 213
  independence referendum 1999 204, 206
  Indonesia occupation 201, 202
  Liquiçá Church massacre 1999 206–11
  national psychological needs assessment 204–5
  role of faith in healing process 213
East Timorese women
  interviews on Liquiçá Church massacre 1999 207–11
  support groups 212–13
  using trauma to recall experiences of occupation 8
Edkins, Jenny 193
Elisa (East Timorese interviewee) 210–11
Elias, Emilia 64
Emmons, Kimberly 223
emotional distress 212, 214
employer–servant relationships
  differences between European and English 63–4
  power imbalance 66, 69–70
employment
  psychiatric diagnosis impact on prospects 89–90, 91

reintegration of POWs into civilian 107–8
endogenous depression 230
episodic amnesia 6

Far East prisoners of war (FEPOWs) 104–6
fascism, *see also* Spanish Civil War
  impact on Italian collective trauma 27, 29–30
Fassin, Didier 6, 19, 103
female humanitarian workers 10, *see also* Odgers, Esme
female hysteria, medical male gaze 1–2
female sexuality, CRU's attitudes towards 110–11
feminist movement
  critique of traditional family structure 225–6, 227, 228, 231
  forum to analyse women's suffering 224
  influence on redefining concepts of trauma 3, 7–8, 222
  influence on reframing sexual assault 146, 148
  second wave 144, 145
Fettell, Alison 226–8
First World War, *see* World War I
flashbacks 4–5
Footscray refugee memorial 189
Forças Armadas da Libertação Nacional de Timor-Leste (FALINTIL) 205
Forum Komunikasi Perempuan (FOKUPERS) 210–11, 212
Foscarini, Ezio 22
Foster Parents Plan for Children 41, 44
Foulkes, S. H. 106
Freud, Sigmund 83–4
  response to sexual abuse claims 7, 8
Freudianism 129
  banned from Soviet Union 124, 126
  family violence framework 146
Friedan, Betty 225
Friedlander, Marion 66
Friedlander, Sophie 65, 66

Gemelli, Agostino 22–3
Gemignani, Marco 195
gender, power inequality 6, 125, 222, 225–6, 227
Gerrard, Hilde 68
Goldschmidt, Annaliese 68
good bloke defence 143
Gorbachev, M. S. 129
Gorlanova, Nina 130, 131
Goscilo, Helena 131, 134–5
Graham, Herta 66, 70–1, 72
Grant, David 84
Graves, Robert 2
Great Britain, *see also* Civil Resettlement Unit (CRU) scheme
  Jewish refugee domestics testimonies 59–73
  1951 post-war refugees study 71
  post-war social policy initiatives 102
  refugee domestic visa programme 61, 64
  repatriation of prisoners of war (POWs) 101–12
  servant shortage crisis 60, 61
  Ugandan army recruitment strategies 165–6, 172
Grekova, Irina 130–1
grief
  ongoing 62, 72, 191
  oral histories 221, 229
  private grief in public domain 186–7
  ways women deal with 193, 194
gross stress reaction 91
group therapy rehabilitation 106–7
Grove, Herta 63
Grunsiet, Ferry 148

Habibie, B. J. 206
Happy Birthday (1988) 135
Herman, Judith Lewis 6, 9, 203
history, contested 189–90, 194–6
Hoa (Vietnamese refugee) 190–1
Hoffman, Hildegard 59–60, 63
Holocaust
  survivor testimonies 71
  victimhood 60
Holstrom, Lynda 8

The Home for Friendless Children 68
humanitarian workers
  impact of witnessing trauma 42
  impact of witnessing trauma (Spanish Civil War) 44–8
  impact of witnessing trauma (WW II) 48–53
humiliated memory 71
hysteria 6, *see also* female hysteria; male hysteria
  as disorder of nervous system 2
  gendered archetypes 223
  performance of 1

identity
  Jewish refugees' loss of 64–5, 72
  Vietnamese diasporic 194
Illinois Psychiatric Society 88
Indonesia
  campaign of terror and intimidation 207
  end of invasion and occupation of East Timor 204
  invasion and occupation of East Timor 201, 202
  Pancasila state ideology 213
  President Suharto resignation 206
Indonesian National Armed Forces (*Angkatan Bersenjata Republic Indonesia*) 202
Indonesian refugee camps, *see* Pulau Galang
insidious trauma 9
International Red Crescent 187
International Red Cross 187, 191
International Rehabilitation Council for Torture Victims (IRCT) 204–5
Ispa, Jean 132
Italian wartime psychiatry 20–3
  common disorders among soldiers 24
  culture towards traumatised soldiers 21–3, 31
  harsh treatment of disorders 25
  rejection of war as pathogenic event 31

Italy, *see also* Caporetto defeat 1917
  collective memory and legacy of WW I   19, 20, 27–31
  fascism impact on collective trauma   27, 29–30
  Psychiatric Centre for Preliminary Collection   23
  refusal to pardon executed WW I servicemen   27–8
  sources of anxiety of soldiers in asylums   24
  struggles of returned disabled soldiers   26
  war neurosis impact on war pensions   25
  war pensions under Mussolini   27
  wartime psychiatric hospitalizations   21

Jakarta Post   188
Janet. Pierre   7
Jensen, Walter   84
Jewish refugee domestic visa programme   59–73
  impact on men's masculinity   69–70, 72
  impact of work on older women   64–5
  literature about   69–70
  loss of identity   64–5, 72
  married couples   67, 69
  ongoing grief and suffering   62, 70–3
  paternalism   69
  single women's testimonies   62–7
  sources of anxiety for women with children   67–8
  testimonies of trauma   70–3
Jina (East Timorese interviewee)   213
Johnston, Francis   89–90

Kaladelfos, Andy   144
Karp, Ivan   126
Kaufman, M. Ralph   81, 84
Kaunda, Kenneth   174
Kent, Lia   211
Kezia, Jaja   172
Kiet (Vietnamese refugee)   192
Kigozi, Richard   168

Kindertransport   62, 67, 69, 72
Kirk, Norman T.   87
Kitende, Julius   176
Kizito, John   175
Kleinman, Arthur   203, 205
Kleinman, Joan   203
Kolk, Bessel A. van der   4
Kriegsneurosen   20
Kutner, Carol   66, 71
Kuttner, Nelly   71
Kyemba, Henry   174

Lago, Enrico Dal   43
The Lancet   109
Langdon-Davies, John   44
Langer, Lawrence   71
language
  adaptation of trauma by Timor-Leste survivors   203–4, 205, 214
  debates over psychiatric terminology   80, 82
  power of words to suggest and condition birth experience   128–9
  social Darwinist terminology around FEPOWs   104–6
  vocabulary used around traumatic births   126
  ways to talk about women's trauma   222
La stampella (The crutch)   26
Leningrad Paediatric Institute   133
letters
  Odgers' testament of Spanish Civil War   45–8
  Odgers' testament of WW II   48–52
  as site of recording emotional responses   42, 53
  as sources of information   43
  written by Spanish refugee children   49
life histories, *see* Australian Generations Oral History project
Lifton, Robert Jay   47
Link, Henry   79
Linton, Susi   63–4

Liquiçá Church massacre 1999 206–11
literature
  British POWs 105
  Jewish refugee domestic experiences 69–70
  medical 147, 148
  Soviet women's writing group 130–1
Lock, Margaret 205
Lomax, Eric 105
Lombroso, Cesare 22
loss, *see* ambiguous loss

McNally, Richard 125–6, 131–2
Madonna/whore complex 111
Makarova, Elena 130
Malaysian refugee camps, *see* Pulau Bidong
male hysteria 2, 7
malingering 7, 147, *see also* railway spine
Malone, Hanna 29
Mama, Amina 163
Mandel, Tina 68
masculinity
  CRU's reaffirmation of POWs' identities 111, 112
  destabilizing effects of WW I and WW II 107–8
  effect of psychiatric language on 81
  Jewish male domestics 69–70, 72
  performative 7
  restorative 163
  self-representations associated with urban 176
  Ugandan men and trauma testimonies 170, 172–7
  warrior ideal 28, 31
Mass-Observation 65
Mate Restu (Remains of the Dead) 212
Mayne, Keith 155
media
  glasnost era articles on birthing experiences 124–5, 129–34
  increased coverage of child sexual abuse 147, 148
  take up of discussion on psychiatric diagnoses 87
Medical Journal of Australia (MJA) 147, 148
memorials
  Caporetto 30–1
  destruction of 187, 188–9, 194
  second generation interpretations 195–6
  as sites of mourning 186, 187
  Vietnamese refugee camp 187–90
memory, *see also* collective memory
  humiliated 71
  personal 19, 31
  public 19, 31
  repressed 226
Memory is Another Country (Nguyen) 191
Menninger, William 83–4, 85, 88
The Mental Health of U.S. Soldiers fact sheet (1944) 86–7
mental hygiene movement 82
mental illness 221–31
  difference between men and women's struggles 232–3
  high profile men's efforts to destigmatize 223, 232
  narrative frames for talking about 221–2
  underlying causes behind 231
Metcalf, Sheila 153–4
Micale, Mark 10, 11
militarization, *see* Uganda
military medical records
  exclusion of psychoneurosis in 87
  use of term 'psychoneurosis' 81
military psychiatry 20
  attitudes towards psychoanalysis 84–5
  challenges to authority 86
  differing opinions about war trauma 90–1
  influence of Freud on 83–4
  Italian wartime 20–3, 24, 25, 31
  rejection of recruits on NP grounds 79–80
Moffett, Helen 168
Morselli, Enrico 21

Mothers and Children (*Materiam i detiam*) (1970) 123
mourning, memorials as sites of 187
Mourning Soldier sculpture 189
Mugenyi, Joyce 168
Muggeridge, Eric 41, 44–5
　Odgers' letters to 45–7, 48, 50, 52
Mukiibi, Zakariya 175
Murray, John 84
Museveni, Yoweri 164, 167
Mussolini, Benito 27, 29

Nakawanga, Grace 169
Nakitende, Rita 167
Namusisi, Julian 167
Namusisi, Rita 172
narcosynthesis 84
National Joint Committee for Spanish Relief 44
national psychological needs assessment 204–5
nervous system disorders 2, 7, 128, *see also* hysteria
　Italian attitude towards 25, 31
Netanyahu, Benjamin 165
neurasthenia 24
neuropsychiatric (NP) rating 79, 80, 83
névrose traumatique 20
nevrosi di guerra 20
New Amazons writing group 130–1, 132
New South Wales court resources 144–5
New South Wales Supreme Court 151–2
New York Times 85
Nga (Vietnamese refugee) 192, 193
Ngo, Phuong 195–6
Nguyen Thanh Thu 189
1944 Family Law 127
nitrous oxide 127
Northfield Military Hospital 106
Novi Novi (Ninety Nine) 212

Obote, Milton 166
Obote, Miria Kalule 171
Odgers, Edwin 44
Odgers, Esme 41, 44–8
　letters as sources of information 43
　letters as testament to witness to trauma 45–8, 52
　on mothers' reactions to separation from children 50
Oedipal Crisis 146
Okazawa-Rey, Margo 163
Opera nazionale per gli invalidi di guerra (National Agency for the War Disabled) 25
operational fatigue 89–90
oral histories 165, *see also* Australian Generations Oral History project
　Vietnamese refugee women 187, 190–4
Orchan, Lisa 67–8
ordinary violence 10
O'Sullivan, Kevin 43
Other People's Houses (Segal) 69–70
Owen, Wilfred 2

Pablos, Eduardo 44
Pablos, Jose G. 44
pain
　management, obstetric 127, 128
　relationship between suffering and 125, 127
　social factors 129
Palei, Marina 130
Pancasila Indonesian state ideology 213
paternalism
　influence on humanitarian activities 50
　Jewish refugee domestics 69
patriarchy 6, 225–6, 227
Pavlov physical psychology 126, 128
personal memories of trauma 19, 31
personal narratives 186
Petrushevaksia, Ludmila 130
Phuong (Vietnamese interviewee) 193–4
physical trauma 125, 148–9, 150
pirate attacks at sea 191–2
Polianskaia, Irina 130
Polish child refugees 51, 52
Polish Relief Fund 52

post-colonial militarization, *see* Uganda
post-natal depression   227, 230
postpartum women   124
post-traumatic stress disorder (PTSD), *see also* complex PTSD
　common symptoms   4
　dominant focus on combat veterans   3
　official inclusion in *DSM-III* (1980)   8, 90, 91, 112, 147–8
　postpartum women suffering from   124
　revision of symptoms   4–5
　revisions in DSM-V (2013)   5
　Vietnamese refugee women   193–4
power relations, *see also* patriarchy
　employers–servants   63–4, 66, 69–70
　gender   6, 125, 222, 225–6
prisoners of war (POWs)   101–12, *see also* Civil Resettlement Unit (CRU) scheme
　Far East (FEPOWs)   104–6
　group therapy rehabilitation   106–7
　role of wives   109, 110–11
　sexual impotence   109–10
Psychiatric Centre for Preliminary Collection   23
psychiatric terminology, debates over   80, 82
psychiatry, *see also* military psychiatry
　division between American and European   83
　Freud's attitudes to childhood sexual abuse   7, 8
　golden age   80, 82
　Italian wartime   20–3
　models focused on family unit reintegration   152
　professionalization in US   82
　testimonies for compensation claims   153
　trauma through language of   6
psychic numbing   47
psychoanalysis   7, 82
　during WW II   82, 83
　military psychiatrists' attitudes   84–5
Oedipal Crisis   146
psychological trauma   125
　collective Ugandan   176
　evolution of understanding   4–5, 112
　redefining   8
　role of medical sciences in defining   20–3
　Uganda women and militarization   167–72
psychoneurosis   4, 80, *see also* combat exhaustion
　contradictory attitudes towards   85–6
　stigma associated with   82, 85
public education, destigmatizing psychiatric diagnosis   80–1, 85, 86–7
public memory, contesting   19, 31
Puigcerda children colony   44, 45
Pulau Bidong
　destruction of memorial   188, 194
　Vietnamese refugee camp memorial   187
Pulau Galang   185
　Camp Vietnam   188
　destruction of memorial   188–9, 194
　Vietnamese refugee camp memorial   187

Quartermaine, Suzie (Australian Generations interviewee)   221, 222, 224, 228–31
Quarter Sessions records   144

Rackley, Mildred   46
The Railway Man (Lomax)   105
railway spine   7
rape
　as form of social control in Uganda   168
　used against Ugandan women to humiliate husbands   173
　Vietnamese refugee women   192
　as weapon of war   10, 168

rape cases
    compensation for trauma   153–4
    courts downplaying impact of trauma   149–52
    reframing psychological harm through moral lens   150
rape trauma syndrome   8, 147
Rate Laek (Without Graves)   212
reactive depression   230
Rechtman, Richard   6, 19, 103
reciprocal induction   128
Rees, J. R.   102
refugee camps, *see* Pulau Bidong; Pulau Galang
Reid, Fiona   26
Report of the Commission of Inquiry into Violations of Human Rights: Verbatim Record of the Proceedings (1995)   164
repressed memory   226
resilience   43, 52, 232
Rickman, John   106
Rivers, W. H. R.   2–3
Robben, Antonius   209, 211
Roberts-Pedersen, Elizabeth   7
Robinson, Geoffrey   206
Robinson, Mary   212
Royal Alexandra Hospital for Children   148

Sakti, Victoria   212
Salvante, Martina   7
Santos, Rafael dos   206
Sanyu, Rita   170
Sassoon, Siegfried   2
Saul, Leon   84
Schneider, Bronka   69
Schneider, Joseph   69
Sebugwawo, David   172
Second World War, *see* World War II
seduction theory   7, 8
Segal, Lore   69
Selective Service examiners   79, 80, 83
self-narrativization culture   223, 231–2
Semambo, Benon   176
Semambo, Samson   176–7
Sentamu, Sifa   170–1

Settling Down in Civvy Street (1945)   104, 105
sexual abuse
    against children   146, 226, 227–8
    Freud's attitudes to women's   7, 8
    medical articles on child   147–8
    repressed memories   226
    trauma from   227–8, 231
sexual assault
    difficulties reporting in Uganda   169–70
    feminist reframing   146
    growing awareness of psychological trauma   147–8, 155
    medical and social focus   145–6, 148
    trauma from   145–8
    Uganda women   167–8, 169
sexual assault criminal trials   9
    court resources and transcripts   144–5
    downplay of psychological harm   143–4, 149–50, 151–2, 155–6
    focus on physical trauma   148–9
    good bloke defence   143
    problematic rulings on consent   150–1
    psychological harm consideration given   151
    reframing psychological harm through moral lens   150
sexual impotence   109–10
sexual violence
    Indonesian occupation of East Timor   204
    legal reforms around   145
    recognition of traumatizing effects   9, 153–4
    ways Ugandan women deflect   169
Shay, Jonathan   5
shell shock   2–3, 7, 108, *see also* combat neurosis
Shephard, Ben   8–9
Silverman, Marione   63
Simkin, Penny   125
single women
    how Ugandan women deflect sexual violence   169

Jewish refugee domestics
  testimonies 61, 62–7
Soviet financial support for unwed
  mothers 127
Skomp, Elizabeth 130
Smith, Catherine 203
social media, culture of self-
  narrativization 223, 231–2
social suffering 205
social trauma 212
Soviet Union, *see also* New Amazons
  writing group
  bans Freudianism 124, 126
  diversity of narratives on traumatic
    births 124–5
  fear in childbirth compared to
    American 132
  fear in childbirth compared to
    American 132
  female combat veterans case
    study 10
  glasnost era diversity of birthing
    stories 124–5, 129–34
  idealized depiction of state care for
    mothers 123–4
  lack of pain management resources
    for labour and birth 127
  maternity care through Pavlov
    lens 126, 128
  maternity wards as contributing
    factor to birth trauma 129–30,
    131, 135
  new mothers bonding in maternity
    wards 134–5
  glasnost era 124–5, 129–34
  1944 Family Law 127
  post-war baby boom 127
  reshaping maternity care and
    experience 133
  social media maternity
    stories 133, 134
  women writing about birthing
    experience 130–1, 132
Spanish child refugees 41, 44–8
  evacuation during WW II
    48–53
Spanish Civil War 41, 43, 44–8
Stamos, John 89
state narratives

Italians contesting WW I
  events 19, 31
Vietnamese refugees
  contesting 194–5
Strecker, Edward 84
stressors 9, 125, 132
Suárez-Orozco, Marcelo 211
suffering
  birth as site of female 130–1
  in East Timor 205–13
  Italian psychiatrists diminish
    soldiers' 22
  Jewish refugee domestics 70–3
  marginalization of women's 9–10
  relationship between pain
    and 125, 127
  sociocultural factors 129, 203
  Soviet men's insight into
    childbirth 134
  trauma as 163
  Ugandan narratives of 177
Sukhanova, Natal'ia 130
Suong (Vietnamese refugee) 192
Supreme Court 144, 153–4
Surgeon General's Office 83, 90
  The Mental Health of U.S. Soldiers
    fact sheet (1944) 86–7
Swain, Shurlee 227

Tai, Hue-Tam Ho 189
Tamburini, Augusto 21
Tavistock Clinic 102, 106
  Marital Unit 108
Tavistock Institute of Human
  Relations 106
Taylor, Christopher 164
therapeutic culture 222, 231, 233
Timor-Leste (post-conflict)
  sociocultural dimensions of
    suffering 205
  sources of enduring tension
    209–10, 214
  women's violence support
    groups 212–13
Timor-Leste Commission for Reception,
  Truth and Reconciliation
  (*Comissao de Acolhimento,
  Verdade e Reconcilição de Timor
  Leste*) 203–4

traditional family, structural
    inequalities 225–6, 228, 231
Tran, Quan Tue 187–8
transhistorical and transcultural
        phenomenon
    CRU's resistance to trauma as 112
    fear in childbirth 132
    trauma as 5, 124
trauma 3–6, 203, *see also* birth
        trauma; physical trauma;
        psychological trauma; war
        trauma
    biography as framework for
        recording 43, 53
    changing socio-medical
        attitudes 147, 151
    collective 176–7, 194
    compensation 152–5
    court trials downplay 143–4,
        149–50, 151–2, 155–6
    CRU's attitudes towards 112
    as depression 222
    direct 9
    dominance of male combat
        tropes 9–10
    emerging areas of studies 43
    maternity wards as sites of
        129–30, 131, 135
    modern conceptualization 3
    nineteenth century context 3–4
    from sexual assault 145–8
    social 212
    stressors 9
    as suffering 163
    through psychiatry lens 6
    through social and cultural
        framework 203, 205
    as transhistorical and transcultural
        phenomenon 5, 124
    as transmittable 210
    as way of understanding effects of
        abuse 222
    ways of uncovering soldiers
        faking 23
Trauma and Recovery (Herman) 6
trauma studies, emerging areas 43
Tuyet (Vietnamese refugee) 190

Uganda 163–77
    British colonisation 165–6, 172
    collective trauma as result of
        monarch's exile 176–7
    importance of oral histories 165
    under Museveni government
        164–5, 167
    under Obote government 166–7
    transition to authoritarian
        state 166
    traumatic testimonies in post-
        colonial 164–5
Uganda army 165–7
    colonial recruitment strategies
        165–6
Ugandan men 172–7
    emasculation during
        colonisation 172
    self-representations associated with
        urban 176
    ways soldiers shame and
        humiliate 170, 172–3, 174–5
Ugandan women
    anxiety over girls' safety 172
    dealing with militarization
        167–70, 177
    deflecting sexual violence 169
    negotiating and dealing with
        soldiers 175
    problematic marriages between
        soldiers and 170–1
    using cultural bodily gestures
        as protective strategies
        175–6
Une leçon clinique à la Salpêtrière
    1, 2
United Nations Commissioner for
    Human Rights 212
United Nations High Commissioner
    for Refugees (UNHCR) 187
United Nations Human Rights Office
    of the High Commissioner for
    Human Rights 206
United Nations Transitional
    Administration in East Timor
    (UNTAET) 203–4
United States
    fear in childbirth compared to
        Soviet 132
    prevalence of rape 10
    professionalization of
        psychiatry 82

psychiatric diagnosis impact on
    employment prospects 89–90,
    91
psychiatric screening
    programme 79–80, 83
psychiatric terminology
    debates 80
Universal Declaration of Human
    Rights 195
Ussher, Jane 231

Vel'vovskii, I. Z. 124, 128–9
Veterans Administration (VA) 89,
    90
victimhood
    female 7–8, 146
    Holocaust 60
    male war trauma 10
    redefining claims 7–8
victim impact statements 154–5
Vietnamese-Australian
    Community 189
Vietnamese diaspora 185, 187, 194
    ways community remember and
        honour 189, 190
Vietnamese government
    destruction of memorials in
        Malaysia and Indonesia 187,
        188–9, 194
    involvement in trafficking
        refugees 190
    post-war state repression in south
        Vietnam 189–90
    reframing of refugee crisis 194
Vietnamese refugees 186
Vietnamese refugee women
    interviews 186, 187, 192–4
    ways to deal with grief 193,
        194
Vietnam veterans
    lobbying for change in war trauma
        terms 91
    mixed responses to suffering
        of 147–8
    redefining psychological
        trauma 7–8
Vietnam War 185–6
    refugee deaths 186
violence, see ordinary violence; sexual
    violence

war neurosis 20, 25
war pensions 20, 25, 27
war trauma 42
    differing opinions about 90–1
    forms of domesticated trauma 53
    gendered 145
    Italian psychiatrists diminish
        impact 22
    psychiatric terminology
        debates 79–90
Weil, Bobby 68
Weil, Marianne 68
Weil, Selma 68
West London Synagogue 68–9
White, Luise 165
Wilcox, Vanda 25
Williams-van Klinken, Catharine
    203
Winter, Jay 20, 25
Wittman, Fritz 68
Wittman, Ilse 68
Wittman, Klara 68–9
Wittmann, Marie 'Blanche' 1–2
Woman's Home Companion 87
women, *see also* East Timorese women;
    Ugandan women; Vietnamese
    refugee women
    counter-narratives of birthing
        experiences 129–34
    Madonna/whore complex 111
    medical tradition of
        disempowering 7
    power of patriarchy over
        lives 225–6
    reluctance to publicly disclose
        mental illness 223, 233
    role as POW wives 109, 110–11
    war and impact on mobility and
        independence 107–8
women's bodies
    medical authority over 125
    patriarchal control over 6
Women's Communication Forum
    (FOKUPERS) 210–11, 212
Women's Day 148
World War I
    Italian psychiatry culture 20–3
    psychiatric screening and services
        79–80, 83
    shell shock 2–3, 7, 108

struggles of returned disabled
    soldiers   26
World War II
    evacuation of child
        refugees   49–52
    humanitarian workers bearing
        witness to trauma   48–53
    Jewish refugee domestics in
        Great Britain   59–73
    professionalization of
        psychiatry   82
    psychiatric screening
        programme   79–80, 83
    psychoanalysis   82, 83
    repatriation schemes for British
        POWs   101–12
Wright, Katie   222

Yeats, Janet   193
Yolanda (East Timorese
    interviewee)   207–8, 209
Young, Allan   5

Zajicek, Ben   10
Zinram, Leopoldine
    Polly   65, 71

www.ingramcontent.com/pod-product-compliance
Lightning Source LLC
Chambersburg PA
CBHW050136240426
43673CB00043B/1684